HOW NATIONS MAKE PEACE

CHARLES W. KEGLEY, JR.
University of South Carolina

GREGORY A. RAYMOND
Boise State University

St. Martin's / WORTH

How Nations Make Peace

Copyright © 1999 by Worth Publishers, Inc.
All rights reserved.
Manufactured in the United States of America.
Library of Congress Catalog Card Number: 98-84988
ISBN: 0-312-16616-8 (paperback)
       0-312-21948-2 (hardcover)
Printing: 1   2   3   4   5
Year: 02 01 00 99

Published and distributed outside North America by:
MACMILLAN PRESS LTD
Houndmills, Basingstoke, Hampshire RG21 6XS and London.
Companies and representatives throughout the world.

ISBN: 0-333-76022-0

A catalog record for this book is available from the British Library.

Executive Editor: James R. Headley
Project Director: Scott E. Hitchcock
Editorial Assistant: Brian Nobile
Production Editor: Douglas Bell
Production Manager: Barbara Anne Seixas
Project Coordination: Publisher's Studio, a division of Stratford Publishing Services
Cartography: GeoSystems Global Corporation
Cover Design: Spinning Egg Design Group
Cover Photo: Michael S. Yamashita/Corbis
Cover Printer: Phoenix Color Corporation
Composition: Stratford Publishing Services
Printing and Binding: R.R. Donnelley & Sons Company

ISBN: 0-312-16616-8 (paperback)   ISBN: 0-312-21948-2 (hardcover)

For information (College):   For information (Scholarly/Reference):

Worth Publishers   **St. Martin's Press, Inc.**
33 Irving Place   175 Fifth Avenue
New York, NY 10003   New York, NY 10010

www.worthpublishers.com   **www.stmartins.com**

ABOUT THE AUTHORS

Charles W. Kegley, Jr. (Ph.D., Syracuse University) is Pearce Professor of International Relations at the University of South Carolina. A past president of the International Studies Association (1993–1994), he has held appointments at Georgetown University, the University of Texas, Rutgers University, and the People's University of China. With Eugene R. Wittkopf, his books include *World Politics: Trend and Transformation,* seventh edition (St. Martin's/Worth Publishers, 1999); *The Global Agenda: Issues and Perspectives,* fifth edition (1998); *American Foreign Policy: Pattern and Process,* fifth edition (St. Martin's Press, 1996); and *The Nuclear Reader: Strategy, Weapons, War,* second edition (St. Martin's Press, 1989). He was also the editor, with Wittkopf, of the first editions of *The Future of American Foreign Policy* (St. Martin's Press, 1992) and *The Domestic Sources of American Foreign Policy* (St. Martin's Press, 1988). He is editor of *The Long Postwar Peace: Contending Explanations and Projections* (1991) and *International Terorrism: Characteristics, Causes, and Controls* (St. Martin's Press, 1990). He has also published many articles in a wide range of scholarly journals.

Gregory A. Raymond (Ph.D., University of South Carolina) is director of the Honors College at Boise State University. Selected as the Idaho Professor of the Year (1994) by the Carnegie Foundation for the Advancement of Teaching, his books include *The Other Western Europe: A Comparative Analysis of the Smaller Democracies,* second edition (1983); *Third World Policies of Industrialized Nations* (1982); and *Conflict Resolution and the Structure of the State System* (1980). He has also published many articles on foreign policy and world politics in various scholarly journals. Raymond has spoken on international issues at numerous professional conferences throughout Europe, the United States, and Latin America.

Together Kegley and Raymond have previously published *A Multipolar Peace? Great-Power Politics in the Twenty-First Century* (St. Martin's Press, 1994); *When Trust Breaks Down: Alliance Norms and World Politics* (1990); and *International Events and the Comparative Analysis of Foreign Policy* (1975). They have also coauthored twenty-one articles in a diverse range of periodicals, including *International Studies Quarterly,* the *Journal of Conflict Resolution,* the *Journal of Peace Research, International Interactions,* and the *Harvard International Review.* Both Kegley and Raymond were Pew Faculty Fellows at the John F. Kennedy School of Government at Harvard University.

For Jeannie,

whose faith and love provide me with peace.

CWK

For Professor Jerzy Hauptmann,

who showed me the path and encouraged me to make the journey.

GAR

CONTENTS

PREFACE

"The problems of victory are more agreeable than those of defeat," observed British Prime Minister Winston Churchill in a speech to the House of Commons on November 11, 1942, "but they are no less difficult." Among the most difficult are those pertaining to how the winners should treat their defeated foes. One school of thought counsels leniency: Victors should be magnanimous to extinguish any desire for revenge by the vanquished. Another school calls for sterner measures: Victors should be harsh to ensure that the enemy's defeat is irreversible. The first approach seeks stability by building trust between adversaries; the second, by eliminating an adversary's capacity to mount a future military challenge. Of these contending approaches, which peace policy between the polar extremes is more likely to yield a lasting peace? Through the ages, philosophers and theologians, novelists and playwrights, as well as journalists and social scientists have debated the relative merits of compassionate versus punitive peace settlements.

The purpose of this book is to stimulate critical thinking about the issues fueling that debate. These issues illustrate the problematic nature of many international-security choices, which often pit competing values and theoretical concepts against one another and rarely produce consensus about the most workable policy choice. But *How Nations Make Peace* is not merely a text on war and its termination; though these are important subjects in and of themselves because the postures victors take when making peace settlements can determine whether a new round of fighting shatters the agreement that ended the war. Instead we focus on the policy problems and moral dilemmas victors face as a vehicle to introduce the obstacles to prudent and principled decision making in the wider fields of foreign policy and international politics. Indeed, we introduce the key concepts and theories used in these fields of study by providing historical cases and comparisons on a timeless problem that can supplement (and make concrete) the ideas surveyed in texts on world politics and world order.

Our experience as Pew Faculty Fellows in International Affairs at the John F. Kennedy School of Government has exerted an enormous influence over the structure of this book. To encourage critical thinking about the consequences of choices between lenient and punitive peace settlements, we have provided the reader with retrospective case studies inspired by the pedagogical methods pioneered at Harvard University. Each case tells the highly textured story of a particular war and the victor's choices for dealing with the defeated. Although space limitations required us to condense these complicated events, we have sought to preserve and illuminate the tangle of historical circumstances that affected the characters in each story. We believe that it is difficult to fathom the choices national leaders make at the end of a war without knowing something about the origins and conduct of the war. By offering a rich narrative, we hope to provide students with a diplomatic context for understanding what happened and why. In addition, we wish to give them concrete referents for the abstract analytic concepts found in theories about war and peace.

The structure of this text has been influenced by several other pedagogical considerations. First, we have attempted to give students a sense of the enduring nature of the debate over alternative kinds of peace settlements by including cases from antiquity to the present day. Although weapons, tactics, and logistics have changed over the centuries, certain perennial questions about the design of peace settlements have been raised in every generation.

Second, because many of these questions are anchored in deeper ethical quandaries, we have highlighted the moral dimensions of postwar policy making. Unfortunately, ethical considerations receive scant attention in most textbooks on international relations. Statecraft, it is often argued, responds to the strategic necessities defined by national interests. Yet invoking necessity does not remove foreign policy decisions from the realm of moral judgment. What one deems necessary will appear compelling only to the extent that certain values are accepted as important enough to warrant sacrificing other values. Choosing one set of values over another entails a moral judgment. By explicitly drawing attention to such judgments, this book helps fill what we regard as a major gap in the literature not only on war termination and dispute settlement, but international decision making generally. The cases provided provoke interest in and awareness of the moral aspects of all controversial policy choices on international issues, so they can be illuminated for instruction.

Finally, while we have emphasized great-power wars that ended with decisive victories, examples of wars between major and minor powers have been included for comparative purposes. Although most readers will disagree little with the wars that were selected, some may wonder about the ones left out or mentioned only in passing. We have chosen to focus on decisive outcomes because they accentuate the unique political and ethical dilemmas facing victors. Given the frequency with which victors have failed to convert battlefield successes into durable peace settlements, these dilemmas deserve our attention. This is not to say that peace building after a military stalemate is unimportant. It is simply another subject, one that introduces a different set of research questions and requires separate treatment.

We have benefited enormously from the assistance of others while writing this book. On a personal level, we wish to thank the two people most important to us, Jeannie Weingarth and Christine Raymond, for their help, patience, understanding, and constant encouragement.

On a professional level, many scholars contributed to our efforts to make this text both informative and interesting. At the project's inception, constructive comments were provided about our prospectus by several anonymous reviewers. Thanks also go to our colleagues who reviewed drafts of the manuscript, including Christopher Joyner, Georgetown University; John Vasquez, Vanderbilt University; Robert Kerstein, University of Tampa; Lawrence Katzenstein, the University of Minnesota; and H. Carl Camp, the University of Nebraska, Omaha.

At the University of South Carolina, we are grateful to the dedicated manuscript preparation assistance provided by Steve Campbell, Ruth Cooper, Fernando Jimenz, Zeric Smith, Homer Steedly, and Zhu Zhiqun. Helpful suggestions were made by Harvey Starr and Dale Thomas.

At Boise State University, Alan Brinton and Stephanie Witt were indispensable in creating a supportive working environment. A sabbatical leave and a grant from the Higher Education Research Council of the Idaho State Board of Education allowed Gregory Raymond to conduct research in various European archives and libraries.

At St. Martin's/Worth, James Headley, our new editor, and Doug Bell, our production editor, offered professional guidance and assistance at every step of the production process. Laura Livingston, Linda DeMasi, and the staff at Publisher's Studio in Albany, New York, contributed significantly to the preparation and polish of the book.

Finally, we are pleased to acknowledge the following people for their contributions at different stages of our research: John Boehrer, Roger Coate, Beth Gillett, Margaret G. Hermann, P. Terrence Hopmann, Addison Lawton, and Alpo M. Rusi.

How Nations Make Peace builds on a quarter century of our friendship and research collaboration. We hope that readers will find this, our latest joint effort, helpful in thinking through the moral dilemmas and policy problems that face nations at the end of wars.

Charles W. Kegley, Jr.
Gregory A. Raymond

PART I

How Nations Make Decisions
for War and Peace

The chapters in this introductory section provide a road map for examining the case histories of war and peace that follow, supplying a framework for identifying important aspects and analyzing how they shaped the outcome of each case. The first chapter outlines the book's goals and organization and presents the key concepts and theories that will be used to investigate the difficult policy problems victors face at the end of a war. Chapter 1 sets out the parameters of the case studies and the principles for interpreting historical events so that they can be placed through comparison in proper context. The contrasting perspectives of the tenets of liberalism and realism on warfare and the means by which peace should be pursued are summarized to introduce these prominent theories about the causes of war and circumstances that can sustain durable peace. The second chapter describes the range of choices available to victors when dealing with defeated adversaries and explains the ethical and pragmatic dilemmas underlying their decisions.

Together, the concepts and theories introduced here furnish tools for exploring the tangle of competing interests, objectives, and values woven throughout the peace process, allowing students to compare wars and peace-making efforts from the earliest to the most recent times.

·1·

WAR AND THE MAKING OF PEACE:
AN INTRODUCTION

The purpose of all war is peace.
SAINT AUGUSTINE

"All history shows," Hans J. Morgenthau once remarked, "that nations active in international politics are continuously preparing for, actively involved in, or recovering from organized violence in the form of war."[1] For observers of world politics like Morgenthau, peace is but a brief interlude between rounds of armed combat. Because these clashes are endemic in a nation-state system lacking global institutions to police aggressors, national leaders must be vigilant and ready to engage any potential adversary on the field of battle.

We do not question the importance of thinking about how preparations for war might affect its likelihood, but believe the traditional emphasis on restraining predators overlooks the equally important dynamics governing how nations make peace. This book is about the linkage between the end of war and the maintenance of peace. Its purpose is to help us to understand the problems of decision making in world politics by focusing attention on a national choice critical to international security: When a war ends, how should victors treat the defeated in order to promote an enduring peace? Battlefield success, no matter how impressive, does not automatically yield a durable peace settlement. The choices national leaders face when wars conclude are among the most consequential they ever make, because winning is not an end in itself. The geopolitical landscape is littered with military victories that never translated into stable political orders.

Perhaps the most famous example of a battlefield success not being crowned by a durable peace settlement occurred over two millennia ago, when King Pyrrhus of Epirus overwhelmed a Roman army at Asculum in 231 B.C.E. The Greek king had recently defeated the Romans at Heraclea, but only after his troops had suffered enormous casualties. Another victory over the Romans, he reasoned, would cement his position on the Italian peninsula and allow him to redirect his attention toward the wealthier cities of Sicily. Pyrrhus achieved victory. After two days of bitter fighting in the woods and marshes around the Aufidus River, some six thousand Roman soldiers lay dead. Yet the victory came at a terrible cost, with his forces again suffering staggering losses. "One more such victory," Pyrrhus grumbled, "and I am undone."[2]

Exhaustion and resource depletion often prevent victors like Pyrrhus from capitalizing on their military accomplishments. However, they are not the only reasons why durable peace settlements are elusive. As we will argue throughout this book, military mastery alone is unlikely to provide an enduring triumph; victors need a coherent political plan for the postwar world. As U.S. President Woodrow Wilson once noted, without a judicious, well-designed strategy for the treatment of vanquished opponents, the terms of peace "would leave a sting, a resentment, a bitter memory . . . [and would rest] upon quicksand."[3]

The underlying theme of this book is that a victor's actions toward the vanquished have a decisive impact on whether the defeated will accept or reject the postwar settlement and whether their role in the postwar world will ultimately be constructive or destructive. How the vanquished are treated can determine whether political defeat will be snatched from the jaws of military victory—or whether a peace treaty is simply an interlude before a bitter foe resumes hostilities. Most scholarship on the decisions undertaken during the waning days of war has focused on the so-called endgame tactics that deal with persuading an adversary to surrender.[4] Our focus in this book is different: We examine the influence different types of peace settlements have had on relations between the former belligerents.

WAR, PEACE, AND THE STUDY OF INTERNATIONAL RELATIONS

World politics can be defined as the pattern of interactions unfolding between and among actors in the global community. The most powerful of these actors are "nation-states" or, as a shorthand for countries or sovereign states, simply **nations.**[5] The relations of national actors are sometimes cooperative, frequently competitive, and often conflictual. Whatever the dominant type of interaction, though, the goal is characteristically "political." The study of international relations focuses largely on efforts by nations to influence the behavior of each other—the very essence of **politics.** To explore international relations, then, is to inquire how nations behave toward each other and to investigate the consequences for peace and prosperity when the general pattern of the political behavior flowing across borders changes.

Politics among nations is a complex and challenging subject in its own right. What makes it even more complicated for students is the fact that scholars do not agree about the best way to study it. The field of international relations is filled with rival theories and methods drawn from the diverse branches of the humanities and social sciences. Politics, economics, history, psychology, sociology, geography, law, philosophy—all offer a unique perspective on international relations. Given the dizzying array of contending approaches to the study of international relations, how, then, should we proceed?

Pedagogical Departures

Rather than cover all aspects of the field, this text concentrates on one issue that illuminates the most significant properties of international relations. And in this respect, there is scholarly consensus about what matters most: War and peace are the principal problems on the global agenda. Without security, other serious threats to humanity cannot be adequately addressed. If nations descend into war's abyss, problems like poverty, environmental despoliation, human rights abuses, and the like become worse. Thus, our point of departure for instructional purposes is to focus on how nations make war and peace. By inspecting the underlying political processes, we concentrate on what is arguably the world's most profound problem and derive from its analysis principles that apply to other dimensions of international relations.

A second way to make the unwieldy subject of international relations more manageable is to take a **decision-making** perspective on war and peace. Highlighting the alternatives available to victors after wars, the options they selected, and the consequences resulting from those selections enables students to explore the limits of rational and moral choice. How individual preferences are formed about specific options, how these preferences are converted through collective processes of policy making into national strategies, and how the strategies chosen by different countries combine to yield international outcomes are generic topics. What we learn about the international, societal, institutional, and psychological influences on peace-making decisions has ramifications for understanding other areas of foreign policy decision making. Choosing among contending postwar strategies exemplifies the larger foreign policy problem of how to make high-stake decisions under uncertain conditions while weighing the trade-offs among multiple competing values and interests.

The third way to focus the scope of inquiry is to emphasize the policy implications of postwar decision making. After a victory, the winner must make controversial choices about how to construct a durable peace. What is the best strategy? Should there be a lenient or a harsh peace treaty? Will an approach entice or coerce the vanquished to behave in ways that serve the victor's national interests? Throughout history, nations have pursued highly divergent policies, informed by different philosophies about the nature of world affairs. Looking at the policy implications of decision making on war and peace thus opens a window for considering the rival theories that speak to the question of how to formulate and implement a successful foreign policy.

A final advantage of examining international relations through peace-making decisions is that such a focus underscores the place of **morality** in foreign policy.[6] Whenever actors have choices, questions of right and wrong arise. There is a tendency to ignore or dismiss discussions of ethical behavior in world affairs, even though questions of injury, retribution, and reconciliation are central to the human condition and, we argue, to most issues on the global agenda. Looking at procedures for bringing wars to just conclusions helps rectify this oversight.

To bring the ethical dimensions of decision making into the study of international relations, we have adopted a comparative case-study approach. Cases of wars and peace settlements that occurred in a variety of settings can cast light on differences that exist across national circumstances and inspire critical thinking about whether there are certain moral principles that hold regardless of period or place. These cases encourage the reader to think theoretically about the consequences of alternative peace-making choices and to develop hypotheses about the conditions under which particular strategies are likely to succeed. The case-study method cannot be used to verify such hypotheses, of course. But it is useful for generating theoretical propositions and policy prescriptions that can subsequently be tested.

Conceptual Overview

To envision the properties that our cases illuminate, it is helpful to think of the transition from peace to war and back to peace as a multistage, branching process. Figure 1.1 depicts the major decision points in this process and the various trajectories a conflict may follow over time. The process begins when a nonviolent conflict of interest occurs between two parties that had previously been at peace. Although conflicts of interest are common in world affairs, most are resolved before either side resorts to heavy-handed tactics. The issue causing the conflict may dissipate on its own, the parties may resolve their differences through bilateral negotiation, or they may use a third-party intermediary to help them reach a settlement through such amicable procedures as **mediation, arbitration,** or **adjudication.**

If the issue is not resolved, the conflict may fester, becoming a chronic source of discord before ultimately being settled or turning more violent. Alternatively, the conflict of interest may rapidly escalate to a serious dispute involving the threat, display, or use of military force. Militarized disputes can evolve in different ways: some are resolved, others fester for generations without resolution, and still others escalate to war. Just as there are numerous causal sequences that can lead a conflict of interest to escalate to a dangerous **militarized dispute,** there are many ways that a militarized dispute can escalate to full-scale war.

Figure 1.2 displays the possible outcomes of a war between two parties.

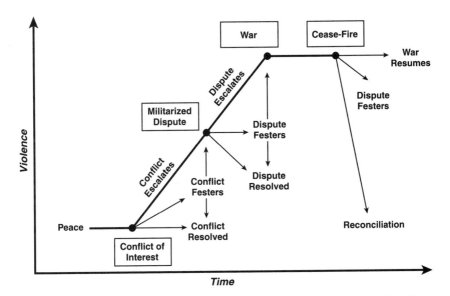

FIGURE 1.1 Phases and Trajectories in the Evolution of Armed Conflicts. Conflicts can move through various stages between peace and war. At each stage there are several divergent paths that the conflict might follow, each leading to different outcomes.

When both sides believe the ratio of expected benefits to costs for continuing the fighting is positive (cell 1), the war will most likely continue. If both are convinced that the ratio is negative (cell 4), a negotiated settlement is probable. But when one side expects the benefits of continued fighting to exceed the costs while the other does not (cells 2 and 3), a cease-fire eventually will be declared with the side making the negative assessment surrendering. As shown in Figure 1.1, once the war is over, (1) the parties may reconcile and resume peaceful intercourse; (2) their conflict may reignite into another round of warfare once the defeated party regroups; or (3) it may fester as a bitter, unrepentant loser resorts to terrorism or other unconventional uses of force short of war to keep pressure on the victor.

The thesis of this book is that *the trajectory of a conflict after one of the belligerents wins a decisive military victory is influenced by the character of the settlement.* Whether a lasting peace emerges depends largely upon how the victor treats the vanquished following a cease-fire. Each of the historical cases presented explores how the postwar policies implemented by the victor in a given war influenced the durability of the peace settlement. As such, they focus on wars terminating with a clear winner and loser (cells 2 and 3 in Figure 1.2), not those ending inconclusively in either a deadlock (cell 1) or a draw (cell 4). Because decisions made by winners on how to deal with the defeated are shaped by the process of escalation and the conduct of the fighting, a brief history of the entire trajectory, from conflict of interest through cease-fire, is

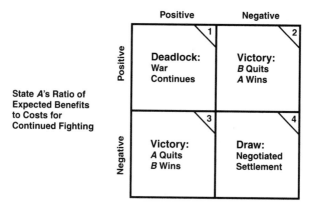

FIGURE 1.2 **War Outcomes Based on Belligerent Cost-Benefit Ratios.** Peace-making decisions are made when a war ends, but the circumstances for choice depend on the way wars conclude. This text investigates situations in which there was a clear winner and loser and evaluates the winner's decisions for dealing with the defeated. Source: Adapted from Stam, 1996.

provided for each war to help readers better interpret each case's peace-keeping choices.

The Plan of the Book

This book is divided into four parts. In Part I, we introduce key analytical concepts for analyzing postwar decision making on the question of how to forge a lasting peace. We devote attention to the various options victors have at their disposal for dealing with defeated adversaries and ways in which certain options are packaged together to create lenient, conciliatory policies while others are combined into harsh, punitive policies.

In Part II, we underscore the timeless nature of the problems inherent in constructing a viable peace settlement by focusing upon the most well-known wars of antiquity. The actions taken by Sparta after the Peloponnesian War are juxtaposed with those undertaken by the Roman Republic following each of the three Punic Wars. Because the Spartans were lenient toward the Athenians but the Romans harshly punished the Carthaginians, this section of the book gives concrete examples of alternative policy choices. Furthermore, because both Sparta and Rome encountered serious difficulties following their victories, the reader is alerted to what can go wrong with lenient as well as with harsh postwar policies. In these and all the cases that follow, we open each chapter with a preview of the key questions to ponder when reading a particular case and close with a consideration of the major controversies suggested by that case.

After using the Peloponnesian and Punic Wars to frame the enduring political and moral dilemmas victors face, in Part III we move into the modern period to compare the settlement policies adopted by the winners of the Napoleonic Wars, the Wars of German Unification, World Wars I and II, and the Persian Gulf War. Though not a random sample of decisive victories, these wars were selected because of their enormous impact on contemporary world politics. Two crucial tests of statecraft are devising and implementing an appropriate political strategy for building a new international order. Because the winners in each of these wars adopted variations of either conciliatory or punitive policies, the chapters in this section of the book evaluate the accomplishments of victors who were lenient compared to those who were harsh, emphasizing how the seeds of future wars may have been sown by the manner in which the vanquished were treated.

Finally, in Part IV we advance a set of moral principles and policy prescriptions for decisionmakers in victorious states to ponder when they weigh the costs, benefits, and risks of conciliatory versus punitive policies. Peace building is a complex and understudied subject. This textbook has been inspired by our belief that without devoting sufficient attention to its dynamics, progress toward a more just and less violent world will be frustrated. Our educational aims will be accomplished if it enables students of world politics to better appreciate the ethical dilemmas intrinsic to making choices about war and peace and to recognize how normative issues affect world politics generally.

THE PERILS AND POLITICS OF PEACE MAKING: WHAT TO LOOK FOR WHEN COMPARING THE CASES

To understand why victors adopted certain policies toward the vanquished, it is helpful to identify the various factors that influence decisionmakers when wars wind down. What factors supported policies that succeeded? What were the obstacles to finding workable solutions? As each case is explored, it is important to dig deeper than the choice itself and search for the roots of success and failure.

As a guide to inquiry, we offer the following framework that groups the factors most likely to affect peace-making success or failure into four master categories. Based on the well-known **levels-of-analysis** distinction in the study of international relations,[7] this framework identifies four categories of variables that can be treated as clusters of causal agents which act in conjunction with one another to shape postwar policy making: the *international* environment, the *societal* setting within the countries who were at war, the domestic *institutional* procedures of governance through which policies are formulated, and

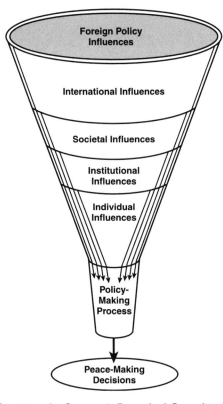

FIGURE 1.3 Making Decisions for Peace: A Funnel of Causality. The factors that influence nations' capacity to make peace settlements can be classified according to four basic levels: international, societal, institutional, and individual. Any and potentially all four levels of influence can modify peace-making decisions.

the *individual* characteristics of national leaders. Inasmuch as these general categories operate collectively and are nested within one another, Figure 1.3 depicts them as the layers of a "causal funnel," with each subsequent layer located closer to the center of decision making where critical peace-making choices are made.

International Conditions and Problem Definition

When a war concludes, political leaders in the triumphant state do not formulate policies strictly in terms of their sentiments about the defeated enemy. Often, their approach is conditioned by their perceptions of the opportunities and constraints created by changes the war may have caused in the structure of the international system. Radical shifts in the distribution of military capabilities and in the composition of military alliances may alter the victor's assessment of how to realize key foreign policy objectives. In effect, the state of the world at the time a war ends rules out certain otherwise attractive options and makes other choices possible.[8]

Examples throughout history demonstrate the need to consider how changes in the international system affected the victor's assessment of objectives and options. Take, for instance, the Great Diplomatic Revolution of 1756. Under Frederick the Great, Prussia sought to increase its military and economic strength by seizing the populous, resource-rich region of Silesia from Austria. Following his country's defeat at the hands of the Prussians, Count Wenzel Anton von Kaunitz, the Austrian foreign minister, organized an unlikely coalition against Frederick comprising three great powers that had previously been competitors: Austria, France, and Russia. Though he had gained Silesia, to his surprise, the victory required Frederick to develop a new strategy for coping with the handicraft of Kaunitz's work. The "great reversal of alliances" that joined the Hapsburgs, Bourbons, and Romanovs in a coalition against the house of Brandenburg illustrates how changes in the state system's configuration after a war can modify the political landscape of victory.

Many theorists of world politics maintain that the international environment determines foreign policy behavior—that changes in the international system's configuration after a war can drive both victors and the vanquished to reassess their vital interests. Because the international system consists of multiple concurrent variables, and because how the winning side perceives the external environment can be as influential as the actual environment, it is difficult to generalize about which of many potentially important global dimensions will most influence the choices and behavior of victors and the defeated. In comparing the cases in this book, it is important to identify the aspects of the international environment that were most influential in shaping the peace policies of the victors. When evaluating individual cases, we recommend asking a series of questions about the conditions that might have affected how the peacemakers visualized their options. How policymakers answer such questions usually influence their decisions about peace settlements. It is instructive, therefore, to assess in each case which of these concerns entered their calculations.

- *Polarity* What was the balance of military capabilities when victors attempted to make peace? As the strength of some states rose and others fell after the war, were military capabilities distributed among several roughly equal great powers in a **multipolar** pattern, were they divided between two great powers in a **bipolar** pattern, or were they concentrated in the hands of one dominate state in a **unipolar** pattern?[9]
- *Polarization* How were states aligned before and after the war? Were there flexible alliances with states frequently shifting partners? Or were alliances petrified in rigid **blocs** with various minor powers clustered around the great powers?
- *Contiguity* What was the geographical location of the warring parties? Did they share common borders? Did the proximity of the belligerents

prompt the victor to seek a harsh peace as a security guarantee against its next-door rival? Were territorial disputes and claims a source of war between neighbors and a factor influencing the durability of a peace settlement?[10] What other kinds of issues were prominent on the postwar political agenda?

- *Commerce* Were economic issues prominent on the postwar agenda?[11] Did hopes for increasing wealth through trade inspire confidence in the future, discouraging victors from enervating adversaries that could easily later become trade partners?
- *Norms* Did shared understandings exist about rules for a peaceful postwar order? Did international legal norms permit or prohibit particular kinds of peace-making strategies? Were there precedents for the peace settlement sanctioned by the international community?

Of course, many other systemic factors can modify the international setting for choice and the willingness to abide by peace settlements.[12] To analyze why some peace settlements succeed and others fail, therefore, we need to consider the existing international system and if and how it influenced victors to make either wise or foolish peace agreements.

Societal Pressures and Goal Selection

Moving down the funnel of causality from international to societal influences on postwar policies, we encounter such factors as the value orientation of the winning side and the attitudes held by the general public toward the vanquished. Peace making has rarely been above domestic politics. The chambers of government where postwar policies are made have at times been swayed by strong societal influences.

When it comes to peace making, politics does not stop at the water's edge. Leaders are forced to confront the national circumstances that prevail as war ends. Faced with the task of charting their nations' destiny in a new milieu, political leaders are tempted to ask themselves, "What are the likely domestic repercussions of reconciliation or retribution? Will the option selected increase or erode my public approval? Might the choice I make convert, perhaps overnight, partisan backers into rabid opponents?" Especially in democracies, heads of government entertain countless questions like these when wars draw to a close. The record of their memoirs underscores the importance leaders give to the likely domestic reactions to any postwar strategy they formulate.

The peace settlements presented in this book require us to question if settlement decisions are primarily based on an almost-obsessive concern about the reactions they would provoke at home. Leaders' preoccupation with their public standing, and their natural desire to be admired, can easily encourage them to make peace in ways that will evoke a positive response domestically. It might even be said that when it comes to peace making, theater on the domestic stage can substitute for rational peace-making choices, with image management an overriding concern. We need to identify when peacemakers have decided to take the popular approach rather than what they really thought was right or wrong for their country in order to estimate the extent to which decisions were influenced by leaders' fear that an unpopular war settlement might cause them to lose a bid for reelection.

This is not to suggest that leaders only make foreign policy decisions designed to curry domestic favor or to divert attention from their failures. That would be an exaggeration. Nonetheless, how often in the past history of peace making have leaders been inclined to approach the task primarily concerned with how their decisions would be evaluated by their constituents and recorded by future historians? In examining the cases, we recommend that you look at the extent to which peace-making decisions were shaped by domestic factors, including:

- *Political Culture* Did deep-seated and widely shared values circumscribe the boundary of choice for leaders, preventing them from pursuing a peace strategy that deviated from the ideals held by the nation? How did beliefs about fair play and human rights affect the peace settlement?
- *Public Opinion* Did public enthusiasm for a vindictive peace settlement drive leaders toward punitive policies, even though they had moral reservations about the wisdom of a harsh settlement? What role did the mass media play in influencing public attitudes about the vanquished?
- *Interest Groups* Were there groups within either nation that aroused hatreds by demonizing the enemy? Did their activities modify peace-making strategies? Were self-serving demands made by powerful business interests that would allow them to make large commercial profits in the postwar era?

There are many variations on the hypothesis that victors make peace in response to domestic pressures. In addition to the factors already suggested, the activities of political parties and lobbying by trade unions and professional associations can also mold the details of a peace settlement.

Which societal pressures singly or in combination shaped decisionmakers' peace policies should be evaluated also in terms of their dependence on conditioning factors. Two such intervening variables deserve particular attention. The first is the winner's level of national prosperity, because the economic health of the victor after a war can affect the overall influence of domestic pressures on treatment of the vanquished, with good times conducive to a compassionate settlement and recession chilling that prospect. A second background factor that can modify the victor's domestic environment and, in turn, influence postwar peace plans is the victor's level of domestic stability. If the victor benefits from the existence of a patriotic, united public, it is likely the peace settlement that leaders craft will be accepted by the wider citizenry. However, conflict at home can easily undermine the success of peace making abroad by diverting leaders' attention from international affairs.

Institutional Impediments and Narrowed Options

The third cluster of factors that influence postwar policy making pertains to the institutional structure of government. Victorious leaders do not make decisions about peace uninhibited by the organizational constraints of the governments they head. Presidents, prime ministers, kings, and emperors must all rely upon vast administrative networks, and they can become prisoners of those networks when agencies within them equate their own organizational interests with those of the country.

Institutional influences on peace making include a plethora of variables. One of the most important is the degree to which the victor's government is organized in a way that concentrates or divides authority over decisions. Does the winning side speak with one or many voices? To what extent do administrative procedures interfere with the capacity of leaders to rule? Who really makes postwar policy?

Policy making is a turbulent process, one that involves complex problems, a chronic lack of information, and a multiplicity of conflicting departments, ministries, and agencies swept up in **bureaucratic politics.** Owing to differences in background and training, members of various foreign policy bureaucracies may disagree on how to deal with a particular policy problem. In addition, because they seek to advance organizational self-interests, bureaucracies and administrative departments may ignore directives they oppose, leak information to sabotage peace proposals from rival organizations, or take stands on issues that are designed to increase their budget, personnel, and functional responsibilities.[13] Because of this highly competitive environment, national leaders must cope with two institutional problems. On the one hand, they may be flooded with narrow, biased analyses from several fiercely competitive agencies. On the other hand, they may obtain a single analysis that is actually a "concealed compromise" produced by a series of lateral agreements among agencies quietly working in tandem to protect their own parochial interests. In neither situation will the leaders receive the full, balanced information they need to formulate a sound peace policy.

> "You know, one of the hardest things in a government this size is to know that down there, underneath, is the permanent structure that's resisting everything you're doing."
>
> —RONALD REAGAN

The impact of large institutions—complex organizations employing thousands or even millions in a maze of channels through which ideas must pass before they become policies—suggests some disturbing propositions worthy of analyses. Although foreign policy bureaucracies were created to increase administrative efficiency, does their size actually reduce the capacity for **rationality**—for making peace policies that are based on a thorough, dispassionate search of the best information available?[14] Did peace making emerge as the end product of a logical chain of reasoning, in which the costs and benefits of reconciliation versus retribution were weighed carefully to pick the strategy most likely to maximize the victor's desired goals? Although many official histories make the circumstances of events sound rational, the participants in the decision-making process have often described something quite different. To participants, as well as to many who subsequently have probed the record of events, postwar policy making is not clearheaded, coherent, and calculated.

Thus, it is fruitful to consider whether certain institutional conditions lead to counterproductive choices. As you read, look for symptoms of dysfunction. Was the victorious government "a finely turned machine controlled by an absolute master,"[15] or was the government its "own worst enemy"?[16] Was the outcome of the policy process a product of rational choice or the result of **muddling through**?[17] Were peace policies formulated according to a vision of the future, or were they the result of inertia and grudging incremental adjustments?

The sheer size of modern governments is only one variable within the cluster of institutional factors that can affect peace making. Among the others to consider are:

- *Regime Type* Democracies are organized institutionally in a way that usually makes it difficult for heads of government to implement foreign policies according to their personal desires (as leaders in authoritarian states can).[18] Did constitutional limitations influence the postwar peace policies of democratic regimes? In presidential systems of separated institutions and shared powers, to what degree did a political struggle between the executive and legislative branches affect policy outcomes? Was the settlement made by a democratic regime different from what would have been reached by an authoritarian regime? Does the size of government exert the same impact on the policy-making process of democracies and nondemocracies?
- *Decision Rules* Large organizations normally handle issues by means of **standard operating procedures** rather than by inventing a new way to deal with each issue that arises.[19] Did bureaucrats defer to precedents established in past peace settlements? If so, did this reliance on past policy prevent leaders from shifting course when a different strategy had a better chance of working?
- *Advisory Groups* When small, homogeneous groups in stressful situations lack impartial leadership and are insulated from outside criticism, social pressures for conformity may lead to **groupthink,**[20] the propensity of the desire for consensus to replace critical thinking. Did the advisers on whom national leaders relied for guidance and emotional support show any of the symptoms of groupthink? Did they discount warnings, take extreme risks, or suppress personal reservations about the moral consequences of the policy recommendations they received?

While it is useful to assess whether peace making is handicapped by government departments that resist control from above while perfecting it from within, it is likewise advisable to evaluate the counterhypothesis that sound postwar policies may be impossible to formulate and implement without a professional bureaucracy and the kind of organizational support that it alone can provide. It is the division of large governments into separate agencies that encourages **multiple advocacy**[21] as leaders hear recommendations by different agencies and, as a result, consider a wide range of options. Moreover, it is only through the assistance of a large administrative staff that leaders can successfully manage a peace policy. While we need to be aware of the problems innate to bureaucratic organizations, we also need to be mindful of how to operate these organizations more efficiently and shape their power to national purposes and worthy ideals. For that, leadership is required. Let us turn, then, to consider our final element in the equation for determining success and failure in the making peace: individual leaders.

Individual Obstacles to Successful Strategies

The last of the four clusters of variables that should be evaluated when identifying the sources of postwar decisions pertains to the individual decisionmaker. National leaders deserve our attention because "all factors that influence what foreign policy organizations actually do must somehow be filtered . . . [through] the attitudinal prisms of decisionmakers."[22] Only by observing the motives of the key policymakers can we fully appreciate how peace-making decisions are made. Theoretically, there is a clear need to evaluate decisions about peace making by focusing on the leaders who make decisions, because

> . . . much of what goes on in world politics revolves around interactions between governments—two or more states trying to gauge the rationales behind the other's actions and anticipate its next moves. Here, the critical issue is how leaders assess the intentions and attitudes of their foreign counterparts. Are these assessments derived from personal interactions with the leaders of the other state, are they filtered through other peoples' lenses, or are they hunches and guesses based on the past behavior of that state, a shared identity, or national interests? Leaders tend to extrapolate from their own perspectives in solving problems when they have had little or no contact with their counterparts on the other side.[23]

The impact of individual leaders is especially noticeable at the end of a successful war, when the time for deliberation is short and the public demands decisive action to ensure that a peace treaty produces sufficient rewards to justify the costs it has borne. If they can take credit for engineering the victory, leaders can sometimes govern without significant restraint. Triumphant leaders, of democracies or dictatorships, often enjoy a honeymoon period during which they can disregard the constraints that normally would restrict their decision making.

Victory gives them a momentary mandate. So it is instructive to observe how their ideas and ideals directed the ways defeated enemies were treated after a decisive victory.[24]

Regardless of the popular adoration leaders experience in the glow of military triumph, they can make grave errors that undermine their nations' long-term security. As historian Barbara Tuchman notes, victorious governments have often pursued peace policies that were contrary to their self-interest, in part because "leaders in government do not learn beyond the convictions they bring with them" and in part because they are "ordinary men walking into water over their heads, acting unwisely or foolishly or perversely as people in ordinary circumstances frequently do."[25] Leaders basking in their achievements can become overconfident and rely too heavily on superficial lessons they have drawn from the immediate past. As one historian has put it, leaders "ordinarily use history badly."[26] They tend to inflate the meaning of their recent successes, embrace information that buttresses their beliefs, and deny or rationalize troublesome facts that contradict their convictions. In short, there is always a danger that the postwar policies promoted by overconfident leaders have been compromised by premature cognitive closure. When examining the cases provided in this text, inspect the material for evidence of the following decision-making pathologies:

- *Satisficing* Did the "rational choice" model of decision making describe the procedures by which leaders made choices about war and peace? Did they engage in a pure cost analysis of the relative merits of all possible options? Or is **bounded rationality** a better description of what occurred because the need to take shortcuts in calculating decision costs encouraged **satisficing**—the acceptance of satisfactory rather than maximal options?[27] What role did leaders' emotions and biases play in the decision-making process?

- *Risks and Sunk Costs* Was the ability to make wise peace-making decisions hindered by leaders' difficulties in abandoning formed opinions[28] and their tendency to overreact in crises? **Prospect theory** informs us that when estimating potential gains and losses, policymakers are likely to be "risk acceptant" with respect to gains but even more stubbornly "risk averse" regarding losses when they refuse to correct costly mistakes.[29] Like investors who take big risks in the hope of making big profits but hold losing investments too long, were policymakers far more concerned with losses than with gains because they viewed the prospects for a new peace policy optimistically but clung to a failed policy long after their deficiencies became apparent? Did they succumb to the "sunk-cost fallacy": Having once made a commitment to a particular kind of peace settlement, did the leaders protect their "investment" in their reputations by refusing to reconsider it even though the chances of it working no longer appeared hopeful?

- *Trade-Offs* Did national leaders select less-than-optimal policy options because they did not feel they could build an international consensus around what they believed were the best possible options? Did some leaders benefit by sacrificing the options they preferred to placate powerful domestic interests that held opposing positions on dealing with the defeated?
- *Policy Momentum* Peace planning often evolves from the cumulative impact of a large number of decisions built up over time. Did principles for action become legitimized by many choices before, during, and after the war and create inertia for a retributive or conciliatory peace settlement that could not be overturned? Unpleasant surprise is a stern teacher. Did any of the leaders exhibit experiential learning after costly mistakes during the course of the war and the peace-making process?

To summarize, the four clusters of factors that we have identified as influences affecting how nations make peace—the structure of the international system, the victorious country's society, its institutions, and its leadership—comprise an analytical framework that organizes the central questions for examining the success or failure of peace-making decisions. No one cluster of factors, by itself, is likely to provide sufficient insight into why peace settlements last. And while the psychological characteristics of national leaders are crucial to explanations of how nations make peace, they are not the only important variables in the equation.

JUSTICE AND EXPEDIENCY IN INTERNATIONAL RELATIONS

This book has raised a question that many decisionmakers face: how, at the close of a war, should the winning country deal with the defeated? It is a question that illustrates the more general challenge of making prudent choices about issues for which there are no compelling solutions. Caught in the ineradicable tension between two aspirations, one for justice and the other for power, decisionmakers must weigh the difficult trade-offs between competing ideals and interests.[30]

The challenge for the policymaker and the scholar is to ascertain which intermediate approach to peace making between the extremes of a lenient or a harsh settlement will most dampen the conditions that might ignite another round of warfare between the same belligerents. Like many other challenges in the field of international relations, it raises ageless philosophical controversies over the proper roles of justice and expediency in statecraft. The following nonexhaustive list of questions illustrates how victors can be pulled one way by the inspiration of moral principles while being pulled another way by the opportunistic quest for advantage:

- **Distributive Justice and Expediency** Despite the fact that conquest can pay,[31] does the victor have any moral duty to disavow the spoils of war that can be seized from the defeated?
- **Retributive Justice and Expediency** Given that repressing the defeated may create significant **opportunity costs** for the victor in the form of forgone gains from trade,[32] should the victor temper the punishment dispensed for immoral or illegal acts committed by the defeated?
- **Corrective Justice and Expediency** Since defeated industrial powers can rapidly resume their antebellum power position unless they are occupied and exploited, [33] should a victor be ruthless and exact a heavy toll from the defeated to retard the vanquished nation's military recovery?
- **Restorative Justice and Expediency** Inasmuch as security threats abound and today's adversary may be tomorrow's ally,[34] should the victor forgo justifiable penalties against the defeated to heal the relationship with its former enemy?

These questions exemplify the dilemmas created by the tension between justice and expediency in world politics. To what higher ideals beyond the pursuit of national self-interests are victors obligated? What duties do they have toward the vanquished? Who has responsibility for postwar policies when they are cobbled together by myriad craftsmen, each of whom may labor only on one element of the overall design?

If we were to peruse what has been written over the centuries about the tension between justice and expediency, we would find that most interpretations have been informed by ideas derived from the intellectual traditions of "liberal" and "realist" thought in international relations.[35] Both traditions purport to explain entrenched behavior patterns and predict future trends; and, most importantly, both offer advice to policymakers on what they ought to do to realize their foreign policy goals. Liberalism and realism have many adherents, and it would

> "Nobody stands responsible for the policy of government . . . a dozen men originate it; a dozen compromises twist and alter it; a dozen offices put it into execution."
>
> —WOODROW WILSON

be unfair to mask the diversity within these traditions by claiming that the members of each respective group all agree with one another. There are many streams of thought within these contending traditions. While it is beyond the scope of this book to trace all of their winding intellectual paths, Box 1.1 describes their core assumptions.

In the chapters ahead, we will encounter a number of policymakers strongly associated with each of these two traditions. For example, Woodrow Wilson after World War I and Franklin Delano Roosevelt in his "Four Freedoms" speech in the closing days of World War II, put into words the major principles of liberalism, while Klemens von Metternich during the Napoleonic Wars and

BOX 1.1
WHAT ARE LIBERAL AND REALIST THEORIES?

The Liberal World View

Liberals hold divergent views of world politics. What joins them is their shared assumptions about reality. Collectively, liberals embrace the following beliefs:

1. Human nature is essentially "good" or altruistic and because people are capable of mutual aid and collaboration, the attainment of moral virtue and justice in international affairs is a meaningful aspiration.
2. The fundamental human concern for the welfare of others makes progress possible.
3. Bad human behavior is the product of evil institutions, global anarchy, and the absence of a global moral consensus that motivates people to harm others.
4. War is not inevitable and its frequency can be reduced by eradicating the anarchical and ethically normless conditions that encourage it.
5. War and injustice are international problems that require collective or multilateral rather than national efforts to eliminate them.
6. International society must reorganize itself institutionally to eliminate the lawless anarchy that makes problems such as war and competitive vengeance likely.
7. Global change and cooperation are possible because history records humanity's continuing efforts to successfully engineer reforms that build collaborative problem-solving institutions.

The Realist World View

Realists also hold diverse views on world politics. Nevertheless, all realists believe that conflicts of interests among nations are inevitable and that the purpose of statecraft is to ensure national survival by acquiring power. The following beliefs comprise the central tenets of realism:

1. History teaches that people are by nature sinful and wicked.
2. Of all people's evil ways, no sins are more prevalent or dangerous than the lust for power and the desire to dominate others.
3. The possibility of eradicating the instinct for power is a utopian aspiration.
4. Under such conditions international politics is, as the sixteenth-century English philosopher Thomas Hobbes put it, a struggle for power, "a war of all against all."

5. The primary obligation of every state in this environment—the goal to which all other national objectives and moral considerations should be subordinated—is to promote the "national interest," defined in terms of survival and national security through power.

6. The anarchical nature of the international system necessitates the acquisition of military capabilities sufficient to deter or subdue any potential rival.

7. Economics is less relevant to national security than military might and is important primarily as a means to acquire national power and prestige.

8. Allies might increase the ability of a state to defend itself, but their loyalty and reliability should not be assumed.

9. International law and international organizations cannot be trusted to preserve peace.

10. International stability results from maintaining a balance of power.

Otto von Bismarck throughout the Wars of German Unification adhered to a realist perspective on war and peace making. To prepare the way for examining the postwar policies advocated by these and other statesmen in historical cases we have assembled, let us briefly take up the question of how liberals and realists respond to the demands of justice and the lure of expediency as wars wind down.

Liberalism

At the heart of liberal theorizing about issues of war and peace is the contention that an unbridled pursuit of national self-interest is destructive. Rather than emphasizing **self-help,** liberalism "seeks to discover ways in which separate actors, with distinct interests, can organize themselves to promote economic efficiency and avoid destructive physical conflict, without renouncing either the economic or political freedoms that liberals hold dear."[36] Power, for liberals, resides in adhering to ethical principles. For them "international behavior and outcomes arise from a multiplicity of motives, not merely security, at least if security is defined solely in military or strategic terms."[37] Following a war, liberal theory counsels against approaching peace making from a **zero-sum** outlook that permits the winner to extract the greatest possible gains at the loser's expense, stressing the principle of reciprocity that is predicated on the expectation that behavior sent will be returned in kind. To maximize the prospects for enduring peace, liberal theorists reason that harsh punishments and staggering penalties will backfire, while clemency and compassion will produce cooperation and compliance.

Realism

"Facts," British Prime Minister Winston Churchill once remarked, "are better than dreams."[38] For realists, liberal dreams of peace through conciliation ignore the nasty, brutish facts of international life: The strong dominate the weak, the powerful take advantage of the powerless, and relations between former enemies are determined more by the military might each possesses than by principled concern for each other's security and status. The core assumptions that lead realists to this conclusion can be summarized as follows:

> To begin with, they consider the central questions to be the causes of war and the conditions of peace. [Second], they also regard the structure of the system as a necessary if not always sufficient explanation for many aspects of international relations. According to classical realists, 'structural anarchy,' or the absence of a central authority to settle disputes, is the essential feature of the contemporary system. It gives rise to the 'security dilemma': In a self-help system, one nation's search for security often leaves its current and potential adversaries insecure; any nation that strives for absolute security leaves all others in the system absolutely insecure; and it can provide a powerful incentive for arms races and other types of hostile interactions. Consequently, the question of *relative* capabilities is a crucial factor. Efforts to deal with this central element of the international system constitute the driving force behind the relations of units within the system; those that fail to cope will not survive. Thus, unlike . . . 'liberals,' classical realists view conflict as a natural state of affairs rather than a consequence that can be attributed to historical circumstances, evil leaders, flawed sociopolitical systems, or inadequate international understanding and education.
>
> A third premise that unites classical realists is their focus on geographically based groups as the central actors in the international system. During other periods the primary entities may have been city-states or empires, but at least since the Treaties of Westphalia (1648), nation-states have been the dominant units.
>
> Classical realists also agree that state behavior is rational. The assumption behind this fourth premise is that states are guided by the logic of the 'national interest,' usually defined in terms of survival, security, power, and relative capabilities. To Hans J. Morgenthau . . . for example, 'rational foreign policy minimizes risks and maximizes benefits.' Although the national interest may vary according to specific circumstances, the similarity of motives among nations permits the analyst to reconstruct the logic of policymakers in their pursuit of national interests—what Morgenthau called the 'rational hypothesis'—and to avoid the fallacies of 'concern with motives and concern with ideological preferences.'
>
> Finally, the nation-state can also be conceptualized as a unitary actor. Because the central problems for states are starkly defined by the nature of the international system, their actions are primarily a response to external rather than domestic political forces.[39]

Realism believes power trumps principles. To the realist, the road to ruin is paved with utopian hopes about the good will of others or the applicability of morality to the ruthless struggle for power in international relations among rival nations seeking self-advantage: "States . . . should not be held to the same moral standards as individuals because to do so subverts their capacity to conduct prudent policy."[40] From this realist ethical posture, peace settlements should not be grounded in expectations that an adversary will reciprocate kindness, because defeated states are likely to interpret generosity as weakness and use lenient treaties as an opportunity to resume the pursuit of power. Apprehensive over the possibility that an indignant loser will try to avenge its battlefield humiliation, realists recommend firm settlements as the only reliable method of maintaining postwar peace.

In Search of a Path to Peace

Within victorious governments, we usually find considerable debate over the advisability of a lenient conciliatory versus a harsh, punitive peace settlement. Liberalism and realism, the two most common theoretical lenses policymakers use when inspecting the political topography of the postwar world, advance diametrically opposed recommendations. Policymakers need a **theory** backed by evidence that answers the questions of how nations should make peace. Which theory—liberalism or realism—offers the strongest basis for developing policy prescriptions to guide peace making in the wake of war?

Over the next several chapters you have the opportunity to look at the dilemmas of peace making through both lenses. History is the social scientist's only laboratory and the moral philosopher's only available object of observation. It is from historical inquiry that we can make better decisions about how nations *ought* to act if they want a lasting peace. To provide a foundation for such an inquiry, in the next chapter we describe a set of analytical concepts that will be used in exploring the subsequent historical cases of how victors treated the adversaries they defeated in war.

NOTES

1. Morgenthau, 1985, p. 52.
2. After the gruesome battle of Malplaquet in 1709, the French drew a similar conclusion about the allied forces arrayed against them. "If it please God to give your Majesty's enemies another such victory," Claude-Louis Hector Villars wrote to Louis XIV, "they are ruined." Weir, 1993, pp. xiii, 95.
3. Speech delivered on January 22, 1917, to the U.S. Senate.
4. See Fox, 1970a; Goldstein, 1991; Hampson, 1996; Iklé, 1991; and Pillar, 1983.
5. For stylistic reasons and to ease communication, we shall use the term "nation" interchangeably with other related terms, such as "country," "state," and other similar concepts used to describe the sovereign-state actors still dominant in international affairs. This is not to suggest that our usage of "nations" is technically correct, even if many scholars use "nations" as we do, as a linguistic convention to describe inter-*national* relations. (Such as Hans J. Morgenthau, 1985, did in his realist classic text, *Politics Among Nations*, recall that this misnomer was also relied on when the globe's premier international organization, the United Nations, was

named.) That said, the reader should keep in mind that "nations" are more accurately groups of people sharing a common culture, language, religion, and culture, in contrast to a legally defined "state"—an independent, sovereign polity possessing a recognized government, territory, and population under its jurisdiction. Furthermore, nations are distinguished from other categories of important actors on the world stage, such as multinational corporations, nongovernmental organizations (NGOs) such as Greenpeace, and intergovernmental organizations (IGOs) such as NATO, that also play active roles in world politics.

6. See Oppenheim, 1991.

7. A multilayered analysis is needed because many of the determinants of peace-making performance are located within an ever larger set of variables, all of which may be operating simultaneously. For a theoretical discussion of the logic behind distinguishing among different levels of analysis, see Singer, 1961; for an alternative statement applied to war and peace, see Waltz, 1954; for a framework widely used in the comparative study of determinants of nations' general foreign policy making, see Rosenau, 1966 and 1984.

8. This interpretation is most forcefully developed in the neorealist "structural" approach of Kenneth N. Waltz, 1979.

9. The assumption that an equitable balance of power promotes peace is a core belief of proponents who advocate promoting the creation and maintenance of this condition. In contrast, proponents of hegemonic stability theory argue that the concentration of military power in one leading state increases the chances of peace because that superpower has the capability to prevent aggression through punishment; see Thompson, 1988. For a structural interpretation, see Kaplan, 1957.

10. For studies demonstrating the importance of territorial issues as a factor influencing the probability of war and durability of peace settlements, see Vasquez, 1995 and 1996, and Goertz and Diehl, 1992.

11. For syntheses and reinterpretations of the impact of international economic conditions on war and peace making, see the "hierarchical equilibrium" theory of Midlarsky, 1989; the "world system" theory of Wallerstein, 1974; and the analysis of economic conditions on peace policies as reflected in such studies as those of Rock, 1989, and Rosecrance, 1986.

12. For example, the proportion of democracies in the system strongly influences the prospects for peace, with increases associated with the declining probability of war. For discussions of the "democratic peace" proposition, see Doyle, 1997; Ray, 1995; and Russett, 1993.

13. For a pioneering definition of the "bureaucratic politics" and "organizational process" models of the institutional barriers to rational peace making, see Allison, 1969 and 1971, and Allison and Halperin, 1989. Discussions of the impact of government type on foreign policy decisions are provided in most texts in the comparative study of foreign policy; see, for example, Ray, 1995; Rosenau, 1966; and Russett, 1993.

14. Rational choice models of decision making emphasize purposeful, goal-directed behavior guided by careful consideration of the costs and benefits of alternative options. Verba, 1969, pictures rationality as the effort by decisionmakers to use the best information and to choose from all potential responses to a problem as the means most likely to maximize national goals. See Bueno de Mesquita and Lalman, 1992, for an application to war.

15. Schelling, 1984, p. 27.

16. Destler, Gelb, and Lake, 1984.

17. For a description of "muddling through" as a process by which rational decision making is compromised, see Lindblom, 1959.

18. The comparative study of foreign policy has demonstrated that democracies make national security decisions differently than autocracies. For discussions of the advantages of democratic governance, see Doyle 1997, and Ray, 1995. For a realist critique of the deficiencies of decisions made through democratic procedures, see Kennan, 1951.

19. See George, 1969, and Kegley, 1987.

20. This concept originated in the research of Janis, 1972, 1982, and 1989; for recent empirical elaborations, see 't Hart, 1990, and 't Hart, Stern, and Sundelius, 1997.

21. A democratic victor will be forced to consider the full range of possible peace-making options, because such polities tend to produce "multiple advocacy": leaders hear advice on behalf of almost every viable peace-building approach. Autocracies do not; few advisers will dare to question the wisdom of authoritarian leaders about the consequences of their peace policy preferences, even if their decisions are doomed to failure. For this reason there is much virtue in reaching wise peace-making decisions through democratic channels of communication that permit, even encourage by their very structure, consideration of all possible strategies. For an innovative rationale for why peace making will be more productive when advocates of differing approaches are able to voice their recommendations, see George, 1972.
22. Hermann and Hermann, 1989, p. 2.
23. Hermann and Hagan, 1998, p. 134.
24. Peace-making decisions have been influenced strongly by whether the victor's government was headed by a "crusader" or "pragmatist"; see Stoessinger, 1985. The more ideological the leaders, the less likely they have been to perceive constraints in peace-making choices; the more pragmatic the leaders, the more responsive they have usually been to the impact of peace-making policies on the defeated.
25. Tuchman, 1984, pp. 23 and 383.
26. May, 1973, p. xi: see also Neustadt and May, 1986.
27. For elaboration of the concept of "satisficing" and the theory of "bounded rationality" in decision making, see Simon 1982 and 1957.
28. The experiments that document this tendency for intellectual and perceptive rigidity from which this observation derives stem from the psychological studies of cognitive dissonance by Festinger, 1957.
29. For a discussion of prospect theory, see Farnham, 1994, and Levy, 1992.
30. As Reinhold Niebuhr, 1932, has aptly described this kind of dilemma, the tension is prone to make for an unresolvable tragedy because no purely moral solution is available for the ultimate ethical issue, but neither does there exist a viable solution that disregards moral considerations.
31. See Liberman, 1996.
32. Aron, 1968, p. 257. Also see Rosecrance, 1986.
33. Organski and Kugler, 1980, pp. 144–145.
34. Kaplan, 1957, p. 23.
35. The literature on the vast diversity of theorizing in international relations is as vast as is its subject. Most, but certainly not all, schools of theorizing and thought can be subsumed by the two dominant traditions: liberalism and realism. For synthesis and summaries of the divergent ideas associated with these two theoretical accounts of the international causes of international war and the conditions of peace, see Doyle, 1997.
36. Keohone, 1992, p. 174.
37. Holsti, 1995, p. 44.
38. In Lefever, 1998, p. 66.
39. Holsti, 1995, pp. 37–38.
40. Monoson and Loriaux, 1998, p. 288.

· 2 ·

APPROACHES TO DEALING WITH THE DEFEATED

A dilemma facing every victor in an interstate war is how to treat the defeated opponent when hostilities end. Should the victor strive for a postwar settlement that addresses at least some of the grievances of the defeated, or should it implement a new status quo that does not acknowledge these grievances? Magnanimity may quell the desire of the defeated power for revenge, but non-magnanimity may prevent the defeated party from acquiring the means to mount future challenges.

STEVEN BRAMS AND BEN MOR

The policy dilemma faced by every national leader fortunate enough to bask in the glow of a hard-earned victory is how to forge a durable peace settlement. It is a difficult task. After examining the outcomes of 311 wars fought between 1480 and 1970, Quincy Wright concluded that stopping warfare does not always end hostilities.[1] To achieve a peace settlement that lasts longer than those who remember the fighting, leaders need an overarching grand strategy that provides adequate guidance on how to deal with the defeated once the opposing armies have disengaged.

At minimum, a *grand strategy* should contain three key elements. It should (1) identify the goals that must be achieved to produce security, (2) describe the military and nonmilitary actions that will result in these goals being attained, and (3) specify how scarce human and material resources will be coordinated to support those actions. Simply put, a grand strategy sets forth a "means-ends chain" of contingent predictions: if we do *A*, *B*, and *C*, the desired results *X*, *Y*, and *Z* will follow.[2] Unfortunately, the "subject of war termination generally has received very little attention in social science and historical literature."[3] There are few guidelines grounded in historical experience that can enable policymakers to safely anticipate and avert potential problems in the wake of war. Rather than crafting a comprehensive, integrated strategy for shaping the contours of the postwar world, most victors simply substitute a defense posture for a comprehensive plan for responding to unfolding events. As Gordon Craig and Alexander George note, "[s]tudents of military strategy have not given much systematic attention to the problem of terminating wars, and military planners have also traditionally neglected this problem."[4]

Given the dearth of evidence on how to convert battlefield success into a satisfactory political outcome, the challenge is to think strategically about the consequences of different policy choices—a challenge that cannot be avoided. At every war's end, victors must decide how they will treat their adversaries. Beyond that, leaders need to carefully think through their options, because their choices will affect national security. Whether or not victors should be magnanimous may seem insignificant as one revels in the applause of a victory parade. Yet the wrong choice can breed the very problem that the war was fought to solve. "It is not enough to win," Napoleon Bonaparte reminds us, "one has to take advantage of this success."[5]

It is the purpose of this chapter to build on the introductory chapter that provided a conceptual road map for investigating past cases of wars and decisions by victors about peace making. Here we look more closely at the range of options available to victors after wars when they make decisions about the treatment of their subjugated enemy. We identify the potential menu of peace making strategies, arrayed on a continuum from the most lenient to the most punitive, with other intermediate possibilities between these extremes. In the cases presented for analysis, we will find that victors have selected from among these options, pinning their hopes for enduring peace on one or a combination of these methods, with outcomes sometimes satisfactory but, more often, disappointing.

To work with this topology or classification system when comparing the cases in Parts II and III, in this chapter we preface our categorization of the options with a discussion of the role of emotion and passion in the calculation of peace-settlement decisions. Passions exert a psychological impact that can undermine the victor's capacity for **rational choice** based on cost-benefit calculations. The chapter also treats the diverse ways armed conflicts may terminate, to encourage inspection of the impact of how wars end on peacemakers' decisions. Throughout this chapter we highlight the role of ethics in decisions for magnanimous or for malevolent treatment of defeated enemies, in the context of the victor's image of the proper conception of justice.

THINKING STRATEGICALLY ABOUT WAR TERMINATION

Wars are initiated for various reasons. Whether inspired by offensive or defensive aims, they breed mutual enmity, which can lead each side to demonize the other as a means of rationalizing violence. Whereas nations take up arms amid conflicting and often quixotic expectations about what the fighting will be like, campaigning against a determined opponent can stagger even the most optimistic soldier. "There is no such thing as 'getting used to combat,' " concluded one psychological study conducted by the U.S. Army. "Each moment of combat imposes a strain so great that men will break down in direct relation to the intensity and duration of their exposure."[6] Despite rigorous training aimed at desensitizing troops to war's horrors, combat "provides the stinging ice of reality both to the soldiers doing the fighting and to the mass populations of the nations at war."[7]

The Impact of Emotion on War-Termination Decisions

Few human activities evoke stronger emotions than combat. Fear, rage, and grief all attend the battlefield. To think about warfare without acknowledging these powerful emotions is to overlook some of the most important forces motivating human behavior, forces that can destroy the prospects of a negotiated cease fire and tear apart the very fabric of a peace agreement. Consider the **enduring rivalry** between Spain and France. Between 1494 and 1683, these neighbors went to war, on average, every 12.6 years. The amount of time that passed between each war was about eight years, and this interval only began to lengthen after the Thirty Years' War in 1648, when the time span between their last three clashes almost doubled (to 15.6 years).[8] Clearly, this sequence of lethal engagements suggests that truces struck between Spain and France were not prompted by a sincere desire to resolve the issues that divided them. They were pauses in an ongoing feud.

Similar patterns of protracted warfare punctuated by lulls can be found among other rivals; "during a span of exactly two centuries—from 1678 to 1878—Russia and Turkey fought one another ten times."[9] Thus, many war termination agreements are merely stop-gap measures. Peace, in these types of long-standing rivalries, rarely endures; it is an interlude during which one side or the other longs for revenge and methodically works to settle old scores.

People harboring an acute sense of injustice do not easily forget the suffering caused by others. Every emotion, argued the philosopher Ludwig Wittgenstein, is its own world. An angry person lives in an angry world. A person deeply resentful over some past injury lives in a bitter world. Emotions are not just physiological reactions to external stimuli that color our view of life, they are feelings about determinate objects that structure how we experience the world.[10] They endow life with meaning and therein alert us to what is important. While at times they may be painful to experience, passions are integral to the human experience. Yet perusing much of what is written in the field of international relations, "one would never suspect that human beings have right brains as well as left"[11]—an intuitive side and a cognitive, logical side, independent but mutually influencing perceptions and decisions. Indeed, "there is a strong tradition in modern scholarship in the human sciences of ignoring emotions as causes."[12] But people do not always behave like the self-concerned egoists found in rational actor models; they can be driven by emotions ranging from love to hate, often disregarding considerations of self-interest. To ignore these grand passions is to imagine that decisionmakers are like the protagonist in Camus's novel *The Stranger*. Unable to savor joy, feel disgust, or fathom grief, such people hardly seem human.

Although emotions may lead people to make poor decisions, sometimes they are grounded in cognitions that are themselves reasonable. Take, for instance, the emotion of fear. A camper in Idaho's Selkirk Mountains might take various precautions when storing food due to a fear of grizzly bears living in the area, and these precautions would be reasonable given the circumstances. On the other hand, additional precautions triggered by a fear of the mythical creature "Sasquatch" would be unreasonable. There can be good or bad reasons for our emotions, and under certain conditions, it is appropriate to act in accordance with our emotions. "The man who is angry at the right things and with the right people," claimed Aristotle, "is praised," and "those who are not angry at the things they should be angry at are thought to be fools."[13]

Since feelings of anger, resentment, and similar intense emotions can be justifiable, and since they can sour relations between former belligerents well after the fighting is over, how can adversaries assuage the rancor of their collective past and restore amicable relations? What policies will promote an enduring peace settlement? It is "easy to patch up a peace which will last for 30 years," warned British Prime Minister David Lloyd George at the end of World War I. "What is difficult, however, is to draw up a peace which will not provoke a fresh struggle when those who have had practical experience of what war means have passed away."[14]

> "Against war it may be said that it makes the victor stupid and the vanquished revengeful."
> —NIETZSCHE

Different Methods of War Termination

Every peace settlement is influenced by the manner in which hostilities conclude. One way they may end is through the mere cessation of combat. With costs mounting and no victory in sight, the belligerents may simply stop fighting. Sometimes a brief "suspension of arms" *(Waffenruhe)* is declared in a given locale for purposes such as tending to the wounded or burying the dead. On other occasions a more general "armistice" *(Waffenstillstand)* may be arranged in order to conduct peace negotiations.[15] And on still other occasions military activities may be halted without any collateral effort to reach a peace agreement. For example, a truce was declared between King Charles XII of Sweden and King Frederick Augustus of Poland in 1716. After each side refrained from attacking the other for roughly a decade, peace was finally recognized de jure by an exchange of letters.

Although various wars have ended through this kind of reciprocal cessation (e.g., in 1720 between Spain and France and in 1801 between Russia and Persia), states usually prefer to bring hostilities to formal closure. By abstaining from an explicit settlement, the issues that initially caused the dispute to become militarized continue festering. Not knowing whether to interpret the claims advanced by each side in terms of the *status quo ante bellum* or the *status quo post bellum (uti possidetis),* other states may find their exchanges with the disputants clouded with uncertainties. What is more, the disputants themselves find it difficult to let go of the past and reconstruct a normal relationship. Thus, settlements are preferred to cessations, even if all of the outstanding issues cannot be immediately resolved. For instance, the Treaty of Ghent, which brought the War of 1812 to a close, provided for the restoration of property and an exchange of prisoners between England and the United States but left various issues open for resolution at a later time.

Figure 2.1 shows the ways in which hostilities between hypothetical states *A* and *B* may be brought to a definitive conclusion. If either *A* or *B* achieves a complete victory, it can demand the "unconditional surrender" of its adversary. In these cases, the losing side grants to the victor "full authority, legal and actual, to do as [it] pleases with the defeated."[16]

While each side may hope for resounding battlefield success, military and financial constraints normally stop the fray before total submission occurs. Table 2.1 lists the arguments typically taken into account when deciding whether or not to terminate hostilities. Of course, the relative importance given to these arguments varies among national leaders as influenced by the myriad possible factors that condition national calculations and choices (recall Figure 1.3). Some decisionmakers might be highly concerned about lost resources, while others might be driven by fears about the deterioration of their domestic support. Even among those motivated by the same kind of argument, different perceptions may exist over which warring nation is stronger,

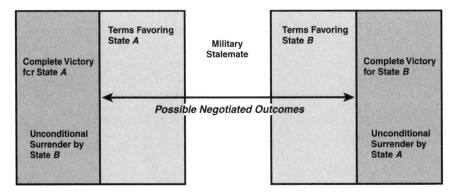

FIGURE 2.1 The Range of Peace Settlements.

TABLE 2.1
The Calculus of War Termination[17]

Arguments Weighing in Favor of Termination	Arguments Weighing against Termination
The situation is deteriorating politically, militarily, or economically.	Circumstances are in our favor or show signs of improving politically, militarily, or economically.
Time is on the enemy's side; cut losses while still possible.	Time is on our side; maintain the pressure on the enemy.
No external support is expected.	External support is forthcoming.
Battlefield casualties are excessive.	The sunk costs are high; the number of lives already sacrificed requires pushing on regardless of the costs.
The domestic situation is unstable; social and political unrest hampers the war effort.	The domestic situation is stable; morale is high and the public continues to support the war effort.
The enemy has offered reasonable terms for concluding the war.	The enemy offers demanding terms for concluding the war.
Participating in peace negotiations will work to our advantage.	Participating in peace negotiations will weaken our position.

and whether the balance of military capability is likely to disadvantageously wane in the immediate future, and if so, how fast that erosion will occur. Hence the decision calculus that encourages state A to disengage may not convince state B that the moment is ripe to stop fighting. Considerations that generate strong incentives for leaders with particular personal characteristics operating within certain types of political systems may not have the same impact on their counterparts.

When neither combatant can conquer the other and both seek a formal end to hostilities, they usually will negotiate a peace treaty. Most treaties are couched in terms of perpetuity, though occasionally they have a fixed time limit. For instance, the 1713 Treaty of Adrianople between Russia and Turkey was limited to twenty-five years. Regardless of the time limit of a peace treaty, each side has an interest in ensuring the other does not violate its terms. A welter of techniques is used to ensure that peace treaties are upheld. They may be sanctified through religious rites (e.g., the 1559 Treaty of Cateau-Cambrésis between Spain and France), secured by an exchange of valuable objects (e.g., the treaties of 1756, 1764, and 1768 between Genoa and France), or guaranteed by third parties (e.g., the 1815 Act of Paris reestablishing the Swiss policy of neutrality). The legal norm **pacta sunt servanda** (treaties are binding) also

TABLE 2.2
Selected Policy Options for Victors

Actions That May Be Used for Retribution	Example
Subjugation	Under the Peace of Vereeniging, which brought the 1899–1902 Anglo-Boer War to a conclusion, the Afrikaner republics of the Orange Free State and Transvaal became extinct as states and thus lost international legal personality.
Partial Annexation	Following the Russo-Ottoman War of 1828–1829, by the Treaty of Adrianople Russia appropriated the mouth of the Danube River and the Black Sea littoral of the Caucasus.
Occupation/ Colonization	In 1849, following the Second Sikh War, the kingdom of the Punjab was placed under British imperial rule in India.
Partition	At the end of World War II, Germany was divided into British, American, Soviet, and French zones and subjected to four-power control. In 1949, the Soviet zone was converted into a separate state, the German Democratic Republic. The remaining western zones became the Federal Republic of Germany.
Neutralization	Under the Austrian State Treaty of 1955, the occupation of Austria, which had been in effect since the end of World War II, was ended contingent upon Austria not acceding to future military alliances.
Demilitarization	Under the 1919 Treaty of Versailles, restrictions were placed on deployment of German military forces in the Rhineland.
Reconstitution	After World War II, the United States imposed a democratic political system upon Japan.
Reparation	Under the terms of the 1842 Treaty of Nanking, China was required to recompense England for costs emanating from the Opium War.

. . . to Promote Reconciliation	Example
Rapprochement	After the defeat of Napoleon in 1815, France was permitted to join the Concert of Europe.
Restoration	Following the Ottoman Empire's victory in the 1861–1862 Montenegrin War, to placate the vanquished, in the Convention of Scutari, the Ottomans restored the frontiers of 1859.
Compensation	After France and Piedmont defeated Austria in 1859, by the Treaty of Zurich Austria was forced to cede most of Lombardy, but, to diminish Austria's humiliation and strengthen peace, Napoleon III in turn ceded Lombardy to Piedmont.
Resuscitation	In 1947, the United States instituted the Marshall Plan to rebuild the war-torn economies of Germany and Italy.

supports the promissory obligations incurred in a formal peace agreement. Indeed, it has long been held that "to recommence a war, by breach of the articles of a treaty of peace, is deemed much more odious than to provoke a war by some new demand and aggression; for the latter is simply injustice, but, in the former case, the party is guilty both of perfidy and injustice."[18]

Peace treaties reflect a complex interplay of many influencing factors, including calculations of the **opportunity costs** or trade-offs of gains and losses among competing options, the amount of domestic and international pressure on the combatants to lay down their arms, as well as the balance of national capabilities, risk-taking propensity, and resolve. Barring a military stalemate, either A or B will enjoy a position of relative superiority and emerge victorious, though the margin of victory can range from modest to decisive. War, as Thomas Schelling reminds us, is "a bargaining process—dirty, extortionate, and often quite reluctant bargaining on one side or both—nevertheless a bargaining process."[19] Almost every bargain that is struck furnishes advantages for victors and disadvantages for the vanquished. The greater the magnitude of the victory, the greater the opportunity for the winner to translate its military gains into favorable treaty terms.

As we noted in Chapter 1, the focus of this book is on those wars in which one warring nation forces the utter capitulation of its opponent (the darkest shaded area in Figure 2.1) or has won decisively enough to obtain peace terms just short of unconditional surrender (the lightly shaded area in Figure 2.1). In contrast to instances of military stalemate,[20] where neither party is in a position to dictate the peace settlement, these two forms of categorical victory allow the winner to impose its will upon the vanquished.

CLASSIFYING THE OPTIONS AVAILABLE TO VICTORS

Victors have many options they can pursue when dealing with the defeated. As shown in Table 2.2, their choices range from actions that can be taken for the purpose of retribution to those that can promote reconciliation. As we shall see in Parts II and III of this book, victors typically combine several of these actions. Moreover, they may at times resort to different combinations when they have engaged the same adversary in successive wars.

Forging a Punitive Peace

The most severe options fall under what the Romans called *deballatio*, a term that had three usages in antiquity: (1) subjugation of the defeated state, (2) occupation of the defeated state until a successor government is established, and (3) controlling portions of the defeated state's territory until it fulfills certain conditions. Of the three, subjugation was the most common usage. Traditionally, it has been defined as the "extermination in war of one belligerent by another through annexation of the former's territory after conquest, the enemy's forces having been annihilated."[21] From the time of Sargon I (2350 B.C.E.), depicted in Akkadian lore as the "King of Battle"and known today as the founder of the world's first recorded empire, armies have obliterated beaten enemies and subjugated their lands. Conquest tended to pay, since ruthless overseerers could extract resources from defeated countries for less than the costs of administration and repression.[22] Moreover, according to custom, conquest gave the victor title to the territory of the defeated.[23]

Francisco de Vitoria, a sixteenth-century Spanish professor of theology at the University of Salamanca, was among the first people to wrestle with questions about the legality and morality of such imperial claims rationalized by the stern realist belief that might makes right.[24] His analysis of the respective rights of Spaniards and the indigenous population of the Americas encouraged a humanitarian reassessment of the long-standing belief that conquerors acquired sovereignty over the conquered. "Arms, of themselves," the Abbé de Mably would later insist in the spirit of liberal thinking, "give no title," a view that did not gain prominence until after World War I with the promulgation of the 1928 Kellogg-Briand Pact, the Stimson Doctrine of 1932, and the 1938 Lima Declaration of the Nonrecognition of the Acquisition of Territory by Force.[25]

Under Article 10 of the League of Nations Covenant and Article 2(4) of the United Nations Charter, involuntary cession by military conquest is now illegal. Still, many students of international law aver that "however meritorious such positions may be from the standpoint of abstract justice, prevailing international practice seems to support the contrary view."[26] Consequently, although the 1970 Declaration of Principles of International Law adopted by the UN General Assembly declares "the territory of a state shall not be the object of acquisition by another state resulting from the threat or use of force," various qualifications to this assertion have been proposed:

1. a State acting in lawful exercise of its right of self-defense may seize and occupy foreign territory as long as such seizure and occupation are necessary to its self-defense;
2. as a condition of its withdrawal from such territory, that State may require the institution of security measures reasonably designed to ensure that the territory shall not again be used to mount a threat or use of force against it of such a nature as to justify exercise of self-defense;
3. where the prior holder of the territory had seized that territory unlawfully, the State which subsequently takes that territory in the lawful exercise of self-defense has, against that prior holder, better title.[27]

Whereas the desires for wealth and glory are among the various impulses that stimulate conquerors, other motives and ethical values also frequently influence how they treat the defeated. "The vanquished can never be the friends of the victors," asserted the harsh realpolitik conqueror Genghis Khan;

"the death of the former is necessary therefore for the safety of the latter."[28] To be sure, numerous conquerors have not annihilated their victims in a genocidal bloodbath. Defeated states have been occupied, partitioned, neutralized, demilitarized, or forced to make reparation payments in retribution for past transgressions and in the name of future defense needs. Yet these acts can create new security problems. A punitive peace often inspires another round of warfare aimed at undoing the harsh settlement. *The Dhammapada,* an early collection of Buddhist verses, tells us that "victory breeds hatred, for the conquered sleep in sorrow." The *Mahābhārata,* an ancient Hindu epic, takes a similar position: "A king should never do such an injury to his foes as could rankle in the latter's heart."[29] "The conqueror can have vengeance or he can have justice," observes Geoffrey Blainey, "but he cannot have both in the same treaty. If he chooses the path of vengeance, he may keep his hobnailed boot on the neck of the vanquished for a generation or so, but this may be the limit."[30]

> "Revenge is its greatest delight and glory. Is it possible that the human heart can find peace and pleasure only in returning evil for evil?"
>
> —MILOVAN DJILAS

Constructing a Lenient Peace

Recognizing the limitations of a boot on the neck, some conquerors have defined national interests in accordance with liberal moral values and not pressed their victories to the point of humiliating the defeated. Rather than establishing a vindictive peace that might fuel an international vendetta, they have sought a restorative peace designed to reconcile former adversaries and would-be belligerents.

One long-standing approach to constructing a restorative peace has been for the victorious party to make symbolic concessions, however minor they might be.[31] Julius Caesar, for example, showed clemency after victory and restored the status of many defeated foes.[32] Similarly, Kautilya, an exponent of ancient Hindu realpolitik, recommended that the conqueror "should never covet the land, things, and sons and wives of the king slain by him." Rather, "he should reinstate in their own estates relatives of the kings slain."[33]

Another approach to establishing a restorative peace involves granting aid to the defeated. Various forms of assistance, ranging from territorial compensation to financial support, have been employed to revive the opponent and allay feelings of bitterness. As suggested in the following Jātaka story titled "Advice to Kings" (*Rājovāda*), compassion is thought to be more beneficial than resorting to retaliation for past injuries:

> The kings of two states meet in neutral territory on a road outside their territorial limits and the question of precedence is raised since it was necessary for one to

give way. Since it is discovered that the extent of territory, military strength, economic resources, nobility of birth are the same, they discuss their policies. The policy of one is: "He meets force with force, mildness with mildness; he wins over the good with good and conquers the evil with evil." The policy of the other is summarized: "He conquers wrath with kindness, evil with good, greed with charity and falsehood with truth." The latter policy is acknowledged as the superior and the former voluntarily gives way.[34]

No leader personifies the tension between retribution and reconciliation better than Alexander the Great. On the one hand, he vented his wrath at Thebes for rebelling, massacred captured Greek mercenaries who had fought on behalf of the Persians at the Battle of the Granicus River (334 B.C.E.), and was ruthless toward Phoenician cities that resisted his march down the coast of Asia Minor. On the other hand, Alexander's treatment of King Poros of India was even-handed; he openly tried to accommodate himself to the lifestyles and customs of each of the regions his Macedonian army conquered, and, during a banquet of international reconciliation at Opis, he prayed for "a union of hearts . . . and for a joint commonwealth in which all peoples should be partners, not subjects."[35]

In sum, when making decisions about national security in the realm of **high politics,** victorious leaders are pulled in opposite directions. Advocates of stern punishment counsel that a punitive peace treaty will disempower the defeated enemy and force it to refrain from future fighting. Proponents of rehabilitative policies proclaim that generous terms will assuage the vanquished, build trust, and secure their cooperation in building a lasting framework of mutual security. As we shall see in the cases presented in the chapters ahead, rationally choosing between these alternatives is difficult for manifold reasons, including "an astounding lack of systematic data on conflict resolution and reconciliation,"[36] and there is little consensus among and between various ethical traditions about the conditions under which either choice is morally justified.

> "Know, my son, with how little wisdom the world is governed."
>
> —COUNT AXEL OXENSTIERNA
> CHANCELLOR OF SWEDEN

CHOOSING BETWEEN RECONCILIATION AND RETRIBUTION

"Victory in the true sense," the strategist Basil Liddell Hart once wrote, "implies that the state of peace . . . is better after the war than before."[37] In an effort to achieve a better peace, victors draw inspiration from a vast reservoir of values when choosing which policy options to pursue as they deal with the defeated. As Box 2.1 displays, some of these values accentuate magnanimity. Defeated troops receive mercy, and noncombatants are treated with compassion. Alternatively, victors may espouse values that downplay clemency in

---

BOX 2.1
CONTENDING VIEWS ON HOW TO DEAL WITH ENEMIES

On Magnanimity

"In war, resolution; in defeat, defiance; in victory, magnanimity."
— Winston Churchill

"Let us never negotiate out of fear; but let us never fear to negotiate."
— John F. Kennedy

"Treat the enemy that has been conquered with courtesy and generosity."
— Kwan-Tsz

On Malevolence

"For great evils, drastic remedies are necessary, and whoever has to treat them should not be afraid to use the instrument that cuts the best."
— Prince Clemens von Metternich

"Nothing should be left to an invaded people except their eyes for weeping."
— Otto von Bismarck

"Bear thou thy foe upon thy shoulders till the time cometh when thou canst throw him down, breaking him into pieces like an earthen pot thrown with violence upon a stony surface. The foe must never be let off even though he addresseth thee most piteously. No pity shouldst thou shew him but slay him at once."
— Kanika

---

favor of harsh punishment. Preoccupied with preserving the gains won in battle, they try to incapacitate former foes. Joseph Stalin's suggestion on how to prevent German military revival after World War II illustrates the kinds of policies derived from this sort of harsh realpolitik value system. According to Winston Churchill, Stalin proposed liquidating the remaining fifty thousand men in the German officer corps.[38]

At issue is whether either of these value positions helps national leaders craft postwar policies that prevent wars from resuming. Desiderius Erasmus of Rotterdam, the sixteenth-century humanist, maintained that "the most disadvantageous peace is better than the most just war."[39] In the midst of war's terrible carnage, a disadvantageous peace might seem preferable to interminable horror. Yet, if peace is to be more than a pause in an ongoing struggle, it must be constructed with forethought. As one student of war termination has put it,

"military success may be a necessary condition for achieving ambitious political war aims, but it is not a sufficient condition for doing so."[40]

"Blessed are the peacemakers," declares the Sermon on the Mount. But
good intentions alone do not assure good results; they must be linked to a well-
designed **grand strategy** under which warfare is conducted with unremitting
attention to the kind of peace that is desired. Yet it is not easy to keep long-
term political objectives in mind during the heat of battle. Former British prime
minister Anthony Eden, reflecting on the failure of national leaders to foresee
the consequences of their actions, once com-
mented that "it is impossible to read the record
now and not feel that we had a responsibility
for always being a lap behind." "Always a lap
behind," he continued, "the fatal lap."[41]

"Peace cannot be kept
by force. It can only
be achieved by
understanding."

—ALBERT EINSTEIN

What makes it difficult to foresee the consequences of adopting policies rooted in either
reconciliation or retribution is that arguments
can be made on behalf of each approach—which
is why various ethical traditions come into conflict with one another on this
age-old controversy. Consider the policy dilemmas as defined by one diplomatic historian.

> Perhaps a war which ended with a moderate treaty was more likely to create a
> lasting peace. Thus, several historians praised the men who shaped the treaties at
> Paris and Vienna in 1814 and 1815 as the creators of a long period of peace. Nev-
> ertheless . . . the praise cannot be carried too far, for many of the important deci-
> sions of 1814–1815 were quickly altered by the eddy of events. In contrast, the
> century's second era of peace followed a treaty which was often regarded as harsh
> and punitive. While the territory and gold which Germany took from France in
> 1871 were later to be singled out as a major cause of the First World War, it is
> salutary to recall that the harsh treaty of 1871 also marked the opening of a
> remarkably long era of peace.[42]

Thus, there seems to be no simple answer to the difficult question of how to
break the chains of successive wars between competitive pairs of states. War
and peace are intimately connected: the Prussian general Karl von Clausewitz
regarded war, a "continuation of politics by other means"; Chou En-lai, a former premier of the People's Republic of China, saw politics as "a continuation
of war by other means."[43] "Politics is war without bloodshed," Mao Tse-tung
once observed, "while war is politics with bloodshed."[44]

Why the answer has remained elusive will be the subject of the cases of war
and peace-settlement decisions in the next chapters in this book. In Part II
we open by comparing two paradigmatic cases from antiquity: (1) the Peloponnesian War between Athens and Sparta in the Greek city-state system and
(2) the more than 150-year three Punic Wars fought between two empires,
Rome and Carthage, to illuminate the perils of prudent decisions in peace mak-

ing. In Part III, we examine in chronological order five cases in the modern global system: (1) the Napoleonic Wars and the peace settlement reached at the Congress of Vienna, (2) the wars of German Unification in the 1870s, (3) the First World War and the Treaty of Versailles that ended it, (4) the Second World War and the series of conferences that sought to negotiate a settlement, and (5) the Persian Gulf War in 1991 and its troubled, uncertain aftermath. These cases allow the various approaches that victors have taken in an effort to construct a durable peace to be compared. As we progress through these historical case studies, our focus will be on the following questions:

- Did the victors seek reconciliation or retribution?
- Was their attempt at engineering either a lenient or a harsh peace supported by a coherent grand strategy?
- If so, what were the elements of that strategy?
- How successful was the strategy?
- What lessons, practical and ethical, do these individual cases suggest about the most productive and moral paths winners should take to peace making with defeated enemies?

Each case tells a different tale and illustrates different aspects of the problems of making rational and ethical decisions about a set of very difficult problems. By asking similar questions about different historical episodes and comparing the choices made by the victors after a series of wars and their consequences, insights can be sharpened about the boundaries of prudent and just choice when nations attempt to make peace. These structured, focused comparisons will facilitate, in Part IV of this book, an effort to glean from the cases inspected some policy prescriptions for national leaders to follow in the wake of war.

NOTES

1. Wright, 1970, p. 58.
2. Posen, 1984, p. 13; Walt, 1989, p. 6.
3. Goodman and Bogart, 1992, p. 3; also Fox, 1970a, p. 2. For summaries of the literature on war termination, see Stein, 1975; Pillar, 1983; and Cimbala and Dunn, 1987.
4. Craig and George, 1990, p. 229. Japan's calculations in 1941 regarding a future armed conflict with the United States exemplify the lack of a comprehensive, well-thought-out plan. Japan entered the war with "no clear conception as to how it was to be won and no realistic analysis of what a long, total war would mean." Morgan, 1983, p. 53.
5. Napoleon, "Pensées politiques et sociales," as reprinted in Freedman, 1994, p. 216.
6. In Dyer, 1985, p. 143.
7. Blainey, 1973, p. 56.
8. Rasler and Thompson, 1994, p. 41.
9. Blainey, 1973, p. 177. History's starkest example of prolonged armed combat interspersed with respites of peace can be found in the Spanish reconquest of the Iberian Peninsula from the Moors. Legend has it that the first Christian victory was won by the Visigothic noble Pelayo

when in 722 he ambushed an Arab patrol in the Cantabrian Mountains. The struggle ended in 1492 with the triumphal entry of Ferdinand of Aragón and Isabella of Castile into Granada. Covering over seven centuries, the reconquest remains an undertaking without parallel in the annals of military affairs. See Fry and Raymond, 1983, pp. 12–14.

10. For an extended discussion, see Solomon, 1976. Other relevant literature includes Gibbard, 1990; De Sousa, 1987; Lyons, 1980; and Rorty, 1980.

11. Welch, 1993, p. 3.

12. Scheff, 1994, p. 63.

13. Aristotle, 1925, pp. 1125b, 1126a. For a fuller account, see Brinton, 1988.

14. David Lloyd George, "Final Draft of the Fontainebleau Memorandum," as reprinted in Gilbert, 1966, p. 189.

15. Unlike a temporary cease-fire, an armistice is viewed as a prelude to peace. Of course, formal peace negotiations can occur without an armistice. During the Thirty Years' War, for example, fighting raged while delegates to the peace congresses at Münster and Osnabrück deliberated. Similarly, the Treaty of Guadalupe Hidalgo (1848) was negotiated while hostilities continued between Mexico and the United States (see Sibert, 1933; Starke, 1991; and Duchhardt, 1993). The legal rules governing an armistice are outlined in articles 36–41 of the Hague Regulations Respecting the Laws and Customs of War on Land, annexed to Convention IV of 1907. For a discussion of the differences among a suspension of hostilities, a cease-fire, a truce, and an armistice, see Smith, 1995, pp. 265–270.

16. von Glahn, 1996, p. 610.

17. Adapted from Handel, 1978, p. 37.

18. Kent, 1866, p. 420. For a discussion of international treaty norms, see Kegley and Raymond, 1990.

19. Schelling, 1966, p. 7.

20. The Korean War (1950–1953) is a modern example of such a stalemate. The armistice signed at Panmunjom represented a truce rather than a peace settlement.

21. Hersch Lauterpacht, following Felix Oppenheim, as cited in von Glahn, 1996, p. 609.

22. Liberman, 1996.

23. See Phillimore, 1879–1888, vol. I, pp. 222–225; Hall, 1917, p. 31; Hershey, 1930, p. 276; and Westlake, 1910–1913, vol. I, pp. 86–118.

24. Vitoria, 1917.

25. Abbé Gabriel Bonnot de Mably, in McMahon, 1940, p. 43. Also see Sagey, 1972, p. 58, and Korman, 1996.

26. Jacobini, 1962, p. 70.

27. Schwebel, 1994, p. 523. Leaving aside the controversial issue of conquest, title to territory may be acquired under international law through either original or derivative means. The former includes the discovery of land unclaimed by any other state *(terra nullius)*, the addition of new land to the territory of a state through the accretion of alluvial deposits, or by prescription—an uncontested exercise of sovereignty over a long period of time. The latter includes the voluntary transfer of territory by purchase, exchange, or gift. Conquest, an involuntary form of cession, is considered to be a source of derivative title. According to the doctrine of *postliminium*, when captured territory is liberated from enemy control, it is assumed to return to its former status.

28. In Montross, 1960, p. 145. On a more grisly note, Genghis Khan also is reported to have said, "Happiness lies in conquering one's enemies, in driving them in front of oneself, in taking their property, in savoring their despair, in outraging their wives and daughters." In Rodzinski, 1979, pp. 164–165.

29. In Pavithran, 1965, p. 619.

30. Blainey, 1968, p. 267.

31. Phillipson, 1916, p. 165.

32. Opponents such as Brutus and Cassius were given honors by Caesar, and the statues of Pompey were restored. Cicero quipped that by setting up Pompey's statues, Caesar "had firmly fixed and established his own." Plutarch, 1958, p. 264.
33. In Sengupta, 1925, p. 13.
34. Jayatillike, 1968, pp. 549–550.
35. Bozeman, 1960, p. 95.
36. De Waal, 1966, p. 64.
37. Liddell Hart, 1967, p. 357.
38. Churchill, 1951, pp. 373–374.
39. In Lamb, 1988, p. 12.
40. George, 1993, p. 100.
41. Eden, 1960, p. 520.
42. Blainey, 1973, p. 15.
43. von Clausewitz, 1984, p. 87; in Green, 1982, p. 18.
44. In Green, 1982, p. 20.

PART II

Making Peace in Antiquity

To see the contemporary relevance of historical cases, we need examples that illustrate the timeless nature of decisions about war and peace making. Historical cases with parallels to the present are especially useful pedagogically when they juxtapose contending ethical traditions and highlight how key theoretical concepts, such as *power transitions* between rivals in the *balance of power,* speak to perennial problems in understanding the dynamics of world politics.

The echoes of the distant past are heard in the present when nations make critical decisions. Every leader relies on history when faced with difficult choices. Two prominent wars and decisions for peace making often referred to, even today, are presented in this part of the book. They provide examples of the limitations on rational choice victors face when deciding how to treat the enemy they have subdued on the battlefield. They also are two classic dramatizations of the moral dilemmas in making difficult decisions and were selected for comparative examination because the victor in the first case chose a strategy that was altogether at odds with the philosophical reasoning underlying the victor's strategy in the second case. Their comparison encourages critical thought about the risks and advantages of lenient versus punitive approaches and the obstacles to making peace when wars end.

Our first case looks back to the Greek world of fifth century B.C.E. Athens, a growing commercial city-state or *polis,* was the cradle of democracy and many other ideas—equality, liberty, adherence to law and justice—that have shaped modern liberal thought about republican civic virtue. Athens was not a hegemon able to exercise its will freely in external relations. It faced a rival power, Sparta, that stood for dissimilar ideals of citizenship based on the nobility of stern military discipline—a value that enabled Sparta to become the strongest military power in Greece. This setting created the conditions out of which the long and bitter Peloponnesian War between Athens and Sparta erupted over power and principle.

The reader will find in the origins, conduct, and climax of this first case a gold mine of information and insight about the politics of war and peace making that suggest important lessons for today. Moreover, this case aptly introduces *realism,* one of the major theoretical traditions for analyzing war and peace. It draws on the famous history of the Pelopponnesian War written by the retired Athenian General Thucydides, which virtually defined the realist approach to world politics that continues today as the primary focus for interpreting international security issues. Thucydides' account of the tragic war between Athens and Sparta, each supported by a vast coalition of allies, colonies, and even former enemies, is a catalyst for understanding many of the core concepts in the contemporary study of world politics. We find here a testimony to the perceived primacy of *power politics* and such other central ideas as competing *alliances, arms races, hegemony,* and, in Thucydides' realist thesis that "what made war inevitable was the growth of Athenian power and the fear which this caused in Sparta," the foundation of what is now known as the *security dilemma* in international politics.

No one can read this case without appreciating the wisdom of Thucydides' belief that theorizing about past decisions can benefit future policymakers. The Pelopponnesian War between 431–404 B.C.E. may be rooted in the ancient past, but it provides eternal lessons about the roles of moderation, trust, revenge, and justice in decisions about peace making.

The second case from antiquity is equally instructive because it offers a striking contrast to the first, while at the same time introducing additional topics and themes in current discourse about international security. The rise of the Greek city-state system was followed by the ascendance of other centers of power. Two vast *empires,* those of Rome and Carthage, rose to eclipse the remnants of the Grecian "golden age." As Roman trade and conquest spread widely, Rome clashed with its only remaining rival for supremacy in the Mediterranean Sea, the Phoenician (Punic) city-nation of Carthage in Northern Africa. Another rival *hegemonic struggle*—this time between two titans— culminated in the Punic Wars during the third and second centuries B.C.E. The three successive wars between Rome and Carthage over a span of 150 years provide an excellent opportunity to investigate the impact of past wars between rivals and their peace settlements on subsequent wars. These three separate wars illustrate an *enduring rivalry* and bring perspective to the recurring dilemmas associated with decisions about lasting peace. Thus, comparisons of these wars, in addition to introducing many central theoretical concepts in world politics generally, vividly reveal an important principle, described by first-century B.C.E. Roman historian Sallust: "It is always easy to begin a war, but very difficult to stop one, since its beginning and end are not under the control of the same man. Anyone, even a coward, can commence a war, but it can be brought to an end only with the consent of the victors."

Taken together, the two cases in Part II set the stage for investigating subsequent wars and peace treaties in the modern era. They provide guidelines for analyses, suggesting the questions to explore when more recent cases are examined in Part III, where we will expand on how rival theoretical and ethical schools of thought approach these perennial choices.

· 3 ·

TARNISHED TRIUMPH:
SPARTA AND THE PELOPONNESIAN WAR

O Huntress who slayest the beasts in the glade,
O Virgin divine, hither come to our truce,
Unite us in bonds which all time will not loose.
Grant us to find in this treaty, we pray,
An unfailing source of true friendship today,
And all of our days, helping us to refrain
From weaseling tricks which bring war in their train.
                              —ARISTOPHANES, *LYSISTRATA*

PREVIEW

Our first historical case focuses on the Peloponnesian War, a titanic struggle between the ancient Greek city-states of Sparta and Athens that lasted from 431 to 404 B.C.E. Most of what we know about this war comes from Thucydides, the author of the first systematic treatise on foreign policy decision making developed within Western cultural tradition. Thucydides was a general who commanded Athenian forces in northern Greece early in the war. Sent into exile because of his failure to prevent the Spartans from seizing the strategic city of Amphipolis, he apparently divided his time between writing a history of the war and traveling throughout Greece to hear public debates over military policy and to interview people who had witnessed major events.

The Peloponnesian War has long been of interest to students of international relations because it was a general, system-transforming war that involved the most powerful states of the day. *Hegemonic* struggles of this type have been the basic mechanism over the millennia for changing leadership within the international system. Though infrequent, they produce an appalling toll of death and destruction. Since many theorists believe that the conditions that precipitate these deadly collisions have not varied significantly since

Sparta and Athens traded blows, the Peloponnesian War has been closely studied in order to learn about:

- rivalries between land powers and sea powers
- coercive diplomacy
- alliance polarization
- power transitions
- imperial overstretch

Thucydides also has been of interest to students of international relations due to his contribution to political *realism* as an approach to explaining the origins of war and the problems of peace making. Not only does his analysis of the Peloponnesian War contain a wealth of insights about the underlying structural conditions that make serious international conflicts likely, but it describes a host of psychological factors that can cause those conflicts to escalate to war.

In addition to telling a tragic tale about war and failed efforts at peace making, Thucydides encourages us to think about ethical questions in international affairs. Through the voices of Pericles and Diodotos we hear pleas for moderation and clemency; through Cleon and Alcibiades we hear exhortations about power politics and revenge. As you read through this chapter, consider how the desires for security, glory, and profit may have affected the way these contending appeals were received.

■ ■

On a beautiful spring day in the year 404 B.C.E.,[1] as the sound of flutes drifted through the crowd, Spartan dignitaries adorned in flowers watched with satisfaction as the once mighty Athenian fleet burned in its home port at Piraeus. Twenty-seven years earlier, Sparta had gone to war with Athens. It was, as the historian Thucydides tells us, the greatest upheaval that had ever shaken the ancient world.[2] Nature itself seemed to agree: the tiny island of Delos, long a center of Greek religious life, was jolted by an earthquake just before the fighting began. No one could remember anything like this happening there before. Was it an omen? Were the gods issuing a warning? Would some terrible tragedy befall Greece once its two most powerful city-states clashed?

Nothing was farther from the minds of the Spartans on that spring day. After dismantling the defensive walls surrounding Athens, they proclaimed all Greeks were free from Athenian imperial control. To commemorate their military triumph, they unveiled a group of bronze statues in Delphi that depicted gods laying wreaths upon Spartan heads. The victors in what we now call the Peloponnesian War could scarcely contain their pride. Not only was peace at hand, but it appeared to be a peace cemented by Spartan **hegemony.** The years of brutal combat and staggering losses were finally over. With an unrivaled army and numerous allies, Sparta was positioned to reshape the Hellenic state system.

But preserving the peace would prove as challenging as winning the war. A clear, constructive strategy was needed to guide the Spartans when they began crafting new rules and arrangements for the postwar world. "Peace," as one student of international history has written, "does not keep itself."[3] If national leaders "concentrate exclusively on victory, with no thought for the after-effect," insists B.H. Liddell Hart, "it is almost certain that the peace will be a bad one, containing the germs of another war."[4] Unless military success is augmented by an effective political design, the prospects for a durable peace diminish.

Could Sparta meet this challenge? Would it be able to translate its battlefield victory into a prosperous, secure future? Or would Sparta's hard-earned triumph be tarnished by a lack of strategic vision and political acumen?

THE HELLENIC STATE SYSTEM

Greece at the time of the Peloponnesian War was not unified; it contained a welter of small, autonomous *poleis,* or city-states, scattered throughout the Balkan Peninsula, the Aegean Archipelago, and what is today western Turkey. Many of these city-states sent colonists abroad, where they established new settlements in Sicily, southern Italy, north Africa, and as far away as the Mediterranean coastlines of France and Spain. When taken together, these geographically dispersed political units comprised the classical Greek, or Hellenic, state system (see Table 3.1). Though fiercely independent and often harboring territorial jealousies, the city-states of fifth-century Greece shared a common culture, language, and religious practices. The strong sense of membership in a larger cultural community combined with an abhorrence of any kind of political overlordship to make these city-states "the first known example" of "independent states that were antihegemonial on principle" and which thought it "unwise to destroy the defeated" or to "support the victor" fully.[5]

While the Greeks were united by shared customs and values, they were divided by rugged limestone and marble mountain ranges. The landscape was one of sharp peaks, narrow valleys, thin soil, and an agricultural mosaic of olive orchards, vineyards, and grain fields. Whereas steep mountain slopes fostered an attitude of stubborn self-sufficiency, the sea discouraged provincialism. Though pirate raids and fierce storms presented constant dangers, the sea facilitated the exchange of goods and ideas among insular Greek communities as well as with the older civilizations of Egypt and Asia Minor.

The typical polis consisted of an urban center and surrounding farmland *(chôra).* Most poleis were small, not exceeding a few hundred square miles and a population of approximately twenty thousand. Sparta and Athens were much larger than the average polis, however. Laconia, the region around Sparta, contained roughly 270,000 inhabitants within an area of over three thousand square miles. Athens boasted a population of approximately 300,000 and an area of some one thousand square miles.[6] Herodotus, touted by many as the "father" of history, indicates that relations between these two powerful

TABLE 3.1
A Chronology of the Hellenic State System

Date (B.C.E.)	Events
c. 1200–800	Dark Ages: collapse of Mycenaean civilization on mainland of Greece; Dorians begin moving overland into southern Greece; Ionians move from northern Greece across the islands of the Aegean Sea and colonize coastline of Asia Minor
c. 750	Greek colonies established in Sicily and southern Italy
c. 735–715	Sparta seizes control of most of the plain of Messenia
c. 700	Athens combines with towns in Attica to form a single political unit
c. 670–650	Spartans solidify hold on plain of Messenia using new hoplite military tactics
c. 624	Drago introduces first code of law to Athens
594	Solon initiates constitutional reforms in Athens
c. 550	The Peloponnesian League established under Spartan domination
553–529	Cyrus the Great conquers Asia Minor (including Ionian Greeks) and Babylonia, transforming Persia into a vast empire
546	Athens ruled by the tyrant Peisistratus
522–485	Darius divides the Persian Empire into twenty provinces (satrapies), introduces reforms including a common currency, regular taxes, and a standing army. Military victories over Egypt (518) and Indus valley region (513); failure against Scythians (512)
507	Democracy restored in Athens by Cleisthenes
499	Ionian Greeks revolt from Persia; suppressed in 494
493	Themistocles elected archon in Athens, begins fortifying harbor at Piraeus
490	Persian invasion of Greece: Athenian victory at battle of Marathon
486	Xerxes becomes King of Persia
483	Rich silver strike at Mount Laurium provides Athens with funds to expand fleet
480	Persian invasion of Greece: Leonidas of Sparta defeated at Thermopylae; Persian fleet destroyed at Salamis; Persian army defeated at Plataea (479)
478–476	Spartans abdicate leadership of Greek states; Delian League formed
466	Delian League transformed into Athenian Empire (treasury moved to Athens in 454)
464	Helot revolt in Sparta
461	Outbreak of war between Athens and Peloponnesian states
458	Athenians build the "long walls" to protect the road to their seaport at Piraeus
445	Thirty Years' Peace
434	Crisis over Epidamnus
433	Athens intervenes in Potidaea
432	The Megarian Decree passed in Athens; Spartan Assembly debates war
431	Outbreak of Peloponnesian War
430	Plague breaks out in Athens; death of Pericles (429)
427	Mytilene surrenders to Athens
425	Spartan soldiers captured at Sphacteria

Date (B.C.E.)	Events
424	Amphipolis revolts against Athens
421	Peace of Nicias
416	Melos destroyed by Athens
415	Athenian invasion of Sicily
413	Athenians defeated at Syracuse
412	Revolt of Athenian allies
411	Rule by the Four Hundred in Athens
406	Athenian victory at Arginusae; peace overtures from Sparta refused
405	Destruction of Athenian fleet at battle of Aegospotami
404	Surrender of Athens to Sparta; beginning of Spartan hegemony in Greece
400–394	Spartan intervention in Asia Minor and northern Greece
395	Corinthian War; Persia finances Greek attacks on Sparta; rebuilding of the "long walls" in Athens with Persian help
387–386	Sparta concludes King's Peace and cedes Ionia to Persia
378	Formation of the Second Athenian League
371	Battle of Leuctra: Thebes defeats Sparta and ends Spartan hegemony in Greece
362	Battle of Mantinea: Epaminondas mortally wounded
359	Philip II becomes king of Macedonians
338	Battle of Chaironea: Philip II subjugates Greece

city-states had long alternated between hostility and cooperation and says that oracles warned the Spartans "many deeds of enmity would be done against them by the Athenians."[7] Stern, authoritarian Sparta and open, energetic Athens were political opposites. For the ancient Greeks, the world was replete with conflicts between opposites. "Fire lives the death of air," insisted Heraclitus of Ephesus, "and air lives the death of fire."[8] Nothing was static; everything belonged to some greater whole. Should the prophecy be fulfilled, and warfare erupt between the great city-states of Sparta and Athens, the outcome would affect the entire eastern Mediterranean region.

SPARTA AND ATHENS

Sparta was located in the Peloponnesus between two mountains on the Eurotas River, a site that provided natural protection and encouraged an attitude of insularity (see Map 3.1). As a result of the First and Second Messenian Wars (circa 735–715 and 670–650), the Spartans gained control of the surrounding region. With few exceptions, those southern Greek city-states that were not conquered became members of the Peloponnesian League, a military **alliance** dominated by Sparta.

Sparta's government was a unique mixture of monarchy, oligarchy, and democracy. Allegedly designed by Lycurgus and expressed in the *Rhetra* (saying),

MAP 3.1 The Hellenic State System of the Late Fifth Century B.C.E. At the onset of the Peloponnesian War, the Athenian Empire consisted of city-states scattered throughout Ionia and the Aegean Sea. Sparta's allies were concentrated in the Peloponnesus.

it contained a dyarchy (joint rule by two hereditary kings from different clans who led military expeditions), a council of twenty-eight elders from noble families *(Gerousia)*, an assembly of the army *(Apella)* which voted on motions brought before it by the council, and, after subsequent reforms, a board of five overseers *(Ephors)* who limited the exercise of royal power. Below Spartan citizens were two other groups: the *perioeci,* free men from the surrounding countryside who engaged in metallurgy and commerce, and the *helots,* conquered peoples forced into serfdom to raise agricultural commodities. The vital economic roles played by these two subordinate groups allowed the Spartans to devote themselves to military activities.

Sparta's reputation was earned by the courage and skill of its soldiers. Their martial spirit was admired throughout Greece and came to be symbolized by a comment attributed to Dïeneces. Prior to a suicidal battle at Thermopylae, where a small Spartan unit was given the task of holding a mountain pass against a massive Persian army, Dïeneces was told the enemy's arrows were so many that when in flight they would hide the sun. He calmly replied, "So much the better, we will fight in the shade." Though eventually overwhelmed, the unit's discipline in the face of certain death inspired Greek forces elsewhere and afforded them the time to mount a successful defense. The valor of this unit was commemorated in an inscription on a memorial later placed on the battlefield: "Stranger, tell the Spartans that we lie here in obedience to their words."[9]

The Spartans excelled at a style of warfare based on the hoplite phalanx. It was a formation of massed heavy infantry, named after the round, convex shield *(hoplon)* soldiers held in their left hands. Any free adult male could be a hoplite if he was able to spend the summer on military campaigns and could afford the weapons, a bronze helmet, a breastplate, and additional armor to protect his shins. Before the onset of the Peloponnesian War, hoplites represented approximately 20 percent to 40 percent of the free adult males of a polis.[10]

The rationale behind the hoplite phalanx derived from the blind spots individuals have when engaged in sword and spear warfare. To compensate for this weakness, soldiers stood shoulder to shoulder in a compact mass, usually eight rows deep. Battlefield success required trust, tenacity, and toughness; members of a densely packed phalanx had to work in unison to win. Since each soldier instinctively sought the protection of his comrade's shield on the right, the result was a predictable angle of attack—each phalanx tended to advance to the right.

The typical hoplite battle was a short, terrifying clash that involved a charge by the opposing phalanxes. Weighed down with some seventy pounds of weapons and armor, the troops sprinted toward one another.

> Each individual would have chosen another as his target at the moment of contact, thrusting his spear point at some gap between shield and shield, and seeking to hit a patch of flesh not covered by armor—throat, armpit, or groin. The chance was fleeting. As the second and subsequent ranks were brought up short by the stop in front, the phalanx concertinaed, throwing the weight of seven men onto the back of the warriors engaged with the enemy. Under this impact, some men inevitably went down at once, dead, wounded or overborne from the rear. That might create a breach in the shield wall. Those in the second or third ranks strove to open it wider . . . to win room in which swords, the hoplite's secondary weapon, might be drawn and used to slash at an enemy's legs.[11]

Once the opposing rank was broken, the defeated hoplites would scatter on foot with cavalry often in pursuit. Escape was difficult. Fortunately for those fleeing, the victors normally did not press their advantage. Instead, a truce would be declared and a battlefield monument erected while the dead on each side were exchanged.

To produce its brave and obedient soldiers, Spartan males progressed through a rigorous system known as the *agogê* (upbringing). Upon birth, all infants deemed imperfect were placed in a gorge outside the city where they soon died from exposure. Physically fit males lived at home until the age of seven, when their formal training began. Spartan boys resided together in a "boot camp" setting—they were issued a single garment to wear, fed a gruel the primary ingredient of which is said to have been pig blood, and prepared for the life of a warrior. At the age of twenty, the young Spartans were assigned to a barracks and declared competent to serve in the army. Ten years later they became eligible for full citizenship as *homoioi* (equals). For the remainder of their lives, Spartan males belonged to one of many small, fraternity-like mess halls where all main meals were taken together. The entire process, from birth through adulthood, was designed to foster resilience and civic unity, with the state controlling every aspect of life. Although other Greek city-states respected Spartan austerity, communal spirit, and *eunomia* (having good laws, well obeyed), none of them adopted this rigid system.

> "The Spartans are not wont to ask how many the enemy are, but where they are."
>
> —AGIS II OF SPARTA

Whereas Sparta was a cautious, methodical land power, Athens was a bold, resourceful sea power. As described by a group of Corinthian delegates to an assembly of the Peloponnesian League, the Athenians were "addicted to innovation" and "adventurous beyond their power." Always "swift to follow up a success," their failures were seen merely as temporary setbacks "soon filled up by fresh hopes." Daring and vivacious, "they were born into the world to take no rest themselves and to give none to others."[12]

Athens and its port, Piraeus, were situated on the Attic Plain. During the early seventh century, political and economic control rested with a group of aristocratic clans known collectively as the *Eupatridae* (having good fathers). After an unsuccessful attempt was made by Kylon to seize power, Drago crafted the first Athenian code of laws (c. 624). Solon revised it roughly a quarter century later. Debt bondage was prohibited, jury courts developed, and any citizen could prosecute public wrongdoing. Cleisthenes initiated another round of reforms between 509 and 507, which ushered in a more radical form of democracy aimed at giving all citizens equal access to political power. Citizenship, however, was limited to a small percentage of the population. Women, slaves, and males who had not come of age were excluded. Freemen of foreign birth were granted citizenship during the time of Cleisthenes, but they too were excluded in later years.

The heart of Athenian democracy was the legislative assembly *(ekklêsia).*

Following the rule of advance deliberation *(probouleusis)*, a council *(boulê)* of five hundred citizens selected by lot discussed pressing matters before they were taken up by the assembly. After speeches were delivered on both sides of an issue, the assembly would vote and then issue a decree.[13] Assembly decrees were implemented by numerous magistrates and boards appointed by lot for a yearlong term. Highly egalitarian for those who were citizens, Athenian democracy contained frequent opportunities for political participation.

Since its economy relied upon maritime commerce, Athenian military power was based on maintaining naval strength. The trireme, a ship approximately 120 feet long and rowed by 170 oarsmen arrayed in three superimposed banks, was the source of that strength. Naval warfare typically involved maneuvering for position so the opponent's vessel could be rammed broadside with an armored beak that protruded from the trireme's bow. If it did not sink, a contingent of marines would board the enemy vessel and subdue its crew.

THE PERSIAN WARS

In many city-states throughout the sixth century, rule by wealthy, aristocratic clans was interrupted whenever ambitious men were able to rally political dissidents under the banner of populism and seize power for themselves. Observing traditional laws only when it was expedient, these so-called tyrants dominated public affairs. Some of them were moderate, others were cruel, and few governed for very long.

Tyranny came to Athens in 546 when Peisistratos took control of the city. Although he was an effective ruler who promoted pride in Athenian cultural achievements, his son Hippias became increasingly oppressive after assuming power upon the deaths of his father and brother.

The Alcmeonids were one of the old, aristocratic clans of Athens whose political position was weakened by the Pisistratid tyranny. In an effort to rid Athens of Hippias, they bribed the priestess at Delphi to command the Spartans to free Athens. In 510, the Alcmeonid family succeeded in enlisting Spartan support and were able to overthrow Hippias. Whereas the Spartans expected Athens to show its gratitude by joining their Peloponnesian League, the Athenians refused and evicted Spartan troops from their city. Fearing **reprisals,** a delegation of Athenians immediately arranged for military protection from Persia. But when counterattacks by Sparta and its allies were unsuccessful, the Athenians saw no need for an alliance with the Persians and repudiated their agreement. For Darius, king of Persia and ruler over the most powerful empire of the day, this unilateral act of annulment was immoral. As a worshiper of Ahuramazda, the Divine Lord of Light and Truth, it was Darius's religious duty to punish the duplicitous Athenians, whom he viewed as agents of the evil forces of Lie and Darkness.[14]

Remember the Athenians

Before Darius could move against the Athenians, he had to deal with civil strife within his own empire. In 499, Miletus, a Greek city-state on the eastern shore of the Aegean Sea, revolted from Persian rule and sought help from the mainland Greeks. Athens sent some twenty warships. Although the Greeks were able to burn the Persian city of Sardis, and the revolt spread to other costal areas of Asia Minor, Darius's forces were able to reimpose control by 493. To punish the deceitful Athenians and dissuade them from supporting future revolts, Darius ordered an invasion of Greece. Three years later, his troops landed on the coastal plain of Marathon, twenty-six miles northeast of Athens. Fighting with verve and using topography as an ally, the vastly outnumbered Athenians enveloped the Persians between the sea and a swampy marsh. Stunned by the ferocious and well-designed attack, the Persian infantry fled in disarray.

Athens had won a striking victory. Roughly 6,400 Persians died, but the Athenians lost only 192 soldiers. Danger still loomed over Attica: The remaining Persian forces hoped to sail down the coast and capture Athens by surprise while its army was camped at Marathon. But a messenger had run the twenty-six miles quickly enough to alert the city. Collapsing from exhaustion in the marketplace, he is said to have proclaimed: "We have been victorious!" Meanwhile, in another heroic feat of endurance, the army marched back in time to prepare for another attack. The Persians, however, disheartened by the prospect of fighting the intrepid Athenian infantry, returned home.

The defeat suffered by Darius's forces was an insult to the great king. So as not to forget the need to avenge the humiliating rout at Marathon, legend has it that a slave was ordered to whisper frequently in his ear, "Remember the Athenians." Darius died before he could take his revenge. His son, Xerxes, who assumed the Persian throne in 486 and was known by the Greeks as the Great King, pledged to vindicate his father by crushing the Greeks.

Now Everything We Love Is at Stake

The instrument of Xerxes' revenge was an immense army composed of troops from across Persia's multinational empire. Numbering in the hundreds of thousands, its size astonished everyone who saw it marching inexorably toward Greece. Stories circulated that the army was so large its soldiers drank entire rivers dry. To feed such a colossal force, Xerxes assembled an equally massive fleet of merchant ships to transport the army's rations, and still another fleet of warships to protect the merchant marine. Initial Greek efforts to stop the Persian juggernaut on land at Thermopylae and at sea near Artemisium failed. Further resistance seemed futile. As the Athenian playwright Aeschylus described the situation: "Now everything we love is at stake."[15]

With public morale ebbing, Themistocles, one of Athens's generals, devised a bold plan. He persuaded the Athenians to evacuate their homeland for refuge on the nearby island of Salamis, while also convincing the jittery commanders of the allied Greek navy to deploy their ships in the narrow straits separating the mainland from Salamis. Meanwhile, Themistocles sent his servant to tell Xerxes that he had accepted the inevitable. If the Great King would hurl his mighty warships against the smaller Greek flotilla at Salamis, the Athenian ships under his control would betray their allies and Persia would be able to destroy the remainder of the Greek navy before it escaped the confines of the straits. Xerxes was so confident that this act of treachery would deliver a swift, decisive Persian victory that he placed his portable throne on a hill overlooking the straits in order to enjoy the naval battle unfolding below.

Themistocles' plan rested on three assumptions: First, the Greeks could not win in open water; only fighting within cramped straits could offset Persia's numerical superiority. Second, Persian warships were difficult to maneuver in heavy swells; by luring the Persians into a morning attack, the Greeks could use the wind to their advantage. Third, the nervous commanders of allied Greek units were in awe of the Persian military; encouraging Xerxes to attack would force the Greeks to fight when they might otherwise have fled southward to the Peloponnese.

Early that fateful September morning in 480, Persia's vast fleet began its dreaded attack. But just as Themistocles had anticipated, a strong wind kicked up heavy swells. Sitting lower in the water than their Persian counterparts, the Greek ships were unaffected. But the taller Persian vessels were swung broadside and suddenly found themselves vulnerable to ramming. Cornered in a tight channel, Xerxes' fleet could not evade its pursuers, nor could it bring its numerical advantage into play. The bulky, less maneuverable Persian warships obstructed one another while the smaller Greek vessels darted among them with impunity. According to local lore, as the battle progressed an immense roar rolled across the land toward the sea where a wondrous mist enveloped the Greek triremes in a veil of supernatural protection. By the end of the day, the Greeks had routed the Persians, destroying as many as 350 ships while losing only forty of their own.

Before the Persian onslaught, the oracle at Delphi prophesied that Athens would be saved by a "wooden wall." Not only had the wall of triremes destroyed Xerxes' navy, but it delivered a fatal blow to his army. Without a fleet to supply it, the Persian army had to retreat. The remnants of Xerxes' land forces were crushed the following year at Plataea by a combined Greek army under Spartan command. With the Great King reeling in defeat, Greek city-states throughout Asia Minor and the eastern Aegean revolted against Persian domination. Athens promptly organized these states into a defensive alliance called the Delian League and drove what was left of the Persian military from the region.

THE THIRTY YEARS' PEACE

The Delian League began as a coalition aimed at deterring future Persian attacks. Based on principles of autonomy and equality, everyone contributed money or ships for collective defense. Over time, however, it became an Athenian empire: key political officers and military commanders were Athenians, the treasury moved to Athens, and tribute was collected from league members for Athenian use.[16] Acting on the advice of Themistocles, the Athenians used league revenue to increase the size of their fleet and construct long, impregnable walls connecting the city with its harbor at Piraeus. As Athens grew in power and prosperity, states including Corinth, Sparta, and Thebes became apprehensive about how that military and economic strength might be used. When, in 465, the Athenians attacked the island of Thasos for unilaterally withdrawing from the Delian League because of a dispute over nearby gold mines, a Spartan counterattack on Attica was only prevented by a helot revolt in Messenia, which forced Sparta to keep its army at home. Subsequent offers by Athens to help defeat the rebels were crudely rebuffed, leading the outraged Athenians to withdraw from the grand coalition that had united the two states since the Persian Wars.

Relations between Sparta and Athens deteriorated further when the Athenians supported Megara in its border conflict with Corinth. Both disputants had been members of Sparta's Peloponnesian League, but Megara offered to defect if Athens helped it defeat Corinth. The Megaran affair revealed how unstable the Hellenic state system had become: so long as Sparta and Athens remained "on good terms, each was free to deal with its allies as it chose; dissatisfied members of either alliance had nowhere to go."[17] Now with Sparta and Athens at odds, opportunistic states could play one side against the other. Moreover, the loss of over two hundred ships and forty thousand men in an unsuccessful Athenian effort to wrest Egypt from Persian control led several states to conclude that the time was ripe to bolt from the Delian League. Great-power rivalry combined with systemic uncertainty to ignite years of sporadic fighting between Athens and a loose coalition of Peloponnesian states. In the end, Megara deserted the Athenians and returned to the Spartan fold. A thirty-year truce was proclaimed, prohibiting states from switching alliances and requiring them to resolve future disagreements through binding arbitration.

The truce was soon challenged by uprisings both on the island of Samos and in Byzantium near the Black Sea. Each revolt involved a Delian League member who opposed Athenian policy. Mytilene, another member, was poised to join the rebellion if Sparta provided support. Yet Sparta decided not to intervene, allowing Athens to suppress dissident allies and maintain its **sphere of influence.**

The next crises to challenge the Thirty Years' Peace did not end with Spartan abstention. Corcyra, a neutral state, and Corinth, a member of Sparta's Peloponnesian League, were naval powers locked in a struggle over Epidamnus, a colony founded by the Corcyraeans. Fearing that as a neutral state it might have to fight Corinth and the Peloponnesian League alone, Corcyra sought help from Athens. Since the Corinthians could change the balance of power between the Peloponnesian and Delian Leagues by seizing the Corcyraean fleet, Athens agreed to a defensive alliance and sent a small squadron to assist this new ally in the battle of Sybota. The Corinthians were irate and sought revenge for what they interpreted as Athenian meddling.

With the specter of war with Corinth now haunting the Athenians, they attempted to buttress their geostrategic position. Potidaea, a Delian League member in northern Greece that had been established by Corinthian colonists, was viewed with particular suspicion by Athens. Anticipating it would back Corinth's quest for revenge, the Athenians demanded that the Potidaeans remove their fortifications. When they delayed, a military expedition was dispatched to tear down the city walls and take hostages.

Simultaneously, the Athenians moved to shore up their position elsewhere. Since Megara, Athens's neighbor to the south, had been assisting Corinth freely, the Athenians issued a decree banning trade between Megara and the Delian League. From the Athenian point of view, **economic sanctions** would pressure the Megarans into cutting their ties with the Corinthians and warn other states that aid to Corinth would trigger economic retaliation.

Sparta's fear of growing Athenian power merged with a series of crises over Epidamnus, Potidaea, and Megara to undermine the Thirty Years' Peace. A resentful Corinth called upon cities in the Peloponnesian League to meet at Sparta and formulate a collective response. At the meeting, the Corinthians warned of an insatiable Athenian appetite for aggression; other poleis would suffer the same fate as Potidaea unless Sparta launched "a speedy invasion of Attica."[18] Sthenelaïdas, a young Spartan ephor, concurred. Acknowledging Athenian service in the Greek cause against Persia, he proclaimed, "They deserve double punishment for having ceased to be good and for having become bad."[19]

Following a vote in favor of war, Sparta sent emissaries to Athens demanding an end to the siege of Potidaea and the economic **embargo** against Megara as the price of peace. At an assembly called to respond to this ultimatum, Pericles, the leading Athenian of the day, urged no concessions: "If you give way," he cautioned, "you will instantly have to meet some greater demand." In a prophetic conclusion to his speech, he professed to being "more afraid of our own blunders than of the enemy's devices."[20]

It would not be easy to dismiss the recommendation of Pericles. He was described by the biographer Plutarch as someone deserving the highest admiration.

> In his military conduct, he gained a great reputation for wariness; he would not by his good will engage in any fight which had much uncertainty or hazard; he did not envy the glory of generals whose rash adventures fortune favoured with

brilliant success, however they were admired by others; nor did he think them worthy of his imitation. . . .[21]

A man of "high spirit" but an "equitable and mild temper," Pericles never succumbed to passion "nor ever had treated any enemy as irreconcilably opposed to him."[22] Convinced by the wisdom of his advice, the Athenians expressed a willingness to arbitrate any outstanding disagreements with the Spartans but refused to accede to their demands. Each side now prepared for war. The so-called Thirty Years' Peace had lasted just fourteen years.

THE PELOPONNESIAN WAR

Hostilities began in 431 when Thebes attacked Plataea, an Athenian ally that had fought against Persia in the battle of Marathon. While Athens assisted Plataea, the Spartan king, Archidamus, prepared to invade Attica. Rather than confront Sparta and its Peloponnesian allies in set-piece hoplite battles, Pericles encouraged people living throughout Attica to abandon their homes for the safety of the walled city. Archidamus might be able to pillage the countryside, but he could not breach Athens's walls or sever the city's maritime links with commercial centers around the Mediterranean and Black Seas. On the other hand, Athens could employ its formidable naval forces to strike anywhere along the coastline of Laconia. If Athens had patience, Pericles reasoned, the Peloponnesian League would exhaust itself in costly, inconclusive campaigns. Furthermore, if it showed restraint by fighting a limited, defensive war, it would be possible to negotiate a peace settlement with those Spartans who feared a protracted conflict.[23]

A Dorian War Shall Come and with It a Plague

Following the first year of fighting, Pericles delivered a eulogy at a state funeral for those Athenians who had fallen in battle. After paying tribute to the dead, he reminded the mourners of their responsibilities in a democracy. "Our ordinary citizens," he noted, "though occupied with the pursuits of industry, are still fair judges of political matters; for, unlike any other nation . . . instead of looking on discussion as a stumbling block in the way of action, we think it an indispensable preliminary to any wise action at all."[24] But the intellectual qualities described by Pericles dissolved when a terrible epidemic struck Athens, killing roughly one-fourth of the population. Fear swept through the city as elderly citizens recalled a prophecy sung in their childhood about pestilence accompanying a Dorian war. With disease ravaging the city and Spartan soldiers laying waste to surrounding farmland, Pericles came under heavy criticism. In his last public speech before succumbing to the plague, he told the Athenians to stop grieving for their private losses and work for the public good. Never before had their city "bent before disaster." Nor, he added, should it buckle now: "They whose minds are least sensitive to calamity, and whose hands are most quick to meet it, are the greatest men and the greatest communities."[25] Persuaded by Pericles' appeals to honor and past glories, the Athenians recommitted themselves to the war effort. Showing phenomenal resilience, they continued to fight even under the most bleak conditions.

The Penalty for Rebellion Is Death

During the summer of 428, Mytilene, the principal city on the island of Lesbos and a privileged member of the Delian League, attempted to break away from an Athens still reeling from the plague. Outraged by this act of betrayal, the Athenians decreed that all Mytilenean men be killed, and all women and children enslaved. The next day, after their anger subsided, many Athenians expressed second thoughts. Cleon, one of the most powerful leaders to emerge after the death of Pericles, disagreed.[26] If Mytilene had succeeded in joining the Spartan camp, other allies might defect as well. Pity should not be shown to turncoats, he argued. The "penalty for rebellion is death."[27]

Diodotus, who opposed such harsh punishment, submitted that not all Mytileneans were culpable. By killing every adult male, Athens would be committing an injustice against those who had played no role in the rebellion. Moreover, with everyone receiving the same penalty as the insurgents, pro-Athenian democrats in other allied cities would have an incentive to back pro-Spartan oligarchs if the latter ever attempted to rebel against Athens. By a slim majority vote, Diodotus prevailed and the Athenians repealed their earlier decree. Fortunately for the Mytileneans, the ship dispatched to inform the Athenians' military on Lesbos of the decision to rescind the original death sentence arrived in time to prevent a massacre.

As the war dragged on, internal disputes within Greek city-states between democrats favoring Athens and oligarchs sympathetic to Sparta became commonplace. The entire Hellenic state system was convulsed with civil strife. In this turbulent environment, Thucydides tells us that the standard criteria of moral judgment were reversed.

> Reckless audacity came to be considered the courage of a loyal ally; prudent hesitation, specious cowardice; moderation was held to be a cloak for unmanliness; ability to see all sides of a question inaptness to act on any. Frantic violence became the attribute of manliness; cautious plotting, a justifiable means of self defense. The advocate of extreme measures was always trustworthy; his opponent a man to be suspected.[28]

The turmoil offered Sparta an opportunity to uncouple city-states from the Athenian empire. Campaigning in northern Greece, the Spartan general Brasidas convinced various cities to renounce their affiliation with Athens.

Meanwhile, Cleon continued to goad the Athenians into a more offensive strategy than the one Pericles had designed. Each side achieved significant victories. Brasidas won over Amphipolis, an Athenian colony and naval base that controlled access to mines, shipbuilding timber, and grain.[29] Cleon captured 290 Spartans on the island of Sphacteria off the west coast of Peloponnesus. But when Cleon spearheaded an effort to regain Amphipolis, both he and Brasidas died in the fighting.

Stung by the devastating losses at Sphacteria and Amphipolis after a decade of fruitless combat, in 421 Sparta and Athens agreed to a cessation of hostilities.[30] Known as the Peace of Nicias, after the Athenian general who directed the negotiations, the agreement amounted to little more than a brief interlude in the fighting. Major powers such as Corinth as well as minor powers such as Chalcidia and Olynthus refused to abide by the terms of the armistice. Sparta and Athens refrained from attacking each other for the next six years, but each state maneuvered to gain advantage over the other in anticipation of the next round of warfare.

The Strong Do What They Can

In the aftermath of the Peace of Nicias, a new leader rose to prominence in Athens. Handsome, charismatic, and daring, Alcibiades was an imaginative military strategist. Yet he also possessed serious character flaws: ostentatious, brash, and self-centered, his behavior offended almost everyone. As one contemporary described him, Alcibiades had a lengthy career "as an adulterer, as a stealer of the wives of others, [and] as a perpetrator of acts of lawless violence in general." Though claiming to be a "friend of the people," he was an extortionist who "made the revenues of the state a means of procuring revenue for himself."[31]

Whereas at the beginning of the war Pericles could boast of free and open political discussion by a knowledgeable citizenry, now passion eclipsed prudence. The moderation of Periclean leadership had given way under the pressure of a long, grinding war to the megalomania of Alcibiades. Reckless ambition led Athenians into "projects both unjust to themselves and to their allies—projects whose success would only conduce to the honour and advantage of private persons, and whose failure entailed certain disaster on the country." Furthermore, "the few who liked it not, feared to appear unpatriotic . . . and so kept quiet."[32]

Two incidents embody these changes in Athenian policy. The first consisted of a ruthless assault on the small island of Melos; the second entailed an ill-fated attack on the larger island of Sicily. Alcibiades, who up to this point had been working to undermine the Peace of Nicias, was behind both incidents.

In 416, the Athenians led a force of approximately three thousand hoplites and archers against Melos, a militarily insignificant polis that wished to remain

nonaligned during the war. Ten years earlier, Athens had sent a smaller expedition to compel the Melians to become a tributary ally. When they refused, the Athenians ruined their crops and sailed away. This time the outcome would be different. Alcibiades recommended that if Melos did not capitulate, it should be obliterated. The Melians argued that such a brutal attack would be unjust since they had not harmed Athens. Moreover, it was in Athens's self-interest to show restraint: destroying Melos would drive other neutrals into the Spartan bloc and set a precedent for how Athens might be treated if it lost the war. Finally, the Melians pointed out that it would be unreasonable to surrender while there was still hope of holding out against an Athenian siege and being rescued by the Spartans. Scornful of these appeals to **justice**, expedience, and reasonableness, the Athenians asserted that in interstate relations "the strong do what they can and the weak suffer what they must."[33] Regardless of the merits of the Melian argument, Athens had the strength to subjugate Melos if it so desired. The Melians chose to resist and were destroyed. Unlike in the case of Mytilene earlier in the war, there was no Diodotus to contest Alcibiades' merciless recommendation. The Athenians killed all adult men and sold the women and children into slavery.

Immediately following the destruction of Melos, Athens embarked upon a larger, more risky military expedition. Attracted by the possibility of acquiring grain, timber, and other resources, Alcibiades began planning an invasion of Syracuse, the most powerful Greek city on the island of Sicily. While opening a new front in the western Mediterranean would not defeat Sparta's heavy infantry on the Greek mainland, a victory over Syracuse would bring Alcibiades personal glory. Opponents of the expedition complained that Athens should not divide its forces and seek new enemies before the military stalemate with the Peloponnesians had been broken. Soothsayers foresaw disaster, based on rumors that a monument in Delphi honoring Athenian military accomplishments against Persia had been pecked apart by ravens, and Alcibiades responded by finding prophets willing to make more favorable predictions. Still, victory would prove difficult to achieve. First, the Athenians had scant intelligence about the island and its inhabitants. Second, the assistance expected from city-states in southern Italy never materialized. Third, the amount of financial support from Athenian allies on Sicily was far less than anticipated. Finally, the military plan suffered from logistical, strategic, and organizational flaws. The expeditionary force was deficient in cavalry; it did not entail a quick, decisive strike; and its command structure was divided among three rivals: Lamachus, who was killed in combat; Nicias, who opposed the expedition; and Alcibiades, who was soon relieved of his command.

Losing Alcibiades, the expeditionary force's most energetic leader, hurt morale and eventually brought Sparta into the conflict. Just before the fleet departed, busts of the god Hermes, which stood before many Athenian houses and public buildings, were mysteriously disfigured. Alcibiades' opponents suspected he was to blame, so they recalled him from Sicily to stand trial. Instead of returning, he fled to Laconia and provided the Spartan general Gylippus with information that would be used to thwart the Athenian drive to conquer Syracuse. After two years of inconclusive campaigning far from home, the Athenian expeditionary force was weakening. In a climactic battle fought in the Great Harbor of Syracuse, it suffered a catastrophic defeat. Nicias was captured and executed. Some of the surviving Athenian troops were held for ransom, but most were sentenced to work under miserable conditions in stone quarries. Estimates place the cost of the Sicilian expedition at approximately forty thousand soldiers and two hundred forty triremes.[34] These losses were so devastating that a group of disgruntled conservatives instituted an oligarchic government called the Four Hundred. Athens's troubles also encouraged many tributary allies to break away from the empire.

She Who Disbands the Armies

In 411, following the disaster in Sicily, the playwright Aristophanes produced the *Lysistrata*. A raucous comedy spiced with scatological language, the play voiced strong objections to the Peloponnesian War and warned the combatants that continued fighting would lead everyone to ruin. In the opening scene, Greek women, led by Lysistrata (whose name means "she who disbands the armies"), agree to engage in a sex strike until their husbands and lovers negotiate a just peace. The impact on Spartan and Athenian soldiers leaves nothing to the imagination. Both sides promptly reach an agreement and celebrate their reconciliation at a lively banquet.

Unfortunately, the antiwar protest embodied in the *Lysistrata* went unheeded. Athens once again displayed amazing resiliency, recovering enough strength to restore democracy, rein in wayward allies, and win several major battles against the Peloponnesians. One of the figures behind these victories was Alcibiades. An affair with Queen Timaia and a contract on his life apparently prompted him to flee Sparta.[35] Upon returning to Athens, he proclaimed his innocence in the sacrilege committed against the god Hermes and blamed everything on the intrigues of people jealous of his abilities. Desperate for someone who could reestablish their military might after the Sicilian debacle, the Athenians designated him "supreme commander with authority over all the other generals."[36] By now, the Persians were financing the construction of a Peloponnesian fleet to contest Athenian naval supremacy. Despite his initial successes against this new challenge, a defeat at Notium, a failed raid on Cyme, and possible lawsuits stemming from allegations of unscrupulous behavior obliged Alcibiades to sail back into exile.

Meanwhile, the Athenians pressed on. As late as 406, they won a decisive victory at Arginusae. Sparta offered peace terms, but was refused. The carnage finally ended the next year when Spartan commander Lysander defeated the Athenians at the battle of Aegospotami. Having recently captured Lampsacus, an ally of Athens dominating the vital shipping route through the Dardanelles to grain fields in the Black Sea region, he was not surprised when the Athenians positioned their fleet on the opposite side of the narrow strait. Each morning, the Athenians would row out to the open sea and offer to fight only to have the Peloponnesians refuse. The Athenians would then sail back to the beach, disembark, and meander several miles to the town of Sestus for supplies. Coincidentally, Alcibiades lived in the area, and he wisely suggested that they move their anchorage down the coast to Sestus. But the Athenians were uncertain about his motives and decided to stay put. On the fifth afternoon, as the Athenian triremes lay virtually unmanned with sailors scattered between the beach and Sestus, Lysander attacked and captured almost the entire fleet. Athens had lost what remained of its once imposing navy. The historian Xenophon described what happened when word of the fiasco reached Athens.

> As the news of the disaster was told, one man passed it on to another, and a sound of wailing arose and extended first from Piraeus, then along the Long Walls until it reached the city. That night no one slept. They mourned for the lost, but more still for their own fate. They thought that they themselves would now be dealt with as they had dealt with others. . . .[37]

Fearing that Sparta would treat them just as they once treated the Melians, the citizens of Athens prepared for a siege. Without food or ships, "they could see no future for themselves except to suffer what they had made others suffer, people of small states they had injured not in retaliation for anything they had done but out of the arrogance of power."[38]

PEACE POSTPONED

With Athens besieged and on the brink of starvation, Sparta convened a conference to decide how to deal with its defeated foe. Erianthus of Thebes proposed leveling the city and converting the land to pasture. Delegates from Corinth suggested enslaving the population. Neither of these punitive measures appealed to the Spartans, however. It is said that after listening to a recitation of poetry from Euripides they declared the city that produced such a writer should never be destroyed.[39] Furthermore, in recognition of what Athens had done for the Greeks during the Persian Wars, its people should not be enslaved. Rather than adopt the punitive measures advocated by Thebes or Corinth, Sparta opted for a relatively lenient settlement: "The Long Walls and the fortifications of Piraeus must be destroyed; all ships except twelve surrendered; the exiles to be recalled; Athens to have the same enemies and the same friends as Sparta had and to follow Spartan leadership in any expedition Sparta might make either by land or sea."[40] Since the Spartans had little regard for democracy, they also backed an oligarchic government in Athens called the

Thirty Tyrants. In addition, they established boards of supervisors over each of Athens's allies and stationed garrisons within their territories to maintain order.

By eschewing a harsh settlement, Sparta's leaders were following advice their predecessors had given to the Athenians at Pylos during the seventh year of the war:

> If great enmities are ever to be really settled, we think it will be, not by the system of revenge and military success, and by forcing an opponent to swear to a treaty to his disadvantage, but when the more fortunate combatant waives these his privileges, to be guided by gentler feelings, conquers his rival in generosity, and accords peace on more moderate conditions than he expected. From that moment, instead of the debt of revenge which violence must entail, his adversary owes a debt of generosity to be paid in kind, and is inclined by honour to stand to his agreement.[41]

Magnanimity, from the Spartan perspective, was in the self-interest of the victor; it was a product of expediency, not pity.

As a lenient peace, the settlement of 404 did not destroy Athenian power, but neither did it moderate Athenian ambitions. Athens "was disarmed but unappeased," and "keeping it disarmed would require strength, commitment, cooperation, and unity of purpose not possessed by the victorious powers."[42] Indeed, the bonds between Sparta and the Peloponnesian League dissolved shortly after the victory celebration as comrades in arms complained little had been done to share the spoils of victory. Although Sparta fought under the banner of liberating the Greeks from Athenian **imperialism,** guided by the neo-imperialist ambitions of General Lysander, it began encroaching on other states. The Spartans had crafted a lenient settlement but they supplemented it with domineering behavior. Lacking a coherent **grand strategy**, they stumbled into confrontations with former coalition partners as well as with a resurgent Athens. And all the while, their hoplite population was gradually being depleted.

> "All arrogance will reap
> a harvest rich in tears.
> God calls men to heavy
> reckoning
> For overweening pride."
> —AESCHYLUS

At the beginning of the Peloponnesian War, King Archidamus spoke about the Spartan virtue of *sōphrosunē*, a form of sobriety or prudence that induces "wise moderation" and prevents one from becoming "insolent with success."[43] After the war, however, its leaders fell victim to arrogant pride and overreaching, what the Greeks called *hubris* and *pleonexia*. Sparta's quest for empire resulted in years of fruitless skirmishing punctuated by untenable truces. As Isocrates described the calamity facing early fourth century Greece:

Already there are many evils which in the course of nature afflict mankind; but we have gone out of our way to discover others beyond those which necessity imposes; we have inflicted on ourselves wars and civil war. Some meet their end in lawless anarchy in their own cities, others with their wives and children move from place to place in foreign lands; many in order to get daily bread are driven to become hired soldiers and die fighting for their foes against their friends.[44]

Peace, as Clinias of Crete quipped, "is nothing more than a name, the truth being that every State is, by a law of nature, engaged perpetually in an informal war with every other State."[45]

The Athenian resurrection began in 403 with the expulsion of the Thirty Tyrants. According to Aristotle, the Thirty initially were "moderate toward the citizens and pretended to be administering the ancestral form of constitution." But before long they "put to death those of outstanding wealth or birth or reputation."[46] Ironically, the uprising against the Thirty was supported by the refusal of the Corinthians and Thebans to back Lysander's efforts to reinforce the Athenian oligarchs, as well as by the intervention of king Pausanias of Sparta, a bitter rival of the general. With democracy restored and Lysander meddling throughout Asia Minor and northern Greece, Athens started rebuilding its Long Walls and, under the leadership of Iphicrates, developed new weapons and tactics for fighting with light-armed troops.

Sparta's increasingly brusque, dictatorial behavior alarmed so many states that it ultimately faced a coalition composed of Corinth, Thebes, Argos, and Athens in the Corinthian War of 395–387. Persia also added its weight in an attempt to weaken Sparta, because Sparta had supported an insurrection against the Persian king. Ever cognizant of the relative balance of power among the Greeks, Persia deftly shifted positions when the anti-Spartan coalition appeared to be gaining strength. In the King's Peace of 386, which brought the war to a conclusion, Sparta granted suzerainty over the Ionian Greeks to Persia and guaranteed the independence of all remaining Greek states in exchange for financial subsidies from Persia.

While Athens and Thebes accepted the King's Peace, both foresaw the need to prepare for future confrontations with Sparta. Despite pledging to uphold the autonomy and independence of other Greek states, Sparta continued its pattern of **military intervention.** The Athenian response was to rebuild its fleet and, in 377, organize the Second Athenian League, a naval alliance that clearly specified the rights of each member in writing so as to avoid the political problems that marred the Delian League. Thebes responded to Sparta's aggressive actions by reorganizing its army around the Sacred Band, an elite infantry unit comprising 150 pairs of lovers (whose personal attachments were thought to make them fight more vigorously than other troops). In combat, the Sacred Band would take its position on the left wing of a charging Theban phalanx. Behind them would be troops arrayed four times deeper than in a traditional hoplite formation. The objective was to use this mass to smash through the enemy line at the point of the Sacred Band's attack. At the battle of Leuctra in 371, Epaminondas, the Theban general responsible for this revolutionary tactic, routed the Spartan army and invaded the Peloponnese. At Mount Ithome in Messenia, he founded a city for helots who had rebelled against Sparta, therein depriving the Spartans of half of their territory and more than half of their serfs.[47]

Sparta would have one more opportunity to reverse its military fortune. At the battle of Mantinea in 362 it faced the Thebans again but experienced another crushing defeat. Thebes, however, could not capitalize on its victory because Epaminondas was mortally wounded and no commander had the skill or stature to replace him. "The result of this battle," noted Xenophon, "was just the opposite of what everyone expected it would be." It was imagined that "the winner would become the dominant power and the losers would be their subjects." Instead, with the Spartan loss and the death of Epaminondas, "there was even more uncertainty and confusion in Greece after the battle than there had been previously."[48]

Perhaps the only thing not uncertain was that Sparta's days as a great power were over. Though they did not recognize it, the Spartans had emerged from the Peloponnesian War with a tarnished triumph. Exhausted by twenty-seven years of fighting, they persevered only with Persian financial assistance. Little thought had been given to designing a political grand strategy for the postwar world. After the peace settlement was concluded, there was no guide for Spartan foreign policy. One mistake followed another until the victor was prostrate. Between 404 and 362, Sparta went from dominance to insignificance. Yet it was not only Sparta that suffered: during the eighty-five years separating the Peloponnesian War from the conquest of Greece by Philip of Macedon, "fifty-five considerable wars were waged by one Greek state against another."[49]

Political leaders must make crucial decisions when wars end. Whereas most leaders claim to have a grand strategy in mind when the fighting begins, their goals are often defined and redefined incrementally as the war unfolds. Leaders typically think of grand strategy in the narrow terms of a military mission designed to coerce the enemy into submission and surrender. Rarely do leaders articulate clear, long-term political goals that military missions ultimately serve.

This inattention to political planning is troublesome because the ways in which allies and adversaries are treated after the weapons are sheathed powerfully influence the prospects for lasting peace. The actions taken by the victor toward the vanquished influence the likelihood that the defeated will accept or resist the postwar order and whether their role will be constructive or destructive. Peace is not something that happens spontaneously when the infernal engine of war is shut off; it must be cultivated and nourished by people of vision. Our aim in this book is to extract lessons from the historical record of war termination that illuminate how this can be achieved. Having looked at a celebrated case involving a lenient peace settlement, let us put our analysis in its proper context by examining an equally famous case involving a punitive peace. In Chapter 4, we will focus on the Punic Wars between Rome and Carthage.

CONTROVERSIES TO CONTEMPLATE

- Various scholars have theorized about the impact of geography on international relations. Alfred Thayer Mahan, Halford Mackinder, and Nicholas J. Spykman are among those who have written about competition between land and sea powers. How did Sparta's position as a land power and Athens' position as a sea power influence the conduct and outcome of the Peloponnesian War?
- Liberal theorists emphasize the impact that societal factors have on foreign policy. In particular, they assert that nations with democratic forms of government behave differently than nations ruled by autocracies. What were the differences in the political systems of Sparta and Athens? How did these differences influence their behavior during and after the Peloponnesian War?
- Realist theories emphasize the impact of international factors on foreign policy. How did changes in the distribution of power in the Hellenic state system following the Persian Wars increase the probability of war between Sparta and Athens? How did international factors contribute to Sparta's downfall after the Peloponnesian War?
- Liberals and realists often debate about the role of morality in international relations. Reflecting upon the behavior of Athens toward Mytilene in 428 and Melos in 416, when do considerations of justice play a role in influencing how powerful states deal with weaker states? What implications do your conclusions have for theorizing about how nations make peace after long, difficult wars?
- Was the collapse of the peace settlement following the Peloponnesian War inevitable? What could have been done differently by the Spartans to cement a durable peace settlement?
- What impact does leadership have on peace making? Imagine that Athens had won the Peloponnesian War. What kind of peace settlement would have been constructed if Pericles presided over an Athenian victory? How might that settlement have been different than a settlement crafted by Cleon or Alcibiades?

NOTES

1. All dates in this chapter are Before the Common Era (B.C.E.).
2. Thucydides, 1951, pp. 14–15.
3. Kagan, 1995, p. 73.
4. Liddell Hart, 1967, p. 353.
5. Watson, 1992, p. 51.
6. Sylvan, 1995, pp. 94–95.
7. Herodotus, 1920, p. 101.
8. In Warner, 1958, p. 26.

9. In Hamilton, 1942, p. 123.
10. Ober, 1994, pp. 14–15.
11. Keegan, 1993, pp. 249–250.
12. Thucydides, p. 40.
13. With the ability to argue effectively before the council, assembly, and the courts an important skill for worldly success, education in persuasive speaking became quite popular in fifth-century Athens. Gorgias, Protagoras, and Thrasymachus were three of the most famous itinerant teachers, called sophists ("men of wisdom"), who offered instruction to young Athenians in the art of rhetoric. By way of contrast, Spartans were trained to be blunt.
14. Strauss and Ober, 1990, p. 23.
15. From his play the *Persians*, reprinted in Agard, 1957, p. 139.
16. Whereas the Peloponnesian League was a loose network of bilateral alliances *(symmachia)* that revolved around the continental power of Sparta, the Delian League evolved into an imperial confederation *(archê)* based on the relationship between a metropolis (Athens) and a periphery (the Aegean city-states) dominated by the maritime might of the metropolis. As such, the Delian League mirrored the vertical structure of domination and submission typically found in an ancient Greek household *(oikos)*. Santoro, 1991, pp. 76–77.
17. Kagan, 1995, p. 30.
18. Thucydides, 1951, p. 41.
19. In Ibid., p. 49.
20. In Ibid, pp. 80, 82.
21. Plutarch, 1864, p. 197.
22. Ibid., p. 211.
23. King Archidamus, a friend of Pericles, counseled against an immediate declaration of war. He recognized that Sparta could not defeat Athens at sea and, without adequate power projection capability, its heavy infantry could not attack Athens's island allies. "Let us never be elated by the fatal hope of the war being quickly ended by the devastation of their lands," he cautioned. "I fear rather that we may leave it as a legacy to our children." Thucydides, 1951, p. 47.
24. In Thucydides, 1951, p. 105.
25. In Ibid., p. 119.
26. Cleon, a populist politician who pressed for an aggressive foreign policy, was criticized for his demagoguery and crass behavior. In Aristophanes' play the *Knights*, a general tells a sausage seller that he has all the qualifications needed to unseat Cleon from power: "low birth, marketplace training, and insolence." Given Cleon's success, the general concludes, "To be a leader of the people isn't for learned men, or honest men, but for the ignorant and vile." Reprinted in Agard, p. 123.
27. In Thucydides, 1951, p. 167.
28. Ibid., p. 189.
29. In 424, Thucydides was the Athenian general responsible for northern Greece. When Brasidas gained control of Amphipolis, Thucydides was on the island of Thasos and thus unable to respond quickly enough to prevent the loss of the city. His punishment was exile from Athens.
30. In addition, Athens experienced a major setback against the Boeotians at Delium in 424.
31. Andocides, 1941, pp. 549, 551. For another glimpse into his character, see Alcibiades' speech on Socrates at the end of Plato's *Symposium*.
32. Thucydides, 1951, pp. 120, 352.
33. Ibid., p. 331. In contrast to Callicles in Plato's *Gorgias* or Thrasymachus in *The Republic*, the Athenians are not simply saying that it is right for the strong to prevail over the weak or that justice is merely what is in the interest of the mighty. Instead, they submit that questions of justice are only relevant when both sides are "equals in power."
34. Woodruff, 1993, p. 153n.
35. Strauss and Ober, p. 66; Thucydides, 1951, p. 477.
36. Xenophon, 1979, p. 72.

37. Ibid., p. 104.
38. Ibid., p. 105.
39. Hamilton, 1942, p. 74.
40. Xenophon, 1979, p. 107.
41. Thucydides, 1951, p. 219.
42. Kagan, 1987, p. 417.
43. Thucydides, 1951, p. 48.
44. In Sinclair, 1967, pp. 117–118.
45. Plato, 1926, p. 7. In describing his own experience during this stormy period, Plato wrote: "Whereas at first I had been full of enthusiasm for public work, now I could only look on and watch everything whirling round me this way and that. . . . In the end I came to the conclusion that all the cities of the present age are badly governed." In Warner, 1958, p. 68.
46. Aristotle, 1935, pp. 101, 103.
47. Liddell Hart, 1967, p. 15.
48. Xenophon, 1979, p. 403.
49. Bozeman, 1960, p. 69.

· 4 ·

CREATING A DESOLATION CALLED PEACE: ROME AND THE PUNIC WARS

A bad peace is even worse than war.

TACITUS

PREVIEW

This chapter is about a particular category of actors in international politics—empires—and the kinds of relationships that tend to result when they come into contact. An "empire" can be defined as an actor so much larger in territory, resources, and military capabilities that all other nations fear its imperial ambitions. Much of world history has been a story of rivalries between such empires as Babylonia and Egypt, the Han and Hsiung-nu in China, and the Ottomans and Hapsburgs. The case to be explored in this chapter will look at the Punic Wars fought between the Roman Empire and the Carthaginian Empire between 264 and 147 B.C.E.

We will look at the determinates of an enduring rivalry over a period of more than 150 years that, in a chain-reaction cycle of three wars ended in tragedy for the loser and, after victory, the erosion of the culture and institutions that formerly had brought glory and power to the Roman Republic. This story contains timeless principles about the factors that influence the onset of war and its termination. We shall find a number of concepts in the contemporary study of international security operative in the tale of the Punic Wars:

- the balance of power
- hegemonic war and hegemonic stability theory
- alliance formation, bandwagoning behavior, self help, and neutrality
- the impact of domestic institutions on the making of choices about grand strategy
- strategic surrender
- enduring rivalries

In addition, this case provokes consideration of the adequacy of rational-actor conceptions of national decision making. The story forces us to put the political psychology of grand passions about feelings of resentment, revenge, and rage into an interpretation of the forces that animate choices about peace settlements. The Punic Wars, like the story of the Peloponnesian Wars between Athens and Sparta a century and a half earlier, speak to the powerful impact of emotions and values as important motives in decisions about peace making. Note that the winners in the case in this chapter chose a different kind of peace strategy than Sparta in the Peloponnesian War. In comparing the outcomes of the Peloponnesian and Punic Wars, this chapter asks you to calculate the cost and benefits of a punitive peace and a lenient peace.

■ ■ ■ ■ ■ ■ ■ ■ ■ ■ ■ ■ ■ ■ ■ ■ ■ ■ ■

Victors in every war face choices. They must define what their long-term political goals will be once peace is restored and devise strategies to realize those goals. In the last chapter we examined the choices made by Sparta after the Peloponnesian War. Under the leadership of Lysander, the general who had delivered the final blow to the Athenians in the battle of Aegospotami, Sparta reneged on its promise to bring freedom to Greece and embarked on a program of imperial domination. Skilled, disciplined, and courageous in warfare, the Spartans proved to be closed minded, reckless, and overbearing in postwar diplomacy. Their experience offers a timeless lesson: unless victory on the battlefield is complemented by a clear, long-term strategy for dealing with allies as well as the defeated, national leaders intoxicated by military success will suffer nasty political hangovers.

Contrary to the ruthless recommendations of Corinth and Thebes, the Spartans treated Athens more leniently than the Athenians had once treated Melos. Nevertheless, Spartan magnanimity had limits. Rather than consolidating their gains and cementing relations with wartime partners, the Spartans adopted policies that hurled them into one debilitating struggle after another. Before long they faced a resurgent Athens backed by its former allies. It is tempting to conclude that victors are better off when they impose harsh settlements on the vanquished. Yet, as we shall see, things are not that simple: a punitive peace also has drawbacks.

To illustrate the nature of a punitive settlement, we will now turn to a **hegemonic struggle** that shook the ancient Mediterranean world almost a century and a half after the defeat of Athens. In contrast to the Peloponnesian War, the so-called Punic Wars between Rome and Carthage came to a cruel, pitiless ending. Defeat meant total subjugation. Nothing but rubble remained where the thriving port city of Carthage once stood. Following three bitter wars in a **chain-reaction cycle** against a shrewd and stubborn foe, Rome was victorious. But what would such a ruthless victory yield?

IMPERIALISM AND THE ROMAN REPUBLIC

Two great empires, Rome and Carthage, collided during the third century B.C.E.[1] Growth in their respective power generated an intense rivalry, which turned violent with wars of twenty-three, eighteen, and three years duration interrupted by a period of peace lasting twenty-two years between the first and second wars and fifty-two years between the second and final wars. **Enduring rivalries** of this sort are common when bitter rivals experience different rates of growth. Sometimes the rising power uses newly acquired military might to muscle ahead of its opponent. On other occasions, the established power lashes out in the hope of arresting its competitor's growing strength. Often these vicious struggles for position exhaust both sides, leading to a temporary cessation of hostilities and ardent preparations for another round of combat.

TABLE 4.1
A Chronology of the Punic Wars, 300–147 B.C.E.

298–295 B.C.E.	Third Sammite War subjects Etruscans to Rome
283	Corsica captured by the Romans
282–272	War between Tarentum and Rome
280	Pyrrhus, king of Epirus, defeats Romans at Heraclea; Rome later defeats him at Beneventium
268	Athens conquered by Rome
264–241	**The First Punic War**
264	Appius Claudius Pulcher defeats Hiero of Syracuse at Messana
256	The Roman fleet defeats Carthaginians at Ecnomus
255	Regulus, attacking Carthage, is captured by Xanthippus the Spartan
250	Unsuccessful siege of Lilybaeum by the Romans
246	Hamilcar Barca takes command of Carthaginian forces in Sicily
241	Hamilcar makes peace with Rome: end of First Punic War
246	Hannibal, Carthaginian general, born, and his father, Hamilcar Barca, begins to educate his son in warfare
238	Carthage begins conquest of Spain; Sardinia becomes part of Roman republic
236	Outbreak of war between Sparta and Achaean League
222	Rome conquers northern Italy, including Mediolanum (Milan)
219–201	**Second Punic War**
218	Hannibal crosses the Alps (Little St. Bernard Pass), invades Italy from the north, takes Turin, and defeats Publius Cornelius Scipio at Ticinus River
217	Hannibal defeats Romans at Lake Trasimene
216	Romans defeated at Cannae, with fifty thousand Roman casualties
216	Philip V of Macedon makes alliance with Hannibal

211	Roman armies defeated in Spain
211	Hannibal leads Carthaginian attempt to attack Rome
207	After the defeat of his brother Hasdrubal on the Metaurus, Hannibal retreats to southern Italy
202	Scipio Africanus decisively defeats Hannibal at Zama
201	Second Punic War ends
200–197	Second Macedonian War
200	Attica ravaged
198	Antiochus III of Syria takes Palestine from Egypt
195	Hannibal flees to Antiochus III of Syria
192	Antiochus III, aided by Hannibal, lands in Greece; war between Sparta and Rome
191–190	Antiochus defeated by the Romans at Thermopylae and at Magnesia
189	Hannibal defeated by Rhodian fleet at Eurymedon River; insurrections in Upper Egypt owing to exorbitant taxes
183	Pisa and Parma in northern Italy become Roman colonies
182	Hannibal commits suicide in exile to avoid extradition by Rome
172–168	War between Rome and Macedon; Roman army defeated by Perseus
168	Romans defeat Perseus at Pydna; Macedon placed under Roman governor
149–146	**Third Punic War**
147	Roman forces destroy Corinth
	Romans destroy Carthage: of 500,000 inhabitants only 50,000 remain alive; survivors sold into slavery
147	Greece comes under Roman control
146	The Roman Empire expands to seven provinces: Sicily, Sardinia, Corsica, the two Spains, Gallia Transalpina, Africa, and Macedonia
133	Asia Minor becomes eighth Roman province
123	Carthage rebuilt by Rome as colony

Table 4.1 summarizes the evolution of the rivalry between the rising power of Rome and the established power of Carthage. A protracted conflict steeped in myth and drama, its outcome would alter the course of Western civilization. The Roman poet Virgil, looking back from his vantage point in the Augustan Age over a century later, wrote: "Fate willed it so." In his epic poem *The Aeneid,* Queen Dido of Carthage was seduced and then spurned by Aeneas, the legendary founder of Rome. Humiliated by her rejection, she cried out: "No love, no peace, between these nations, ever!" After imploring her people to "hate, and hate forever" Aeneas' descendants, the distraught queen committed suicide.[2]

From Virgil's perspective, war between Rome and Carthage was inevitable. Let us trace the tragic history behind his colorful story about the origins of the Punic Wars in order to ascertain what lessons can be derived about peace settlements.

The Heirs of Cincinnatus

At its zenith, the Roman Empire "comprehended the fairest part of the earth and the most civilized portion of mankind."[3] Its emergence as one of the world's largest and long-lasting empires would not have been predicted by geopolitics. The city possessed meager resources and lacked natural frontiers. For the first two and a half centuries after its founding in 753, Rome fought numerous invaders, losing as often as it tasted victory. While many factors helped turn this vulnerable city-state into a great **empire,** two were particularly important: a civic culture emphasizing duty, dignity, and virtue, and a military code that fostered discipline, valor, and tenaciousness. Romans often recounted the story of Cincinnatus, a man embodying these traits, who left his plow to fight an invader and returned to it after triumphing.[4]

Over time, the Romans succeeded in dividing and isolating many of their enemies, which allowed them to win military victories with increasing frequency. Nowhere was their patriotism and dauntless courage better exemplified than in the response of Gaius Mucius to the siege of Rome by Lars Porsinna, king of Clusium. According to the historian Livy, Mucius infiltrated the enemy camp but was captured after mistakenly stabbing someone other than the king. Upon hearing that his prisoner was just one of many determined assassins, Porsinna threatened to throw him into a nearby fire unless he revealed their names. Mucius retorted that his comrades would bear any hardship to slay Porsinna, whereupon he thrust his arm into the flames and held it steady without showing pain until his right hand was burned off. Shocked by this demonstration of resolve, the flustered king decided it would be prudent to end the siege and evacuate Roman territory. Gaius Mucius was subsequently honored for his bravery and given the name Scævola, or "lefty."[5]

The story of Gaius Mucius illustrates the Roman admiration for heroism. It was not unusual for soldiers who lost a sword to throw themselves into an enemy formation, hoping they could recover their weapon or escape humiliation by death. Unlike most of their adversaries, the Romans learned from military setbacks and adapted their tactics to fit new circumstances. Ultimately this martial spirit was combined with rigorous training and an outstanding logistical system to create an awesome fighting machine. Roman legionaries "inflicted heavy casualties even when they were defeated" and "[a]gainst untrained troops, they simply could not be defeated, even when they were greatly outnumbered."[6]

The Roman Empire may have grown by force of arms, but its rulers recognized the contribution defeated adversaries could make to Rome's security. "Once victory has been secured," wrote the Roman philosopher Cicero, "those who were not cruel or savage in warfare should be spared."[7] To encourage the vanquished to accept Roman rule, conquered Latin cities that demonstrated their loyalty were given *civitas sine suffragio*—the same rights enjoyed by Roman citizens, except for the vote. Rome also rewarded these cities by exempting them from taxation and granting them a share in the plunder from subsequent conquests. Leniency paid handsome dividends, as defeated cities were systematically converted to allies. No state had ever been so successful at winning the allegiance of such diverse people. By constructing an elaborate network of roads, Roman legions could march at great speed to defend these new allies. Between 323, when Rome launched its drive to conquer peninsular Italy, and 275, when this goal was achieved, the peasants and shepherds who once lived in scattered villages on the hills above the Tiber River had gradually positioned themselves to expand throughout the Mediterranean basin.

An Oligarchy of Merchants

Roman expansion was not unopposed. After the death of Alexander the Great, the Hellenistic world had crumbled into three centers of power: Macedon, Egypt, and the Seleucid Empire in Syria. These eastern states posed no real threat to Rome, but the same could not be said about Carthage. Founded just before 800 by a Phoenician queen known as Dido, Carthage (called "New City" to distinguish it from the mother city of Tyre) encompassed most of what is today northern and central Tunisia. The city boasted an excellent harbor, a large market square bordered by rows of six-story houses, and surrounding lands planted with olive and fig trees. The entrepreneurial Carthaginians traded with peoples from Sierra Leone to the Brittany coast and gradually acquired control over commerce throughout the western Mediterranean basin (see Map 4.1).

Carthage was "an aristocratic republic, reserved and well ordered, in which the individual [was] subject to laws administered by the well-disciplined and austere rich."[8] Conquered peoples were treated harshly, however. By extracting heavy reparations from those they defeated, the Carthaginians could expand their navy and hire mercenaries to augment their army. During its early years, the major security concern for Carthage came from Greek expansion into nearby Sicily. As early as 730, Corinthians and Megarans were settling along the east coast of Sicily, where they displaced the indigenous Sikels and founded such city-states as Syracuse and Hyblaea. Simultaneously, migrants from Crete and Rhodes founded Gela on the southern coast, and, in later years, Carthage established a commercial center of its own at Akragas. Carthage ultimately collided with the Greeks on Sicily, suffering a disastrous loss to Syracuse in the Battle of Himera (480). Not until the end of the century was Carthage able to avenge its defeat. Landing on the southwest coast of Sicily in 409, the Carthaginians quickly overran the Greek city of Selinus and then moved on to destroy Himera. Whereas these victories reestablished Carthaginian supremacy in the western Mediterranean, a frenzy of looting after the victories combined with the grisly religious practice of human sacrifice to earn the Carthaginians a reputation for butchery.

MAP 4.1 Empires in the Mediterranean, About 240 B.C.E. The struggle for domination in the Mediterranean had shifted following the collapse of Alexander the Great's Empire, which splintered into the Macedon, Egyptian, and Seleucid (Syrian) empires. In the West, the Roman Empire and the Carthaginian Empire were expanding.

Syracuse was able to hold out against this Carthaginian onslaught, but its military grip over the island was shattered. A century later, under the leadership of Agathocles, Syracuse would again threaten Carthage, but intermittent civil strife prevented the city from recovering its past glory. In short, Carthage eclipsed its Greek competitors and became the greatest sea empire of its day.

Although Roman anxiety had been mounting as Sardinia, Corsica, Malta, and the Balearic Islands fell under Carthaginian suzerainty, Carthage still did not seem to be Rome's principal problem. Relations with Carthage had been peaceful for centuries and Rome was preoccupied elsewhere.[9] In the year 509, following the expulsion of the Etruscan kings from Rome, Carthage signed a treaty with the nascent Roman Republic, the text of which proclaimed that "there shall be friendship between the Romans and their allies, and the Carthaginians and their allies."[10] Under the terms of this treaty, two **spheres of influence** were established: "The Romans could not sail west of Carthage [and could] trade elsewhere in Africa and in Sardinia only under the supervision of the Punic authorities. The Carthaginians pledged in return to respect Roman interests in the Latin towns and not to pursue colonial ambitions in Latium."[11] A new Romano-Punic Treaty in 348 expanded Carthaginian dominions while prohibiting Roman commerce in North Africa, Libya, and Spain. Rome consented to these terms in order to consolidate its position along the coast of what is today France, as well as in the eastern Mediterranean where Greek power had collapsed. Rome was preoccupied with struggles with her immediate neighbors, and Carthage, seeing its interests advanced by the imposition of order, pledged the assistance of Punic pirates in Rome's battles with Latin states. These agreements prohibiting either party from intruding on each other's domain were generally followed, and each side expected that the peace would last.

A TRAGEDY IN THREE ACTS

Relations deteriorated, however, when the two expanding empires clashed in Sicily, after the departure of a Greek army under Pyrrhus. When Carthage finally subjugated Sicily in 241, the Romans began to reconsider the value of their old **alliance** with Carthage. Of critical importance was the potential threat to Roman interests at the heel and toe of Italy, from which Carthage could now easily cross into Italy. In 262 the Roman Assembly voted to expel the Carthaginians from Sicily, and the First Punic War (named after the Latin name for the Carthaginians, *Poeni,* a contracted form of Phoenician) began.

The decision to repel the Carthaginians was justified by the call of Messana for assistance. Failure to defend an ally asking for protection would have undermined the Roman reputation for safeguarding its protectorates. The loss of credibility could have eroded the faith other allies had in Rome, destroying the basis for their political compliance and economic cooperation. A breach of principle would be costly; therefore, Rome reacted to prevent its honor from being tarnished. The "long tradition of friendship uniting Rome and Carthage" came to an end, despite the fact that "before 264 nothing seemed to foreshadow or justify a death struggle between the two powers which controlled the western Mediterranean."[12]

At first glance, war between Rome and Carthage would seem akin to the Peloponnesian War. Like Sparta, Rome was a continental power with a fearsome infantry but virtually no maritime forces. On the other hand, Carthage resembled Athens in that it was a mighty naval power with a far less formidable army. Rather than acceding to a standoff between one military designed to operate on land and the other at sea, the Romans built a fleet and relied on their larger population to wear the Carthaginians down in a grueling war of attrition.[13] In the end, Roman pressure eroded Carthage's financial resources.

Indeed, Rome's military response to Carthage was extraordinary. "It had cost more in materials and supplies and had lasted longer than all the wars of Alexander [the Great] and his successors."[14] In one of the most severely contested wars in history, the Roman militia was depleted, as was the Roman treasury. To defeat the seemingly invincible Carthaginian navy, Rome built vessels modeled after a Punic warship that had been captured after it ran aground near Messana. In what proved to be a decisive innovation, they added grappling hooks and boarding bridges to these vessels so troops could assault enemy ships through hand-to-hand combat. Although inexperienced Roman sailors lost many fleets to storms in the Mediterranean, through daring and pure tenacity they took command of the sea and drove the leader of the Carthaginian armed forces, General Hamilcar Barca, into retreat at a fortress in western Sicily. Exhausted, both empires were now prepared to negotiate a truce.

Act One: Forging a Peace Settlement

Great endeavors often unleash intense emotions, and the conclusion of the Punic War in 241 was no exception. Both parties were embittered. The victorious Romans faced the decision of how to vent their anger toward Carthage without imposing on it terms so spiteful that they might stoke the fires of revenge. High principles were at stake, touching at the very core of the old Roman policy of generosity toward defeated foes. But the showdown with Carthage differed from Rome's earlier campaigns on the Italian peninsula: it was an exhausting ordeal that Rome did not wish to repeat. Given this situation, what would be the prudent course of action? What would be just?

> "Certain peace is better and safer than anticipated victory."
>
> —LIVY

The Romans recognized that the cost of continued fighting was prohibitive. But would peace best be secured through a resuscitative settlement inspired by the traditional Roman code of fostering alliances with the vanquished or a retributive settlement driven by recrimination? Cogent arguments could be made on behalf of either approach, in the name of empire (de imperio), the satisfaction of grievances for honor (laus or praise), or to safeguard protectorates (according to fides Romana toward allies). The choice was further complicated by the fact that without a fleet to protect the remaining Carthaginian stronghold in Sicily, "Hamilcar Barca was given the task of concluding a peace on the best terms he could get."[15] In this emotionally charged but confused climate, the Roman Senate, unable to come to grips with the dilemmas posed by alternative conceptions of an appropriate peace strategy, put the choice to the Assembly to vote on the alternatives of revenge or magnanimity.[16] They chose retribution. This quest for punishment in the final armistice proved, ultimately, to have fatal consequences. As one student of this choice comments:

> The Roman Consul G. Lutatius Catulus offered Hamilcar a generous peace. The Carthaginians were required to leave Sicily and to promise not to make war on Hiero of Syracuse, who had joined the Romans early in the war, or his allies; to return Roman prisoners; and to pay an indemnity of 2,200 silver talents over twenty years, a sum Carthage could afford to pay. Hamilcar agreed, but the treaty had to be ratified by the Roman people, and they refused to accept it. Instead they sent a commission of ten men to make revisions, and they added a thousand talents to the indemnity—to be paid immediately—cut the time available to pay the rest to ten years, and required Carthage to evacuate not only Sicily but also the Lipari and Aegates islands that lie between Italy and Sicily. Perhaps they were stirred to this action by the jealous rivals of the Consul, eager to discredit his achievement, but the Roman people clearly thought that victory in so long and difficult a war deserved a greater reward.[17]

The Roman Assembly, consumed by a zeal for revenge, reversed a previous promise to Carthage and replaced a charitable peace treaty with one that exacted heavy financial, territorial, and psychological costs. The new terms resulted in the loss of Sicily, the retention of which had been a cornerstone of Punic policy "for so long that it had become second nature to record it as a matter of life and death."[18] According to Polybius, the second Roman vindictive peace of Lutatius "exasperated the anger of Hamilcar, [which] became one of the causes of the Second Punic War."[19] Instead of solving the source of conflict, the second Roman "settlement" exacerbated the Carthaginian feelings of discord and anger, while at the same time leaving Carthage in a position from which it could avenge its sense of unjust injury. "The peace [the Roman victors] finally imposed on Carthage in 238 was of the least stable kind: it embittered the losers without depriving them of the capacity for seeking revenge and without establishing a system able to restrain them."[20]

Act Two: The Oath of Hannibal

Boiling with resentment over the peace terms but encouraged that his army had not been beaten by the Romans on land, Hamilcar Barca began planning for the day that Carthage would get even with Rome. Revenge is said to be sweet, but it is not always swift. Various obstacles hampered Carthage's recovery, including a bloody insurrection known as the Truceless War. Thousands of mercenaries who had fought against Rome revolted when the Carthaginians could not (or would not) pay their back wages. Joined by Libyans and

Numidians who resented being exploited by their Punic overlords, the rebels attempted to seize the city of Carthage. Although Hamilcar Barca ultimately organized a citizen army and defeated the mercenaries, Rome took advantage of the chaos by snatching the strategically important island of Sardinia, which Carthage had been allowed to retain under the treaty ending the First Punic War. When the Carthaginians protested, the Romans threatened war and demanded higher reparations payments. According to one analyst of the period, "The seizure of Sardinia and the outrageous claim for an indemnity nipped in the bud the possibilities of a reconciliation between the powers."[21]

Five years after the First Punic War ended, in 246, Hamilcar fathered a son named Hannibal (the "favorite of Baal," an important god) and schooled him in the hatred of Rome. There is no precise way to measure the depth and intensity of the emotions that inspired Hamilcar, but Polybius claims that Hannibal once told King Antiochus of Syria about an oath he swore at the age of nine during a religious ceremony involving his father:

> The sacrifice successfully performed, my father poured the libation and went through the usual ritual. He then bade all the other worshippers [to] stand a little back and, calling me to him, asked me affectionately whether I wished to go with him on his expedition. Upon my eagerly assenting and begging with boyish enthusiasm to be allowed to go, he took me by the right hand and led me up to the altar and bade me lay my hand upon the victim and swear that I would never be friends with Rome.[22]

The expedition Hannibal joined was a campaign by his father to expand Carthaginian holdings in southern Spain. Hamilcar assured the Romans that he had no hostile intent toward them; acquiring territory in Spain was necessary for Carthage to pay the heavy indemnity imposed by Rome. Preoccupied by other security concerns, the Romans accepted his explanation.

The Second Punic War started in 219, just twenty-two years after the end of the First Punic War. Frustrated over the revised terms of the peace settlement, outraged by Rome's seizure of Sardinia, and galled by the subsequent demand for more reparations, war became a means of redressing what was perceived as unjust and humiliating treatment: "The Carthaginians were a proud people with a high sense of their own honor, accustomed for centuries to ruling others. The arrogant behavior of the Romans must have made many Carthaginians, not only the fiery Barcids, contemplate revenge."[23]

In 229, during the siege of Helike in southeastern Spain, the gallant Hamilcar Barca died in battle. The Carthaginians appointed his son-in-law to succeed him as the commander of their operations on the Iberian peninsula, but he was assassinated by a slave eight years later. As a result, Hannibal Barca, now twenty-six years of age, became the new military leader and began developing a daring plan to extract revenge from the Romans. His plan hinged on a series of assumptions: (1) Roman maritime strength and control of the islands between Africa and Italy prevented Carthage from mounting a credible naval threat; (2) speed and mobility could be used by the Carthaginian army to out-flank, envelop, and destroy larger, slower Roman units; (3) a string of dramatic victories over the Roman army on Italian soil would cause Rome's allies to unite with the Carthaginians; (4) defections by its allies would deprive Rome of almost half of its manpower, thereby reducing its capacity to wage another war of attrition; (5) since Carthage had a small fleet devoid of logistical support, troops and supplies for an assault upon Italy could not be transported by sea; and (6) the most promising invasion route extended overland from Carthage's resource base in Spain, through France, across the Alps, and down into northern Italy.

It was not long before Hannibal had the opportunity to implement his plan. Following the First Punic War, Rome recognized a Carthaginian sphere of influence south of the Ebro River in Spain. In 221, the Romans ignored this line of demarcation and supported an anti-Carthaginian faction during a civil war in Saguntum, a Spanish costal town well within Carthage's sphere of influence. When neither side accepted the claims of the other regarding the political status of Saguntum, war was declared.

Hannibal departed from Spain in the spring of 218 with his veteran army, an impressive cavalry, and trained elephants. His march must have seemed to the Romans an audacious endeavor lacking a reasonable expectation of success. Between Hannibal and Italy stood the treacherous, snow-capped Alps—mountains never before crossed by an army with war elephants. As Hannibal's forces struggled through the passes, mountain tribes attacked the troops from above. How Hannibal found enough food for his men and animals remains a mystery. Just as winter approached, Hannibal brought his half-starved and half-frozen army down into the Po Valley, where they found potential allies among Rome's ancient enemies, the Gauls. Twenty thousand soldiers, six thousand horses, and many of the elephants had miraculously survived the journey, but nearly half of the original contingent of troops died in the mountains.

Alarmed that their cunning adversary had reached northern Italy in 217, the Roman Senate sent forces to stop Hannibal at the Trebia River near Genoa. Hannibal's cavalry was superior to that of the Romans, and he used it masterfully. He could not overwhelm the Romans in a frontal assault across the river, so after dark his cavalry crossed a few miles up river while a small contingent remained behind making enough noise to convince the Romans that the Carthaginians were still in camp. At dawn Hannibal surprised the Romans from the rear, pinning them against the river. The overconfident Romans suffered a humiliating defeat, losing some thirty thousand troops. Hannibal now turned his attention toward central Italy.

The Roman Senate responded by marshaling new forces to block the Carthaginian advance. With Roman soldiers lying in wait along the eastern and western roads to their city, Hannibal did the unexpected. He evaded detection by leading his forces for several days through a swamp and eventually reached the hills beside Lake Trasimine, which often were shrouded in morning fog.

When the Romans finally located him, they thought he was trapped at the end of a narrow valley. But once they attacked, the Romans discovered Hannibal had lured them into an ambush. Most of the Carthaginians were hidden on the misty hillsides, where they showered the Romans with javelins before swooping down on their unprotected flanks. Once again, Hannibal had devastated a massive army, killing approximately twenty-five thousand Roman soldiers.

Emboldened by his lopsided victory, Hannibal marched on southern Italy, expecting Rome's allies to revolt and join him. Although many Italian cities and colonies were sympathetic to the Carthaginians, who promised to liberate them from Roman rule, Hannibal's hopes were unfulfilled. While twelve of the thirty Latin colonies refused to supply soldiers for the Roman army,[24] no weak nation that had **bandwagoned** by allying with the strongest power, the Roman Empire, deserted Rome after the Carthaginian victories in the north. Convinced that just one more stunning victory would induce Rome's allies to defect, Hannibal sought an opportunity to deliver what he believed would be the decisive blow.

Conversely, most Roman senators were sure the devious Hannibal would not succeed if he had to fight in open terrain. At the Trebia River and Lake Trasimine, they asserted, he had won by ruses. Once Hannibal was flushed out, no tricks could save him from the ferocious Roman infantry.

The showdown came in 216 near the village of Cannae, a Roman supply depot on the Aufidus River in southeastern Italy. Vastly outnumbered, Hannibal deployed his troops in a convex formation with the apex facing the Romans. When the Romans surged forward, the Carthaginians fell back into a concave formation whose outer cavalry wings encircled the surprised legionaries. By encouraging the Romans to advance against what seemed to be the most vulnerable point in his unorthodox alignment, Hannibal had duped them into expending their energy in the wrong place, thus turning a fake retreat into a double envelopment of the charging Roman infantry. With cunning, Hannibal strategically had nullified his opponent's numerical superiority, since only those legionaries along the perimeter of the densely packed mass of soldiers could reach the Carthaginians with their swords. Of the roughly eighty thousand Romans who took the field that day, some fifty thousand were killed. Hannibal, on the other hand, lost less than six thousand of his thirty-five thousand troops. Yet, despite his magnificent victory at Cannae, few major cities on the Italian peninsula were willing to join him, and the disappointed Hannibal never acquired adequate strength to capture Rome itself.

Finally recognizing Hannibal's brilliance as a field commander, the Romans henceforth avoided set-piece battles. Under the leadership of Fabius Maximus, they adopted a defensive strategy: Roman legions would harass Hannibal's forces, deny them access to supplies, and ruthlessly punish any Italian city that defected to Hannibal's side. Although the Romans did not win any morale-boosting victories, their strategy of exhausting the Punic army had two important effects: (1) because Hannibal's men could not disperse and plunder on a large scale, Hannibal was unable to raise the funds needed to purchase additional mercenaries, and (2) because Hannibal's army remained relatively small and lacked a powerful siege train, it remained unable to coerce Rome's allies into defecting.[25]

At the same time, Rome continued to control the seas. Hopes for a second front in Illyria vanished when Carthage's ally, King Philip V of Macedon, was intimidated by the Roman navy. Lacking an offensive naval capability, Hannibal watched helplessly as Rome took the offensive in Spain, drove the Carthaginians out of the Sicilian stronghold of Syracuse, and recaptured Tarentum in southern Italy. Hasdrubal, Hannibal's younger brother, attempted to relieve the pressure on the Carthaginians by bringing reinforcements from Spain across the Alps into Italy. But before the brothers could join forces, the Romans intercepted Hasdrubal and routed his army in 207 at the battle of the Metaurus River. After fifteen years of fighting on Italian soil, Hannibal was called back to Africa to defend Carthage, which had come under attack. Hannibal finally would face a Roman general who was his equal, the talented Cornelius Scipio (later known as "Africanus" for his triumph over Carthage).

In 204, Scipio marshaled a huge expeditionary force for his invasion of north Africa. Containing many of the disgraced soldiers who survived the battle of Cannae, the historian Coelius claimed it was so large that birds tumbled from the air whenever the troops shouted in unison. Prior to setting sail, Scipio prayed to the gods of land and sea so his men would return "home again safe and sound, enriched with spoils and laden with plunder to share my triumph when the enemy has been defeated." He asked for "the power of vengeance upon those whom we hate and our country's enemies" and requested the "means to inflict upon the Carthaginian state the sufferings which the Carthaginians have labored to inflict on ours."[26] Hannibal had taken the initiative in the opening stages of the war, establishing a dominant position in the Italian theatre. The Romans then seized the initiative with victories in the subsidiary theatres of Spain and Sicily.[27] Now, behind the tactical genius of Scipio, they were threatening the Carthaginian homeland.

Before the showdown between Hannibal and Scipio near Zama in 202, Hannibal undertook a desperate effort to make peace in the hope that his reputation would deter the Romans. It was to no avail. The titanic battle began with almost one hundred Carthaginian war elephants charging the Roman line. Hannibal assumed the charge would disrupt Scipio's forces, but the Romans responded by quickly shifting into columns, which opened wide alleys for the thundering beasts. As the elephants rumbled through these alleys, archers shot their riders and the columns rotated back into a normal attack formation. Scipio then unleashed his infantry in a frontal assault while using the superb cavalry he brought from Spain to outflank Hannibal's troops. After nearly a day of fighting, the veterans of Cannae regained their honor. Hannibal suffered the first major defeat of his military career, losing approximately twenty-five thousand soldiers compared to only two thousand for the Romans.[28] Given his losses, Carthage had no choice but to adopt a policy of **strategic surrender.** When a young noble in the Carthaginian Assembly urged his fellow citizens to reject the crushing terms dictated by Rome, Hannibal leaped on the speaker's rostrum and yanked him to the ground. He later apologized, professing an ignorance of parliamentary methods.[29]

Following the rout at Zama, the best thing Carthage could do "was live peacefully from the proceeds of her trade and agriculture, as a client city of Rome. . . . One of the greatest proofs of Hannibal's intelligence and self-control is his comprehension and acceptance of the fact that it was better for his country to follow this rather inglorious but peaceful line of conduct than be exterminated."[30] The triumphant Scipio announced that his aims were to establish Roman hegemony that could dominate the entire Mediterranean. But for this, Scipio rejected the view that Carthage's annihilation was necessary. He wished to avoid weakening the Punic economy so much that it could not contribute to the richness and glory of Rome. Thus, while the peace treaty of 201 destroyed Carthage's capacity to threaten Rome again, it did not leave Carthage in ruins. After disarming the Punic army, Rome imposed an indemnity, and

> Carthage was held liable for a sum of ten thousand talents of silver payable by installments over fifty years. For a city of vast resilience and wealth-accruing capability, it was hard but not ruinous. Worse were the territorial clauses. On the one hand, Carthage was to surrender all lands which had ever belonged to Masinissa and his ancestors [in Africa]. . . . On the other hand, she was forbidden to make war, even in Africa, without Roman consent. Whether this precluded resort to arms in defense of her own boundaries was ambiguous, but it certainly ruled out retributive or pre-emptive movements across them. Thus, plainly exposed to contentious claims, Carthage no longer had the right of direct redress. With such despair did some regard these terms that there was talk of continued resistance.[31]

Resistance did not resume, however. The Carthaginian peace negotiators bargained from a position of extreme weakness and pleaded for mercy. They accepted Rome's terms, convinced that nonviolence was preferable to nonexistence.

Act Three: Punishment without Pity

Carthage paid a high price for the Second Punic War. All that remained of the great empire was the city itself and about thirty miles of surrounding territory. If the residue of its once proud military ever left that area, Rome would retaliate. Though humbled into client status, Carthage nonetheless recovered economically and was able to pay off the war indemnity within ten years, despite losing all overseas territories. With the resurgence of Carthaginian prosperity, some leaders in Rome began to fear that Punic imperial ambitions might also resurface.

The pleadings of Marcus Porcius Cato about the potential dangers of a Carthaginian revival struck a responsive chord among the landed gentry of Rome, who feared Carthage's recovery and possible aggression to avenge past losses. Many of these wealthy Romans had acquired fertile land along the coast of north Africa after the Second Punic War, and they were irritated at the prospect of competing with Carthaginian merchants. Still, Carthage posed no real threat to Rome. It had been reduced to the status of a Roman protectorate, without the means to defend itself from attacks by its neighbors. Tied by the terms of the disarmament clause of the 201 peace settlement, Carthage was militarily vulnerable.

Carthaginian vulnerability was revealed not only by the deference Carthage paid Rome, but also by the inability of Carthage to withstand the expansionist policies of its Numidian neighbor. Led by an ambitious leader named Masinissa, the Numidians took possession of territory in the Bagradas Valley, and Rome permitted the seizure despite Carthaginian pleas for Roman military assistance. Encouraged by the success of his initial raids, in 174 Masinissa confiscated over seventy Carthaginian towns and outposts, and Rome let the loss stand. Carthage was weak and defenseless, and, after Scipio died in 168, "increasingly the protective imperialism expressed in his philosophy gave way to a bullying, ruthless [Roman] foreign policy."[32]

In this climate, during which a **long peace** lasted for many decades, Carthage did what it could to reignite its powerful economy while expressing continued frustration over its inability to stop armed incursions by its neighbors. Appeals to Rome for help and protection proved of little avail. In desperation, beginning in 160, Carthage became more militant in its approach to the Numidian aggressors, which continued to absorb territory the 201 peace treaty had assigned to Carthage. A series of border skirmishes followed, including Punic raids into the lands taken by Masinissa. The Numidian leader retaliated by occupying the plains of Souk el Kremis adjacent to Carthage. Rome now had to respond, and in 153 sent a commission of inquiry to Africa. It was headed by the 81-year-old Cato who, a half-century earlier, had fought the Carthaginians at the decisive battle of Zama. His position was to produce fatal consequences.

> "We are now suffering the evils of a long peace. Luxury, more deadly than war, broods over the city, and avenges a conquered world."
>
> —JUVENAL

Most historians reject the view that a third, final armed conflict in the enduring rivalry between Rome and Carthage was inevitable and believe that the two former adversaries "could have avoided the final showdown, since there was no basic conflict of interest between the two powers."[33] But passion, not cool calculations of interest, produced the outcome that was to unfold a half-century after the Second Punic War.

The elderly Cato held strongly anti-Punic views. He was embittered by memories of battle scenes in the Second Punic War. Moreover, he harbored nearly paranoid fears of Carthaginian power; images of a large, united empire emerging in Africa played heavily on his imagination. Indeed, the "anger and horror experienced as a young man may easily have revived as potent and obsessive forces in the mind of an octogenarian."[34] Observing firsthand Carthage's growing prosperity as a member of the Roman commission of inquiry sent to to hear complaints about Masinissa's expansionism, Cato became consumed with the fear that renewed Punic rivalry with Rome would occur unless drastic steps were taken. He would end every speech by proclaiming: "*Ceterum censeo Carthaginem esse delendam* [As for the rest, I am of the opinion that Carthage must be destroyed]."[35]

> "Of war men ask the outcome, not the cause."
>
> —SENECA

Rome heeded Cato's advice. A pretext was found in the claim that Carthage had breached the peace treaty of 201 by resisting the encroachment of the Numidian King Masinissa, a Roman ally. Two earlier Roman delegations, one led by Scipio Africanus and the other by his son-in-law, Publius Scipio Nasica Corculum, had tried to restrain Masinissa and urged lenient treatment for Carthage. But Cato's pleadings proved decisive: Rome declared war in 149 and blockaded the city. Appian, a Greco-Egyptian writer of the second century C.E., described the desperate Carthaginian struggle for survival:

> All the sacred places, the temples, and every other wide and open space, were turned into workshops, where men and women worked together day and night, on a fixed schedule, without pause, eating in turns. Each day they made one hundred shields, three hundred swords, one thousand missiles for catapults, five hundred javelins and spears, and as many catapults as they could. For the torsion ropes to fire them, the women cut off their hair for want of other fibers.[36]

Compared to the two previous wars between Rome and Carthage, the Third Punic War ended quickly. Not only was Carthaginian power destroyed, but Carthage itself was annihilated by Scipio Africanus Minor, who conquered the city block by block, house by house. Picture, if you will, the plight that confronted the city of Carthage on the eve of its annihilation. The Romans pursued a pitiless campaign, and then, on the seventh day of brutal fighting for survival, the Carthaginians pleaded for mercy. As one historian paints the scene, a party of the city's defenders approached the Roman General Scipio,

> asking for the lives of those who surrendered; Scipio agreed and 50,000 men, women and children, half starved, filed out of the citadel. Nine hundred deserters from the Romans, who could expect crucifixion as a punishment, continued to resist with [the Carthaginian general] Hasdrubal in the enclosure of the temple of

Eshmoun until forced to retreat into the building, on the roof of which they took up their final position. At this point the courage of Hasdrubal, who had often proclaimed his determination to fight till death, collapsed, and he came out with his wife and two children to ask for Scipio's mercy. The deserters who saw this asked Scipio for a few moments' respite during which they hurled insults at the Carthaginian general, after which they fired the temple and died in the flames. Hasdrubal's wife also turned on her husband after thanking Scipio for granting their lives, and calling Hasdrubal a coward and traitor threw herself and her children into the burning temple.

For ten days or more the fires raged in the city. Reserving the gold and silver and sacred objects for the state, Scipio allowed his troops to plunder. Those who had surrendered were sold into slavery and all the arms captured were ceremonially dedicated to Mars and Minerva and burned. Finally, everything that was still standing was levelled; Scipio pronounced a curse over the remains, a plough was drawn over the site and salt sown in the furrow, to signify that it was to remain uninhabited and barren forever.

Such was the end of the city of Carthage after an existence of about six centuries. . . .[37]

After the slaughter of nearly a half-million Carthaginian citizens, the remaining 10 percent who survived were sold into slavery, and the territory of Carthage was absorbed by Rome. Carthage, totally devastated, was not reoccupied for another hundred years, when Julius Caesar established a Roman colony there.

Rome was changed by its act of **genocide** as well. The prudence that had previously converted conquered peoples to willing allies of the Roman Empire was replaced by a creed that put the worship of power above honor. The Romans had substituted annihilation for assimilation. "They create a desolation," Calgacus, a Caledonian tribal chief would later say, "and call it peace."[38]

As Scipio Aemilianus viewed the total destruction of Carthage, he is said to have wept and and quoted Homer: "The day shall be when holy Troy shall fall, And Priam lord of spears, and Priams's folk." When asked what he meant, he explained to the historian Polybius, "I feel a terror and dread, lest someone someday should give the same order about my own native city."[39] Perhaps this led Polybius to conclude that "it is not the object of war to annihilate those who have given provocation to it, but to cause them to mend their ways."[40]

The annihilation of Carthage "opened the flood gates to a river of vices in the Roman state," with "a real deterioration in the standards of political behavior by all classes in the state."[41] According to the historian Diodorus Siculus,

so long as Carthage survived, the fear that she generated compelled the Romans to live together in harmony and to rule their subjects equitably . . . but once the rival city was destroyed, it was only too evident that there would be civil war at home, and that hatred for the governing power would spring up among all the allies because of the rapacity and lawlessness to which the Roman magistrates would subject them. All this did indeed happen to Rome after the destruction of Carthage, which brought in its wake the following: dangerous demagoguery, the redistribution of land, major revolts among allies, [and] prolonged and frightful civil wars.[42]

The Punic Wars placed an enormous strain on the Roman Republic. Fighting for almost a century without respite, the Romans financed warfare on a scale never before attempted. Not only did the sheer magnitude of the Punic Wars transform the Roman economy, but they ultimately shattered the political structure of the Republic.

Hannibal's campaign ravaged the agricultural infrastructure of southern Italy. Small, rural landowners who had been conscripted into the Roman army could not tend their fields. When the Punic Wars ended, soldiers mustered out of the army returned to devastated, debt-ridden farms. Wealthy aristocrats, enriched by the spoils of war, purchased these farms and combined them into vast estates *(latifundia)* worked by slave labor. Whereas hardy, independent subsistence farmers had once been a central component of the Roman citizenry, now resentful, landless army veterans began crowding into the city from the countryside. To address their grievances, Tiberius Gracchus, a patrician and war hero elected tribune in 133, sought to enact a program of land reforms in the Senate. When another tribune attempted to cast a veto, Tiberius's supporters carried him away so the bill would pass. Outraged by this unprecedented use of force for political ends, a group of conservative senators later clashed with some of Tiberius's followers and, in the bloody riot that ensued, Tiberius was murdered.

A decade later, Gaius Gracchus, the younger brother of Tiberius, was elected tribune and initiated a new package of social welfare reforms. By this time, Rome's rich had grown richer while its poor had become poorer. Friction between haves and have-nots ultimately ignited another riot in 121, and the military was called into the city by the Senate. In the melee that followed, several thousand Gracchan supporters were killed, along with Gaius Gracchus. Now that the army was entwined with Roman politics, it would prove impossible to remove.

Rome suffered through a prolonged period of revolutionary strife after the Punic Wars. Despite the need for reform, the Senate seemed oblivious to the rising tensions, with the result that violence became a tool for circumventing the constitution. Following the murder of the Gracchi, political life degenerated into a class conflict between the Populares (a faction that appealed to the masses by calling for radical change) and the Optimates (a faction bent on maintaining the prerogatives of the wealthy). Each side had its own military champion. Gaius Marius, who distinguished himself in wars against King Jugurtha of Numidia (112–104), stood with the Populares. Lucius Cornelius Sulla, Marius's former lieutenant in the Jugurthine War, sided with the Optimates. The confrontation between these generals would drag Rome through a gruesome civil war that ended with Sulla coercing the Senate in 82 to declare him dictator for life. Once in control, he terrorized Rome by posting lists of enemies and offering rewards to those killing anyone on the lists. The limited use of political violence initiated in 133 by Tiberius Gracchus had now evolved into a monstrous system of political purges. Upon Sulla's death in 78, the question was not whether the Republic would be supplanted by imperial rule,[43] but which ambitious military commander would use the army to inaugurate that rule. The answer would come several tumultuous decades later, when Julius Caesar vanquished his rival, Pompey, and assumed absolute power.

CONTINGENT BEHAVIOR AND REPETITIVE WARS

The tragic relations between Republican Rome and Carthage present the modern student of world politics with a puzzle: What motivates the participants in **enduring rivalries**? It is a question that transcends the ages and encourages us to ask whether conflagrations like the Second and Third Punic Wars can be avoided. If the settlement at the end of the First Punic War had been different, would Roman-Carthaginian relations have followed a more peaceful trajectory?

The tendency of most self-proclaimed realists is to look for the solution to this puzzle in the anarchic structure of the state system. Foreign policy, realists note, is conducted in an environment that lacks a central arbiter. States are sovereign: they have supreme authority over their territory and populace, and no higher authority stands above them wielding the legitimacy and coercive capability required to undertake the extractive, regulative, and distributive functions that governments normally perform in domestic political systems. Varying in strength, growing at different rates, and uncertain of one another's intentions, they rely on **self-help** to cope with relentless competition from potentially threatening rivals. Security in a world under the shadow of conflict is a function of power, and power is primarily a function of military strength. Prudent leaders, realists insist, use peace settlements to enhance their relative power, positioning themselves to repel an attack whenever the dogs of war are unleashed.

Certainly **balance-of-power** considerations loomed behind the territorial disputes between Rome and Carthage over Sicily, Sardinia, and Spain, and various Roman leaders sought security by attempting to eradicate Carthaginian military capability. Beyond these considerations of raw power politics, however, were a welter of psychological factors that inflamed the passions of Romans and Carthaginians alike, robbing them of the judicious calculations of reason of state that realists celebrate. Both states engaged in a form of emotionally charged contingent behavior, where each side's actions were a reaction to the other side's actions. Indignities suffered in the past had serious consequences for ensuing behavior.[44] Emotions such as anger, hatred, and malice

CONTROVERSIES TO CONTEMPLATE

- What caused the enduring rivalry between the Roman and Carthaginian Empires?
- What factors were the most influential in driving the decisions of Rome and of Carthage about war and peace?
- To what extent did the experience of the First and Second Punic Wars and the way they concluded influence the thinking about Rome in the Third Punic War? Were the wars repetitive because of the peace-making strategies that were chosen?
- In the wars between the Roman and Carthaginian Empires, was grand strategy interpreted as military strategy? If so, what were the consequences?
- What role did passions such as anger, hatred, and rage play in the making of decisions about war and peace? To what extent did considerations about justice and injustice fuel these emotions?
- What is the moral of this story? Does this case suggest policy principles that apply to peace making in the modern international system?

pushed these rivals in directions not predicted by realist theories of national self-interest.

Warfare is an imprinting experience. Potent images are born during these harrowing times. Atrocities in battle, genocidal slaughtering of innocents, the imposition of a perceived unfair peace settlement, or the desire to reclaim lost territory—**irredentism**—may all evoke shrill calls for obtaining **justice** on the field of battle, calls which encourage retribution rather than reconciliation. When stung by feelings of injustice, political leaders may respond in terms of resentment and rage. These grand passions are compelling forces that can distort the shape of a peace settlement. Contrary to the **rational actor** accounts of realist theory, emotive language is not merely bombast and bravado; it reflects "sentiments that at one time or another have entered into the calculations of foreign policymakers."[45]

A desire to even old scores is understandable, but the story of the Punic Wars suggests that it has enormous costs. Postwar arrangements like those crafted after the First Punic War simply hasten the day of another military reckoning: they rub dignity raw while failing to deprive the defeated of the means for satisfying their desire for revenge. Of course, annihilating an enemy prevents retaliation, but such genocidal acts ultimately haunt a state's political life. Consider, for example, the results of the Second and Third Punic Wars. Rather than delivering peace and domestic tranquility, these wars were catalysts which accelerated socioeconomic processes that eventually undermined the Roman Republic.[46] Rome would dominate Western civilization for centuries to come, but the Republic was doomed.

Victors frequently claim to be lovers of peace.[47] Yet as we have seen, it is not always easy to construct a durable peace settlement. Neither the Spartans at the end of the Peloponnesian War nor the Romans at the end of the Punic Wars succeeded. Both the former's leniency and the latter's severity were implemented in the absence of a political **grand strategy.** Without an overarching set of principles to guide statecraft, diplomacy lacks a sense of direction, foreign and defense policies loose touch with one another, and military victory becomes an end in itself.

Vae victis (woe betide the defeated), Romans lamented after their city was sacked by the Gauls in 390 C.E. But the Peloponnesian and Punic Wars reveal that woe also plagues victors who squander their opportunities to craft an enduring peace. As these two cases from antiquity show, the policy options available for treating defeated adversaries are arrayed along a hypothetical continuum, ranging from magnanimity to annihilation. To place these analyses of critical choices about grand strategy and war termination in their contemporary context, Part III will describe the arguments for and against each of the major options between the polar extremes on this continuum and their relative success in peace-building efforts during the modern era of world politics.

NOTES

1. All dates during the rivalry between Rome and Carthage in this chapter are Before the Common Era (B.C.E.).
2. Virgil, 1951, pp. 4, 109. Another version of this legend can be found in the *Bellum Poenicum* by Naevius. Other foundation myths relate the origins of Rome to the twins Romulus and Remus, who allegedly were nurtured by a she-wolf.
3. Gibbon, 1952, p. 27.
4. Roman society was structured according to a patriarchial system, where individuals belonged to tightly knit extended families that were linked to other people through patron-client relations. Patrician families with numerous clients had enormous power and status. The authority of the father *(patria potestas)* in Roman families was absolute. Like Cincinnatus, he should exhibit diligence *(industria)* and good judgment *(consilium)*. All family members were expected to give deference to the traditions of their ancestors *(mos maiorum)* and show respect to the law *(ius civile)*.
5. Livy, 1919, pp. 255–261.
6. Ferrill, 1991, pp. 77–78. In contrast to the Greek hoplite model discussed in the previous chapter, the Roman legion fought in a checkerboard formation to allow for greater movement than was possible in a tight phalanx. Each *maniple* (or company) in the formation contained soldiers wearing iron ring armor and armed with javelins (the *pilum*) and swords. Usually, the Romans would attack in a series of waves, in which troops from the rear of the formation would rotate with those on the front line throughout the battle to make the most efficient use of manpower. The best soldiers became centurions, company leaders who served as the first professional officer corps in antiquity.

7. Cicero, 1991, p. 15. To emphasize this point, Cicero mentions the granting of citizenship to the Tusculani, Aequi, Volsci, Sabini, and the Hernici after they had been defeated by Rome.

8. Picard and Picard, 1968, p. 125.

9. Harris, 1979, p. 41. Carthage had other problems as well. Since the late fifth century it had feuded with Greek colonies in Sicily and thus hoped to use Rome as a check on their expansion.

10. In Picard and Picard, 1968, p. 72.

11. Lloyd, 1977, p. 110.

12. Picard and Picard, 1968, pp. 182–183.

13. With the exception of Brindisi, Naples, and a few other ports, Italy lacked natural harbors. Rome itself was built at the first ford of the Tiber River, some fifteen miles from the sea, and thus did not possess the maritime tradition of Carthage. Consequently, when Gaius Duilius unexpectedly defeated the Carthaginians in the naval battle of Mylae in 260, a triumphal column was erected in honor of Rome's first victory at sea and a flutist played whenever Duilius dined in public. Soren et al., 1990, p. 95.

14. Picard and Picard, 1968, p. 200.

15. Warmington, 1960, p. 162.

16. The three political pillars of the Roman Republic were the Senate (containing three hundred members selected from the heads of major families), the Popular Assembly (which represented all citizens), and a Magistracy composed of *consuls* who served as generals in the army, *praetors* who adjudicated legal disputes, *censors* who guided public morals, and *quaestors* who oversaw financial matters.

17. In Kagan, 1995, p. 252.

18. Warmington, 1960, p. 162.

19. In Kagan, 1995, p. 254.

20. Ibid., p. 255.

21. Warmington, 1960, p. 168.

22. In Soren et al., 1990, p. 101.

23. Kagan, 1995, p. 271.

24. Warmington, 1960, p. 183.

25. Strauss and Ober, 1990, pp. 148–149.

26. Livy, 1965, p. 601. Despite Scipio's rhetoric of vengeance, it is said that the peace terms he offered defeated states would place him "on a pinnacle among the world's greatest conquerors—his entire absence of vindictiveness, his masterly insurance of military security with a minimum of hardship to the conquered, his strict avoidance of annexation of any civilised State. They left no festering sores of revenge or injury and so prepared the way for the conversion of enemies into real allies." Liddell Hart, 1994, p. 278.

27. Dorsey and Dudley, 1972, p. 149.

28. Caven, 1980, p. 252.

29. Bradford, 1951, p. 203.

30. Picard and Picard, 1968, p. 266.

31. Lloyd, p. 19.

32. Ibid., p. 35.

33. Lazenby, 1978, pp. 243–244; see also Picard and Picard, p. 289, and Astin, 1978, p. 284.

34. Astin, 1978, p. 284.

35. In Adcock, 1970, p. 77.

36. In Armstrong, 1965, p. 10.

37. In Warmington, 1960, p. 208.

38. In Seldes, 1985, p. 64.

39. In Soren et al., 1990, p. 120.

40. In Hartmann, 1983, p. 150.

41. The Greek commentator Poseidonius, as cited by Warmington, 1960, p. 212.
42. Diodorus of Sicily, 1967, p. 131.
43. After the fall of the Republic, various writers contrasted the high moral standards of Rome's early days with the corruption and excesses of the Empire. The biographies of Suetonius, the epigrams of Martial, and the satires of Petronius and Juvenal portray the sordid side of Roman life in this new age.
44. Several empirical studies of crisis behavior have shown that states look backward to previous conflict episodes to decide upon the appropriate behavior in later encounters. See Hensel, 1994; Leng, 1993; and Anderson and McKeown, 1987.
45. TRB, 1966, p. 6; also see Welch, 1993.
46. Lazenby, 1978, p. 253.
47. See Blainey, 1973, p. 109.

PART III

Peace Building in Modern History

Historians differ over the best point in time to date the advent of the modern era of world politics. Some see the present age beginning in 1648 at the end of the Thirty Years' War in Europe, when the Treaty of Westphalia created a system of independent and sovereign nation-states with no higher authority, such as the Roman Catholic Church, to manage their relations. However, many other historians don't see the modern system crystallizing until the late 1700s, when the so-called age of democratic revolutions altered the characteristic ways nation-states interacted and the rules they accepted for diplomatic conduct. *How Nations Make Peace* uses that latter date as our point for departure for examining decision making regarding war and peace in the contemporary system.

The five case studies in Part III were chosen for their significance, variety, and ability to collectively capture the inherent tensions across time between contrasting philosophies for making successful peace settlements. The divergent settings and results force comparisons of successes and failures and give a clearer picture of the preconditions for successful strategies.

Three of the cases are widely known global-transforming *general wars* which concluded with peace treaties that, for better or worse, transformed not only the worldwide hierarchy of power by redistributing wealth and territory between the victors and vanquished, but also created new rules and institutions for the postwar system. The Napoleonic Wars that threatened to revolutionize international affairs until that revolution was defeated by the leading greatpowers at the 1815 Congress of Vienna comprises our first modern case study. World War I and the 1919 Treaty of Versailles provide a second case of general war that was settled by the embrace of a radically different approach. And World War II, with its protracted settlement during the ensuing Cold War, provides the third case for analysis.

These three widely known system-transforming wars and peace settlements epitomize the wisdom, or folly, of the kinds of approaches that might be taken at peace conferences. But there is more. First, juxtaposing these three major general wars in chronological order invites consideration of the possibility that the seeds of past wars, and the ways in which they are settled, will sow either a durable peace or a new global war. Second, comparing these three epic struggles provides a basis for reaching conclusions about the validity of prescriptions for peace making informed by the rival *realist* and *liberal* theoretical traditions and the adequacy of their ethical visions about justice. The peace treaties of all three virtually redefined realist and liberal thought, as witnessed by the realist reformulations after the 1815 Congress of Vienna and after World War II and the Wilsonian reconceptualization of liberal ideals after World War I. A comparison of the adequacy of both theoretical traditions forces evaluation of important questions. Which theory best accounts for the variation and outcomes across cases? Are there moral principles that these cases suggest apply across period, place, and global circumstance? Or do the cases illustrate the contingent nature of policy prescriptions, forcing us to conclude that the applicability of inferred lessons about workable peace-making rules is restricted to particular types of global conditions and actors? If so, what are those circumstances?

To broaden the picture and balance the sample, Part III expands the inventory of types of wars and peace settlements presented for comparison by providing two other cases that capture important properties not observable when major system-transforming wars and peace treaties are inspected. The notorious if less-familiar Wars of German Unification in the latter part of the nineteenth century add a regional case to our sample and disclose many concepts generic to the onset and resolution of wars—the impact of *nationalism, bureaucratic politics, mirror imagining,* to name a few. They raise questions about the determinants of successful and failed peace strategies and the trade-offs between available peace-making options. When compared chronologically with the Congress of Vienna that preceded them and World War I which followed, the Wars of German Unification invite closer examination of the hypothesis that the terms by which they were settled were the kindling that ignited the conflagration of the globe's first truly worldwide war in 1914.

Our final case, the Persian Gulf War of 1991 and its troubled aftermath, opens the door to analyzing wars and peace treaties between contemporary enemies who are unequal in power. By looking at the first great-power effort to collectively enforce peace in the post–Cold War era, we are afforded an opportunity to assess the realism of realpolitik and the practicality of collective security by the growing liberal democratic community. This case, an *asymmetrical war* far different in scope, duration, and destruction, represents the world's most recent example of a great-power versus non-great-power armed conflict and illustrates properties and principles not exhibited in the other cases, including controversies about peace making, preventive diplomacy, and peace building by collective global institutions like the United Nations or NATO.

Together, the five cases presented in Part III provide detailed information about how national interests and ethical values are woven into the process by which peace-making decisions are made. And in the blow-by-blow accounts of these disputes, we can see the tangle of factors that condition the victors' decisions when war making ceases and peace making commences.

The cases in Part III thus present the raw materials from history—however partial—from which policymakers can extract lessons about how to make a peace that lasts. In Part IV of *How Nations Make Peace,* we will put many of the pieces in this perplexing peace puzzle together when we will advance some policy recommendations for future peacemakers and interpret, from the standpoint of the realist and liberal theoretical traditions, the moral dilemmas involved with building a just and lasting peace.

· 5 ·

VISIONARY VICTORS?
THE NAPOLEONIC WARS
AND THE CONGRESS OF VIENNA

Better a lean peace than a fat victory.
ENGLISH PROVERB

PREVIEW

This chapter looks at one of history's "turning points" when, between 1792 and 1815, Napoleonic France waged wars to spread its influence, ideals, and institutions throughout Europe. That bid to overturn the ancien regime, or old order, marks the beginning of the modern era. The Napoleonic Wars were revolutionary in three of the major ways by which international systems are transformed, because they were fought (1) in pursuit of revolutionary ideological objectives, (2) by a new type of national actor mobilizing *nationalism* in a fight to overthrow monarchies and dynasties, and (3) with huge mass military armies armed with highly destructive weapons.

This is the story of the reaction that an imperial power with hegemonic ambitions provoked. The response of the other great powers threatened by the revolutionary aspirations of France is traced from the outbreak of war to its dramatic climax at the Congress of Vienna when the victors convened to create new rules for managing the postwar peace.

The terms of that settlement stand as a paragon of a lenient treaty toward the vanquished. But, as shall be seen, the peace treaties that emerged were guided less by sentiments of compassion than by *realpolitik* thinking about the *balance of power.* We shall also inspect the consequences in the nineteenth century of the rules that were created and the ways the Concert of Europe sought to act on them to police the system.

This case illuminates how nations conceived of their interests and ideals as they wrestled with the competing values and moral principles that colored their thinking about prudent, expedient, and practical approaches to maintaining international stability. The narrative introduces many core concepts in contemporary world politics, including

- alliances and coalition formation
- the balance of power
- a "balancer" role in the maintenance of power balances
- multipolar distributions of power
- nationalism
- popular sovereignty and liberal convictions about democratic governance
- a "concert" of the great powers to manage international affairs

These and other concepts within *realist* and *liberal* theories about international security are prominent in this chapter, where we will pursue questions about the conditions under which, in different situations, those theories explain the choices before, during, and after wars about war making and peace making.

■ ■ ■ ■ ■ ■ ■ ■ ■ ■ ■ ■ ■ ■ ■ ■ ■ ■ ■

Durable peace settlements are not neatly packaged by history. The past is cluttered with numerous treaties, some which lasted a long time and some which were quickly broken as the signatories prepared for a new war with one another. In order to fit the various fragments of historical evidence together in a coherent pattern, it is useful to begin with the big pieces first and try to figure out how they might be linked. In this part of the book we will inspect several of the largest pieces of the war-termination puzzle in the modern world system: the Napoleonic Wars (1803–1815), the Wars of German Unification (1862–1871), the First (1914–1918) and Second (1939–1945) World Wars, and the Persian Gulf War (1991). National leaders often cite the ways these wars ended when drawing lessons from modern history about whether to treat their prostrate enemies with compassion or with vengeance. Over the next five chapters we will present comparison cases to gain more insight into the costs, risks, and benefits of conciliatory versus retributive peace settlements.

AFTER ME THE DELUGE

The seventeenth and eighteenth centuries were an age of dynasties. Monarchs ruled over territories that often resembled confederations of provinces tied together through crisscrossing marriages among noble families. Religion played a waning role in the politics among nations. In its place stood *raison d'état* (reason of state), the realist notion that any act advancing state security interests was warranted no matter how morally repugnant it might seem. To realist theoreticians at the time, royal power was absolute. As expressed by French King Louis XIV, *"L'etat, c'est moi"* [I am the state].

Widespread agreement existed among this small, homogeneous group of monarchs over how the game of international politics ought to be played. They shared common experiences and held the same basic values and thus tended to feel more comfortable with fellow rulers than with lower-class citizens from their own states. In this aristocratic environment foreign policy was "a sport of kings, not to be taken more seriously than games and gambles, played for strictly limited stakes, and utterly devoid of transcendent principles of any kind. Since such was the nature of international politics, [all strategies and actions] were executed according to the rules of the game, which all players recognized as binding."[1] These monarchs understood that they were competitors with one another for power and believed that national survival frequently depended on forming flexible alliances with any nation in order to maintain a rough balance of power. They all agreed on the divine right of all kings to rule at home as they saw fit and to follow a transnational code of conduct when dealing with one another. Reputation and personal honor precluded doing unseemly things to others who held the same station in life.

This **multipolar** system of many contending great powers survived until the French Revolution. To be sure, during its previous history Europe had experienced numerous wars, some of which dismembered once powerful states.[2] Yet the ebb and flow of countervailing alliances prevented any single power from conquering the rest. When an aspiring hegemon appeared within reach of military preponderance, other states coalesced to block its designs. The tacit rules of this balance-of-power game neither eliminated human rapacity nor prevented the collision of contending national interests; they merely prevented competition from degenerating into pure bedlam by specifying how the rivalry among dynastic states would be conducted.

The pillars of this laissez-faire, self-help system began to crumble in the late 1700s from a weakness that the ruling monarchs did not fully appreciate. Dynastic power declined more from internal causes than from external aggression. Nowhere was this more apparent than in France. Located at the center of the intellectual movement of the Enlightenment, and benefiting from the growing industry, commerce, and capital that its reform-minded and expanding middle class was generating, France was the most advanced country on the Continent. Yet its despotic government was reeling under the pressure generated by an inefficient system of taxation. As King Louis XV, who held power from 1715 until 1774, predicted: *"Après moi le déluge"* [after me the deluge].

LIBERTY, FRATERNITY, AND EQUALITY

In eighteenth-century France, everyone belonged to an "estate" or "order" that defined his or her legal rights. The First Estate consisted of the clergy, the Second Estate the nobility, and the Third Estate included the remainder of the population. Whereas the first two estates were privileged, the third was not and remained subject to a land tax called the *taille*.[3] Dividing French society into three categories, with the third combining such disparate groups as peasants, urban workers, merchants, financiers, physicians, and attorneys, aroused serious tensions. On the one hand, the wealthy commercial and professional classes in the Third Estate resented being classified together with impoverished laborers and lashed out at feudal privileges retained by the nobility. On the other hand, the nobility bemoaned what they saw as the pretensions of a rising bourgeoisie and sought to protect their long-standing social and political privileges.

Meanwhile, peasants throughout the French countryside and proletarians working at menial jobs in the cities harbored economic grievances. Heavily taxed by an inefficient government, they suffered without hope of relief. As Victor Hugo's moving historic novel *Les Miserables* captured it, the daily struggle for survival for the common person was extremely difficult, especially if he or she relied upon wages rather than selling handicrafts or agricultural products at market prices. Not only was income unevenly distributed, but the classes with the least wealth paid the bulk of the taxes.

The financial collapse of the French government precipitated a mass rebellion that became the French Revolution. King Louis XVI's intervention in the 1778–1783 War of American Independence had exhausted the French treasury, and to replenish it the king required tax burdens to be shouldered by the entire nation. When the well-to-do resisted, the king called for a convocation of the Estates General in May 1789 at Versailles, the first such assembly since 1614. The initial plan was to have representatives from each of the three estates sit in different chambers and cast votes separately; however, the Third Estate, possessing as many representatives as the other two estates combined, shrewdly called for all delegates to be combined in a single legislative house where they would hold the majority. The nobility refused and pressured Louis XVI to close the building where the Third Estate had been meeting. In response, representatives of the Third Estate gathered in a nearby indoor tennis court, where on June 20 they swore an oath proclaiming themselves to be the National Constituent Assembly charged with drafting a constitution.

> "The outcome of the greatest events is always determined by a trifle."
>
> —NAPOLEON BONAPARTE

For those who had taken the "Oath of the Tennis Court," the king's actions revealed he was siding with the hated nobility against the commoners. As a result, many of them argued for a constitution that kept the monarchy weak. Louis considered dissolving the Assembly, but eventually ordered the two other estates to join this new legislative body, though he never reconciled himself to the role of a constitutional monarch and continued working to undermine the Assembly. Indignant over their loss of privilege, many of the nobility emigrated to neighboring countries where they urged their hosts to overthrow the new regime.

Compounding the political problems now facing the monarchy were the wrenching economic consequences of a poor harvest and a decline in foreign trade. Unemployment, rising food prices, and labor unrest staggered French society: waves of panic swept across the country. On July 14, 1789, a Parisian mob stormed the royal fortress and prison, the Bastille, and organized a revolutionary municipal government. Outside of Paris, manors were looted, private estates occupied, and landlords murdered. Some revolutionaries were appalled by the violence; others insisted on even more extreme actions. Internal resistance among many clergy to sweeping reform combined with the threat of foreign intervention to push the revolution along a more radical, nationalist course.

On August 26, 1789, the Assembly issued the Declaration of the Rights of Man and Citizen as a guide to the new political system it was creating. "Men are born, and always continue, free and equal in respect of their rights," asserted Article I. According to Article II, these rights were "liberty, property, security, and resistance of oppression." "The nation is essentially the source of all sovereignty," continued Article III, "nor can any individual, or any body of men, be entitled to any authority which is not expressly derived from it." Inspired by the liberal ideas of the eighteenth-century philosophes,[4] the authors of the declaration had articulated a set of principles that would replace the last vestiges of feudalism in France with a political order based on *liberté, égalité, fraternité* (liberty, equality, fraternity).

The Society of Friends of the Constitution, known as the Jacobin club because they met in a Jacobin monastery, were among the most militant of the French revolutionaries. The Girondins, then the dominant faction within the club, believed the revolution would not be secure at home until it was exported abroad. Arguing that the French army would find allies among the oppressed populations of adjacent countries, they envisioned war as a crusade against monarchy. Ironically, the king and many of his conservative supporters also expected war to deliver them from their political problems. If revolutionary France lost, the powers of the Bourbon dynasty would be restored. By 1792, various royal courts across the Continent began preparations to prevent the spread of revolution to their own territories. As international tensions mounted, Franco-Austrian relations rapidly deteriorated, leading the National Assembly to approve a declaration of war on April 20 with only seven dissenting votes.

TO ARMS, TO ARMS, YE BRAVE

Contrary to Girondin predictions, the war began badly for France. Prussia joined the Austrian side, French defenses were weakened by the desertion of officers drawn from the nobility, and within a year the British joined this first coalition against France. When the Duke of Brunswick, commander of the Austrian and Prussian forces, issued a manifesto threatening retribution against anyone who harmed the French royal family, rumors circulated throughout Paris that King Louis XVI was assisting the invaders. On August 10 an armed mob attacked the Tuileries Palace and forced the royal family to flee. A revolutionary "commune" assumed control of the government in Paris and ordered the election of a new legislative body, the National Convention.

Authority now passed from the Girondins to more violent men. A Committee of Public Safety was established in 1793 to secure the home front by executing counterrevolutionaries. Under Maximilien Robespierre, a fanatical Jacobin who had once served as a small-town lawyer in northern France, it unleashed the Reign of Terror that sent Louis XVI and his queen, Marie Antoinette, to the guillotine. Over the next fourteen months, hundreds of thousands of people were arrested and approximately forty thousand were killed. The strength of popular government lies in virtue, Robespierre thundered in a speech to the Convention on February 5, 1794. But, he continued, virtue is powerless without terror. The campaign to uproot domestic conspiracies against the revolution eventually devoured Robespierre. He was executed five months later, along with several of his closest associates.

To deal with foreign threats, the Committee of Public Safety ordered a *levée en masse* (universal conscription). By the spring of 1794, it had raised 800,000 troops. Unlike other armies of the day, this was a national armed force composed of enthusiastic citizen-soldiers who marched to battle singing, "To arms, to arms, ye brave," the rousing lyrics to "La Marsellaise," which later became the French national anthem. Commanded by officers who had risen through the ranks according to merit, France now possessed a formidable military machine.

Napoleon Bonaparte was one of the most talented officers in this machine. A short, temperamental man from the Mediterranean island of Corsica, he gained the attention of the Jacobins by brilliantly expelling British forces from Toulon in 1793. Napoleon claimed that his mind was like an ordered chest of drawers: each drawer contained a vast amount of information on a particular topic, and he could open any of them whenever necessary to inspect their contents without missing a single detail. On October 5, 1795, when some twenty thousand royalists marched against the Convention, the twenty-six-year-old officer dispersed the crowd by firing at it with grapeshot from a cannon. Less than two weeks later he was appointed to the rank of brigadier general.

The following year, Napoleon received command of an army. He forced the Austrians out of Italy, and, in the 1797 Treaty of Campo Formio, he obtained the Austrian Netherlands and the Ionian Islands. From there, Napoleon's armies pursued an expansionist policy that sought to surround France with dependent countries modeled after Republican France. These actions precipitated a Second Coalition against France in 1798, composed of Great Britain, Austria, and Russia. Building on his popular support and rising national pride after the intervening "triumvirate" period, Napoleon seized control of the government in 1799 in a coup d'état that secured his position as supreme military commander. On December 4, 1804, his personal power increased even more when he assumed the title "Napoleon I, Emperor of the French." The French Republic was now a personal dictatorship.

Napoleon Bonaparte had come to power on the heels of a revolution inspired by the twin forces of liberalism and **nationalism.** The Napoleonic Wars, which ravaged Europe from 1803 to 1815, were undertaken to establish a new international order, one that would impose political unity on the Continent and reform the way European leaders ruled their tributary states. Napoleon sought to establish a single code of law, a public school system, and to implant liberal ideals in constitutions of the countries he conquered. His reforms generated several movements for national unification and republican administration. However, his methods were at times ruthless, and victory on the battlefield sometimes led him to violate many of the liberal principles that he espoused. Occasionally he installed members of his own family as the rulers of subjugated lands.[5]

Napoleon's Grand Empire reached its zenith in 1810 (see Map 5.1). Beyond France (which included Belgium and lands on the left bank of the Rhine) were layers of dependent states and political allies. The former encompassed what is today the Netherlands, Spain, Switzerland, western and southern Germany, most of Italy, and parts of Poland. The latter included Austria, Prussia, Denmark, Sweden, and Russia. All of these countries were part of Napoleon's Continental System, a mechanism designed to crush Great Britain by prohibiting the importation of British goods into Europe. By interrupting this trade flow, Napoleon hoped to dry up a major source of London's revenues and establish France as the economic hub of Europe. Since its naval victory over the French in the 1805 Battle of Trafalgar, Britain had been able to retain control of the seaborne commerce, thwarting Napoleon's military ambitions outside of Europe.

Napoleon's pursuit of hegemony stalled after 1811. The economic sacrifices demanded by the Continental System bred resentment from Zeeland on the North Sea to the distant shores of the Baltic Sea. Simultaneously, France began to suffer serious military setbacks. Although Napoleon had sent military units to Spain several years earlier to suppress a revolt against French rule, his forces were unable to defeat or pacify the country. As savage fighting with local guerrillas continued, he committed over 250,000 troops to what he called his "Spanish ulcer." Yet the French never tasted victory in this Peninsular War, despite the vast resources they hurled at their opponent.

More resources were drained by the June 1812 invasion of Russia. Determined to punish Czar Alexander I for withdrawing from the Continental System two years earlier, Napoleon assembled an enormous multinational force for the campaign. Despite defeating the Russians at Borodino and occupying Moscow on September 14, he could not compel them to surrender. Overextended, with limited supplies, and facing an opponent who engaged in "scorched earth" tactics, Napoleon confronted the unsavory prospect of being isolated in the smoldering ruins of Moscow as cold, harsh weather arrived. Realizing it would be difficult to feed and equip his Grande Armée under these

MAP 5.1 Europe in 1812. In 1812, Napoleon had subdued continental Europe and the occupying French armies aroused nationalism in the territories they occupied.

conditions, he ordered a withdrawal. Relentlessly harassed by the Cossack cavalry, the Grande Armée retreated slowly through the snow, icy wind, and seemingly eternal darkness of the Russian winter. Of the 611,000 troops who invaded Russia, roughly 400,000 died from exposure, starvation, and battle wounds. Another 100,000 men were taken prisoner. When the frozen tatters of what remained of the Grande Armée crossed back into Poland, it was no longer a disciplined fighting force.

With Europe no longer in awe of Napoleon, another coalition consisting of Great Britain, Russia, Prussia, and Austria was forged against French expansionism (see Box 5.1). Napoleon's empire finally collapsed after the Waterloo Campaign of June 12–18, 1815, but its fate had been sealed in defeats France

BOX 5.1
THE STEPS TOWARD A SETTLEMENT
OF THE NAPOLEONIC WARS

- During 1800, French forces inflict crushing defeat on the Second Coalition in Italy and southern Germany, and Austria sues for peace; the 1801 Treaty of Lunéville terminates the provisions of the Campo Formio armistice.
- In March 1802 Great Britain and France sign the Treaty of Amiens, which accepts the Lunéville Treaty settlement and adds a British promise to restore all the colonial conquests engineered during the war (with the exception of Ceylon and Trinidad).
- In May 1803 Great Britain renews hostilities in response to the French refusal to cease its interventionary pursuits in Italy, Switzerland, and the Netherlands.
- Third Coalition formed in 1805 by Great Britain, Austria, Russia, and Sweden to overthrow Napoleonic France. In December, Napoleon's victories at Ulm and Austerlitz force Austria to abandon the Third Coalition, and the Treaty of Pressburg gives Venetia to Italy and recognizes Napoleon as its king. This humiliating treaty reduces Austria to a second-rank power by severing it from its former dominions in Italy, Switzerland, and the Rhine region.
- In 1806 Prussia declares war on France, but Napoleon's armies inflict disastrous defeats in the battles of Jena and Auerstädt. In triumph, Napoleon occupies and takes possession of most of Prussia.
- In June 1807 Napoleon defeats the Russians at Friedland, and Czar Alexander sues for peace. In the Treaty of Tilsit, Napoleon unexpectedly offers Alexander magnanimous terms, asking for no Russian territory in exchange for Alexander's pledge to help prevent British trade on the Continent. However, this treaty extracts from Prussia half of the territory it controlled in Poland and requires Prussia to pay France a large indemnity—a provision that makes Prussia a third-rate power and destroys the Third Coalition, with the effect that opposition to French dominion on the European continent is provided only by Great Britain and Sweden.
- In April 1809 Austria launches a war of national liberation, but at the battle of Wagram in October 1809, Napoleon forces the Austrians to accept the harsh terms of the Treaty of Vienna (or Treaty of Schönbrunn), which costs Austria 4.5 million subjects, a forced disarmament to 150,000 soldiers, heavy indemnities, and a pledge not to trade with Great Britain.
- The Treaty of Bucharest (May 28, 1812) suspends Russia's war with the Ottoman Empire, and Russian borders are extended southward to the Pruth River.
- Napoleon's forces cross the Niemen River on June 24, 1812, and begin the invasion of Russia. In September, Napoleon takes possession of Moscow, but the lack of supplies in the burning city forces Napoleon on October 22 to evacuate Moscow and retrace his tracks toward the Niemen, where a

mere remnant of his starving and frozen army crosses the river on December 13. Czar Alexander I proclaims the liberation of Europe, and Prussian and Swedish forces join Russia in a new allied effort to vanquish the French.

- In May 1813 Austrian chief minister Klemens von Metternich mediates an armistice and proposes a general European peace settlement between the faltering French and the allied armies, with territorial transfers and the reconstruction of Prussia. Seeking a decisive victory with expected French and Italian reinforcements, Napoleon stalls, and on August 12, 1813, Austria formally joins the coalition against him.
- The Treaty of Gulistan, which cedes to Russia the region of Georgia between the Black and Caspian Seas, is signed on October 12, 1813, by Russia and Persia.
- An unofficial, unsigned offer of peace is sent on November 9, 1813, to Napoleon from Frankfurt, asking France to withdraw behind the natural frontiers of the Rhine, the Alps, and the Pyrenees. Napoleon conveys his consent to this agreement through his minister for foreign affairs, but the outbreak of a rebellion in Holland means that France can no longer control the mouth of the Rhine. This causes the allies to change their thinking about the terms they should request from France. On December 5, 1813, the members of the Quadruple Alliance promulgate the Declaration of Frankfurt, which withdraws their previous offer in regard to the frontiers, and the Alliance begins instead to aid the revolt of Holland and pursue a policy of alienating Napoleon's friends in France and abroad. The allied armies cross the Rhine into France on December 21, 1813, and the main allied army invades from Switzerland through Lorraine.
- By the terms of the January 14, 1814, Treaty of Kiel, Denmark, which had been an ally of France, is forced to cede Norway (united with Denmark for the preceding four hundred years) to Sweden. The Norwegians refuse to accept the Treaty of Kiel, declare themselves independent, establish a liberal constitution, and offer the Norwegian throne to the Danish crown prince Christian Frederick, who holds the Norwegian throne only from May 17 to August 14, 1814 (Frederick later was to become the king of Denmark between 1839 and 1848).
- The Treaty of Chaumont, signed March 9, 1814 by Great Britain, Russia, Prussia, and Austria, strengthens the allied offensive against France and establishes a unified effort to police European politics. The combined allied armies deal Napoleon a decisive defeat at Laon, northeast of Paris, March 9–10, 1814.
- Austrian, Prussian, and Russian troops enter Paris on March 30, 1814. On April 1 Charles-Maurice de Talleyrand convokes the Senate, which until then had been a tool under the control of Napoleon; on April 2 the invading armies demand Napoleon's abdication, but the emperor continues to resist.
- The French troops under General Soult are defeated on April 10, 1814, by the Duke of Wellington at Toulouse, France, in the last battle of the Peninsular War (1808–1814). On April 11 Napoleon signs the Treaty of

Fontainebleau and abdicates his title as Emperor of France; in exchange the allies grant Napoleon sovereignty over the island of Elba off the coast of Italy.

- The First Treaty of Paris, signed on May 30, 1814, between France and Austria, Prussia, Russia, and Great Britain (the Quadruple Alliance), establishes a preliminary peace in Europe. The French minister of foreign affairs, Charles-Maurice de Talleyrand, receives extraordinary leniency in exchange for the pledge to restore the Bourbon monarchy to the throne in a "limited" rather than absolute monarchy: French boundaries are to be kept to those of 1792, and France is not required to pay any reparations. France also is allowed to keep the colonial possessions taken by Great Britain, except for Mauritius and the Seychelles Islands in the Indian Ocean and the West Indian islands of St. Lucia and Tobago. The treaty confirms Great Britain's possession of Malta.

- Louis XVIII, the brother of Louis XVI and king of France in exile since 1795, is restored to the French throne June 4, 1814, as a result of the negotiations of Talleyrand and the acquiescence of the allies. (The boy king Louis XVII, who was born in 1785 and became king in name on January 21, 1793, when his father Louis XVI was guillotined, was said to have died from mistreatment on June 8, 1795, in a revolutionary prison.)

- The Congress of Vienna convenes in September 1814. Representatives from all European states in existence prior to the Napoleonic Wars gather to settle territorial disputes and establish a perpetual balance of power in Europe to be overseen by the members of the Quadruple Alliance (Russia, Prussia, Austria, and Great Britain). The congress remains in session until June 9, 1815, when the Final Act of the Congress of Vienna is signed.

- On February 26, 1815, Napoleon escapes from Elba and is warmly received by the French people who, inspired by Napoleon's slogan "War to the palaces, peace to the cottages," join his bodyguards to recreate an army, Napoleon claims, to "save France from the outrages of the returning nobles [and] to secure to the peasant the possession of his land and to uphold the rights won in 1789 against a minority which had sought to reestablish the privileges of cast and the feudal burdens of the last century." The monarchies then debating treaty provisions in Vienna put aside their disputes and, in the name of unity, renew their alliance.

- On June 18, 1815, Napoleon wages his final battle and is dealt a crushing defeat in the Battle of Waterloo. Three days later he abdicates his power for the second and final time to the French provisional government, and on July 7 the allies' armies reoccupy Paris and restore the Bourbons by putting the aging Louis XVIII at the head of the French government. Napoleon surrenders to the commander of a British warship on July 15 and is sent to a prison on St. Helena, where he lives for the next five and a half years while writing his memoirs.

- Three months after Waterloo, on September 15, 1815, at the urging of Czar Alexander I, Austria, Prussia, and Russia sign the Treaty of the Holy Alliance in which they vow to "remain united by the bonds of a true and indissoluble fraternity" and "on all occasions and in all places, lend each other aid and assistance. . . ."

- Less than a month later, these victorious states expand the alliance by including Great Britain in postwar planning and reaffirm the pledge of cooperation that all four had previously made in the Treaty of Chaumont and the first Treaty of Paris to repel French aggression. In addition, they resolve to hold periodic congresses "for the purpose of consulting upon their common interests. . . ." This agreement thus stipulates the goal of creating a league among the great powers to collectively maintain European peace through a concert system for collective security.
- On November 20, 1815, the Second Treaty of Paris is signed. It renews the Quadruple Alliance for twenty years in order to prepare the way for the members to jointly manage international relations. Moreover, it modifies the previous understandings by increasing the penalties to France. The treaty's provisions require France to remain within its 1790 borders, return the art treasures Napoleon had taken from other countries, prohibit Napoleon and members of his family from gaining the throne of France, pay an indemnity of seven hundred million francs, and allow foreign occupation troops to make use of France's major fortresses for a period of five years. Article 6 of this treaty provides for future conferences to promote peace and lays the groundwork for the postwar Concert of Europe.

suffered in the preceding three years. Following a series of treaties and armistice agreements, the victors met in Vienna to craft a peace settlement with France.

WHAT EUROPE WANTS IS NOT LIBERTY BUT PEACE

Napoleon's defeat at Waterloo concluded a period that had battered Europe for almost a quarter century and left over 2.5 million combatants dead. When measured by battle deaths per population, the toll exceeded all previous wars fought during the preceding three centuries.[6] The carnage inspired pity in people of compassion and horror in people of prudence. It galvanized a consensus among the victors who met at the Congress of Vienna about the need to prevent another great-power death struggle from again erupting.

The Congress of Vienna

Vienna was famed for its charm and beauty. As the site for the peace deliberations, it played host to a dazzling assemblage of people: monarchs and their servants, diplomats and their deputies, generals and their aides, as well as wives, mistresses, spies, pickpockets, and hangers-on. Numerous banquets, teas, and balls were organized to delight the city's guests. Despite being almost bankrupt, the Austrians spent over fifteen million dollars providing entertainment. Among the cultural events was the first performance by the German musician Beethoven of his Seventh Symphony.[7]

While the festivities went on, statesmen toiled over more than just ending the roar of artillery. As the Austrian chancellor Prince Klemens von Metternich proclaimed in an opening session, the Congress of Vienna had as its mission goals beyond those of previous peace congresses.

> It does not require any great political insight to see that this Congress could not model itself on any predecessor. Previous meetings which have been called congresses have confined themselves to making treaties of peace between parties which were either at war or ready to go to war. This time the treaty of peace is already made, and the parties are meeting as friends, not necessarily having the same interests, who wish to work together to complete and affirm the existing Treaty. The matters to be negotiated are a multifarious list of questions, in some cases partly settled by previous discussions, in other cases, as yet untouched. The Powers which made the Treaty of Paris will determine the meaning which they wish to attach to the word Congress, and will also decide the form which would seem most appropriate for reaching the goals they have set themselves. They will use this right of determination equally to the advantage of the interested parties, and thus, to the good of Europe as a whole, and the plenipotentiaries at Vienna will deal with matters in the most efficient, prompt and confidential way. Thus the Congress is brought into being of itself, without having received any formal authority, there being no source which could have given any.[8]

The victors in the Napoleonic Wars operated from an unusually high level of agreement about the rules that should govern their future relations. The world they restored was a conservative world defined with an unusual clarity of purpose and consistency of vision. Napoleon's quest for **hegemony** had challenged not only the existing distribution of power on the European continent, but also the self-help system of legitimized competition among sovereign great-power equals that policymakers inspired by realist theory advocated. Napoleon embraced an imperial vision of international order with himself at the apex of authority; he had tried to recreate the quasi-world government that had operated throughout the medieval system prior to the 1648 Peace of Westphalia, which ended the Thirty Years' War and that had established the system of territorial states independent of the authority of the Church or any other supranational institutions.[9] But with the defeat of Napoleon came the defeat of his vision for a new international order. Metternich, backed by Russian czar Alexander I,

> "One must, if one can, kill one's opponent, but never rouse him by contempt and the whiplash."
>
> —KLEMENS VON METTERNICH

Prussian king Frederick William III, and British foreign minister Castlereagh, tried to restore as much of the pre-Napoleonic map of Europe as possible and return to the laissez-faire rules so that the old Westphalian game could be played again.

The bargains struck among the victorious powers about territorial matters reflected the realpolitik belief that conflict was a natural component of inter-state interaction. Disputes were bound to arise just as friction results from objects in contact. Whereas they might not be able to prevent future disputes, realist leaders assumed that they could reduce the likelihood of such disputes escalating to war by preserving an equilibrium among the **great powers.** In effect, the final act of the peace settlement of the Congress of Vienna redrew the map of Europe, guided not just by the goal of rewarding the victors for their sacrifices, but, more importantly, of making Austria, Russia, Prussia, Great Britain, and France approximately equal in their capacity to wage war. A stable **balance of power** was sought, with territorial boundaries altered so that no single state would be in a position to threaten the rest.

To attain this goal, the negotiators bargained long and hard to delineate a new set of borders that would allow the invisible hand of the balance of power to work. The biggest prize went to Russia, as Poland was again partitioned with the Czar gaining the largest slice. Russia also received Finland from Sweden, which had gained Norway from Denmark. To build a counterweight to France, Prussia gained a portion of Saxony, all the German territories Napoleon had taken from it, as well as land in Westphalia and the Rhineland. For similar reasons, Austria regained the Tyrol and other formerly held land, including territories in wealthy and strategically important regions of Italy, as compensation for its willingness to accept the suspension of claims on the southern Netherlands. The Vienna settlement also permitted the Vatican's recovery of its former possessions in central Italy, and Switzerland was made a neutral state. In addition to these and other changes in Europe, modifications were made in colonial possessions, again with the aim of fine-tuning the overall equilibrium. For example, Great Britain returned to the Netherlands all the overseas territories seized in 1806, except for Ceylon, the Cape Colony in Africa, and part of the Guyana coast of South America east of Venezuela. In compensation, the various settlements on the Atlantic coast (including the colonies of the Essequibo River, Berbice, and Demerara) were united in 1831 to form the Crown Colony of British Guiana, the only British colony in South America.

The Bourbon Restoration

The most memorable aspect of the peace settlement was its resuscitative policy toward the defeated power, France, which had tried to establish universal dominion. Article 32 of the first Treaty of Paris provided for French representation at Vienna, but a secret clause excluded France from the actual decision making. However, Charles-Maurice de Talleyrand, who represented France at the congress, was able to use discord among the victors to leverage French participation in the negotiations. France, it was finally concluded, would be needed as a **balancer** to help police the new order, and its exclusion, partition, or forced demise could easily become the seed of a subsequent war. A conciliatory attitude toward France was seen as prudent because a Bourbon government in Paris could help shore up monarchical rule elsewhere in Europe.

Talleyrand's appeals to the "sacred principle of monarchical legitimacy" helped to prevent his nation from remaining a pariah. The former Bishop of Auteuil, who had forsaken the Catholic Church during the Revolution only to abandon the Revolution for Napoleon, was famous for his caustic wit and cleverness. It was said that he had both the laughers and the thinkers on his side.[10] Upon arriving in Vienna, he insisted that with Napoleon gone, the victors had no right to exclude Bourbon France from the deliberations. His reiteration of the mantra of legitimacy eventually resonated with conservatives, who feared the Continent might suffer a relapse into revolutionary turmoil. As Metternich put it, what Europe wanted was not liberty but peace.

The Concert of Europe

To maintain peace after the congress ended, the diplomats in Vienna established the Concert of Europe, an oligarchic system of great-power consultation and policy coordination. The assumption behind the **concert** was that discussion and consensus building among those at the apex of the global hierarchy would produce multilateral decision making on divisive issues. Compromise and collaboration, rather than the thrust and parry of unbridled competition, would yield outcomes acceptable to all of the great powers. Not only would rule by this self-appointed coalition help control rivalries among the mighty, but it would provide a vehicle for enforcing peace among the smaller states, whose conflicts and civil wars could draw the great powers into combat.

Although theorists had in earlier times advocated various organizational schemes for orchestrating such collective responses to common problems, none were ever implemented. What made the climate of early-nineteenth-century opinion different was shared great-power fear of the strife unleashed by the French Revolution. Democratic ideals had taken root in a political landscape populated by monarchies adhering to strict realist conceptions of rules for peace keeping. The consequences for European royalty were profound:

> Decision makers no longer felt more loyalty to each other than to their own people. Fewer social and cultural ties united decision makers of different countries, and correspondingly more social and cultural ties grew between each country's decision makers and its general populace. The willingness to use more force and less restraint against other states increased as members of the system became

geographically dispersed and culturally heterogeneous. Increases in speed of transportation and communication did more to tie nations together internally than promoting cooperation among states. Xenophobia, the fear and hatred of foreign states, became a force . . . in almost every state. Where [before the French Revolution] the classical decision maker had difficulty in engendering patriotism among nations, the decision maker [after the French Revolution] had difficulty in controlling patriotism in order to follow a flexible foreign policy.[11]

From this setting emerged a **security regime** that took a different posture toward rules regarding the use of force for promoting security than had existed in the seventeenth century. Intervention in the internal affairs of states, for example, was uncommon in the eighteenth century; but since Revolutionary France had overturned the constitutions of conservative states, reactionary statesmen like Metternich and Friedrich Gentz now proclaimed the right to use forcible methods to suppress revolutionary uprisings within other nations' borders.[12] United in a common cause to combat rebellion from within, the victors experimented with the idea of collective intervention. For instance, at the Congress of Aix-la-Chapelle in 1818, Czar Alexander I of Russia proposed an alliance to intervene on behalf of rulers who were threatened by insurrection.

However, great-power unanimity proved to be elusive. While the British were willing to help the three Eastern monarchies stem military aggression aimed at overturning the post-Napoleonic balance of power, they did not countenance **military intervention** to prop up tottering autocrats. Foreign Minister Castlereagh, for example, refused Metternich's invitation in 1819 to approve the Carlsbad Decree and in 1829 rejected the Protocol of Troppau. In the first instance, the burning of conservative books and the murder of a conservative journalist by members of the German nationalist student movement prompted Metternich to convene a meeting of the larger German states at Carlsbad, where he coerced those leaders to promulgate measures he had drafted in order to suppress liberal nationalist ideas.[13] In the second instance, revolts in Spain and Naples led the three Eastern courts to agree at the Congress of Troppau that force could be used against states that had been transformed by internal upheaval and were threatening to their neighbors. Although Castlereagh was sympathetic to the fears held by his counterparts across the Channel, he resisted the use of the congress system to regulate other states' domestic affairs. Castlereagh, observed the Austrian ambassador in London, "is like a great lover of music who is at church; he wishes to applaud but he dares not."[14]

Despite British refusal to police sociopolitical disturbances, Austria, Prussia, and Russia were determined to use the Concert of Europe to prevent revolution. Therefore, at the Congress of Laibach the three conservative powers sanctioned Austria's intervention into Naples and Piedmont to suppress liberal revolts, and the following year at Verona they agreed to a French proposal to crush rebels in Spain.

THE LEGACY OF THE COACHMAN OF EUROPE

Metternich's dexterity at guiding events during this turbulent period earned him the title "Coachman of Europe." For him, no lasting peace was possible "with a revolutionary system, whether with a Robespierre who declares war on chateaux or a Napoleon who declares war on Powers."[15] Leery of **popular sovereignty** (the belief that citizens should have a voice in governmental policies and governments should be accountable to the public), Metternich preferred discipline and social order. The story is told that having observed an eclipse of the sun from the garden of his castle on the Rhine, a "great sense of relief came over him when the moon finally completed its path across the sun and the temporary darkness was dispelled. There was 'order' again in the world."[16]

Still, despite Metternich's best efforts, popular attacks on absolute monarchy occurred after the Vienna settlement. On July 29, 1830, after an unsuccessful attempt to exert royal control over the French press and legislature, Charles X lost his throne to Louis Philippe, who had fought in the republican army of 1792. Shock waves reverberated across the Continent: the Belgians revolted against King William I of Holland; the Polish diet declared their country independent of Russian control; and the rulers of Brunswick, Hesse-Cassel, and Saxony were forced to abdicate their thrones. In response, the Austrian and Russian emperors and the crown prince of Prussia met at Münchengratz in 1833 to voice support for collective great-power cooperation and to exercise the declared right to use force to contain civil rebellion.[17]

Successive congresses of the Concert of Europe were convened over the next five decades (see Table 5.1), and additional proposals were advanced to coordinate a collective great-power response to the threat of the moment. These conferences also sought to amend the understanding reached at the Congress of Vienna in order to accommodate it to changing international circumstances.

Though Britain's insular position sometimes led it to differ with Austria, Prussia, and Russia over the peace-keeping rules of the Concert of Europe, at critical junctures the great powers were able to agree upon a normative framework that prevented serious disputes from escalating into wars. To be sure, many conflicts later arose as the great-power struggle for influence continued, and mutual suspicions eroded confidence in what has been called "the scheme for the continuous management of the international system."[18] However, these fears were generally overcome, as the spirit of cooperation instilled at the Congress of Vienna went a long way in preserving peace.[19]

The fragile normative consensus underlying the Vienna settlement managed to persist for three decades—an extraordinary achievement, given the past record of common purpose vanishing after a common enemy was defeated. Nonetheless, it was eventually challenged. The liberal revolutions that swept Europe in 1848 undermined both the governments and the rules for international conduct that the victors had advocated when the Napoleonic wars

TABLE 5.1
Significant Great-Power Conferences, 1815–1870

Date	Location	Issues on the Agenda
1814–1815	Vienna and Paris	Peace Treaty, Quadruple Alliance
1818	Aix-la-Chapelle	France, Quadruple Alliance
1820	Troppau	Naples revolution
1821	Laibach	Naples revolution
1822	Verona	Italy, Spain, "the Eastern question"
1830–1832	London	Belgian independence
1831–1832	Rome	Papal States Government
1838–1839	London	Belgium (implementation of Treaty of London)
1839	Vienna	Egyptian insurrection
1840–1841	London	Egypt and the Straits
1850–1852	London	Schleswig-Holstein
1853	Vienna	Turkey
1855	Vienna	Crimean War Settlement
1856	Paris	Crimean War Peace Treaty
1858	Paris	The Principalities (implementation of Paris Treaty)
1860–1861	Paris	Syrian revolution
1864	London	Schleswig-Holstein, the Ionian islands
1866	Paris	Navigation on the Danube
1867	London	Luxembourg
1869	Paris	Cretan revolution

ended. The outbreak of the Crimean War in 1854 signaled the ultimate demise of the accords struck at the Congress of Vienna, which had required constant lobbying for them to work. That in itself is symptomatic of the inherent fragility of any peace program, however creative in design and durable its initial application.

The intellectual climate following the collapse of the Metternichean concert to collectively manage international affairs elevated national self-interest far above the old ideal of a common European interest. Instead of promoting collective action, it led the great powers to return to a security strategy based on flexible, short-term countervailing alliances.[20] The consensus that had constrained international rivalry in the first three decades after the Battle of Waterloo dissipated, bringing to a close a remarkable experiment in peace making.

To place the achievements of the Vienna settlement in their proper perspective, it is useful to compare the concert period of 1815–1848 with the postconcert period of 1849–1870. The concert period witnessed roughly the same number of serious interstate disputes as did the postconcert period, but between 1815 and 1848 there were fewer disputes between great powers and none escalated into wars. This is especially noteworthy given the greater frequency of interventions and reciprocated military actions during the reign of the concert system. In contrast, during the postcongress era between 1849 and

1870, no less than half the serious great-power disputes resulted in war, and, as we will see in the next chapter, some of these drastically altered the European balance of power.[21] The ostensible harmony at the congresses in London (1850, 1864, 1867), Paris (1856, 1858, 1860, 1869), and Vienna (1853, 1855) masked the unraveling of Metternich's security regime. The conservative solidarity that provided the normative underpinning for the Concert of Europe had collapsed. By the end of the Crimean War, no major power remained committed to preserving the rules emanating from the Vienna settlement. On the contrary, various political leaders actively sought to replace the agreement of the great powers to act collectively with a new set of rules that permitted each to act unilaterally in pursuit of its own perceived interests. As rivalries intensified, the consensus for cooperative peace keeping in the Concert of Europe broke down and balance-of-power politics reemerged.

> "Eternal peace lasts only until next year."
> —RUSSIAN PROVERB

THE POWER OF PRINCIPLE IN PRESERVING PEACE

The Vienna settlement stands in history as a paragon of a conciliatory peace that produced large dividends for the victors. It suggests that the prospects for a durable peace settlement can be enhanced by giving the vanquished enemy a stake in preserving the new order. To quote one famous contemporary realist theoretician on policy making, Henry Kissinger,

> In dealing with the defeated enemy, the victors designing a peace settlement must navigate the transition from the intransigence vital to victory to the conciliation needed to achieve a lasting peace. A punitive peace mortgages the international order because it saddles the victors, drained by their wartime exertions, with the task of holding down a country determined to undermine the settlement. Any country with a grievance is assured of finding nearly automatic support from the disaffected defeated party.[22]

Minimizing potential resentment requires a statesmanship of self-restraint. Defeated powers, this exceptional case suggests, must not be humiliated; neither should they be denied their legitimate rights, nor have their honor impugned.[23] Yet even with a conciliatory peace, a proud nation "sustains a deep wound from which there is no full recovery. . . . However much resilience the nation may retain outside the field of politics, a spring has been broken which cannot be welded together again."[24]

Offering a conciliatory peace, however, should not be confused with being ambivalent about whether the settlement will be vigorously upheld. A generous peace, realpolitik counsels, must still be a firm peace. By itself, a conciliatory settlement is no guarantee against revisionism. Victors must be capable of marshaling the military resources needed to convince the vanquished that efforts to overturn the status quo carry grave risks.

CONTROVERSIES TO CONTEMPLATE

- Did Republican France's effort to spread of liberal ideals in national governance and international affairs create the modern world system?
- Why did France under Napoleon pursue an imperial policy of expansionism that ravaged Europe? What were the ideas, ideals, and interests behind this quest for hegemony?
- What motives united the alliances that opposed each other in the European balance-of-power system?
- What national interests and ideals were uppermost in the minds of the leaders of the victors when they convened at Vienna and Paris to negotiate the terms of a peace treaty and devise new rules for the maintenance of world order? What was the prevailing philosophy of the victors?
- Was the consensus of the victors at Vienna about peace-making principles morally just? Why? What are the criteria by which such evaluations are best judged?
- How did nationalism and ascendant liberal values such as popular sovereignty influence international relations in the late eighteenth century?
- Why did realists at the Congress of Vienna create the Concert of Europe and endorse conciliation and compassion toward a vanquished expansionist power, France, as a prudent and practical peace policy?
- Did the Congress of Vienna settlement succeed? What are the preconditions for successful peace making?

In 1807 Napoleon Bonaparte observed, prophetically, "If they want peace, nations should avoid the pin pricks that precede common shots."[25] One of the most difficult tasks in statecraft is anticipating the issues that potential adversaries will likely see as so important that they will take up arms, if necessary, to resolve them to their own satisfaction. As adept as the negotiators at the Congress of Vienna were in preventing the rapid onset of another major war, deficiencies marred the final peace settlement and led, over time, to the gradual erosion of the foundation on which the Concert of Europe rested. As one student of the period notes,

> the Vienna peace settlement was backward-looking. The problem of the future was assumed to be the problem of the past: French revolutionary expansionism. . . . The drafters created a successful system to cope with the problem of hegemony-seeking. That is not an insignificant accomplishment, but the threat of hegemony was not to arise for many more decades. In the meantime, the problems of national liberation, national unification, and liberal institutionalism were already on the horizon. They would become the most important sources of war

throughout the nineteenth century, but the 1814–1815 settlements ignored them. The statesmen of the great powers created a static system for a world of change . . . and a peace system that anticipated for the future little more than a recurrence of a problem they had already resolved.[26]

Peace treaties are not self-enacting; all parties must work energetically to guarantee that their provisions are carried out, and they must address divisive issues that may later arise. As prescient as it was, the Vienna settlement still failed to identify two "pin-prick" issues that would precede the cannon shots fired during the second half of the nineteenth century: liberal reform movements and hypernationalism.

Controversies remain about the transferability of lessons derived from this historical episode. What do the events of 1814–1815 tell us about the viability of future peace settlements? For some nations, the Congress of Vienna laid the groundwork for a lengthy peace; for others, it stifled democracy and national self-determination and thus sowed the seeds of subsequent trouble. To draw lessons about the most effective means of achieving durable peace settlements, we need to broaden our coverage and look at other cases for additional evidence. In Chapter 6 we take up this challenge by examining the Wars of German Unification.

NOTES

1. Morgenthau, 1985, p. 210.
2. Poland, for example, was partitioned three times (1772, 1793, and 1795) and ultimately disappeared as an autonomous state, until reconstituted at the end of World War I.
3. Because the bourgeoisie generally found ways to avoid paying this tax, most of the revenues were collected from the peasantry.
4. The philosophes were men of letters who popularized the ideas of the Enlightenment. Drawing upon the previous work of Francis Bacon, Rene Decartes, John Locke, and Isaac Newton, they were confident in the power of reason to discover the laws of nature and promote human progress. Within France, the center of this intellectual movement, Condorcet, Diderot, Helvétius, Montesquieu, Quesnay, Rousseau, Turgot, and Voltaire were the most renowned figures.
5. For example, his brother Joseph was made king of Spain, Louis served as king of Holland, and Jerome became king of Westphalia, an artificial state cobbled together from Prussian and Hanoverian territories. Napoleon's sister Caroline was named the queen of Naples, and his stepson became viceroy of the Kingdom of Italy.
6. Levy, 1983, p. 58.
7. Lane, Goldman, and Hunt, 1959, p. 341.
8. In Langhorne, 1986, p. 318.
9. Miller, 1985, p. 31.
10. Kissinger, 1973, p. 148.
11. Coplin, 1971, p. 305.
12. Rosecrance, 1963, p. 29.
13. Nicolson, 1946, p. 265.
14. Kissinger, 1973, p. 275.

15. In Kissinger, 1973, p. 12.
16. Pinson, 1966, p. 56. Metternich's last words in 1859 revealingly were, "I was a rock of order." In Green, 1982, p. 25.
17. The right to intervene in lesser powers' internal affairs was also rationalized by goals other than the conservative purpose of preserving monarchies and the status quo. Under Castlereagh's successor, George Canning, the threat of British sea power was used to support the independence movement in Spanish America; later, under Lord Palmerston, the British supported constitutionalist causes in Spain and Portugal. Intervention and forcible procedures, in other words, also had become tools of liberal statecraft, as progressive thinkers like Stratford de Redcliffe and John Stuart Mill advocated their use to liberate oppressed peoples and engender democratic reform. For a history of the rise and decline of the nonintervention principle in international law since 1816, see Kegley, Raymond, and Hermann, 1998.
18. Langhorne, 1986, p. 317.
19. For example, when peace was threatened by an uprising in Belgium in 1830, the great powers were able to resolve their differences despite King William's plea to the conservative states for help, a plea which threatened to expand to war when Russia responded with an offer of sixty thousand troops to assist in restoring him to his throne.
20. Hinsley, 1963, p. 238.
21. See Schroeder, 1986; Wallace, 1979.
22. Kissinger, 1994, p. 81. Schroeder, 1994b, p. 477, elaborates, characterizing the peace that the victors launched as testimony to the capacity to achieve, "or at least approach, consensus on a sane, practical concept of peace. This was the product of learning, of changing previous concepts of peace and victory to fit reality."
23. Elrod, 1976, p. 166.
24. Dehio, 1962, p. 173.
25. In Seldes, 1985, p. 305.
26. Holsti, 1991, pp. 136–137.

· 6 ·

BLOOD AND IRON:
THE WARS OF GERMAN UNIFICATION

The statesman is like a man wandering in a forest
who knows his general direction, but not the exact
point at which he will emerge from the wood.
OTTO VON BISMARCK

PREVIEW

The Peloponnesian, Punic, and Napoleonic Wars were system-transforming struggles that pitted the most powerful states of the day against one another to determine whose vision of international order would prevail. To place these hegemonic wars in perspective, we turn our attention in this chapter to the Wars of German Unification—a set of shorter, less destructive clashes that helped pave the way for World War I, history's next system-transforming war. Fought early in the second half of the nineteenth century, they were an important link in the chain of events that led the victors of World War I to design a peace treaty that was far more harsh than the settlement crafted a century earlier at the Congress of Vienna.

The Wars of German Unification were dominated by the towering personality of Otto von Bismarck. His *realist* approach to statecraft accepted military force as a tool of foreign policy to be unleashed whenever the value of what could be won exceeded the costs of fighting. In wars against Denmark (1864), Austria (1866), and France (1870–1871), he skillfully used military force to achieve his political goals. Once these wars were over, he sought to preserve their cumulative outcome by building a network of alliances that would solidify the new *balance of power* in Europe. A study of the Wars of German Unification thus gives us an avenue for exploring how war and peace making are influenced by:

- nationalism
- power politics

121

- technology that rewards taking the offensive
- irredentism
- secret diplomacy
- alliances

When reading this chapter, note how Bismarck deftly isolated an opponent before hostilities were initiated and how each victory positioned him to undertake another war against a different opponent. In addition, contrast his settlement of the war with Austria with the settlement that terminated the war with France.

■   ■

On September 24, 1862, Count Otto Eduard Leopold von Bismarck-Schönhausen was appointed minister-president of Prussia by King William I. The king was desperate. His decision to undertake a comprehensive reform of the Prussian military had precipitated a constitutional crisis, pitting the crown against liberal members of parliament. The proposed reforms would expand the officer corps and double the size of the army, both costly undertakings that required the legislature to authorize a substantial tax increase. When liberal legislators balked at providing the necessary appropriation, a somber William briefly considered abdicating, but he turned instead to his new minister in the hope that this self-proclaimed man of action could break the political deadlock over funding the military reforms.

Bismarck was a tall, broad-shouldered man with deep loyalty to the Prussian state. For him, domestic politics were subordinate to questions of foreign policy. Like Karl von Clausewitz, the Prussian general who had fought against Napoleon half a century earlier, Bismarck saw war as an instrument in the conduct of foreign policy.[1] Without a modern, effective military force, Prussian foreign policy would lack an essential tool. A practitioner of **realpolitik,** during his first appearance before the legislative Budget Committee on September 30, he declared, "The position of Prussia in Germany will be determined not by its liberalism but by its power." In his opinion, "Prussia must concentrate its strength and hold it for a favorable moment." "Not through speeches and majority decisions are the great questions of the day decided," he concluded, "but through iron and blood."[2]

During Bismarck's era at the helm of Prussian foreign policy, his policy of iron and blood resulted a series of wars, collectively known as the Wars of German Unification. In this chapter we will examine the character of these wars, compare the peace settlements that were constructed in their aftermath, and evaluate the consequences that resulted from the philosophies of statecraft that shaped the policies of the victors.

THE RISE OF BRANDENBURG-PRUSSIA

The first German empire, or *Reich,* had its origins in the vast lands once controlled by Charlemagne, the Frankish king who conquered much of western Europe during the ninth century. Following his death in 843, these lands were inherited by his only surviving son, Louis the Pious, who spent half of his life trying to figure out how to distribute the territory among his own sons. Following a series of civil wars, Louis's holdings were subdivided: one son took the west, another took the east, and the third received a corridor stretching from the North Sea to Rome (including modern Belgium, Alsace, Lorraine, the Rhineland, Switzerland, and the Po valley). Much of European history ever since has involved a struggle between the west (contemporary France) and east (contemporary Germany) for control of this middle kingdom.

The Holy Roman Empire

The eastern Frankish region came to be known as the Holy Roman Empire of the German Nation. A conglomeration of many different tribes speaking various dialects, this First Reich suffered from an ever-growing tension between central authority and the power of local princes. As central control gradually decayed, a feudal structure took its place. What we today call Germany was a mosaic of political units: duchies, free cities, bishoprics ruled by churchmen, and minuscule fiefdoms controlled by an assortment of counts and barons, each nominally the vassal of some higher lord. Certain frontier principalities called *Marken* (or marchlands) were given special privileges for defending the borders of the empire. The most important of these were Brandenburg in the northeast and Austria in the southeast (see Map 6.1).

In a process termed *Drang nach Osten* (drive to the east), Brandenburg accumulated territory largely at the expense of the neighboring Slavs. In 1618, it inherited the duchy of Prussia when the male line of the dukes died out. An area along the coast of the Baltic Sea, Prussia had been colonized by the Knights of the Teutonic Order in the thirteenth and fourteenth centuries,[3] but was acquired by Poland after the order was defeated twice during the fifteenth century. When the Hohenzollern dynasty of Brandenburg inherited Prussia, it initially recognized the overlordship of Poland. But due to warfare between Poland and Sweden, the House of Hohenzollern was able to gain complete sovereignty over the duchy and ultimately renamed it the Kingdom of Prussia. Before long, all of the Hohenzollern possessions throughout Germany were referred to as Prussia.

Under Hohenzollern rule, Prussia developed an efficient bureaucratic machine that turned landed aristocrats known as Junkers into administrators. Though relatively poor and lacking in natural resources, Prussia was fortunate to have been led by several skilled monarchs, most notably Frederick William

(1640–1688) and Frederick the Great (1744–1786). The Hohenzollerns demanded discipline and sacrifice from their subjects. Through their leadership, Prussia emerged in the eighteenth century as "a new state prototype in Europe, a state with a drillmaster administration based on principles of unquestioning obedience and total regimentation, directed toward the development of unbridled and unlimited military power."[4] It became "not so much a State which possessed an army as an army which possessed a State."[5]

While many Germans living to the west and south of the Prussian capital of Berlin had misgivings about this upstart kingdom, they faced a greater threat in Napoleonic France. As discussed in the previous chapter, Napoleon Bonaparte invaded German territory in 1806 and replaced the region's kaleidoscope of petty principalities with larger units of government (see Table 6.1). Prussia, too, was overwhelmed by the French juggernaut. At the Battle of Jena, it suf-

TABLE 6.1
A Chronology of the Wars of German Unification

Year	Event
1806	Dissolution of the Holy Roman Empire following Napoleon's invasion of central Europe; Prussia defeated at the Battles of Jena and Auerstädt and loses its western territories under the Treaty of Tilsit
1813	Napoleon defeated in the Battle of Leipzig, marking the end of French control over German territory
1814	Convocation of the Congress of Vienna, which established the German Confederation under the presidency of Austria
1834	Creation of the Zollverein, a Prussian-sponsored customs union that excluded Austria
1848	Political uprisings throughout Europe, including liberal revolts in Berlin, Frankfurt, and Vienna
1850	The "humiliation" of Olmütz: the Prussian attempt to establish a political union of German states blocked by Austria and Russia; Prussian constitution revised
1852	London Protocol gives international recognition to the Danish position on the provinces of Schleswig and Holstein
1861	William I crowned King of Prussia
1862	Otto von Bismarck appointed minister-president of Prussia
1863	Alvensleben Convention between Russia and Prussia regarding the Polish question
1864	War waged by Austria and Prussia against Denmark
1865	Gastein Convention provides for Austrian administration over Holstein and Prussian administration of Schleswig
1866	The Seven Weeks' War of Austria against Prussia
1867	Establishment of the North German Confederation
1870–1871	Franco-Prussian War; creation of the Second Reich

fered a catastrophic defeat, resulting in the loss of roughly half of its territory. Over the next decade, a group of Prussian reformers headed by Baron Karl Freiherr vom Stein and General Gerhard von Scharnhorst began planning a war of revenge. From their perspective, future military success depended on mobilizing the entire population as a citizens' army in service of the state. This emphasis on strong, centralized bureaucratic government took precedence over all other concerns.[6] It led to the creation of a general staff within the military, various social and educational changes, and a ministerial system designed to advise the king on issues of foreign and public policy, the very system that Bismarck would someday head as minister-president.

The German Confederation

After Napoleon's defeat in 1815, the units of government he had established were consolidated into a loose-knit confederation of thirty-eight states known as the German Confederation, or *Deutscher Bund*.[7] The diet of the confederation was located in Frankfurt and functioned like a standing conference, with permanent emissaries representing their respective states. Since the confederation required unanimous approval of any significant policy initiative, it was not an active organization. Nevertheless, it provided a stage where the drama of German national unification would soon be performed.

The liberal ideas of liberty, fraternity, and equality that crossed the Rhine River with Napoleon's armies took root in the fertile soil of German **nationalism.** So long as Germany was splintered into more than three dozen small states, Germans would be at the mercy of their larger neighbors.[8] "We Germans have never lacked natural strength," noted the eminent historian Ludwig Dehio:

> But if German power at times towered up like a cloud bank, it also dissolved again in rolling mists. Unformed in formless territory, our power was without core or sequence, always developing, never developed. Its forces boiled over across our frontiers, and at the same time turned against one another within them.[9]

According to German liberal nationalists, the remedy was to unite under a constitutional monarchy that would provide security against external attack and protect civil rights against the capricious acts of petty princes. As advocates of citizen participation in policy making, the liberal nationalists were distrusted by the conservative aristocrats leading Prussia. When the liberals met in Frankfurt in 1848 and petitioned King Frederick William IV of Prussia to become the head of a new unified German state governed by a parliamentary monarchy, he refused because he saw it as an offer "molded out of the dirt and dregs of revolution, disloyalty, and treason."[10] Still, efforts to forge German national spirit

MAP 6.1 The Medieval German Empire. Following the death of Frederick II in 1250, the Holy Roman Empire was a mosaic composed of hundreds of small, quasi-autonomous principalities. German territory remained fragmented politically until the nineteenth century.

continued. Glee clubs, debating societies, and various professional associations were organized across regional lines, all for the purpose of building solidarity among people whose political loyalties had long been to their local princes.

Prussia and Austria were the two major powers within the German Confederation. Rivalry between them had festered since Frederick the Great wrested the resource-rich province of Silesia from the Austrians in a series of wars (1740–1742, 1744–1745, 1756–1763). Perhaps nowhere could the intensity of this rivalry be shown more starkly than in a letter Bismarck wrote in 1856:

Germany is clearly too small for us both [Austria and Prussia] . . . Austria will remain the only state to whom we can permanently lose or from whom we can permanently gain.

For a thousand years intermittently . . . the German dualism has regularly adjusted the reciprocal relations [of Austria and Prussia] by a thorough internal war; and in this century also no other means than this can set the clock of evolution at the right hour.

I wish only to express my conviction that, in the not too distant future, we shall have to fight for our existence against Austria and that it is not within our power to avoid that, since the course of events in Germany has no other solution.[11]

Bismarck's prediction highlighted the tension between two schools of thought about German unification. Whereas advocates of "Great Germany" *(Grossdeutschland)* hoped to forge strong ties between Austria and the other German states, those calling for "Little Germany" *(Kleindeutschland)* argued that Austria should be excluded from the unification process. Well before this debate was settled on the battlefield, Prussia took the initiative by establishing a **customs union** *(Zollverein)* with Hesse, Bavaria, Saxony, Thuringia, and Württemberg. By reducing tariffs on trade among member states and raising them on imports from nonmembers, the customs union fostered economic interdependence within Little Germany while undermining Austria's position in central Europe.

TWO IRONS IN THE FIRE

By 1862, when Bismarck became Prussian minister-president, the economic influence of Prussia had become so great that many of the smaller German states began to see Austria's Hapsburg dynasty as a counterweight to the growing power of the house of Hohenzollern. To capitalize on these fears of Prussia, the Austrians proposed a series of changes in the German Confederation that would have weakened Prussian influence within the organization. Their plan was thwarted, however, when Bismarck persuaded King William to boycott the 1863 Frankfurt Congress of Princes, where the Austrian reforms were to have been proposed.

Unlike the Austrians, who as early as 1850 had proposed a union of the northern German states, Bismarck had no preconceived plan to unify Germany. For him, unification remained less important than advancing Prussian power in the face of Austrian opposition. The minister-president of Prussia might not have been a liberal nationalist, but he recognized the wave of nationalism sweeping across German lands as a potent source of political **power** that could be mobilized to achieve his policy goals.

Bismarck came from the Junker class of old Brandenburg. A master of bluffing, intrigue, and alliances of convenience, at various times he had held important diplomatic posts, representing Prussia at the court of Czar Alexander II of Russia, Emperor Napoleon III of France, and in the diet of the German Confederation in Frankfurt. A loyal servant of his king, Bismarck believed in duty and order. To his critics, however, he appeared obstinate, arrogant, and an unscrupulous reactionary. Indeed, during his tenure, Bismarck undertook many actions that inspired this reputation. For example, when faced with the political deadlock between the king and parliament over funds for the proposed military reform, he simply initiated the reforms and collected the needed taxes without parliament's approval. "World history with its great events does not pass by like a railway train at a constant speed," he once said. "No, it goes forward by fits and starts, but then with irresistible force."[12] The dilemma for the statesman was to know when to act at the right moment.

In addition to his assertive and often abrasive style, Bismarck had an uncanny ability to isolate his opponents and defeat them one at a time. No better illustration of this ability can be found than in the prelude to the 1864 war with Denmark, ostensibly fought over the duchies of Schleswig and Holstein. The status of the duchies was extraordinarily complicated. Lord Palmerston, the British prime minister, once claimed only three people understood its intricacies: one had died, another had gone crazy, and he himself, the third, had forgotten it all.[13] Though neither duchy was part of Denmark proper, both were possessions of the Danish crown and had been politically united for centuries. Schleswig, the province immediately south of Denmark, was inhabited by both Danes and Germans; Holstein, adjoining Schleswig, was predominantly German and held membership in the German Confederation. Neither duchy had much economic importance, though both had geostrategic significance.

On November 13, 1863, a new constitution was promulgated for Denmark that included provisions that would lead toward the eventual incorporation of Schleswig into that country. Just over a decade earlier, hostilities had arisen over this very issue. In 1848 the duchies erupted in revolt when the Danes tried to make Schleswig a part of Denmark. Whereas Danish nationalists maintained that the Eider River dividing Schleswig from Holstein was Denmark's natural frontier, German nationalists responded by identifying the more northern Königsau (or Kongeaa) River separating Schleswig from Sonderjylland as the appropriate boundary. Ultimately thirty thousand troops from Prussia and other members of the German Confederation poured into the duchies to support the German nationalists. Denmark appealed to the **great powers**, and pressure from England and Sweden soon prompted a Prussian withdrawal. The Convention of Malmö appeared to settle the matter, but this peace treaty proved to be a brief truce as hostilities flared up again during the following spring. After the British and Russians exerted further pressure, the 1850 Treaty of Berlin restored Denmark's control and the London Protocol of 1852 gave international recognition to the Danish position.

When King Frederick VII died on November 15, 1863, two days after the Danish parliament had approved the new constitution, his successor, Christian IX, signed the document. Austria and Prussia then protested that this action violated the 1852 agreement and thereupon issued an **ultimatum** for Denmark to rescind those terms of the November constitution that affected Schleswig and Holstein. The Danes refused, and on February 1, 1864, Austro-Prussian forces swarmed into Denmark.

"Great crises," Bismarck once observed, "represent the weather which is conducive to Prussia's growth, when we use them without fear and perhaps very ruthlessly."[14] Although Danish troops mounted a stout defense at Dybbøl and their fleet was victorious at Heligoland, Denmark was vastly outnumbered by the combined Austro-Prussian forces. After a brief truce did not yield a peace settlement, the fighting resumed. On June 29 Prussia captured the island of Als, and over the next few weeks advance units reached as far as Frederikshavn. By July 20, King Christian had acknowledged his cause was hopeless and agreed to a new truce. Five days later a peace conference began in Vienna. A preliminary agreement was reached on August 1, and a final peace treaty was signed on October 30. Under the Treaty of Vienna, Denmark renounced all rights to Schleswig and Holstein.

Once Denmark relinquished its control over the two duchies, the question arose over their future disposition. On August 14, 1865, Austria and Prussia concluded the Gastein Convention by which Austria would administer Holstein while Prussia took Schleswig. This formula portended problems between the victors since Holstein was a virtual enclave within Prussian territory. Soon tensions mounted over rights of passage and Prussian encroachments in Holstein. While feigning a willingness to negotiate, Bismarck felt content to let the dispute escalate to armed conflict. More had been at stake in the war with Denmark than the future of the duchies. The design of the Treaty of Vienna and the Gastein Convention gave Prussia an opportunity to create a diplomatic incident over the occupation of Schleswig and Holstein, discredit the Austrians, and settle old scores on the battlefield without appearing to be the aggressor. As Bismarck later put it, "One must always have two irons in the fire."[15]

> "Pointed bullets are better than pointed speeches."
>
> —OTTO VON BISMARCK

THE SEVEN WEEKS' WAR

Since Bismarck doubted that Vienna's influence among the German states could be curtailed without unsheathing the sword,[16] he sought to isolate the Austrians so military action could be taken without worrying whether another nation might come to their aid. In October 1865, Bismarck met Napoleon III in Biarritz and offered him vague promises of territorial "compensation" in western Germany if France remained neutral during a war between Austria and Prussia. Bismarck also gained the support of Italy by concluding a secret agreement that would permit the Italians to annex the Austrian-ruled region of Venetia if Prussia was victorious. Russia was expected to remain on the sidelines owing to earlier Prussian support for the Czar's repression of a Polish uprising in 1863. Finally, England probably would not interfere due to trade concessions granted by Prussia.

Meanwhile, Austria reacted to growing Prussian influence in Holstein by unilaterally appealing to the diet of the German Confederation, where it hoped to gain support from the other German states. Declaring that this violated the Gastein Convention, which called for the two powers to decide all issues pertaining to Schleswig and Holstein by common consent, Bismarck accused the Austrians of aggression and sent troops into Holstein on June 7, 1866. The Hapsburgs responded by calling upon the diet to assemble a confederal army and punish the Prussians.

Prussia, a state of 18 million people, now faced an empire almost twice as large. Under the leadership of Helmuth von Moltke, chief of the general staff, Prussia won a crushing victory on July 3 at Königgrätz (also known as Sadowa), with the Austrians suffering 42,812 casualties among their officers and troops to just 9,153 for the Prussians.[17] The Prussian breech-loading needle gun gave Moltke's troops superior firepower over the Austrians, which relied upon antiquated muzzle-loading rifles and outmoded shock tactics. Breechloading rifles revolutionized infantry tactics by allowing soldiers to reload on the move or in a prone position rather than only while standing.[18]

An Italian attack on Austria's southern border aided Prussia's war effort. Nevertheless, the Austrians defeated the Italian army at Custozza on June 24 and might have been able to move additional forces north if they had more time. If the Hapsburgs had rebounded from their losses at Königgrätz and continued fighting, France or Russia might have intervened on their behalf. Bismarck moved swiftly to foreclose either possibility. He persuaded King William to relinquish any possibility of further battlefield triumphs and offer Austria lenient peace terms, even though the king and many of his generals had hoped to march in triumph through the streets of Vienna. In his memoirs, Bismarck wrote:

> We had to avoid wounding Austria too severely; we had to avoid leaving behind in her any unnecessary bitterness of feeling or desire for revenge; we ought rather to reserve the possibility of becoming friends again with our adversary of the moment, and in any case to regard the Austrian state as a piece on the European chessboard and the renewal of friendly relations with her as a move open to us. If Austria were severely injured, she would become the ally of France and every other opponent of ours; she would even sacrifice her anti-Russian interests for the sake of revenge on Prussia.[19]

An armistice was reached on July 22 and a preliminary peace agreement was signed at Nikolsburg four days later. Under the terms of the final peace treaty, signed in Prague on August 23, Austria agreed to pay an indemnity of 40 million Prussian talers, but its territorial integrity was respected.

Defeat for the Hapsburgs not only ended their long-standing role in Germany but served as a catalyst for reshaping their multinational **empire**. Under the *Ausgleich* (compromise) of 1867, Hungary became a semi-independent kingdom with its own capital and parliament, though Francis Joseph served as emperor of Austria and king of Hungary. This system of dual monarchy left some problems untouched, however. In particular, many Slavs were indignant because they did not attain the same political status as the Hungarians.

Additional treaties were signed in Berlin during August and September with the southern German states who had supported the Austrians. Prussia solidified its boundaries by annexing those states which lay between its Rhenish and Elbian territories. Hanover, Hesse-Cassel, Nassau, and Frankfurt were all absorbed, and an indemnity was imposed on the remaining defeated states.

The Italians received Venetia despite their defeat at Custozza and a naval defeat at Lissa. Counting on a protracted war, Napoleon III of France was unable to respond to the rapid movement of events. The German Confederation was dissolved and Austria was excluded from Germany. All states north of the Main River joined a North German Confederation under Prussian leadership while the south German states remained independent. When Napoleon III insisted upon compensation for staying **neutral,** and his ambassador indiscreetly put his demands in writing, Bismarck touted this request as proof of Napoleon's aggressive intent. More fearful of France than of Prussia, the southern German states of Bavaria, Baden, and Würtemberg responded by forming military alliances with Prussia.

THE FRANCO-PRUSSIAN WAR

The creation of the North German Confederation in 1867 increased Prussian military strength. Together with the political unification of Italy (1859–1861), this league presented new risks for France since previously there had been only divided minor powers on its borders. To make matters worse, French intervention in Mexico proved disastrous. French troops, which were part of a larger European force sent to Vera Cruz in 1861 to collect debts owed to European bondholders, failed in an ill-conceived attempt to make Mexico a French satellite. Napoleon III was called the "Sphinx of the Tuileries" because many people believed he had been working in secret to devise an elaborate scheme aimed at restoring French domination in Europe. In truth, his foreign policy was foundering; he needed a resounding diplomatic triumph to quell a rising tide of criticism.

Public apprehension over Germany soared after the Luxembourg crisis of 1867. The Grand Duchy of Luxembourg had been given to the Netherlands after the Napoleonic Wars as part of the Vienna peace settlement discussed in Chapter 5. Though not part of Bismarck's North German Confederation, the Grand Duchy was garrisoned by Prussian troops. When the French approached King William III of the Netherlands to purchase Luxembourg, the king replied that the sale would be contingent upon Prussian approval. Bismarck rejected the French request, and hostilities between Prussia and France were only avoided when the Grand Duchy was **neutralized.**

Although the Luxembourg crisis had been defused, people in both countries anticipated war. During the summer of 1870, the Spanish government invited a German prince, Leopold of Hohenzollern-Sigmaringen, to assume the vacant Spanish throne. Two years earlier, an insurrection had driven Queen Isabella II into exile. Finding it difficult to obtain a suitable replacement, the Spanish turned to Leopold, a Roman Catholic married to a Portuguese princess. Leopold's candidacy spoke to the dream of someday uniting the Iberian peninsula. Yet when news of the invitation reached Paris, it prompted fears of a Prusso-Spanish alliance because Leopold was a member of the Prussian ruling family.[20] Just as Charles V, the Hapsburg Holy Roman Emperor, had ruled over Austria, Germany, and Spain during the sixteenth century, many feared that Bismarck would encircle France once again.

The French statesman Adolphe Thiers once remarked that "the highest principle of European politics is that Germany shall be composed of independent states connected only by a slender federative thread."[21] In line with this principle, the French ambassador to Berlin, Vincente Benedetti, was instructed to insist that Leopold should decline the crown. The withdrawal of the prince's candidacy failed to placate the French, however. During an interview at the resort of Bad Ems, Benedetti pressed King William I of Prussia for an apology and future guarantees. The king politely declined and sent a report of the conversation to Bismarck. Seeing the chance, as he put it, to wave a "red flag to the Gallic bull,"[22] Bismarck published an account of the interview that gave the false impression of a rude encounter, which led to further antagonism between Paris and Berlin.

With national honor and pride now at stake, the French declared war on Prussia. The Franco-Prussian War lasted six months and ended with a shattering defeat for the French. Once again, Bismarck was able to isolate an adversary.[23] Rather than side with Paris, the Italians used the opportunity created by the withdrawal of French troops from Rome to occupy the Eternal City. The Russians maintained neutrality and used the distraction created by the war to refortify their Black Sea bases. The British declined to act as well. Annoyed with Napoleon III's policies, they were satisfied with promises from Prussia that Belgian neutrality would be respected. Finally, Bismarck published the 1866 French demands for territorial compensation in the Rhineland to rally the southern German states to the Prussian cause.

Devoid of allies, the French marched on to inevitable defeat. By September 2, 1870, Napoleon III himself was captured at Sedan with 39 of his generals, 2,700 officers, and over 80,000 troops. A second French army of 173,000 under Marshal Bazaine surrendered at Metz on October 27. Although the minister of war had claimed his country was ready down to the last detail, the French were woefully unprepared. Mobilization was chaotic, commanders disagreed on strategic questions, and the Prussians made innovative use of technology. Although the French possessed the *mitrailleuse,* a thirty-seven barrel machine gun, and their *chassepot* rifle was superior to the Prussian needle gun, the Prussians were better trained, had more artillery, and were able to use the railroad to give their troops speed and mobility.

Prussia's victory has been described as "a triumph of planning."[24] For years, Prussian officers disguised as tourists painting the French landscape had studied the sites of probable battles.[25] Rather than fight a protracted war of position, the Prussians devised a war of movement aimed at encircling a stunned opponent. So important were the Prussian railroads for military operations that as early as 1860 half of them were owned by the state. During the 1866 war with Austria, the benefits of rail transportation became obvious: "The Prussian Guard Corps was deployed within a week, in twelve trains a day from Berlin to the front."[26] Railroads thus presented commanders with new strategic opportunities. According to General von Moltke, the "difficulties of mobility grow with the size of military units" and "the closer one gets" to the battlefield, "the essence of strategy consists in the organization of separate marches, but so as to provide for concentration at the right moment."[27] By relying on the railroad, Prussian forces from multiple locations could mobilize rapidly, move to the front from opposite directions, and converge upon a slower-moving opponent with numerical superiority at the point of attack. Within the first two weeks of fighting, the Prussians mobilized 1,180,000 troops, compared to only 330,000 for the French.[28]

The news from Sedan toppled the French government. Napoleon III was dethroned and republican leaders, headed by Léon Gambetta, proclaimed a Government of National Defense. The republican government desperately tried to raise new armies to reverse their fortunes on the battlefield. The French simply could not believe they had been beaten. Refusing to credit the Prussians with any virtues whatsoever, they insisted that their losses were due to trickery and to Prussia's substitution of technology for courage.[29] German forces laid siege to Paris on September 19, forcing the city to surrender four months later. As a result, a newly elected French National Assembly met in Bordeaux and voted for peace. On January 22 the French asked for an armistice. It was implemented six days later and peace negotiations began. On February 26 a preliminary agreement was reached, and on March 3 the final treaty was signed.

Parisians were more resistant to making peace than were most other French citizens. Radical leaders in Paris denounced the Bordeaux Assembly and, in a gesture of defiance, the Parisian National Guard refused to surrender its weapons. An independent government, called the Commune of Paris, was declared. With many of the streets of Paris barricaded by insurgents and the city inflamed by insurrection, the Assembly decided to subdue the rebellion. In June, after weeks of bloody fighting, rebel resistance was broken. Estimates place the number of people killed at over twenty thousand.

The emotions unleashed in Germany by victory over France were over-whelming. Rather than crafting the kind of lenient peace that had been im-plemented following the Seven Weeks' War with Austria, the triumphant Prussians took a series of humiliating actions against their prostrate oppo-nents, including holding a victory parade that entered Paris by way of the Pont de Neuilly, proceeded to the Arc de Triomphe, and continued down the Champs Élysées. As one historian has concluded, "the peace that France had to sign blocked the restoration of friendly relations between France and Germany for the foreseeable future."[30] Convinced that "lasting hostility between Paris and Berlin" remained inescapable, Bismarck acceded to demands to weaken France.[31] "An enemy, whose honest friendship can never be won," he agreed, "must at least be rendered somewhat less harmful."[32]

Under the terms of the Treaty of Frankfurt, France ceded Alsace and part of Lorraine to Germany. From a military point of view, control of the Vosges mountains and the fortress of Metz were critical for German defenses. But whereas Alsace had been under German control prior to the 1648 Treaty of Westphalia and contained a substantial German-speaking population, the people of Lorraine spoke French. The loss of Alsace and Lorraine embittered the French for years to come. France, as one government official put it, "could forget Sedan, she could forget a military disaster; she could not forget the wrong done to the liberty of her nationals."[33]

In addition to accepting the annexation of two provinces, France pledged to pay Germany an indemnity of five billion francs. The first billion was to be paid in 1871 and the remainder over the next three years. Most German occu-pation forces would be withdrawn after the initial two billion francs were paid, with the remainder withdrawn once the total indemnity was discharged.

Deputies in the French National Assembly called the terms of the peace treaty a "sentence of death."[34] The terms were harsh, but not nearly as harsh as those the French had imposed on the Prussians in 1807.

> There was no attempt to interfere with the internal affairs of the country. No limit was imposed on the size of the armed forces which France might keep up; no cession or destruction of naval vessels was demanded; and in spite of agitation among the mercantile interests of Hamburg and Bremen, Bismarck left French overseas possessions intact. Whatever her losses and her humiliation, France remained a Great Power: too great, indeed, for German peace of mind during the coming forty years.[35]

Bismarck's adroit diplomacy and Moltke's peerless armies brought the frag-mented German lands together and shaped them into a centralized state (see Map 6.2). On January 18, 1871, leading German princes acclaimed William I of Prussia German kaiser or emperor in the Hall of Mirrors in the Palace of Versailles. In structure, the new empire became an extension of the North German Confederation, with the southern German states of Bavaria, Würt-temberg, Baden, and Hesse-Darmstadt added. With approximately forty-one million inhabitants, the Second Reich, as the new German empire was called, possessed a dynamic, growing economy and the most powerful army in Europe. Yet something was amiss. Writing in his diary, Crown Prince Frederick William III lamented, "We are no longer looked upon as the innocent victims of wrongs, but rather as arrogant victors, no longer content with the conquest of the foe, but determined to bring about his utter ruin."[36]

Bismarck was quickly appointed the imperial chancellor for the Second Reich. Having accomplished his foreign policy goals, Bismarck turned his attention to internal politics, where he tried under the so-called *Kulturkampf* to reduce the influence of Catholic orders and

> "What our sword has won in half a year, our sword must guard for half a century."
>
> —HELMUTH VON MOLTKE

clergy, especially in education. As socialism gained ground, it too was repressed. Within less than a decade, the new German Reich was an industrialized, authoritarian state in which powerful conservative groups could steer policy behind a facade of representative government.

WORSE THAN A CRIME

Bismarck's genius resided in his ability to entertain multiple courses of action, explore all of their permutations, and move on several fronts simultaneously. No single move was an end in itself; each positioned him to advance in another direction. "One cannot play chess," he insisted, "if from the outset sixteen of the sixty-four squares are out of bounds."[37] A tenacious advocate of Prussian interests, he could see the opportunities presented by different configurations on the diplomatic chessboard. To exploit them, he was willing to be disingenuous and, at times, even ruthless. "If it hadn't been for me, there wouldn't have been three great wars, 80,000 men would not have died, and parents, brothers, sisters, and widows would not be in mourning," he once admitted. "But that I have to settle with God."[38]

Before the Wars of German Unification, Prussia was the smallest of Europe's great powers; afterward, it held a semi-hegemony over the continent. With an excellent educational system, skilled labor, and unparalleled electrical, chemical, and steel industries, the new united Germany was an economic powerhouse. To be sure, it had liabilities. Located in the center of Europe, Germany lacked abundant resources and the natural protection of formidable mountains or vast oceans. In other words, it was "too weak to go it alone, too strong to be left alone; with enough muscle to best any single comer, but too exposed to defy them all at once."[39] To make matters worse, the manner in which the Second Reich was created produced both enemies bent on revenge and bystanders wary of its military might. On the one hand, France still felt humiliated and sought to avenge the loss of Alsace and Lorraine. On the other hand, Russia

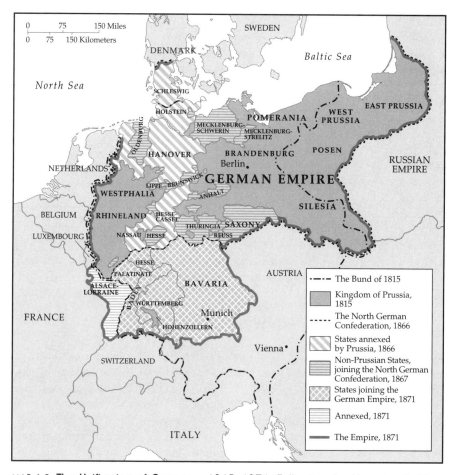

MAP 6.2 The Unification of Germany, 1815–1871. Following the Napoleonic Wars, the German Confederation (or Bund) replaced the old Holy Roman Empire. After Prussia's victory over Austria in 1866, the states north of the river Main joined Prussia in the North German Confederation. Once France was defeated in 1871, all non-Hapsburg southern German states merged with the North German Confederation to create the Prussian-led Second Empire.

became suspicious of Berlin's territorial aims and worried about possible expansion to the east. While Bismarck went on to build an intricate network of secret alliances to keep France and Russia from making common cause against Germany, his successors lacked the vision and skills to prevent a protracted two-front war that would divide German forces.

A resentful France would now bide its time for an opportunity to reverse its fortunes on the battlefield. In the words of a popular slogan of the day, "Never speak of it, always think of it." In a symbolic gesture, the statue of Strassburg on the Place de la Concorde was draped in black. Expressing the emotions of a wounded nation, the novelist Victor Hugo told the National Assembly "the day would come when France would rise again invincible and take back not only Alsace and Lorraine but the Rhineland."[40] The Reverend W. Gibson, an English Methodist working in France at the time, anticipated what would come from the demand for vengeance he witnessed among Parisians. "Germany," he wrote, "when within the next few years she again encounters France in arms, will find a very different foe from the France of 1870; and who knows but that before the end of this century there may be a similar triumph in Paris to that which is now being celebrated in Berlin?"[41]

The Gospel of Offensive Power

Flush with victory, most Germans saw a different future. "We Germans today are in a happy position," wrote Field Marshal von der Goltz. "The star of the young Empire has only just risen on the horizon; its full course lies still before it."[42] The writer Friedrich Naumann agreed. The German nation, he proclaimed, "feels the spring-time juices in its organs."[43] This heady atmosphere even intoxicated German liberals. Heinrich von Treitschke, once a prominent liberal spokesman turned to realism and reveled in the glory brought by Prussian militarism. Writing about the provinces of Alsace and Lorraine, he boasted:

> These provinces are ours by the right of the sword, and we shall dispose of them by a higher right—the right of the German nation. . . . With joyful wonder, we have watched the immortal progress of these moral forces of history.[44]

The Wars of German Unification and the peace settlements they produced transformed the political landscape of Europe. Bismarck subsequently installed a huge statue of Germania on a hill above the vineyards of Assmannshausen and Rüdesheim in the Rheingau to commemorate this transformation. Few people scanning the horizon on the day the monument was dedicated could see the storm clouds building in the distance. Bismarck's wars had fostered the belief that modern technology gave an advantage to the attacking side by increasing the speed and maneuverability of combat units. Offense, in other words, was thought to be the best defense. Lured by the presumed superiority of offensive doctrines and fearing that an adversary might move first and capture the battlefield initiative, commanders across the continent formulated meticulous plans that required rapid mobilization at the instant a conflict began. The relentless pressure of these rigid, intricate military timetables produced an atmosphere of urgency whose deleterious effect on foreign-policy decisionmakers was magnified by the assumption that future wars would be won by whoever possessed an army massive enough to make a decisive thrust in the shortest possible time. By the end of the century, German spending on arms had risen some 80 percent and its war establishment had grown to 3.4 million personnel. Similar trends unfolded elsewhere. Russian spending climbed at a rate approximating the German increase, to support roughly 4 million men under arms. French military expenditures expanded by 45 percent, and troop strength was doubled to 3.5 million.[45] As Winston Churchill summarized the situation, "when mighty populations are impelled on each other . . . when the resources of science and civilization sweep away everything that might mitigate their fury, a European war can only end in the ruin of the vanquished and scarcely less fatal dislocation and exhaustion of the conquerors."[46]

The Departure of the Iron Chancellor

The way peace was made after the wars of 1866 and 1870 had serious consequences for Europe's future. By forging a lenient settlement at the end of the Seven Weeks' War, Prussia was able to cultivate a working relationship with an Austro-Hungarian Empire worried about future conflict with Russia. In fact, "so perspicaciously were Austrian interests respected that Austria remained neutral during the Franco-Prussian war four years later and within another decade was prepared to conclude the Dual Alliance and become Germany's staunchest ally."[47] Alternatively, the harsh settlement imposed upon the French crippled relations between Paris and Berlin. **Irredentism** became the cornerstone of French foreign policy toward Germany. Periodic German attempts to justify incorporating Alsace and Lorraine into the Second Reich merely reopened "the wound that the annexation had left in the French national soul."[48] Although the 1871 Treaty of Frankfurt was punitive, it did not weaken France enough to eliminate it from the ranks of the great powers and thus from the heart of German defense plans. French willingness to stand alone in a war for the lost provinces would ebb with the passage of time, but Germany could still count on France throwing its weight on the side of any great power who might someday confront German troops on the battlefield.

No political order is self-maintaining. At the end of the Wars of German Unification, Bismarck assured his contemporaries that Germany was a satisfied power, willing to play the role of an "honest broker" in mediating threats to the international status quo. By following this pragmatic policy of moderation and restraint for the next twenty years, Bismarck became "one of the rare leaders of mighty states who chose to limit his ambitions."[49] With France isolated due to Germany's secret arrangements with Austria and Russia, Bismarck believed the danger of war was remote.

But the structure of the Bismarckian order did not long outlive its architect. Following the death of William I in 1888, and the death of his son Frederick III shortly thereafter, Frederick's son William II became the new German emperor. Impulsive, insecure, and insistent on being his own chancellor, the young kaiser dismissed Bismarck and unveiled a "new course" of *Weltpolitik* (world policy), under which power projection capabilities were expanded and colonies sought. Germany now saw itself as more than a continental power. Demanding

CONTROVERSIES TO CONTEMPLATE

- The foreign policies pursued by Otto von Bismarck fall within the realist approach to international relations. Austrian chancellor Prince Clemens von Metternich, one of the architects of the peace settlement forged during Congress of Vienna, also was guided by political realism. Were there any significant differences between Bismarck and Metternich in their strategies for dealing with defeated adversaries? Does realism offer national leaders clear guidelines on how victors should design a peace settlement?

- Long before he was appointed minister-president of Prussia, Bismarck had argued that war between Prussia and Austria was inevitable. Despite his belief that Austria should be excluded from the process of German unification, he offered a lenient peace settlement to the Austrians after they were defeated in the Seven Weeks' War. On the other hand, a harsh settlement was imposed upon the French after the Franco-Prussian War. What accounts for the differences in Prussian policy at the end of these two wars?

- Realist theory advises political leaders to heed strategic necessities when formulating their foreign policies. They must do whatever they can to advance national interests, regardless of whether their actions contravene the moral values that guide people in everyday lives. Was the goal of German unification justified? Did Bismarck violate any moral standards by employing the means that he used to attain the goal of unification? Under what specific circumstances do which kinds of foreign policy goals justify which means?

- Prussia defeated its adversaries in the Wars of German Unification by engaging in thorough planning and by harnessing modern technology to give their forces speed, mobility, and firepower. How did the manner in which the Prussians won these striking battlefield victories create new problems for maintaining peace in the postwar era?

a redivision of great-power **spheres of influence** around the globe, Germany became a dissatisfied, expansionist state, bent on changing the international status quo. As friction between Germany and other great powers mounted, the linchpin of Bismarck's **grand strategy**—the isolation of France—fell to the wayside. When William II allowed Germany's secret reinsurance treaty with Russia to lapse, the Russians formed a military alliance with the French. Similarly, Great Britain responded to Berlin's heavy-handed behavior by jettisoning the long-standing policy of "splendid isolation" and reconciling its differences with both France and Russia. While not an immediate cause of the First World

War, the harsh peace settlement embodied in the Treaty of Frankfurt set the parameters within which Bismarck had to work. Owing to the outcome of the Franco-Prussian War, all efforts to build a lasting peace were impaired by a feud over lost territory. Moreover, the punitive, humiliating peace of 1871 would provoke French retaliation when the tables were turned after World War I. It is for this reason that one historian has said the annexation of Alsace and Lorraine "was worse than a crime, it was a blunder."[50]

NOTES

1. To underscore this point, he wrote in his memoirs that fixing the objectives in warfare is "a political function" which "cannot be without influence on the method of conducting the war." Bismarck, 1966, p. 106.
2. In Pinson, 1966, p. 128.
3. During the crusades of the twelfth and thirteenth centuries, the popes bestowed privileges upon various religio-military orders. The Knights Templars were dedicated to the protection of pilgrims. The Knights Hospitallers were devoted to the care of the sick.
4. Manuel, 1951, p. 105.
5. Howard, 1991, p. 52.
6. Gillis, 1978, pp. 320–323.
7. The membership of the German Confederation rose to thirty-nine in 1817 with the addition of Hesse-Hamburg.
8. The Thirty Years' War (1618–1648) provides a horrifying example of the devastation that occurred on German land. Once one of the most prosperous regions of Europe, German territory was ravaged by religious warfare that ultimately resulted in troops from France, Denmark, Spain, and Sweden fighting on German soil. The following passage, excerpted from a sermon preached in Nuremberg during 1638, underscores the misery experienced by German burghers and peasants alike:

   Our dear country, that was once so rich, so full of plenty, so abounding with multitudes of people, so glorious for arts, so renowned for pleasantries, for strength, for our many great and beautiful cities, for our large and graceful churches. . . . But these times are gone; oh, how my soul mourns to see her excellence thus departed!

   When the fighting finally ended with the Peace of Westphalia, roughly one-third of Germany's population had perished. In Württemberg alone, 318 castles and 36,100 houses were destroyed, and the number of men capable of bearing arms dropped from 65,400 to 14,800. King Gustavus Adolphus of Sweden, the architect of the Protestants' most significant battlefield victories, explained why the toll was so grim: "We have been obliged to carry on the war *ex rapto,* with great injury and damage to our neighbors," he wrote to his chancellor Axel Oxenstierna. "We have nothing to satisfy the soldiers except what we have taken by pillage and brigandage." In Weir, 1993, p. 68; also Friedrich and Blitzer, 1957, p. 95; *The Tears of Germany,* 1963, p. 238.
9. Dehio, 1962, p. 210.
10. In Detwiler, 1976, p. 113.
11. Bismarck, 1948, p. 220.
12. In Joll, 1984, p. 203.
13. Pinson, 1966, p. 133.
14. In Carr, 1991, p. 70.
15. In Pflanze, 1963, p. 91.
16. In Pinson, 1966, p. 135.

17. Craig, 1964, p. 166.
18. Hammond, 1993, p. 82. Increased firepower made old shock tactics obsolete. "Close order, with advance of the line ending up with the bayonet charge became suicidal. . . . So also did frontal attacks." Finer, 1975, p. 159.
19. He also commented that it would be a political mistake "to endanger everything that has been achieved by trying to get from Austria a few square miles of territory or a few millions more indemnity." Friedjung, 1966, p. 287.
20. Prince Leopold belonged to the Sigmaringen branch of the Hohenzollern family and was actually more closely related to Emperor Napoleon III of France than to King William I of Prussia.
21. In Craig, 1982, p. 21.
22. In Carr, 1991, p. 196.
23. Bismarck had previously hinted that it would be possible to create the image that the Prussians were on the defensive: "Mobilization, national manifestations in Germany and Italy, over relations with Belgium or even with Spain, would give us the opportunity of a diversion which would bring us into the war without giving the appearance of an aggressive . . . war." Steefel, 1962, p. 10.
24. Taylor, 1962b, p. 114. The Prussians were aided by the "inferiority of force and stupidity of mind" of their opponents, adds British military strategist B.H. Liddell Hart. "In preparation for war, any strategist would be rash to base his plans on the supposition that his enemy would be as weak in brain and body as the Austrians of 1866 and the French in 1870." Liddell Hart, 1967, p. 137.
25. Mann, 1968, p. 190.
26. Keegan, 1993, p. 307.
27. In Holborn, 1943, p. 178.
28. Ziegler, 1993, p. 26. Trains had become such an important element in military mobilization that German staff officers once watched the visiting Ringling Brothers circus load its railway cars to learn more efficient ways of moving troops and supplies to the front. Quester, 1977, p. 79.
29. Kranzberg, 1950, p. 15.
30. Holborn, 1969, p. 221.
31. Raff, 1988, p. 142.
32. In Pflanze, 1963, p. 479.
33. Raymond Poincaré as cited in Welch, 1993, p. 102.
34. Giesberg, 1966, p. 119.
35. Howard, 1962, p. 449.
36. In Crankshaw, 1981, p. 299.
37. In Carr, 1991, p. 59.
38. In Craig and George, 1995, p. 279.
39. Joffe, 1995, p. 101.
40. In Pinson, 1966, p. 148.
41. In Horne, 1965, p. 427.
42. Von der Glotz, 1992, p. 252.
43. In Kennedy, 1987, p. 211.
44. Treitschke, 1948, p. 226.
45. Bartlett, 1984, pp. 6–7.
46. In Ibid, p. 88.
47. Ibid., p. 127.
48. Welch, 1993, p. 102.
49. Kagan, 1995, p. 101.
50. Fay, 1966, p. 51.

· 7 ·

A WAR TO END ALL WARS?
WORLD WAR I AND THE TREATY OF VERSAILLES

It must be a peace without victory. . . .
Only a peace between equals can last.
WOODROW WILSON

PREVIEW

The assassination of Archduke Franz Ferdinand in 1914 touched off a series of actions that ultimately embroiled the world's most powerful nations in a gruesome war of attrition. There are numerous explanations for why this happened. Many scholars emphasize how certain underlying conditions made the world ripe for a violent flare-up. Virulent nationalism, intense military and economic competition among the great powers, a polarized system of alliances, and offensive strategic doctrines built around rigid mobilization schedules created a volatile international environment that would have eventually ignited a war regardless of whether the archduke was assassinated. Other scholars stress more immediate causes, pointing to the inability of political leaders in Berlin, London, Paris, and Saint Petersburg to douse the flames of war before they spread beyond Austria-Hungary and Serbia. According to this view, misperceptions about the capabilities and intentions of rival states prevented these leaders from extinguishing the crisis sparked by the assassination.

In retrospect, various factors contributed to the outbreak of the First World War. Remembering the short, decisive wars fought by Bismarck to achieve German unification, few people believed it would last very long. But by the time what came to be called the "Great War" ended four years later, Europe was devastated. France, which had sought revenge for its humiliating loss to Germany in 1871, was particularly hard hit since most of the major battles on the western front occurred on its soil. Not only were the French staggered by a frightening number of casualties, but national reconstruction was hampered by the need to service the enormous foreign debt incurred to finance the war effort. Recalling the harsh peace treaty imposed upon them by the Germans, the French under Premier Georges Clemenceau pushed for a peace settlement that would weaken Germany so it no longer posed a military threat.

The French demand for ironclad security guarantees to keep Germany at bay collided with the *liberal idealism* of Woodrow Wilson. The American president's exhortations for a new international order were initially received with enthusiasm by the traumatized, war-weary population of Europe. People hoped their suffering had not been in vain. Democracy, open diplomacy, national self-determination, and a League of Nations would allegedly usher in an era of perpetual peace.

France's enthusiasm for dismembering Germany also clashed with the interests of Great Britain, its other major wartime partner. With the German navy no longer menacing the sea lanes that sustained the British empire, policymakers in London declined the French request for a formal military alliance aimed at Germany and returned to their traditional policy of promoting a *balance of power* on the continent. Germany, they calculated, would once again become an important market for British manufactured goods as well as a potential counterweight against any land-power that might seek to dominate Europe.

Thus, despite the euphoria surrounding the opening of the Paris Peace Conference in January 1919, there were serious differences among the victors about how to deal with Germany. As you read this case, think about how the following issues drove a wedge between the French and their Anglo-American allies:

- territorial boundaries
- reparations payments
- disarmament
- collective security

In addition to examining the cleavages that divided the victors, consider the reaction of the vanquished to the Treaty of Versailles. Since Germany had routed the Russian army in the east and relinquished its position in the west without having lost territory to the Allies, how would the German population respond to a harsh peace settlement? How could demagogues within Germany use this response to their political advantage? What were the consequences of creating a group of weak, unstable states on Germany's eastern border? Marshal Ferdinand Foch of France once said the Treaty of Versailles was not a peace settlement; it was merely an armistice for twenty years. Was he correct?

■ ■

The day's activities began at a small Orthodox chapel on the edge of the Scheveningen Woods. Attired in ceremonial uniforms and accompanied by a magnificent escort, the Russians attended mass before proceeding to the opening ceremony at a splendid chateau on the outskirts of the Hague. They were joined that afternoon by representatives from more than two dozen other countries. With colorful flags rustling against an azure spring sky, the delegates to the International Peace Conference of 1899 began grappling with such issues as **disarmament**, arbitration, and the law of war. According to one delegate, it was "a place in which to forget old passions and prejudices and the grosser forms of selfishness; a place for good consideration, courtesy, patience, and the philosophic mind."[1] When the conference concluded at the end of July, those in attendance believed they had taken an important step toward regulating interstate violence.

Optimism ran high at the beginning of the twentieth century. The marriage of science and industry spawned one technological innovation after another, international commerce generated extraordinary amounts of wealth in trading countries, and, at the Hague peace conference of 1899, the world community developed new rules to control the use of force. Europe had avoided a military showdown between major powers since the end of the Wars of German Unification. Now almost everyone thought it would continue to enjoy peace throughout the new century.

Global optimism was nourished by faith in progress. Andrew Carnegie, a wealthy industrialist and philanthropist who had emigrated in his youth from Scotland to the United States, gave much of his fortune to educational programs aimed at abolishing war, which he saw as "the foulest blot upon our civilization."[2] Maintaining that the ancient dream of perpetual peace was now within reach, he provided funds to build a "Peace Palace" in the Hague that would house a court for the pacific settlement of international disputes. The British writer Norman Angell also saw a bright future: in *The Great Illusion,* he asserted that economic development made preventing war mandatory, because its costs were prohibitive.[3] To Carnegie, Angell, and many others, progress had bestowed peace and prosperity upon the twentieth century.

In just over a decade, however, Europe was engulfed by the flames of war. The conflict ignited in the Bosnian city of Sarajevo on June 28, 1914, when a Serbian nationalist assassinated Archduke Franz Ferdinand, a successor to the throne of Austria-Hungary. Seeking to punish Serbia, the Austrians delivered an **ultimatum** on July 23 that was deliberately worded so Belgrade would reject it. Five days later Austria declared war, setting in motion a series of moves by other states who distrusted one another's intentions. Before the assassination at Sarajevo two hostile alliances had already existed, pitting Germany, Austria-Hungary, and the Ottoman Empire against France, Great Britain, and Russia. When Russia mobilized against Austria to support fellow Slavs in Serbia, Germany attacked France, and Britain entered the fray to counter the Germans. Like a chain reaction, the dispute between Austria and Serbia rapidly expanded across the continent to involve every major power.

By the time World War I ended, nearly twenty million people were dead, empires had crumbled, and new states were born. It was hardly the buoyant future that had been predicted for the twentieth century. What caused this unanticipated spasm of carnage? Could a durable peace be built on its ashes? Would this titanic struggle serve as a war to end all wars?

THE EUROPEAN TINDERBOX

How can such a catastrophic war be explained? Although the answers appear numerous, many converge around psychological explanations regarding the motives and emotions of the major players in this tragedy. Some historians maintain that World War I was an **inadvertent war,** inspired by passions, hatreds, and misperceptions, and not the result of anyone's master plan. It was a war bred primarily by the participants' fearful confusion and their inability to overlook insults—a war that none wanted or expected, but one which resulted from their failure to recognize how others would react to their own retaliatory actions. A review of the steps taken prior to the war suggests just how uncoordinated are the processes through which nations often stumble in their efforts to make and keep peace (see Table 7.1).

Many historians believe that the great powers' prior rearmament efforts also played a major role in the onset of World War I. It might seem obvious, on the surface, that one state's acquisition of arms would make others feel frightened and less secure, but few of the actors engaged in the European **arms race** appeared to take that psychological reaction into account. The Europeans proceeded by assuming that their own armaments would gain them respect rather than arouse suspicions about their expansionist motives. This belief was espoused most by France and Germany, which raced against each other in establishing superior schools for officers, requiring in peacetime compulsory military training for development of military engineering and supply capabilities, and manufacturing improved cannons, rifles, and machine guns. Whenever one made an advance in military preparedness, the other country felt it had to follow—unaware of the possibility that disarmament and **arms-control** agreements to alleviate fears might produce greater security for both.

By 1914, Germany had taken the lead in developing its armed forces, building military

> "Till the world comes to an end, the ultimate decision will rest with the sword."
>
> —KAISER WILHELM II

roads and railroads, and planning future campaigns down to the smallest detail. But other powers besides the Franco-German rivals were also participants in the armaments race. At the turn of the century, Great Britain could still proudly sing "Britannia rules the waves." Command of the seas had long been necessary to feed the people and the industries of the British Isles and to protect the distant parts of the British Empire. To counter Great Britain's maritime pre-eminence, Germany began to build a navy that could challenge the

TABLE 7.1
A Chronology of Peace Treaties and Peace-Disrupting Events, 1899–1939

Date	Settlement/Conference
1899	First Hague Peace Conference
1901	Peace of Peking ends Boxer Rebellion
1902	Triple Alliance between Germany, Austria, and Italy renewed
1903	Britain and France sign "Entente Cordiale"
1905	William II of Germany and Nicolas II of Russia sign Treaty of Bjorko pledging mutual security pact in Europe
	Anglo-Japanese alliance renewed for ten years
1906	Algeciras Conference grants France and Spain control of Morocco
1907	Second Hague Peace Conference
1908	Austria and Russia agree to Austria's occupation of Bosnia and Herzegovina
1910	Japan annexes Korea
1911	Kaiser William II's Hamburg speech proclaims Germany's "Place in the Sun"
1912	Montenegro declares war on Turkey; armistice signed also by Bulgaria and Serbia ends crisis
	Italy and France sign Treaty of Lausanne
	German-Austrian-Italian alliance renewed
1913	Balkan War ends with signing of London Peace Treaty between Turkey and Balkan states; Second Balkan War ends with armistice signed at Bucharest
1914	World War I erupts with assassination of Archduke Franz Ferdinand and his wife, June 28
1917	Czar of Russia abdicates throne, March 16
	United States declares war on Germany in response to submarine attacks in violation of its neutral status
	German-Russian armistice signed at Brest-Litovsk
1918	Woodrow Wilson proposes Fourteen Points for world peace
	Brest-Litovsk Treaty between Russia and Central Powers; Soviet government assumes power in Moscow, cedes large portions of Russian territory
	Rumania signs peace treaty with Central Powers
	Pittsburgh Agreement signed between Czechs and Slovaks
	Germany and Austria agree to Wilson's demand that their soldiers retreat to their own territory before an armistice is signed
	Allies agree to truce suspending fighting with Austria-Hungary, November 3
	Pre-armistice agreement signed between Allies and Germany, November 11, to end the fighting and begin negotiations for peace settlement based on Fourteen Points
	Allies agree at Versailles on peace terms for Germany; Germany consents to establish an electorally based republic
	Polish republic proclaimed
	Austria becomes an elective republic
	Montenegro united with Serbia
	Serbo-Croatian-Slovene kingdom of Yugoslovia proclaimed
	Woodrow Wilson arrives in Paris for Versailles Peace Conference

Date	Settlement/Conference
1919	Peace conference opens at Versailles, convenes between January and June
	President Wilson presides over first League of Nations meeting in Paris
	Hapsburg dynasty exiled from Austria
	Finnish-Soviet War erupts
	Treaty of Versailles signed, June 28
	Treaty of St. Germain forces Austria to surrender 73 percent of its territory, pay reparations, and limit its army to thirty thousand, September 10
	Treaty of Neuilly cedes Bulgarian territories to Yugoslavia and Greece, November 27
1920	After Greece invades Asia Minor in May 1919, the abortive Sévres Peace Treaty of August 10, 1920, wrests control of Thrace and Asia Minor from the Ottoman Empire and internationalizes the Straits to shipping
	U.S. Senate votes against joining the new League of Nations, leaving the fledgling international organization without its most enthusiastic advocate
	Treaty of Trianon forces Hungary to accept huge territorial losses and heavy reparations payments, June 4
1921	Paris conference of Allies sets schedule for German reparation payments
	Treaty of Riga moves the resurrected state of Poland to the east of the Curzon Line established at the Paris Peace Conference following the Polish-Soviet war, March 18
	London Imperial Conference
	Washington Conference produces Four-Power Treaty committing the United States, Great Britain, France, and Japan to consultations in the event of any threat of aggressive action against the rest, November; the Five-Power Treaty establishes disarmament to maintain naval parity; Nine-Power Treaty pledges respect of China's independence, November
1922	Treaty of Rapallo between Germany and the Soviet Union provides for mutual diplomatic recognition, reciprocal trade and cancellation of prior financial claims and permits Germany to train its army in the Soviet Union in violation of the Versailles Treaty, April 16; Germany cedes Upper Silesa to Poland
	Austria denounces Anschluss in Geneva Protocol
1923	Hitler's "Beer Hall Putsch" attempt to overthrow democratic institutions in Germany and acquire power for Nazis fails
	Treaty of Lausanne revises the Treaty of Sévres, July 24
	U.S. Senate votes to withdraw American occupation forces from the Rhineland
1924	Pan-American Treaty, to prevent international conflicts, signed
	London Conference approves Dawes Report to resolve controversies about German reparations following Germany's default on its payments and French occupation of the Ruhr, April
1925	Lucarno Conference seeks to cooperatively amend Versailles agreements to keep the peace, guarantee Germany's western frontiers, December 1
1927	Inter-Allied military control of Germany ends
	Geneva economic conference of fifty-two nations fails to reach agreement
	Germany's economy collapses on "Black Friday"

Date	Settlement/Conference
1928	Kellogg-Briand Pact, signed by sixty-five nations, outlaws war as an instrument of national policy
1929	Inter-American Treaty on Arbitration signed in Washington
	The Young Plan revises the 1924 Dawes Report, reducing Germany's reparations and rescheduling payments until 1988
1930	Treaty settling ratios on tonnage of permissible naval fleets signed by United States, Japan, France, and Italy
	Last Allied occupation troops leave Rhineland
1932	Stimson Doctrine protests Japanese invasion of Manchuria, declares that the United States will hereafter not recognize territorial changes resulting from use of armed force
	Global disarmament conference fails to produce agreements
1933	"Enabling Law" gives Hitler dictatorial power in Germany; Nazi persecution of Jews intensifies
	United States extends diplomatic recognition to the communist regime in the Soviet Union
	International economic conference collapses
1935	Nazi regime in Germany repudiates Versailles treaty and reintroduces compulsory military service
	Italy invades Ethiopia
	Anglo-German Naval Agreement
1936	The Montreux Convention supersedes the 1923 Treaty of Lausanne governing commercial shipping in the Straits, July 20
	German troops occupy Rhineland
	Italy, Austria, and Hungary sign Rome Pact
	London Naval Convention signed by the United States, Britain, and France
	Mussolini and Hitler announce formation of "Berlin Axis" alliance
1937	Italy and Yugoslavia sign Belgrade Pact
	London Imperial Conference
	Japan invades China, seizes Peking
	Germany guarantees Belgium inviolability
	Italy joins anti-Comintern (Communist international) Pact of Germany and Japan
	Italy withdraws from League of Nations
1938	Munich Conference, September
	Germany occupies Sudentenland of Czechoslovakia, October 10
1939	Germany invades Poland, September 1
	Britain and France declare war on Germany
	The Soviet Union invades Poland
	Britain and France reject Hitler's "peace feelers"
	In Molotov-Rippentrop Pact, the Soviet Union and Nazi Germany agree not to initiate aggression against each other
	The Soviet Union invades Finland and is expelled from the League of Nations in its last act as an international organization

British. France, Italy, the United States, and Japan also built powerful navies, but the British navy continued to be the largest, and to Germany, Great Britain justifiably appeared to be the biggest obstacle to its desire for status, for what the kaiser called its deserved "place in the sun." In short, the quest for ever more arms had transformed Europe into a tinderbox that would be ignited by the Austro-Serbian confrontation.

Another key argument about the origins of World War I assigns blame for the outbreak of the war to the anxieties that coalition formation unleashed. Many historians contend that, in addition to an unrestrained arms race, the **polarized** system of alliances and counteralliances (the Triple Alliance of Germany, Austria-Hungary, and Italy versus the Triple Entente of Russia, Britain, and France) engendered a chain reaction following the 1914 Austrian reprisal against the Sarajevo assassination, where prior commitments pulled one European state after another into a continental war.

A key factor in the outbreak of the First World War was Germany's challenge to British strength in the overall geostrategic balance of power and the fears this action aroused. Although Germany did not become a unified country until 1871, the German Reich had prospered and used its growing wealth to build a formidable military machine. As the predominant military and industrial power on the European continent, Germany sought to compete for international position and status; as Kaiser William II put it in 1898, Germany had "great tasks . . . outside the narrow boundaries of old Europe."

The Germans attempted to expand their empire under Kaiser William II, who reigned between 1888 and 1918 and whose ambitious plan for the expansion of German power and prestige superceded the policies of Otto von Bismarck. Under the kaiser's concept of *Weltpolitik* (world policy), Germany began building a strong navy that would command respect for the German flag around the globe. Fearing that Great Britain, Russia, and France were encircling Germany, William II insisted that a larger military was necessary to protect German interests.

Germany was not the only newly emergent power at the turn of the century, however. Russia was also expanding, and becoming a threat to Germany. The decline in power of the Austro-Hungarian Empire, Germany's only ally, heightened that threat. Russian nationalists glorified the distinctiveness of their country; they hailed "Holy Russia" as the rightful inheritor of the old Byzantine religion and culture. Consistent with this haughty patriotism, and governed by their "endemic refusal to forget a slight,"[4] the Russian Czars dedicated themselves to expanding their empire's power and prestige. Germany responded with apprehension and looked for an opportunity to block the Russian drive for pre-eminence. For William II, the opportunity came with the assassination of Archduke Ferdinand. He was convinced that a short, localized, and victorious Balkan war was possible and feared that an unfavorable shift in the **balance of power** would occur in the event of a long war. Austria-Hungary had to be preserved, since the disintegration of this neighboring empire would have left Germany isolated, without an ally. As a result, Germany gave Austria-Hungary a "blank check" to crush Serbia, so that it could undercut Russia's ally and thereby weaken Russian influence in Europe. Germany's unconditional support proved, however, to be a serious miscalculation, as it provoked an unexpected reaction from France and Russia, the two allied powers on Germany's western and eastern borders.

In the so-called Schlieffen Plan, Germany's generals had long based their military preparations on the premise that in the event of German war with both Russia and France, German troops would first quickly defeat the French and then turn against the larger but slower-moving Russians. The quickest way into France was through neutral Belgium. When the Germans marched into Belgium, Britain declared war, thus joining France and Russia in opposing Germany.

Although Britain's immediate objective was to defend Belgian **neutrality,** the war later expanded across the globe when on August 23 Japan complied with its alliance commitment to Britain by declaring war on Germany (taking advantage of the situation by seizing some important German colonial possessions in Asia). The war's enlargement proceeded in October when the Ottoman Empire in Turkey and, later, Bulgaria, joined Germany and Austria-Hungary. These four nations became known as the "Central Powers." Although a member of the Triple Alliance, Italy decided not to join Germany and Austria-Hungary in the war. Italy declared its neutrality, and later allied itself with the Triple Entente alliance composed of Russia, France, and Great Britain. Japan, Rumania, and many other countries also joined this expanding coalition to form a partnership referred to as the "Allies." On April 6, 1917, the war expanded further when the United States entered the conflict. Outside Europe, Britain remained supported by its vast empire. In time, China and some South American countries joined the Allies. Before World War I ended, thirty-two countries on six continents were at war. For the first time ever, war had become truly global in scope.

WAR BECOMES TOTAL

World War I differed from any previous war in several ways other than the number of participants and its geographical scope. Science and technology made the conflict a war of machinery: old weapons were improved and produced in great quantities, new and far more deadly weapons were rapidly developed and deployed. Widespread universal military conscription drew soldiers from nearly every family and touched the lives of every citizen. Huge armies had to be fed, and therefore agricultural production was a necessary part of national efforts to wage war. Equipping the armies with machine guns, cannons, and shells made factories vital to victory. Thus, whole national populations, including women and children, became part of the war effort, with the result that mass mobilization and communication made public opinion and nationalistic sentiments a potent factor in the way warring nations approached one another.

The hatreds incited by wartime propaganda must also be placed into this mix. The adversarial governments expended great effort attempting to persuade their populations of the righteousness of their cause and the malevolence of their enemies. The Central Powers' propaganda emphasized that the Allies had been trying for years to deprive them of their just share of the world's trade and colonies. The Allies' propaganda claimed that the Germans, assisted by their allies, were trying to conquer the world and that the authoritarian government in Berlin was hostile to Western democracy and international law. Allied propaganda vehemently condemned the German march through Belgium in violation of prior treaty provisions and alleged that the Germans had committed terrible atrocities against the Belgian population. Both sides told their populations that the enemy had started the war, and both sides distorted facts in their propaganda. "In war," said one Allied statesman, "the first casualty is the truth."[5]

The U.S. publicist Henry Adams noted in 1907, "Politics as a practice has always been the systematic organization of hatreds."[6] This statement may be an exaggeration in times of peace, but in wartime it is accurate. Demonization of the adversary would prove instrumental in the conduct of the war as well as its conclusion. Passions of hatred rationalize the sacrifice of life and property in an exhaustive, protracted war. But by vilifying the entire population of enemy nations, a compromise settlement became difficult. In effect, the war was total: doing whatever was necessary for victory became permissible, surrender unthinkable. What was expected to be a short war continued mercilessly, with no end in sight and no willingness on either side to terminate the slaughter at the bargaining table.

> "We must dictate the peace and I am determined to continue the war until the Central Powers are destroyed. . . . No Congress or mediation for me!"
>
> —CZAR NICHOLAS II

By the third year of the war, soldiers were dying by the thousands on the western front without a hope of breaching enemy lines. The Allies were demoralized and angry. Russia was ripped apart by the Bolshevik revolution which, during the next year, forced it to withdraw from the war. In the Treaty of Brest-Litovsk (March 3, 1918), Germany annexed one-third of Russia's European territory and established a protectorate over the Ukraine. Germany was disinclined to treat its vanquished foe charitably; it saw in Russia's partition a just and deserved dividend for the cost of warfare, to which it was entitled. Having defeated its foe in the east, Germany was free to turn all of its forces westward. As the war continued, mutiny began to spread in the French army—to such an extent that at one point only two French divisions between Soissons and Paris were considered reliable enough to continue in the struggle. But the Germans, outnumbered to begin with, were also in desperate straits. Huge losses on the western front undermined the German commanders' confidence. To worsen the situation, the British naval blockade was exerting a devastating effect on German morale. Despite strict rationing and the ingenuity of German scientists, ammunition shortages developed and long lines of people waited for dwindling stocks of food. Worried German leaders observed that, for the first time, Allied propaganda was beginning to weaken the German army's spirit.

Early in 1917, desperate German leaders announced the resumption of unrestricted submarine warfare. Like other Americans, President Woodrow Wilson had been drifting toward the conviction that war with Germany was necessary to protect American interests. The toll that Germany's return to submarine warfare would take on American shipping led the United States to declare war on Germany in April 1917. The United States' entry into the war gave the weary Allies an enormous boost at the very time Germany was fighting without additional reserves and with allies whose armies were disintegrating. By the end of 1917 a fresh, well-equipped American army of almost three million soldiers was expected to join the fight. Meanwhile, the German population neared starvation. Revolution began to sweep through the land, and groups within Germany started lobbying for peace.

Germany's leading general, the Prussian Junker Paul von Hindenburg, felt it necessary to end the state of belligerency and asked President Wilson for an armistice. General Hindenburg's willingness to agree to a truce settlement was shaped by his awareness that, as Napoleon Bonaparte put it in 1802, "to negotiate is not to do as one likes."[7] Hindenburg had incentives beyond military necessity for surrendering. He expected the offer to result in fair treatment for Germany, as a bargain struck between equals, based on principles of equity and **reciprocity**. Hindenburg approached his grim task, therefore, with a sense of remorse but also with hope and spoke on behalf of the country for which he had fought (the kaiser had fled to Holland, and Hindenburg was the appointed defender of German national interests). In French general Foch's special train in the forest of Compiégne, early in the morning of November 11, 1918, Hindenburg consented to a prearmistice agreement. In precisely the same car in which the Franco-Prussian armistice was negotiated in 1871, Hindenburg's "cease fire" order ended a war that had killed thirteen million soldiers and sailors, approximately the same number of civilians, and injured some thirty million people.

The prearmistice contract had been signed under duress, but the cease-fire agreement was accepted primarily because of Germany's expectations of accommodation: "The Germans had laid down their arms after receiving solemn assurances that they could be granted a peace of justice based on Wilson's Fourteen Points."[8] Those principles outlined a framework for a lasting and just peace on which the Germans felt they could rely (see Box 7.1). As events

BOX 7.1
PRESIDENT WOODROW WILSON'S PLAN
FOR A LASTING PEACE
(ADDRESS TO THE U.S. SENATE, JANUARY 22, 1917)

In every discussion of the peace that must end this war it is taken for granted that the peace must be followed by some definite concert of power which will make it virtually impossible that any such catastrophe should ever overwhelm us again. Every lover of mankind, every sane and thoughtful man must take that for granted.

. . . It will be absolutely necessary that a force be created as a guarantor of the permanency of the settlement so much greater than the force of any nation now engaged or any alliance hitherto formed or projected that no nation, no probable combination of nations, could face or withstand it. If the peace presently to be made is to endure, it must be a peace made secure by the organized major force of mankind.

. . . The equality of nations upon which peace must be founded if it is to last must be an equality of rights; the guarantees exchanged must neither recognize nor imply a difference between big nations and small, between those that are powerful and those that are weak. Right must be based upon the common strength, not upon the individual strength, of the nations upon whose concert peace will depend. . . . Mankind is looking now for freedom of life, not for equipoises of power.

. . . I am proposing, as it were, that the nations should with one accord adopt the doctrine of President [James] Monroe as the doctrine of the world: that no nation should seek to extend its polity over any other nation or people, but that every people should be left free to determine its own polity, as its own way of development, unhindered, unthreatened, unafraid, the little along with the great and powerful.

I am proposing that all nations henceforth avoid entangling alliances which would draw them into competitions of power, catch them in a net of intrigue and selfish rivalry, and disturb their own affairs with influences intruded from without. There is no entangling alliance in a concert of power. When all unite to act in the same sense and with the same purpose all act in the common interest and are free to live their own lives under a common protection.

I am proposing government by the consent of the governed, that freedom of the seas which in international conference after conference representatives of the United States have urged with the eloquence of those who are the convinced disciples of liberty, and that moderation of armaments which makes of armies and navies a power for order merely, not an instrument of aggression or of selfish violence.

These are American principles, American policies. We could stand for no others. And they are also the principles and policies of forward-looking men and women everywhere, of every modern nation, of every enlightened community. They are the principles of mankind and must prevail.

unfolded, that expectation would be dashed by the angry emotions unleashed after years of bitter fighting.

TRUST BETRAYED

The document signed on November 11, 1918, was only a preliminary armistice. It nonetheless set the stage for the peace conference that would eventually come and explicitly established the ambitious goals that would be pursued. As David Lloyd George, the British prime minister, announced, "I hope that we may say that thus, this fateful morning, come to an end all wars."[9] The British prime minister shared Woodrow Wilson's vision of World War I as "the culminating and final war for human liberty"[10] and perceived the rules for international conduct that would emerge from the peace negotiations as the dawning of a new age.

To craft the final peace terms, a conference assembled in Paris during the following winter with representatives from twenty-seven allied states, accompanied by hundreds of advisors and clerks. In addition to the official delegates, representatives from a host of dissatisfied peoples who wished to place their claims before the world also attended, including the Irish, the Ukrainians, the Finns, the Albanians, the Armenians, and the Koreans. The result was by far the largest, most widely reported peace conference ever convened. After four years of carnage, the attention of people throughout the world was riveted on Paris, where they hoped the participants would find a formula to keep such destruction from ever occurring again.

> For most Europeans, the Great War had been a source of disillusionment. . . .
> When it was all over, few remained to be convinced that such a war must never happen again. Among vast populations there was a strong conviction that this time the parties had to plan a peace that could not just terminate a war, but a peace that could change attitudes and build a new type of international order. . . .
> For the first time in history, broad publics and the peacemakers shared a conviction that war was a central problem in international relations. Previously, hegemony, the aggressive activities of a particular state, or revolution had been the problem. In 1648, 1713, and 1815, the peacemakers had tried to resolve issues of the past and to construct orders that would preclude their reappearance. But in 1919 expectations ran higher. The sources of war were less important than the war itself. There was a necessity to look more to the future than to the past. The problem was not just to build a peace, but to construct a peaceful international order that would successfully manage all international conflicts of the future.[11]

The war's destructiveness prompted many people to question the **realpolitik** philosophy that had rationalized weapons acquisition, secret alliances, and power politics. The time was ripe for a different approach to building world order. Instead of establishing a new balance of power, the American president Woodrow Wilson preached the need for a peace plan rooted in the idealism of liberal international relations theory.

Wilsonianism Ascendant

President Woodrow Wilson personally led the American delegation to the peace conference. Many people regarded Wilson as the architect of a better world. In Italy, along Wilson's route to the conference, people threw flowers at his feet. When he arrived in France, bands escorted him down the broad boulevards of Paris and a palace was put at his disposal. From Eastern Europe to the Far East, war-sick and impoverished peasants placed Wilson's picture beside their religious symbols.

Many months before the war ended, Wilson had urged in eloquent speeches that World War I must be "the war to end all wars," that the peace must benefit all and hurt none. He had put his ideals into specifics earlier in his widely proclaimed Fourteen Points speech of January 22, 1917. Some of these points concerned boundary lines or other specific arrangements, but seven key points heralded bold new principles for making peace: (1) "open covenants openly arrived at"—that is, the end of secret treaties; (2) a settlement of all territorial claims on the basis of **self-determination** to permit each nationality to determine the flag under which it wanted to live; (3) disarmament to reduce war-breeding weaponry in all nations; (4) the cutting of protective tariff barriers to free trade, which had encouraged imperialistic rivalries and inhibited economic growth; (5) the promotion of democratic governance within states, based on the belief that democracies would resolve their disputes through **mediation** rather than war; (6) strengthening international law; and (7) creating a League of Nations to guarantee the independence and territorial integrity of all states. These seven principles shaped the thinking of nations during debate among the participants at the peace conference.

Before substantive issues could be debated, however, it was necessary to settle various procedural matters. Because no formal agenda had been established prior to the conference, on January 12, 1919, meetings began to hammer out organizational issues. Ultimately it was decided that the key decision-making body would be a Council of Ten, composed of the foreign ministers and heads of state from France, Great Britain, the United States, Italy, and Japan. Not long thereafter, the foreign ministers were dropped, thus leaving a Council of Five. Since Japan only participated when the council dealt with a topic pertaining to the Pacific region, most of the decisions were made by a Council of Four (which became a council of France, Great Britain, and the United States when Italy withdrew at the end of April). Because council members lacked detailed information about most substantive issues they addressed, fifty-eight commissions of experts were established to study specific problems and make recommendations. Council deliberations over these recommendations were held in secret, and only eight plenary sessions involving all delegates to the peace conference were held.

Idealism versus National Self-Interest

As the delegates to the conference approached their historic mission, they were also influenced by the fact that the Germans had asked for a peace grounded in Wilson's Fourteen Points. The Germans believed such a peace would be based on reconciliation rather than recrimination because Wilson had preached that "only a peace between equals can last."[12] However, once the Allies began their work, the knives of national interest began to whittle away at the **liberal** internationalist philosophy underpinning the Fourteen Points. Although many were moved by the Wilsonian program, each state expected their leaders to pursue their own parochial concerns.

Many European politicians believed the Fourteen Points were merely utopian dreams built on illusions about human nature and the willingness of nations to sacrifice for the larger collective good. These leaders remembered that during the war the Allies had made many secret (and occasionally conflicting) agreements concerning territories they hoped to obtain. Not ideals, but the quest for land, defensible frontiers, ports, and supplies of raw materials shaped the bargaining. Statesmen grounded in realpolitik remained reluctant to accept Wilson's idealism and were offended by the pontificating American president and his preaching style. "God was content with Ten Commandments," growled Georges Clemenceau, the cynical French prime minister. "Wilson must have fourteen."[13] Statesmen's behavior at the bargaining table showed that they were only willing to support those particular principles of the Fourteen Points that served their national interests.

Clemenceau, a disciple of the realist premise that wars were inevitable, evaluated all proposals for a peace settlement on the basis of how much they strengthened France and weakened Germany. Great Britain's policy was guided by Prime Minister David Lloyd George, who, like Woodrow Wilson, was himself something of a reformer; nonetheless, Lloyd George believed in the necessity of preserving Britain's freedom of decision and had his ear attuned to the public's cry for a peace treaty that would put British interests ahead of grand global ideals. Lloyd George did not see the need for charity toward external enemies, having campaigned in the 1918 election with the slogan "We will squeeze the orange till the pips squeak."[14]

> "I wish to be buried standing, facing Germany."
>
> —GEORGES CLEMENCEAU

As negotiations at the conference proceeded, Clemenceau's stark realpolitik thinking prevailed. His philosophy was rooted in the politics of revenge, although he gave his consent to Wilson's fourteenth point—the need to create the League of Nations to keep the peace through **collective security** instead of the discredited balance-of-power process, which had shown itself unreliable. If the League were established, Wilson believed, it would allow the victors to deal with serious flaws in the Versailles peace treaty, help nations become accustomed to resolving their disagreements peacefully, and provide the machinery by which future disputes could be settled without war.

How the League would be structured remained an issue of vigorous debate, however. Should it be designed in accordance with the theory of collective security, or should it have a permanent staff and an international army? What roles and responsibilities would the great powers have in comparison to small- and medium-sized countries? Although Wilson had asked his trusted adviser Colonel E.M. House to prepare a blueprint for the new organization, other countries advanced their own ideas. Lord Phillimore of Great Britain, Léon Bourgeois of France, V.E. Orlando of Italy, and Jan Christiaan Smuts of South Africa all offered different proposals. The American president may have commanded enormous popular attention on the topic of a League of Nations, but the organization would only emerge through a patchwork of compromises with allies striving to protect their competing national interests. After considerable wrangling among the victors, a combined Anglo-American draft was issued by Cecil Hurst and David Hunter Miller, which then served as the basis for the Covenant of the League.

Wilsonianism in Decline

The League of Nations that had been advocated so vigorously by Woodrow Wilson was written into the peace treaty with Germany as the first of 440 articles. The rest of the settlement became largely a compromise among the ambitious, self-interested demands of the other victors. Agreements were not openly arrived at because the important decisions were made behind closed doors. The central issues of the final settlement were settled through bargaining among the victors, with the vanquished and the other affected states excluded from full representation. Furthermore, no agreements were reached to lower tariffs or reduce armaments. As the pursuit of self-advantage dominated the debate, the Versailles peace conference increasingly began to resemble a victor's peace instead of the "peace without victory" that Wilson had championed.

In thinking about the ways the Germans should be treated in defeat, the Allies could not help but to take into consideration how, had Germany won the war, it probably would have treated its victims. The victors shuddered over the March 13, 1918, Treaty of Brest-Litovsk between Germany and Russia. Its terms were so exploitative that the Russian negotiator, Leon Trotsky, at first refused to sign the armistice, in reaction to the German demand that would deprive Russia of 26 percent of its population, 27 percent of its arable land, and 33 percent of its manufacturing industries. Trotsky was overruled by his comrade, Vladimir Lenin, who was willing to accept these enormous Russian losses in order to allow the Bolsheviks the opportunity to consolidate their control within Russia. The Allies concluded that, if victorious, the Germans would have imposed the same kind of harsh terms against them. These fears undermined sympathy for the surrendering Germans and made it difficult for the Allies to contemplate treating the Germans in a manner the Germans were unlikely to have treated them if the outcome were reversed. As a result, the Allied powers responded with a vindictive settlement that mirrored the punitive policy of Germany toward Russia after Russia's surrender. Lloyd George, for example, publicly demanded in his November 1918 "Khaki" campaign for office that Germany pay for the entire cost of the war.

The settlement finally reached is known as the Treaty of Versailles because it was signed in the glittering Versailles palace—the same hall in which Louis XVI had held court during his reign as king prior to the French Revolution and where Prussian chancellor Otto von Bismarck had imposed terms on France in 1871 after the Franco-Prussian War. The newly created republican German government headed by its socialist president, Friedrich Ebert, submitted to the agreement on June 28, 1919. The final draft departed from the approach Woodrow Wilson had originally recommended. It was a punitive peace settlement best known not for what it created, but for what it destroyed: the spirit of conciliation that the belligerents had pledged to respect when the prearmistice pact on November 11, 1918, had been signed in the celebrated "boxcar" truce.

The treaties that ended World War I ratified the end of the kaiser's rule in Germany, as well as the dissolution of the Austro-Hungarian and Ottoman empires. Inspired by revenge, the settlement was an act of retaliation rather than reconciliation. "No quarrel ought ever to be converted into a policy," David Lloyd George had once admonished,[15] but this sentiment was ignored at Versailles as the victors redrew the map of Europe to prevent Germany's recovery. As Map 7.1 shows, in the follow-on Treaty of St. Germain (September 10, 1919), Austria was allowed to retain only 27 percent of its former territory (ceding South Tyrol, South Styria, and the Sudetenland). Its army was limited to thirty thousand soldiers, and Austria had to pay a large indemnity. Likewise, the Treaty of Neuilly (November 27, 1919) forced Bulgaria to cede four strategically important areas to Yugoslavia and its Aegean coastline to Greece. The Treaty of Trianon (June 9, 1920) required Hungary to surrender 71 percent of its territory, pay reparations to the Allies, and reduce its armed forces to thirty-five thousand soldiers. Similarly, the Treaty of Sèvres (August 10, 1920) dismantled the Ottoman Empire, with Greece gaining ground in Thrace and Asia Minor, and Arab provinces placed under League of Nations mandates. Beyond these territorial adjustments, the Versailles treaty forced Germany to relinquish various holdings. Specifically, it was required to give

- Alsace-Lorraine to France
- North Schleswig to Denmark
- West Prussia, Posen, portions of East Prussia, Outer Pomerania, and Upper Silesia to Poland

- Eupen and Malmedy to Belgium
- the Memel district to Lithuania

Moreover, the Versailles peace treaty mandated the Saar region to the adminis-trative control of the League of Nations and made Danzig a "free city" in which Germany had no jurisdiction. In addition, Germany was prohibited from uniting with Austria.

In addition to the boundary revisions, the Germans suffered the humiliating presence of military occupation forces on their territory and the forced reform of their governing institutions. The Versailles treaty called for a special tribunal to try Kaiser William II for offenses against international morality and the sanctity of treaties and obligated Germany to create a democratic government ruled by the consent of the governed. To make matters even more difficult, Germany was assessed an astronomical thirty-three billion dollar (1,452,360 billion Reichmarks) indemnity by the Reparations Commission in 1921. In interpreting the fantastic level of this indemnity, and the improbability that Germany could ever hope to repay it, one should keep in mind that the German government's annual revenue at the time was less than three billion Reichmarks.

Many historians believe that this extreme approach might have been avoided if, as originally planned, the United States had taken its seat on the Reparations Commission. This is not to argue that the victors were divided about the kind of peace that should be made once the conference got under-way, with Wilson on one side and the other Allies in opposition. At the confer-ence Wilson himself shifted from his prior light-handed position, keeping his options open concerning the provisions of a final settlement. In fact, from the start Wilson had viewed Imperial Germany as "the epitome of evil in the mod-ern world"[16] and had harbored no sympathy for its militarism and autocracy; his disdain for Germany helps to explain why "the salient feature of American diplomacy from April 1917 to October 1918 was Wilson's attempt to impose a moratorium on political consultation with the Allies"[17] about the way the Ger-mans should be treated after victory.

As early as September 27, 1918, Wilson had begun to voice his support for a settlement among the Allies that would exclude the enemies' participation; instead of **negotiations,** Wilson insisted that the settlement should be imposed by the victors:

> We are all agreed that there can be no peace obtained by any kind of bargain or compromise with the governments of the Central Empires. . . . They have con-vinced us that they are without honor and do not intend justice. They observe no covenants, accept no principle but force and their own interest. We cannot "come to terms" with them . . . Germany will have to redeem her character, not by what happens at the peace table but by what follows.[18]

As a result of Wilson's posture, "the Paris Peace Conference became the first European multilateral war settlement that was not negotiated between all the

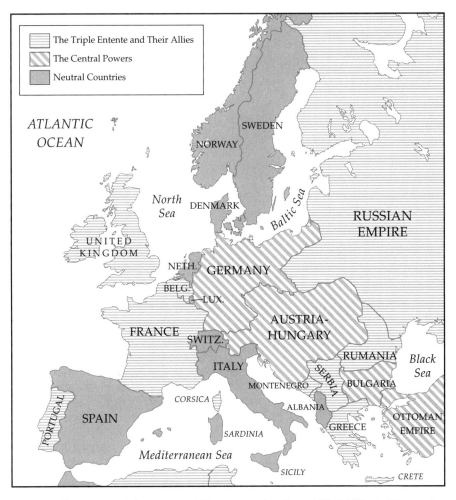

MAP 7.1A Empires and Competing Alliances on the Eve of World War I. Prior to the First World War, the major powers in Europe had separated into two opposed coalitions, the Triple Entente and the Central Powers, with only a handful of neutral states avoiding entanglement in these alliance networks. When the war erupted, this bipolarized balance-of-power distribution engulfed the entire continent.

MAP 7.1B The New Distribution of Power after the Versailles Treaty's Border Changes in 1919. When World War I came to an end, the winners redistributed territories at the expense of the defeated. Empires were reduced to shadows of their former selves, and the boundaries of Germany were stripped of territories to which German nationalities had long laid claim. The wisdom, or folly, of this settlement was to be shown by subsequent developments.

belligerents. Whatever the pretensions of the peacemakers that their work represented leniency and justice and that it could serve as a basis for an enduring peace, it was a *diktat*—as most Germans were to claim from the day it was signed."[19]

Moreover, although there remained much disunity and even competition among the victorious allies at the bargaining table, Wilson was not "prepared to insist on a peace of reconciliation,"[20] and as a consequence the defeated powers were forced to accept the heavy burden that the victors imposed on them. There seemed little recognition of the possible rewards that might result from leniency, despite some professions by the peacemakers of the importance of treating the vanquished as equal members deserving of respect in the community of nations. "Germany and the other defeated belligerents would have to serve a probationary period, earning their way to membership through their foreign policy behavior, even though they otherwise met the only specific membership requirement in the Covenant, that a state be 'self-governing.' "[21]

The final terms of the lengthy text of the Versailles treaty made the victors' true intention—to strip Germany of its status as a great power—abundantly clear. Germany, though defeated, was allowed to remain an independent sovereign state, but the peace terms were intentionally so burdensome as to ensure Germany's decline and, with Poland created as an independent buffer state between Germany and Russia, to also guarantee that Germany's potential resurgence would be contained. As one historian summarizes:

> Germany's military and naval power was drastically curtailed; Allied soldiers could occupy the left bank of the Rhine for up to fifteen years; Alsace and Lorraine were returned to France; German colonies were divided among the victors; East Prussia was separated from Germany proper by the new Poland. The German government was obliged, moreover, to pay reparations for the physical and human suffering of the war, reparations that soon became a major political and economic stumbling block to Europe's recovery and stability.[22]

The harsh terms of the Treaty of Versailles provoked resentment in the Germans, who felt betrayed by the victors' refusal to honor their prior promise to grant Germany a voice during the deliberations. On learning of the provisions the Germans were told to accept, the exiled German kaiser is said to have declared that "the war to end wars has resulted in a peace to end peace."[23]

THE RISKS OF VENOMOUS VICTORY

The victors' mood after World War I was driven by the spirit of revenge. With nightmarish visions of trenches, poison gas, barbed wire, and mechanized slaughter fresh in their minds, the victors assembled at Versailles approached the task of making peace in a state of anger. They sought revenge against an enemy that, in the words of French foreign minister Georges Clemenceau, had "flung aside every scruple of conscience" to wage a brutal war "hoping for a peace of enslavement under the yoke of militarism destructive of all human dignity."[24]

At Versailles, the victors did not just blame the leaders of their defeated adversaries for their aggression. They blamed their entire populations, holding them collectively accountable for the crimes committed. "War guilt" was assigned to the German people and their allies: the famous Article 231 of the Treaty the German authorities were forced to sign stipulated that "Germany accepts the responsibility of Germany and her allies for causing all the loss and damage to which the Allied and Associated Governments and their nationals have been subjected as a consequence of the war imposed upon them by the aggression of Germany and her allies."[25]

WHAT GOES AROUND COMES AROUND

What were the consequences of the punitive peace-keeping strategy that the victors embraced at Versailles? Many feel it backfired, producing the very outcome it sought to prevent. In 1928 the Kellogg-Briand Pact (or Pact of Paris) had outlawed the right of states to make war, but the Versailles peace settlement failed to extinguish Germany's hopes for global status and influence. On the contrary, some have argued that the vengeance of Versailles and the blame it assigned was the kindling that led to the global conflagration that erupted in 1939.

Germany's hegemonic ambitions were renewed in the helter-skelter atmosphere of the 1920s and 1930s. Incited by resurgent nationalism, **irredentist** calls for the recovery of lost territory focused on the plight of Germans living in Austria, Czechoslovakia, and Poland. The rise of fascism in Germany can be attributed, in part, to the angry emotions unleashed following the conclusion of the First World War. Adolf Hitler's meteoric rise to power, and subsequent German aggression under him, were fueled by many Germans' resentment over the harsh conditions imposed upon them after the war. "Hitler exploited the Versailles Treaty as a symbol of a vindictive Western policy designed to hold down a defeated Germany—rhetoric that pushed onto the Western allies the blame for Germany's domestic misery."[26] Since no foreign army had reached German soil during World War I, many felt that the German army had not been defeated; it was stabbed in the back by traitors within Germany itself.

Germany's armed forces were reduced by the peace settlement to 100,000 volunteers, the navy was cut to six cruisers, and it lost 13 percent of its prewar territory and colonies overseas. Yet Germany was also denied membership in the League of Nations until 1926. When Germany defaulted on the war reparations payments in 1922, France sent troops to occupy the German industrial area of the Ruhr Valley. In 1925, in response to the German delay in adhering to the disarmament provisions of the Versailles treaty, the French postponed the scheduled evacuation of their occupation troops. The crisis was momentarily defused by the efforts of German foreign minister Gustav Stresemann.

> He proposed a set of nonaggression and arbitration treaties, principally among France, Britain, Italy, and Germany. These countries, as well as Belgium, Czechoslovakia, and Poland, met in the Swiss town of Locarno in the fall of 1925 in an omnibus negotiation of a pact to remove the scourge of war from Europe. A treaty on the Rhineland provided for that region's full demilitarization, pledging France, Germany, and Belgium to refrain from resorting to war against each other, except for a flagrant breach of the Locarno Pact itself or as a part of a League of Nations action against an aggressor state. France also signed two special treaties of guarantee with Poland and Czechoslovakia providing for mutual assistance against Germany in case that country should violate her new obligations. Finally, Germany signed arbitration treaties with each of the other countries, agreeing to submit her disputes with them to a conciliation commission and then, if necessary, to the World Court and the Council of the League. As the icing on the cake of peace, Germany was admitted to the League of Nations.[27]

The so-called hopeful spirit of Locarno succeeded in adjusting the terms of the Treaty of Versailles, in large part because the government in Paris came to the reluctant conclusion that "France's relative position vis-à-vis Germany was declining and . . . that reconciliation with Germany represented France's best hope for long-term security."[28] With France prepared to relax its punitive policies, a window of opportunity opened for a retreat from the Versailles provisions. On September 27, 1926, France agreed to return the Saar coal region to Germany without the plebiscite that had been required in the Treaty of Versailles and removed its occupation forces from the Rhineland the next year.

This spirit of cooperation and conciliation did not last long, and further serious efforts to amend the Versailles peace treaty were not undertaken. The efforts by the great powers to work together, through the League of Nations, to collectively keep the peace, sputtered. Realpolitik returned, spawning the very behaviors that Wilson and others had sought to expunge at Versailles: unilateral initiatives and the struggle for national power and position through secret treaties pitting one set of states against another. Alliance formation became frantic and reached epidemic proportions as national leaders sought protection not through international organization but through arms and military alliances. As Hans J. Morgenthau observes, in the period after the First World War, "the principle of the balance of power was supposed to have been superseded by the League-of-Nations principle of collective security," but in fact that principle was put "under the sign of the balance of power by alliances and counteralliances."[29] France, for example, sought to buttress its security by forging alliances with Belgium, Poland, and the so-called Little Entente of Yugoslavia, Rumania, and Czechoslovakia. The frequency with which states entered into formal alliances between 1923 and 1933 warrants the label for this period: "the era of pacts."[30] The plan to make peace through concerted international cooperation was stillborn. Ironically, the United States, which had fathered collective security under Woodrow Wilson, refused to join the League of Nations.

War clouds gathered in a relatively short amount of time after the Versailles conference. Symptoms of the gathering storm included the failures of the global economic conferences in 1927 and 1933, as well as the inability of the League of Nations to respond effectively to the 1931 Japanese invasion of Manchuria, the Chaco War of 1932, and Italy's 1935 invasion of Ethiopia. By the late 1930s it appeared another great-power war was about to erupt. Not prepared themselves to enforce the peace, the victors in World War I responded to German rearmament with an **appeasement** policy aimed at pacifying potential aggressors with concessions. Adolf Hitler, the German dictator who came to power in 1933, pledged not to expand German territory by force, and this encouraged the democracies to withdraw from the challenge of peace maintenance in the false hope that war could be avoided without active engagement. Hitler betrayed his promise when in March 1938 he forced Austria into union with Germany in violation of the terms of the Versailles treaty. Shortly thereafter Hitler insisted upon the annexation of the German-populated area of Sudentenland in Czechoslovakia. The fears that German expansionism provoked led to the final Allied effort to prevent another European war. At the September 1938 Munich Conference, Britain, France, and Italy agreed to Hitler's territorial demands. Their decision was rationalized by noting that Hitler's request fell under the right of national self-determination and, once the Sudentenland was given to Germany, Berlin would issue no more territorial demands.

Rather than satisfying Germany, appeasement encouraged further efforts at overthrowing the international status quo.[31] Between September 1, 1939, when Germany invaded Poland, and December 7, 1941, when Japan launched a surprise assault on the United States at Pearl Harbor, the world slid back into a global war. Just two decades after the Versailles peace conference, the world was again in flames. If Versailles teaches us anything, it is the scope and complexities of the peace-making endeavor. To succeed, the victors must tighten the bonds among themselves, cultivate a consensus on goals and strategies, and persevere in their efforts to implement and adjust the peace plan on which they agree. Ideally, allies should begin negotiations while the war is still being waged and mobilize public support for the plans they create to enable them to abide by the agreements they pledge. It is critical for the victors to adhere to the provisions they declare in the armistice so that the vanquished will not feel betrayed and be tempted to reverse the settlement by force at a later date. To be sure, almost "every treaty which brings a war to an end is, in one sense, a dictated peace; for a defeated Power seldom accepts willingly the consequences of its defeat. But in the Treaty of Versailles the element of dictation was more apparent than in any previous peace treaty of modern times. . . . At the ceremony of signature, the two German signatories were not allowed to sit with

CONTROVERSIES TO CONTEMPLATE

- Was World War I inevitable? If not, what could policymakers have done to avoid war?
- How did wartime propaganda and electoral rhetoric of political leaders in the Allied nations affect the provisions of the peace settlement?
- The president of the United States, Woodrow Wilson, attended the Paris Peace Conference in person and, despite complaints from members of the U.S. Congress, remained in Europe for six months to negotiate the details of the final settlement. What are the drawbacks of having heads of state negotiate the details of peace settlements?
- Was the Treaty of Versailles a failure because of its inherent defects or because it was never fully implemented?
- What were the consequences of imposing a war indemnity on Germany but not specifying in the peace treaty the sum to be paid? What were the problems of having a Reparations Commission draw up the bill years later?
- Whatever the faults of the Treaty of Versailles, Woodrow Wilson believed they could be rectified by the League of Nations. Why was it problematic to expect the League to correct any flaws in the peace treaty?
- John Maynard Keynes, a British economist and former Treasury official who attended the Paris Peace Conference, complained that French premier Clemenceau saw international politics as a perpetual prize fight. Germany was victorious in 1871, now France had won in 1918, but this was not likely to be the final round. To what extent did the peace settlement after World War I contribute to the outbreak of World War II?
- After the initial feelings of righteous anger toward Germany faded, many British citizens expressed misgivings about the Treaty of Versailles. David Lloyd George, the British prime minister involved in negotiating the treaty, later commented that the war resulted from botched decisions by all sides, not from the master plan of the Kaiser. How did second thoughts over the cause of the war and the harshness of the peace settlement influence British foreign policy toward Germany during the interwar years?

the Allied delegates at the table but were escorted in and out of the hall in the manner of criminals conducted to and from the dock."[32] These humiliations linked the new Weimar Republic in Germany to a feeling of national disgrace and helped to create the belief that the provisions of the treaty were not morally binding.[33]

Finally, the tragic case of Versailles illustrates the need for victorious nations to distinguish realizable goals from unobtainable ideals. As Henry Kissinger concludes, the victors assembled in Paris felt so eager to avoid what they considered to be the mistakes of previous settlement plans that they embraced a set of terms that

> mortgaged the new international order instead of helping to create it. . . . What they finally produced was a fragile compromise between American utopianism and European paranoia—too conditional to fulfill the dreams of the former, too tentative to alleviate the fears of the latter. [The terms of the Treaty of Versailles] were too onerous for conciliation but not severe enough for permanent subjugation.[34]

It proved exceedingly difficult to strike a balance between satisfying and subjugating Germany. Ultimately, neither occurred.

Given the failure of the Allies to forge a durable peace settlement after World War I, renewed emphasis was placed on the issue of war termination by the Allies following World War II. In Chapter 8 we will examine what the victors did differently and whether they were any more successful than the delegates to the Versailles peace conference.

NOTES

1. In Eyffinger, 1988, p. 21.
2. Ibid., p. 52.
3. Angell, 1910.
4. Kissinger, 1994, p. 214.
5. Lane, Goldman, and Hunt, 1959, p. 567.
6. In Green, 1982, p. 12.
7. In Bailey, 1968, p. 144.
8. Bailey, 1968, p. 268. Wilson's Fourteen Points proposal was one of several peace plans that surfaced toward the end of the war. Prime Minister David Lloyd George of Britain issued a Declaration of Aims on January 5, 1918, which listed conditions his government saw as necessary for peace. In addition, numerous agreements had been reached among different allied nations throughout 1916 and 1917 over how specific issues (such as the disposition of lands held by the Ottoman Empire) would be handled after the war.
9. In Link, 1957, p. 100 ff.
10. In Hunt, 1996, p. 22.
11. Holsti, 1991, pp. 175–176, 208–209.
12. In Bailey, 1968, p. 268.
13. Lane, Goldman, and Hunt, 1959, p. 571.
14. In Craig and George, 1995, p. 45.
15. In Bailey, 1968, p. 8.
16. Esposito, 1996, p. 5.
17. Fowler, 1969, p. 5.
18. In Holsti, 1991, p. 198.
19. Holsti, 1991, p. 199.
20. Kissinger, 1994, p. 229.
21. Holsti, 1991, p. 199.
22. Williamson, 1993, p. 989. For a full account of the terms of the Versailles settlements and a highly critical realist assessment of the fallacious hopes on which the liberal-idealist peacemakers based their thinking, see Carr, 1947.

23. In Bailey, 1968, p. 267.

24. In Holsti, 1991, p. 191.

25. At the end of the war, public opinion in many of the victorious countries demanded a formal condemnation of Germany. The original intent of Article 231 was to indicate that while Germany was morally responsible for the war, it was only legally liable for more narrowly defined damages. By embracing *collective guilt* in asserting that the German nation was morally responsible, the victors "in the passion of the moment, failed to realize that this extorted admission of guilt could prove nothing, and must excite bitter resentment in German minds. German men of learning set to work to demonstrate the guiltlessness of their country, fondly believing that, if this could be established, the whole fabric of the treaty would collapse." Carr, 1947, p. 46.

26. Dean, 1996, p. 18.

27. Brown, 1994, p. 170.

28. Kissinger, 1994, p. 277.

29. Morgenthau, 1985, p. 212.

30. Langsam, 1954, p. 79.

31. Disillusioned with Western liberalism and the Paris settlements, and suffering economically from the effects of the Great Depression of the 1930s, Japan also embraced militarism. Inspired by Germany's imperialistic quest for national aggrandizement, Japanese nationalists took Japan on the path to imperialism and colonialism. When Japan invaded China in 1937 after subjugating Manchuria (1931–1935), this accelerated the momentum for still more aggression. Italy attacked Ethiopia in 1935 and absorbed Albania in 1939, and both Germany and Italy intervened in the 1936–1939 Spanish civil war on the side of the fascists headed by General Francisco Franco.

32. Carr, 1947, pp. 4–5.

33. Ibid., pp. 44–45.

34. Kissinger, 1994, pp. 240, 242.

· 8 ·

THE LONG, COLD PEACE:
THE AFTERMATH OF WORLD WAR II

Too often in the past, each war only planted the seeds of the next. We celebrate today the reconciliation . . . that has liberated us from that cycle of destruction.

JOHN F. KENNEDY

PREVIEW

In 1919 the victors, in what was then called the "Great War," met in Paris to design a peace settlement that would prevent such a human tragedy from ever happening again. Just twenty years later, the liberal idealist plan for lasting peace was shattered when the second world war of the twentieth century broke out. This chapter will examine the path to the outbreak of World War II and, in particular, the impact of the Versailles peace treaty on Germany's foreign policy. The chapter then reviews the conferences held by the Allies during the war to construct a new, more durable peace settlement. Next, the divergent interests among the Allies and growing distrust they had of one another are charted in order to explain the different ideas that surfaced regarding the treatment of the vanquished Axis powers. The chapter concludes by describing the forces that splintered the Allies into opposing blocs in what was to become a forty-year Cold War that postponed a final settlement to the Second World War until the collapse of communism in the period between 1989 and 1991. The material covered in this case highlights the following concepts from a *structural realist* approach to the study of war and peace making:

- balance of power
- arms races
- security dilemma
- spheres of influence

When reading this case, give particular consideration to how decisionmakers in 1945 tried to avoid what they saw as the mistakes of 1919. In what ways did the peace settlement of World War II differ from the settlement of World War I? Did those differences improve the prospects for a durable peace?

▪ ▪ ▪ ▪ ▪ ▪ ▪ ▪ ▪ ▪ ▪ ▪ ▪ ▪ ▪ ▪ ▪ ▪ ▪ ▪

Germany's defeat in World War I did not extinguish its desire for global status and influence. On the contrary, defeat and humiliation became the soil from which sprouted an intensified desire for recovery and revenge. Beginning in the 1930s, Germany, joined by Japan and Italy, began pursuing an aggressive course, which resulted in the twentieth century's second worldwide conflict.

World War II personified a hegemonic struggle for power that pitted a fascist coalition striving for world supremacy—the Axis trio of Germany, Japan, and Italy—against the "grand alliance" of four great powers—Great Britain, France, the United States, and the Soviet Union. The Allies united although they espoused incompatible ideologies—communism in the case of the Soviet Union and democratic capitalism in the case of Britain, France, and the United States. Their victory was achieved over a six-year ordeal, but at a catastrophic human cost: Each day twenty-three thousand lives were lost, and the war resulted in the death of sixty million people worldwide.

> "In starting and waging a war it is not right that matters, but victory."
>
> —ADOLF HITLER

To appreciate what the victors did at the end of World War II, one must first recall the atmosphere and attitudes that prevailed prior to the onset of what became the biggest and most destructive war in history. This atmosphere was to shape the thinking of the victors toward the vanquished after they repelled the Axis threat to conquer the world.

THE PATH TO WORLD WAR II

Germany's hegemonic ambitions were driven by hypernationalism, which stimulated that country's latent **irredentist** effort to recover provinces ceded to others after World War I and to expand its borders to absorb Germans living in Austria, Czechoslovakia, and Poland. The Nazi regime's fascist ideology championing race, flag, and fatherland preached the most extreme version of realism, **machtpolitik** (power politics), to justify the forceful aggrandizement of the state. What helped to make this political philosophy acceptable to many Germans was their resentment of the harsh terms imposed at the 1919 Paris peace conference. As described in Chapter 7, the settlement insisted on the destruction of Germany's armed forces, the sacrifice of territory (such as Alsace-Lorraine, which Germany had acquired following the Franco-Prussian War of 1870), and the imposition of heavy reparations to compensate the Allies for the damage exacted by the German military. Denied membership in the League of Nations until 1926, Germany was not accepted as an equal member of the state system. Affronted by this treatment, Berlin sought by force of arms to restore its perceived rightful status as a great power.

As German preparations for war gathered speed in the 1930s, the other great powers ignored the signs of danger. The United States retreated to isolationism and Britain and France each maneuvered to their advantage. Whereas France wanted to prevent Germany's revival, Britain, by contrast, saw Germany as a counterweight to balance growing Soviet power on the European continent. By viewing a revitalized Germany in these terms, London underestimated the threat posed by growing German strength and ambition.

A circumstance poisoning the prospects for international cooperation was the collapse of the international economic system during the 1930s. As a result of the costs of fighting World War I, a weakened Great Britain could not continue to perform leadership and regulatory roles in the world political economy. Although the United States appeared the logical successor to Britain as world economic leader, Washington refused to exercise leadership. The Depression of 1929–1931 was followed in 1933 by the abortive World Monetary and Economic Conference. This meeting failed to address the chain reaction of retaliatory trade protectionism and beggar-thy-neighbor tariff walls that were emerging. The advent of trade wars and the financial decline they precipitated worldwide contributed to interstate hostility and rivalry. In this depressed global environment, disgruntled countries sought a remedy in **imperial** expansion.

Acquiescence to German rearmament was justified in Great Britain by a policy of **appeasement,** designed to pacify dissatisfied countries with concessions. Adolf Hitler, the dictator who by this time controlled the German government, claimed to have limited territorial objectives that were supported by the principle of national **self-determination.** He betrayed that declaration in March 1938 by forcing Austria into a union with Germany (the *Anschluss*). Shortly thereafter he began pressuring Czechoslovakia, which led to the September 1938 Munich Conference attended by Hitler, British prime minister Neville Chamberlain, and leaders from France and Italy (Czechoslovakia was not invited). Under the erroneous conviction that appeasement would halt further German expansionism, Chamberlain and the others agreed to Hitler's demands to annex the German-populated area of Sudetenland in Czechoslovakia.

Complacency followed by appeasement encouraged Hitler to press for further revisions in the international status quo. He was joined in this effort by Japan and Italy. The former invaded Manchuria in 1931 and China proper in 1937; the latter absorbed Abyssinia (Ethiopia) in 1935 and Albania in 1939. Furthermore, both Germany and Italy intervened in the 1936–1939 Spanish civil war on the side of the fascists, headed by General Francisco Franco. The failure of the League of Nations to mount an effective response to German, Japanese, and Italian acts of aggression revealed the hollow promise of **collective security.** International institutions were powerless to dispel the gathering war clouds.

These acts of aggression paved the way for the century's second massive war. After Germany occupied the previously unannexed area of Czechoslovakia in March 1939, Britain and France reacted by joining in an alliance to protect the next likely victim, Poland. They also opened negotiations in Moscow in hope of enticing the Soviet Union to join the alliance, but this attempt failed. Then, on August 23, 1939, Hitler and the Soviet leader Joseph Stalin shocked the world by announcing that they had signed a nonaggression pact.[1] Certain that the Western democracies would not intervene without Soviet assistance, Hitler promptly invaded Poland on September 1, 1939. Honoring their pledge to defend the Poles, Britain and France declared war on Germany two days later. World War II had begun.

The war expanded rapidly as Hitler turned his forces loose on the Balkans, North Africa, and westward. Powerful, mechanized German units invaded Norway and marched through Denmark, Belgium, Luxembourg, and the Netherlands. They swept around France's defensive barrier, the Maginot Line, and forced the British to evacuate a sizable expeditionary force from the French beaches at Dunkirk. Paris itself fell in June 1940, and in the months that followed, the German air force pounded Britain in an attempt to force it into submission as well. Instead of invading Britain, however, the Nazi troops turned against Hitler's former ally, attacking the Soviet Union in the surprise blitzkrieg operation known as Barbarossa in June 1941.

The next phase of the war's expansion was even more rapid. On October 17, 1941, the first American casualties were taken when a German torpedo hit the USS *Kearny;* this was followed by another German submarine attack on the USS *Reuben James,* even though the United States was still officially neutral. American **neutrality** ended on December 7, 1941, when the Japanese launched a surprise attack on the U.S. Pacific fleet anchored in Pearl Harbor, Hawaii. The next day President Roosevelt asked Congress for authorization to declare the existence of a state of war with Japan, and an angry Congress passed that resolution with only a single negative vote. Three days later (for reasons that remain mysterious), Adolf Hitler declared war on the United States, and Italy followed suit. On that same day, the U.S. Congress passed a resolution recognizing that a state of war existed with Germany and Italy, thereby ending years of American **isolationism** and neutrality.

Under the claim of racial superiority, Hitler waged war to create an empire that could settle the historic competition among the great-powers in Europe by eliminating all rivals. The Nazi vision had few limits.

The broad vision of the Thousand-Year Reich was . . . of a vastly expanded—and continually expanding—German core, extending deep into Russia, with a number of vassal states and regions, including France, the Low Countries, Scandinavia, central Europe and the Balkans, that would provide resources and labor for the core. There was to be no civilizing mission in German imperialism. On the contrary, the lesser peoples were to be taught only to do menial labor or, as Hitler once joked, educated sufficiently to read the road signs so they wouldn't get run over by German automobile traffic. The lowest of the low, the Poles and Jews, were to be exterminated. . . .

To Hitler . . . the purpose of policy was to destroy the system and to reconstitute it on racial lines, with a vastly expanded Germany running a distinctly hierarchical and exploitative order. Vestiges of sovereignty might remain, but they would be fig leaves covering a monolithic order. German occupation policies during the war, whereby conquered nations were reduced to satellites, satrapies, and reservoirs of slave labor, were the practical application of Hitler's conception of the new world order. They were not improvised or planned for reasons of military necessity.[2]

Italy and Japan, intoxicated by dreams of glory, found the quest for empire equally irresistible. Their victims had reason to recognize the magnitude of the security threat but failed to do so until the Axis rush toward worldwide war was almost irreversible. The failure of the French, British, Russians, and Americans to recognize the danger is perplexing. All received ample signs of the looming threat; indeed, all had extensive evidence of German, Italian, and Japanese intentions, as conveyed by the words and deeds of those states. As shown in Box 8.1, the Allied powers had a clear basis for alarm about the conduct of the three members of the Axis coalition. This failure to recognize the danger, together with the brutality of the acts of violence committed by the Axis states when a full-scale state of war erupted, helps to account for the emotional calls for unconditional surrender. Once engaged, the Allies sought not just defeat of the aggressors, but revenge, and each had psychologically powerful reasons to demonize their adversaries and to wage **total war.**

WARTIME PLANNING FOR A POSTWAR PEACE

Although they were far from confident of victory, at the onset of World War II the Allies almost immediately began to search for principles to underpin a stable postwar world order. Determined not to repeat the failure associated with the Treaty of Versailles, they concurred about the need for unity. Within less than a month of the Japanese attack on Pearl Harbor, on January 1, 1942, the United States, the Soviet Union, Great Britain, China, and twenty-two other states signed the United Nations Declaration, which pledged to proceed with a united front employing all available resources to defeat Germany, Italy, and Japan. The declaration also established the agreement for no signatory to make a separate armistice or peace. This convention, to which an additional twenty signatories later agreed, set the stage in the war's final days for the April 1945 conference of fifty states to draft the United Nations Charter in San Francisco.

A series of other agreements were negotiated during the war at various conferences. Operating under the strong conviction that they could not afford to wait until the war was over to plan for a postwar peace, the United States, Great Britain, and the Soviet Union also accepted the principle of mutual

BOX 8.1
ALLIED GRIEVANCES AGAINST THE AXIS POWERS
PRIOR TO WORLD WAR II

The acts that led the United States, France, Great Britain, and the Soviet Union to despise the Axis powers were varied. Among the steps that led the Allies to stereotype their adversaries as evil and undeserving of forgiveness were:

Germany

- after his 1933 election, Adolf Hitler's conversion of the German democracy into a military dictatorship
- the Nazi regime's withdrawal from the League of Nations, suppression of trade unions, and persecution of the Jews (culminating in the Holocaust)
- Hitler's March 7, 1933, reoccupation of the demilitarized Rhineland, in violation of the Treaty of Versailles
- Germany's forced merger of Austria and annexation of the Sudetenland of Czechoslovakia
- the German attack of Poland on September 1, 1939
- to the Soviet Union, Germany's June 21, 1941, Operation Barbarossa invasion in violation of the von Ribbentrop pledge of nonaggression

Italy

- Benito Mussolini's establishment of a military dictatorship in 1922 after his Fascist party came to power
- Italy's invasion in 1935 of Ethiopia without a declaration of war

Japan

- Japan's suspension of the liberalizing democratic reforms, such as the introduction of universal male suffrage and governance by major party rule in the 1920s, and in the 1930s its dissolution of political parties and trade unions as Japanese leaders moved to create a militarized state
- the 1931 Japanese invasion of China's northeastern province of Manchuria, which the Japanese renamed Manchukuo
- the 1932 Japanese invasion of Shanghai
- the 1937 Japanese invasion of mainland China and siege of Nanking, the provisional capital of the Chinese leader Chiang Kai-shek (the conquest of that city became known as the "Rape of Nanking" because of its brutality)
- Japan's December 7, 1941, surprise attack on Pearl Harbor
- for the Soviet Union, Japan's defeat of Russia in the 1904–1905 war, its termination of the Neutrality Pact, and Japan's July 1938 and May 1939 attacks at the Manchukuo-Soviet border

responsibility for maintaining world order. The two western democracies were especially cognizant of the need to work together. Four months prior to the United States' official entry in the war, President Roosevelt and Prime Minister Churchill agreed to the 1941 Atlantic Charter while meeting on a ship off the coast of Newfoundland. This vital document "reiterated a number of Wilsonian principles: the right of self-determination; prohibition against any aggrandizement, territorial or other during the war; abandonment of the use of force in postwar international relations; a commitment to economic collaboration; and a reference to a postwar international security system."[3] In particular, the Atlantic Charter firmly established support for the view that competition among the allies should be eschewed; the Allies were to work in tandem to preserve world order in accordance with specific rules of conduct.

Particularly critical to the successful operation of such a **security regime** became the resolution of the troublesome issue of the governments the Allies would install in Germany, Italy, and Japan after the war. The Soviet Union especially dedicated itself to eradicating fascism since "Nazi hatred of Communists and Nazi racist definitions of Slavic peoples combined to turn the German war against the U.S.S.R. into an attempt at the annihilation of a society."[4] Although Britain and the United States found fascism equally repugnant, the Allies nonetheless found themselves mired in the sticky issue of whether fascism should be replaced by liberal democratic capitalism or communistic planned economies—a question that threatened to divide the United States and Great Britain from the Soviet Union. Agreement on a solution to this dilemma was reached, however, when the Allies decided to reaffirm the classic **noninterference principle** prohibiting external interference in the internal affairs of states, which under international law permitted all states to choose their own systems of government without outside intervention. The Atlantic Charter explicitly endorsed this "hands off" principle as a partial solution to the problem, proclaiming "the right of all peoples to choose the form of government under which they will live," even while it qualified that principle in spirit by accepting, in President Roosevelt's words of May 27, 1941, that the Allies would "not accept a world . . . in which the seeds of Hitlerism can again be planted and allowed to grow."[5] This posture led the Soviet Union on September 24, 1942, to notify "London and Washington that a consistent application of those principles will secure the most energetic support on the part of the Government and the Peoples of the Soviet Union."[6]

Acting largely in concert, the Allied powers established coordinating committees to refine and extend their understandings about unity, mutual responsibility, and **military intervention**. Table 8.1 describes a series of additional meetings that were designed to clarify these understandings.

These meetings produced a general consensus about the aims and preferred strategies for reconstructing a world destroyed by war. Yet beneath the surface uncertainties percolated about the best path for postwar peace. How should the Axis powers be treated? Should they be forgiven, so that their reconciliation and collaboration in postwar peacekeeping would be possible? Or was a

TABLE 8.1
Postwar Planning during the War: Declarations and Doctrines

Date(s)	Conference/Declaration	Key Doctrinal Principle(s)
January 14–24, 1943	Casablanca Conference (French Morocco)	Roosevelt and Churchill issue declaration pledging that the war would end only with the unconditional surrender of the Axis states
October 1943	Moscow Foreign Ministers Conference (Four Power Declaration)	Allied unity and establishment of a global organization to maintain peace and security
November 28– December 1, 1943	Teheran Conference	Allied unity to preserve order, with U.S. air and naval support for Soviet and British soldiers for peace keeping in postwar Europe
July 1–22, 1944	Bretton Woods system (United Nations Monetary and Financial Conference)	Rules and institutions created near the end of World War II to govern international economic relations in the postwar world capitalist economy under U.S. leadership; this conference resulted in the creation of the International Monetary Fund (IMF) and the International Bank for Reconstruction and Development
August– September 1944	Big Four (including China) Conference at Dumbarton Oaks (Washington, D.C.)	Draft for negotiations to create the United Nations
September 1944	Quebec Conference	Roosevelt and Churchill agree on goal of reducing Germany to an agricultural economy, without any "war-making industries"
February 4–11, 1945	Yalta Conference (Crimea, Soviet Union)	Confirmed policy of unconditional surrender and complete demilitarization of Germany, division of Germany into four zones of occupation (U.S., British, French, Soviet) under unified control commission in Berlin, war crimes trials of Nazis, and study of reparation question. Secret agreements also accepted veto system for voting in future UN Security Council and for the Soviet Union to enter the war against Japan within three months of Germany's surrender (with territorial concessions pledged to the Soviet Union for its participation)

Date(s)	Conference/Declaration	Key Doctrinal Principle(s)
April 25–June 1945	San Francisco Conference	Design of United Nations Charter; Big Four responsibility for preserving postwar order, with China's inclusion; dismemberment and disarmament of Germany, which would be de-Nazified through occupation
July 17–August 2, 1945	Potsdam Conference/ Potsdam Declaration of July 26	Four powers discuss new procedures for disarming Germany and preventing its resurgence as a military power and encouraging free elections; all former German territory east of the Oder and Neisse Rivers transferred to Polish and Soviet administration; the level of possible reparation payments and policies were considered, and a Council of Foreign Ministers was created to evaluate a peace settlement, as well as the Allied Control Council to administer it. In addition, Japan was given the ultimatum of choosing between unconditional surrender or total destruction, and the Soviet Union promised to enter the Pacific War once Germany was subjugated

vindictive peace prudent, to prevent their recovery and, with it, their possible resumption of forceful expansion?

Responses to these pressing questions varied from Washington to London to Moscow. The Allies recognized that "as war is fought in order to make peace possible, foreign policy should be conducted in order to make peace permanent."[7] But which policy would best ensure a permanent peace—a compassionate or a punitive one?

THE POSTWAR BARGAINING PROCESS

On the threshold of victory, the Allies voiced enthusiasm for the doctrines and principles they had previously negotiated. Each Allied leader hoped the others would adhere to their prior agreements and act in concert after the war. For example, after the Yalta Conference, on March 1, 1945, President Roosevelt concluded that the meeting "was a successful effort by the three leading nations to find a common ground for peace. . . . It spells—and ought to spell—the end of the system of unilateral action, exclusive alliances and spheres of influence, and balances of power and all other expedients which have been tried for centuries and have always failed."[8]

A Vindictive Mood

At first, common ground appeared to exist in the American, British, and Soviet perceptions about the need to penalize the Axis for its offenses. Fighting had heightened hostility and resolve. As victory neared, the Allies insisted that war crimes had to be punished; German and Japanese atrocities could not be overlooked. Indeed, as the war moved toward its climax, Allied behavior took on the characteristics of blood revenge. The American and British firebombing of Dresden, an act that targeted "city-center churches and palaces packed with refugees" and "roasted at least twenty-five thousand of its inhabitants in the notorious firestorm" in a single night of bombardment[9] seemed more a product of vengeance than of **military necessity.** So too, did the March 9–10, 1945, firebombing of Tokyo, which took some eighty thousand lives, as well as the American carpet bombing of thirty-six other Japanese cities, which "killed an estimated four hundred thousand civilians."[10] Similarly, the Soviet Army zealously annihilated a despised enemy that had shown no compassion toward Russian prisoners of war and had slaughtered about 3.25 million Soviet soldiers in Nazi custody.[11,] The mood of revenge had become so pronounced by the time the United States dropped atomic bombs on Hiroshima and Nagasaki that U.S. general Omar N. Bradley observed that man had "grasped the mystery of the atom and rejected the Sermon on the Mount."[12]

> "When you are winning a war almost everything that happens can be claimed to be right and wise."
>
> —WINSTON CHURCHILL

The demand for revenge that colored Allied thinking during the closing phases of the war fed off a diabolical image of the enemy. Take, for example, the implicit assumption of **collective guilt** in the "Morgenthau Plan" for Germany, which Roosevelt and Churchill accepted in principle at the September 1944 Quebec postwar preparation conference. This plan called for "not just reparations, but Germany's return to its eighteenth-century 'agricultural and pastoral' economy, minus all 'war-making industry.' "[13] Germans, it was believed, were all warlike; hence they should be deprived of the tools for waging war.

Growing Allied Discord

On May 2, 1945, Berlin surrendered to the Russians, and on May 7 in Reims, France, the Germans agreed to the complete and unconditional surrender of all their forces. On August 14 the Japanese surrendered unconditionally on the

U.S. battleship *Missouri,* following Emperor Hirohito's announcement that "it is truly unbearable for the officers of the Army and Navy to surrender their arms and face the occupation of the country. . . . However, compared with the complete disappearance of Japan, even if only a few seeds survive, this would allow us to envisage recovery and a brighter future."[14]

At this point the victors faced a monumental challenge: how to overcome the exhilaration that followed the **strategic surrender** of their adversaries and begin to construct a postwar peace plan that all the Allies could accept. This challenge proved beyond the Allies' capacity, as their interests pushed them in divergent directions. Division rapidly replaced the harmony that had characterized the Allies' postwar peace discussions. As Winston Churchill lamented in his March 5, 1946, "Iron Curtain" speech in Fulton, Missouri, "a shadow [had] fallen upon the scene so lately lighted by Allied victory."[15]

That latent differences should emerge among the victors regarding the precise terms of the peace settlement is not surprising, because changes in global circumstances historically have preceded redefinitions of national interests, allegiances, and eventual realignments. However, at the end of the war there still remained a basis for the Allies' hope that they would continue to cooperate to build a stable world order: they had successfully overcome their differences during the war. This hope was exhibited in the high level of agreement that had attended the planning at various summit conferences for a new postwar structure of peace even as the war raged. As early as 1943 the Four Power Declaration advanced principles for Allied collaboration in "the period following the end of hostilities." The product of the Allies' determination to create a new international organization to manage the postwar international order—the United Nations—was conceived in this and other wartime agreements, to ward off any collapse of their collective spirit. Consistent with the expectation that the great-powers would collaborate to manage world affairs, China was promised a seat on the United Nations Security Council along with France. Recognizing the benefits of inclusiveness in an attempt to implement **collective security,** the purpose was to guarantee that all of the victorious great-powers would share responsibility for keeping the peace.

In practice, the United States and the Soviet Union became most influential because they were the most powerful. However, their ideological differences about capitalism and communism undercut the prospects for their continued solidarity. Still, Franklin Roosevelt and Joseph Stalin had made repeated promises to work together. Upon returning to Washington from the summit conference in Teheran, for instance, President Roosevelt told a national radio audience: "I got along fine with Marshal Stalin. . . . I believe that we are going to get along very well with him and the Russian people—very well indeed."[16] At the Yalta Conference fourteen months later, Stalin echoed Roosevelt's optimism. According to James F. Byrnes, director of the Office of War Mobilization, Stalin had been lavish in his praise of the United States; in fact, "Joe was the life of the party."[17]

Yet the period between the 1943 Teheran and 1945 Yalta summit conferences would mark the apogee of Soviet-American cooperative relations. The vague promises of continued unity voiced in these summits concealed many problems, and history would show that the party would end in sobering gloom. When their armies met on April 25, 1945, at the Elbe River, the common military threat had been destroyed. Nonetheless, long-gestating mutual suspicions in Moscow and Washington began to harden almost immediately into policy disagreements over the future of the postwar world. Following the death of Roosevelt in April and Germany's unconditional surrender, the United States, now represented by Harry S. Truman, met again with the Soviet Union and Great Britain at Potsdam in July 1945. The meeting ended without agreement over specifics or the larger issues beyond the transfer of territorial boundaries in Europe. The facade of Allied unity began to fade.

Interallied problems notwithstanding, an air of accommodation prevailed when the victory celebrations commenced. The victors arrived at agreement on some preliminary principles after the truce, in part as a consequence of the thoroughness of the Allied victory. Surrender was unconditional, and the devastated Axis powers were in no position to bargain. Taking advantage of their position of strength, the victors decided to remove Germany and Japan from the ranks of the great-powers. Germany was partitioned into four occupation zones that later were used as the basis for creating the Federal Republic of Germany (West Germany) and the German Democratic Republic (East Germany). Japan was occupied by the United States and divested of its conquests in Indochina and Korea.

Partitioning Germany into separate states was not a part of the victors' original peace plan. They had agreed to treat Germany as a single state, with the Allied Control Council in charge. However, the decision to divide Germany into four zones of occupation, with the military commanders-in-chief of each victor given complete administrative authority, had the unintended consequence of preventing any treatment of Germany as a single unit. The Allies' peace policy was therefore not **rational** in the sense that it could be described as a logically consistent and coherent decision. The step-by-step formula did not link means to goals, and the agreement to permit each occupying power to control reparations in its respective zone contradicted the original aim of overseeing Germany as a whole. This inconsistency made the outcome almost a foregone conclusion, when four years later the United States, Great Britain, and France decided to combine their zones in the west to create a central democratic government, freeing the Soviet Union to impose a communist regime in its **sphere of influence** in the remaining zone in the east. Differences among the leaders and within their nations about the best way to make a lasting peace also undermined allied harmony and pushed decision making about a postwar settlement in divergent directions.

Nonetheless, all the victors shared a conception of **justice**—about what was prudent and moral with regard to suitable punishment of Germany for its aggression and war crimes. The victors agreed that Germany should pay for its sins, and they agreed on four principles to carry out a retributive policy. First, they would destroy the remnants of Nazi ideology; Nazi leaders were tried as war criminals for crimes against humanity at the special court established at Nuremburg, which condemned twelve of them to death. Second, the victors agreed to demilitarize Germany, insisting on complete disarmament. Third, the victors undertook a coordinated effort to control and dismantle German industry, under their conviction that deindustrialization was necessary to ensure that Germany's remarkable engineering and technological talents could not be used for weapons production. And finally, at the urging by the West, the Allies agreed to a program of building democratic institutions within Germany as a deterrent to the rise of another totalitarian government under a new autocrat like Hitler. Although in implementation these principles were compromised, they defined the major ideals of the victors.

Most problematic was the issue of territory—who would obtain and control what. A Council of Foreign Ministers was created at the Potsdam Conference for the purpose of working out the terms of surrender in a way that was mutually satisfactory to the victors, but to little avail. Mistrust and acrimony divided the winners, and as **zero-sum** thinking about which victors deserved to gain at the other victor's expense, disagreement over the German question led to a settlement that proved unacceptable to all. This division bred a fierce competition that paralyzed collective decision making for many decades. Allied discord and distrust became the seeds from which the Cold War was to grow, as international borders were redrawn across the Eurasian landmass. Out of this redistribution of territorial boundaries the Soviet Union gained nearly 600,000 square meters of territory in the west from the Baltic states of Estonia, Latvia, and Lithuania and from Finland, Czechoslovakia, Poland, and Romania—territorial changes that enabled the Soviet Union to recover what Russia had lost after World War I. Poland was compensated with land taken from Germany.

Italy, too, was targeted for punitive treatment, although the perpetrators of Italian aggression were no longer on the scene when the final major peacemaking decisions were taking place. Italy ceased to be a real player in the war after Sicily fell to Anglo-American forces, and this sealed the fate of Il Duce, Benito Mussolini, and his fascist troops and collaborators. Fearing that Italy would defect to the Allies, Hitler had sent reinforcements to carry on the fight and watch over the king and Mussolini, whom Hitler restored as a puppet dictator. Mussolini did not survive long enough to see his German ally go down to defeat; he was captured and executed by Italian partisans. This took the sting out of the debate about how to treat Italy and the other minor states that had aligned with the Axis powers. At Potsdam, the Council of Foreign Ministers were assigned the task of negotiating the peace settlement with Italy and the other states that had been aligned with the German-Japanese Axis (Romania, Bulgaria, Hungary, and Finland) when they surrendered. The border and territorial transfer options considered by the Allies quickly became wrapped up in the larger controversies that poisoned the relationship between Moscow and its allies in Washington and London, as they searched in vain for a bargain to safeguard their goodwill and make a satisfactory peace settlement.

Finally, pro-Soviet regimes with the U.S.S.R.'s support assumed power throughout Eastern Europe (see Map 8.1). In the Far East, the Soviet Union took the four Kurile Islands, or the "Northern Territories" as Japan calls them, from Japan, and Korea was divided into Soviet and U.S. occupation zones at the thirty-eighth parallel.

World War II thus produced a massive redistribution of power based on landmass. The United States was the only one of the great powers whose economy grew during the war and surged to equal that of the rest of the world combined—the United States was not just wealthier than anyone, it was wealthier than everyone. The Soviet Union, though economically exhausted, possessed the largest army in the world, and its annexation of the northern half of East Prussia, along with its expanding sphere of influence, catapulted it to the status of a superpower. As the French political sociologist Alexis de Tocqueville had foreseen in 1835, the Americans and Russians fulfilled their national destinies and now held in their hands the fates of half the world's populaton. In comparison, all other states were dwarfs.

All alliances are inherently fragile, and even wartime allies tend to quarrel despite the bond of a common enemy. In this regard, the victorious "Grand Alliance" was never altogether "grand" while it collectively sought to engineer victory. The United States, Great Britain, and the Soviet Union had interests that were not always convergent, and this had become apparent at times even while the three Allies worked together to subdue Germany, Japan, and Italy. In fact, during the war, rivalry between the United States and the Soviet Union became evident, as distrust lingered that each was not truly an ally but, rather, had secret intentions to treat the other as the next enemy. For example, while still a U.S. senator, Harry Truman had fueled Soviet suspicions when he expressed the hope that, following Hitler's invasion of Russia, the Nazis and communists would destroy each other, declaring bluntly, "Let's help the Russians when the Germans are winning and the Germans when the Russians are winning so each may kill off as many as possible of the other."[18] Thus, the hostility felt by the American and Russian allies for one another, while glossed over during the war when the need to suppress the discord was overwhelming, was always recognized as a probable danger. Victory only magnified the growing distrust that each great power harbored about the others' motives in a turbulent environment pulsating with ill-defined borders, altered allegiances, power vacuums, and economic ruin.

Let us inspect more closely how the peace settlements struck at the end of World War II influenced Russian-American relations and with them international stability over the next fifty years. This was an era during which the Cold War unfolded, while Germany and Japan rose from the ashes of defeat to become prosperous economic powers without military ambitions. It is necessary

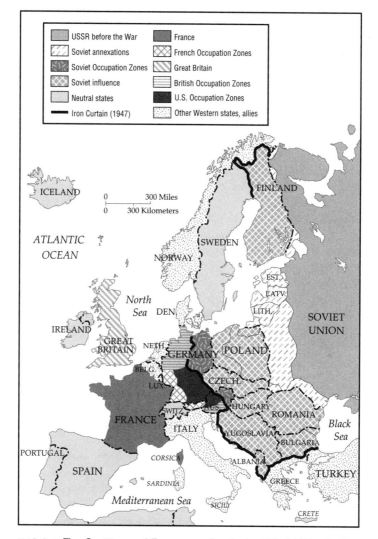

MAP 8.1 The Partitions of Europe at the End of World War II. The Allied victory in Europe shifted the European geostrategic landscape, as borders were redrawn and each of the victors dominated the zones their armies occupied when the fighting stopped. Discord among the winners over territorial issues led to the division between East and West as the so-called "Iron Curtain" separated the new rivals in the Cold War.

to review the policy redirections that took place in Washington and Moscow at the end of World War II when the two major victorious powers struggled to find a formula for peacefully managing international affairs.

The Origins of a Forty-Year Peace Settlement Process

The pre-eminent status of the United States and the Soviet Union at the top of the international hierarchy at the end of World War II gave each superpower reason to be wary of the other. However, their collision was not predetermined. After victory had been achieved, new efforts were made by both superpowers to construct rules for continuing cooperative engagement. These efforts proceeded crabwise, with zigs and zags in different directions through a series of agreements (see Table 8.2). Unfortunately, they did not succeed in reaching agreements; many issues (such as the future of Germany) were simply postponed without resolution. A final settlement was not reached until the Cold War ended a half-century later.

Why did the superpowers fail to reach a conclusive and permanent peace settlement that all the Allied victors could accept? To answer that question, we must put the problematic role of disagreements about how to treat the defeated nations of Germany and Japan into the equation. The Soviets and Americans came to very different conclusions on this fundamental issue, and those differences became the primary source of the failure to arrive at a final peace settlement for another four decades.

RESURRECTING GERMANY AND JAPAN

Despite their deep resentment of the German and Japanese aggressors, the United States and Great Britain began in the early postwar period to radically shift their thinking about the value of retribution. Recalling that the harsh terms of the Versailles treaty had contributed to the rise of fascism, "Churchill and Roosevelt threw their weight behind a more moderate policy, closer to the precept Churchill later quoted in his memoirs, 'In victory, magnanimity.' "[19] They repudiated vengeance in favor of a policy guided by forgiveness, in the expectation that assistance with the restoration and reform of Germany and Japan could repair those prostrate states and permit them to play a constructive role in the new world order. Rather than require reparations, the United States and Great Britain undertook steps to resuscitate their former enemies— much to the dismay of the Soviet Union, which clung tenaciously to the Allies' prior agreement to exact revenge. Clemency was not an option for Joseph Stalin.

TABLE 8.2
A Chronology of Postwar Peace Plans, 1945–1951

Date(s)	Proposed Plan	Goals
1945–1946	Nuremburg and Tokyo war crimes trials	Individual Nazi and Japanese policy-makers held accountable for their crimes against humanitarian international law
June 14, 1946	Baruch Plan to create the new UN Atomic Energy Commission	Creation of an international authority that would exercise monopoly control over all atomic energy production and use for war purposes (proposal was not accepted unanimously, with the Soviet Union leading the opposition)
February 10, 1947	Treaties of Paris	Italy loses its colonial empire, which became UN mandates, and cedes territory on the Adriatic Sea to Yugoslavia and the Dodeconese Islands to Greece
1947–1952	Marshall Plan (European Recovery Program)	Massive $50 billion U.S. foreign assistance program to rebuild Europe's war-torn economy, in order not only to ensure a market for American exports but to strengthen Europe's capacity to resist communist subversion and Soviet domination
1950	NSC 68	Top-secret U.S. strategic plan that called for increased military spending and a U.S. counteroffensive against the Soviet Union that endorsed the use of covert economic, political, and psychological warfare to incite unrest and revolt in countries aligned with the Soviet Union
September 8, 1951	Treaty of San Francisco	In agreement with forty-eight allied states, Japan accepts the loss of all territory acquired in its past wars since 1895 and consents to an imposed constitution which declares that "the Japanese people forever renounce war as a sovereign right of the nation"

Resuscitating Germany

Britain and the United States began to lose confidence in and patience with Joseph Stalin and against this background found it increasingly prudent to question the wisdom of a punitive approach to Germany and Japan. Given Russia's perceived intransigence, its prompt institutionalization of Russian regional hegemony over the eastern half of Europe (which had been liberated by the Red Army, with Roosevelt's tacit support[20]), and the heavy reparations it extracted in its zones of occupation, the United States began to rethink its prior punitive peace settlement philosophy toward Germany and Japan. At the same time, the United States was facing the reality of growing Soviet ambitions and the collapse of unity within the Allied Control Commission. The Soviets appeared intent on reaping the fruits of war and expanding their power, and, in light of this, U.S. leaders came to the conclusion that rising Russian influence needed to be balanced. That goal, in turn, required a different plan—one that replaced the impulse toward revenge with a policy seeking reconciliation with Germany and Japan. The spirit of Yalta and Potsdam quickly evaporated, and the interallied tension level escalated in the first few years after the surrender of Germany and Japan (see Box 8.2).

The signal of the U.S. change of heart was conveyed dramatically by U.S. Secretary of State James F. Byrnes. "The gamecock from South Carolina," as he was known, was in a fighting mood—not toward America's former enemy, but its former ally. In a major turning-point speech in Stuttgart on September 6, 1946, Byrnes drew a sword, which the Soviets promptly interpreted as not only an intentional breach in the Soviet-American relationship, but a declaration of enmity. In that speech (delivered in the only building of any size left standing in the city, the State Opera House), Byrnes declared that a policy of reform, rehabilitation, resuscitation, and reconciliation would now define U.S. policy toward West Germany. Germany, he informed the audience, would be allowed to earn its way back into the international community, and the United States would assist the reconstruction and democratization program. As Byrnes explained, the United States eschewed revenge and had chosen to seek Germany's renewal and reform, backed by financial assistance and the promise of U.S. military protection. After the American military band welcomed Byrnes to the podium with the rousing chorus of "Dixie," the secretary of state from South Carolina announced to his audience that the

> American people have no desire to enslave the German people. The American people want to return the government of Germany to the German people. The American people want to help the German people to win their way back to an honorable place among the free and peace-loving nations of the world.

Linking this initiative to political goals, Byrnes pledged that the United States would actively participate in the promotion of Germany's revival, declaring, "We will not shirk our duty. We are not withdrawing. We are staying here, and will furnish our proportionate share of the security forces."[21] In addition, Byrnes called for the "prompt formation of a provisional government with authority to administer the entire country so that Germans could once again manage their own affairs." In a repudiation to prior agreements, Byrnes refused to recognize the Oder-Neisse frontier between Germany and Poland, throwing American support behind the German people's wish for the restoration of the

BOX 8.2
THE END OF THE SOVIET-AMERICAN WARTIME ALLIANCE

1945

- United States rejects Soviet request for $6 billion reconstruction loan
- Churchill, Roosevelt, and Stalin sign Yalta agreement
- United States approves transfer of Kurile Islands to Soviet Union
- Moscow formally abrogates 1925 Turko-Soviet Friendship Treaty, makes territorial demands
- Truman cancels Lend-Lease allocations and shipments to the Allies
- Truman sends Harry Hopkins to Moscow to discuss postwar settlement
- Allied Control Council establishes four-power occupation of Berlin and right to determine Germany's boundaries
- San Francisco Conference approves UN Charter
- Korea partitioned into Soviet and American occupation zones
- Churchill, Stalin, and Truman attend Potsdam Conference
- United States drops atomic bomb on Hiroshima
- Chiang Kai-shek and Molotov sign Sino-Soviet friendship treaty
- Soviet-Polish treaty recognizes Oder-Neisse line as Poland's western border
- Council of Foreign Ministers meets in London
- Iranian rebellion, supported by Soviet arms, erupts; civil war resumes in China
- Big Three meet at Moscow Conference; Secretary of State James F. Byrnes agrees to recognize Romanian and Bulgarian satellite governments

1946

- People's Republic of Albania proclaimed
- Soviet Union protests British role in Greek civil war
- United States protests the continued presence of Soviet troops in Iran
- United States leads UN involvement in Iranian crisis over Soviet protest
- Stalin announces new Soviet Five-Year Plan making rearmament a priority for defense against foreign encroachment
- Churchill delivers militantly anti-Soviet Iron Curtain speech in Fulton, Missouri
- Council of Foreign Ministers convenes Paris Peace Conference
- General Lucius Clay stops reparations to Soviet zone of Germany
- Soviets reject Baruch Plan to destroy atomic weapons and place control of nuclear energy in international hands
- United States protests Soviet economic exploitation of Hungary
- Secretary of State Byrnes outlines U.S. policy for German war recovery in Stuttgart speech
- Nuremburg Tribunal sentences twelve Nazis to death and others to life imprisonment

- Japan's wartime leaders (including Emperor Hirohito) imprisoned or hanged following Tokyo trials
- United States signs treaty of friendship and commerce with China
- Iran crushes independence movement in Azerbaijan with U.S. aid
- Treaties at New York Foreign Ministers Conference confirm U.S. recognition of Soviet control in southeastern Europe
- War breaks out in Vietnam

1947

- The United States and Great Britain merge their occupation zones in Germany, January 1
- United States charges violation of Yalta agreement following communist electoral victory in Poland
- Britain and France sign a fifty-year Treaty of Alliance and Mutual Assistance at Dunkirk
- Truman Doctrine pledges aid to Greece, Turkey, and others resisting communism
- Big Four Foreign Ministers Conference in Moscow concludes without agreement
- Communists smash Hungarian ruling party
- Secretary of State George C. Marshall announces European Recovery Program (Marshall Plan)
- Under Soviet pressure, Poland and Hungary decline Marshall Plan assistance
- George F. Kennan's "X" article proposing U.S. containment of Soviet communism, based on 1946 telegram sent from Moscow, published in *Foreign Affairs*
- NSC-68 blueprint moves U.S. foreign policy from containment to confrontational strategy against Soviets
- Soviet Union charges that the United States threatens war
- General Agreement on Tariffs and Trade (GATT) treaty signed by twenty-three countries
- Rio Pact for collective defense of Western Hemisphere commits the United States and Latin American republics to mutual assistance against aggression
- United States, Australia, and New Zealand conclude ANZUS tripartite security treaty
- Comintern revived by Soviet Union and greatly expanded as Cominform
- London Council of Foreign Ministers ends without agreement on mutual administration of occupation zones in Germany

1948

- Communist coup occurs in Czechoslovakia
- Soviet Union withdraws from the Allied Control Council, March 20
- Brussels Treaty calls for cooperation among Belgium, France, Luxembourg, the Netherlands and the United Kingdom; creates Brussels Pact military alliance to repel attack

- Soviet Union imposes a blockade on Berlin (from June 20, 1948, until May 1949) after the Western powers implement currency reform in their occupation sectors of Germany
- United States and Great Britain supply West Berlin with a massive airlift
- Organization of European Economic Cooperation (OEEC) established to disburse Marshall Plan funds
- Organization of American States (OAS) created to replace the Pan American Union
- Vandenberg Resolution pledges U.S. support for Brussels Treaty and defense agreements in Europe
- Brussels Treaty powers, Canada, and the United States meet in Washington to create North Atlantic defense treaty

1949

- "Point Four" of Truman's inaugural address promises aid to developing countries
- Council for Mutual Economic Assistance (Comecon) is created for Soviet assistance in Europe
- Negotiating powers invite Denmark, Iceland, Italy, Norway, and Portugal to adhere to the North Atlantic Treaty
- Soviet Union protests that prospective North Atlantic Treaty Organization (NATO) is contrary to UN Charter
- NATO formed with signing of North Atlantic Treaty
- London Ten-Power Agreement creates the Council of Europe
- Berlin blockade lifted; separate West and East German governments established when Western powers' occupation zones are merged to form the Federal Republic of Germany and the Soviets establish the German Democratic Republic in their zone (Berlin remains under four-power occupation until the reunification of Germany in 1990)
- Mao Tse-tung unifies mainland China and proclaims People's Republic of China
- Greek civil war ends in communist defeat
- Mutual Defense Assistance Act pledges U.S. aid to countries vulnerable to communist pressure

1950

- United States announces intention to build hydrogen bomb
- Soviet Union begins eight-month boycott of UN Security Council
- Soviet Union and Communist China sign thirty-year Mutual Aid Pact
- National Security Council issues Memorandum No. 68
- North Korean forces invade South Korea and capture Seoul; U.S. troops enter Korea with orders to defend Formosa and prevent Chiang's forces from attacking mainland China
- United States invades North Korea; South Korean troops cross thirty-eighth parallel
- U.S. proposes to British and French that German divisions be added to NATO, though Potsdam agreement had forbidden German participation in Western European defense

- Greece and Turkey accept North Atlantic Council invitation to participate in Mediterranean defense planning
- East German-Polish treaty ends dispute over border
- UN General Assembly passes the Uniting for Peace Resolution

1951

- Secretary of State Marshall tells Senate that Chinese Nationalists were beaten by communists due to lack of public support and "the character of their government"
- San Francisco peace treaty ends state of war with Japan (Russia and China not included)
- Treaty establishing European Coal and Steel Community (ECSC) signed
- Mutual Security Act pledges U.S. military assistance throughout the world
- Korean truce line (thirty-eighth parallel) accepted at United Nations

sizable territory Germany had been required to cede to Poland (to compensate Poland for the territory it had been forced to cede to the Soviet Union).

The message to the relieved and applauding Germans was one of compassion. America would live up to the most charitable liberal ideals in its heritage, treating all others as equals in the community of nations. However, parochial self-interest also appeared as a U.S. motive: "This was a straightforward message to the Soviet Union that the United States was not going to permit Germany to be completely absorbed into any communist sphere."[22] This balance-of-power realpolitik policy was geared toward a clear geostrategic objective: to remove the Soviet Union from the path of the peace process and clear the way for the recovery of Germany, and with it, the rest of Europe.

With this turnabout in U.S. policy toward a conciliatory approach to the Germans, U.S. policy toward the Soviets had also changed and become combative. The wartime Allies would now proceed separately, acting independently in their respective spheres of influence. With the breakup of this wartime partnership, the European geostrategic landscape shifted, and the way was paved for the division of Europe into two blocs, with the east controlled by Moscow and the west dominated by the United States.

Resuscitating Japan

The new U.S. policy of assisting in the recovery of Germany did not mean that a nonretributive peace philosophy would remain confined to the European continent. The United States also abandoned a vindictive approach for a conciliatory one in the Far East. In Japan, "the Americans arrived not to conquer but to reform."[23] General Douglas MacArthur, the commander of the U.S.

occupation forces, built a recovery and reform program on the principle that, in a country in which "face" matters greatly, America's long-term interest did not sanction the humiliation of the Japanese. In August 1945 MacArthur stated his goals, and the liberal peace-making philosophy that would define U.S. policy in postwar Japan, when he directed the occupation forces he commanded to

> First, destroy the military power. Punish war criminals. Build the structure of representative government. Modernize the constitution. Hold free elections. Enfranchise the women. Release the political prisoners. Liberate the farmers. Establish a free labor movement. Encourage a free economy. Abolish police oppression. Develop a free and responsible press. Liberalize education. Decentralize political power. Separate church from state.

Overcoming the temptation to exact revenge, the United States embarked on a systematic reform and reconstruction program for the devastated enemy, whose colonial empire had been relinquished. Permitting the emperor to retain his position of prestige to facilitate Japanese compliance, the United States dismantled the country's feudal system and built new democratic institutions in its place. MacArthur's staff drafted a new constitution for Japan. It went into effect May 3, 1947, and sought to remake Japan in America's image. "The Occupation tried to import three things . . . : One, demilitarization and anti-militarism. Two: egalitarianism. And three: individual freedoms."[24] Article IX of the Constitution pledged that Japan would "forever renounce . . . the threat or use of force as a means of settling disputes" and prohibited Japan's right to maintain "land, sea, and air forces, as well as other war potential." Similarly, U.S. reform policy redistributed land from baron families to tenant farmers, gave women rights equal to men, and encouraged the formation of powerful trade unions. The Constitution also established a parliamentary form of democratic government similar to the British system and instituted procedures to protect civil liberties such as a free press and free speech.

Consistent with this reform program, the U.S. occupation forces exercised respect for those the United States had vanquished. Japanese customs and courtesies were honored, and MacArthur encouraged his own troops (whom he disarmed to lessen Japanese anxieties and resentment) to fraternize with the Japanese people and educate them about the meaning of democracy.

Behind the ideals inspiring the United States' compassionate policy of revival and reconciliation was a stronger, ulterior motive. The United States had powerful geostrategic interests in assisting Japan's recovery, because of its

> fear that an economically weak, militarily vulnerable Japan would become a tempting target for Soviet intimidation once the American occupation forces had been withdrawn. Thus in 1948–1949 the United States removed all restrictions on Japan's economic recovery, halted the requisition of capital equipment for reparations, abandoned plans for the forced decentralization of Japanese industry, and

began to furnish financial assistance to promote Japan's economic growth and social stability.[25]

Reconciliation and resuscitation, in short, served U.S. interests as well as its ideals; the compassionate postwar peace plan emerged from a combination of American faith in liberal democracy and the United States' need for a strong Japan which could be shaped into a faithful American ally. The philosophy practiced by the United States—treat the former enemy forgivingly, in conformity with the Golden Rule—bred Japanese goodwill and appreciation that paid huge dividends to the future Japanese-American diplomatic relationship.

The Treaty of San Francisco that was signed on September 8, 1951 (without inclusion of the Soviet Union, which did not issue a declaration ending its state of war with Japan until October 19, 1956), terminated the state of war with the United States and forty-eight other states and allowed the American occupation force to exit Japan on April 28, 1952. The treaty contained no demands for reparations or restrictions on Japan's foreign policy. The Treaty signaled the forceful conversion of Japan to a liberal democracy dedicated to peace. Japan's climb to the top of the global pyramid of economic power began. In addition, by reorganizing Japan's right to defend itself militarily, the Japanese peace settlement transformed the global **balance of power** and, by so doing, completed the break between the American and Soviet wartime allies.

> Very soon after the Occupation years, the United States became . . . more worried about keeping Japan both non-Communist and anti-Soviet than about any other aspect of its development. Emphasizing the essentially positive nature of Japan's post-Meiji development was useful from the Cold War perspective. China had been set up as the major counterexample in Asia, under the Soviet thumb at the time and committed to communism. The Japanese example could show a better path: toward both prosperity and democracy, in alliance with the United States.[26]

In conjunction, the U.S. shift from retaliation against to assistance of Germany and Japan produced changes of massive proportions. Both of these defeated foes soon became steadfast members of the community of liberal democratic and free-market capitalist states and the most reliable allies of the United States. Fed by vast sums of U.S. financial assistance under the shield of the U.S. nuclear umbrella, Germany and Japan also became economic giants. They were freed from the burden of heavy defense expenditures, and both were liberated from the legacy of their imperial traditions.

Germany's and Japan's active participation in the liberal economic order as U.S. allies undoubtedly contributed to the stability of the emerging **multipolar** system and its continuing prosperity in the free-trade regime among the industrialized deomcracies of the Global North. Despite the disorder that has afflicted, and continues to afflict, the zone of turmoil in the less-developed countries of the Global South, the achievement of the longest period of great-power peace in the past half-millennium testifies to the payoff that the compassionate reconstruction policies of the Western Allies provided. History has few cases of successful peace settlements that approximate this remarkable accomplishment—the most enduring **long peace.** By permitting Germany and Japan to reenter the liberal community of democratic nations, the United States allowed these states to build stable governments, provide leadership in the integration of a globalized political economy, and to participate in the defense of liberal values. Both former enemies became among the most faithful allies of the United States and major partners in trade, investment, and development-assistance ventures. In retrospect, the rewards and returns of this reconciliatory policy were remarkable and provided the basis for a **democratic peace** predicated on the principle that democratic governance, if it spreads, will be an antidote to war because democracies rarely wage war against each other.

This outcome of this resusitative policy should not automatically lead to the conclusion that the rewards of reconciliation between the Western Allies and the Axis powers came without substantial costs. The schism that culminated in the Cold War between the East and West exacted an enormous toll and became a primary consequence of the goodwill that allowed Germany and Japan to become members of the Western bloc that united in solidarity throughout the Cold War.

> "Peace, like war, can succeed only where there is a will to enforce it and where there is available power to enforce it."
>
> —FRANKLIN D. ROOSEVELT

That a compassionate peace settlement between Germany and Japan and the United States could cause a Cold War to break out between the United States and the Soviet Union presents a puzzle. Is intra-allied discord and disunity a likely price in the aftermath of victory? Was the Soviet-American conflict necessary? Did the differences in the postwar peace goals and philosophies of the victors produce this colossal hegemonic struggle between two titans and postpone final resolution of a post-World War II settlement for over forty years?

THE POST–WORLD WAR II ORIGINS OF THE COLD WAR

Lacking the glue of a common external threat, the Grand Alliance of World War II began to dissolve amidst distrust, apprehension, and recriminations. Stalin insisted in 1946 that the defeat of Germany did not eliminate the danger of foreign aggression, and his heir apparent, Andrei Zhdanov, in 1947 identified American expansionism as the major threat to world peace. On the other hand, W. Averell Harriman, U.S. ambassador to the Soviet Union, warned of a probable "barbarian invasion of Europe"[27] from America's former wartime ally.

The United States and the Soviet Union, former partners in war, ceased to remain allies and became foes. Each superpower acted in accordance with the realpolitik premise that the only language a recalcitrant rival understands is military might. President Truman, a staunch realist, for example, argued that "unless Russia is faced with an iron fist and strong language, another war is in the making."[28] Secretary of State James F. Byrnes agreed, maintaining, "The only way to negotiate with the Russians is to hit them hard."[29]

The Cold War originated in part because of the superpowers' mutual disdain for their rivals' political system and way of life. As U.S. Secretary of State James F. Byrnes argued at the conclusion of World War II, "There is too much difference in the ideologies of the United States and Russia to work out a long-term program of cooperation." Such assumptions were widely held in both Washington and Moscow, and these ideological differences converted the rivalry from a conflict of interests between two powerful states to a conflict between two opposed philosophies for organizing systems of governance and economics within states. Whether real or imagined, U.S. fears of Marxism stoked the flames of anticommunism at home and ignited a global crusade to remove the communist ideology from the face of the earth.[30] The rupture in U.S.-Soviet relations occurred bit by bit, ultimately producing a schism that would place the competitors for global hegemonic leadership in the throes of a classic **security dilemma** that reduced their sense of safety, and placed the rest of humanity on the edge of nuclear destruction. As UN Secretary-General Trygve Lie lamented on September 23, 1947, in his plea for a return to the spirit of Yalta and San Francisco, "The very cornerstone of the UN, Big Power cooperation and understanding, is being shaken."[31]

American leaders acted on the perception that the triumph of communism in one country would cause the fall of its neighbors, and still others in turn. This prediction, which became known as the **domino theory**, maintained that, like a row of falling dominoes, a chain reaction would bring the entire world under communist domination unless checked by the power of the United States and its allies. Similarly, Soviet policy was energized by the assumption that in the long run capitalism could not coexist with communism. "A funeral dirge will be sung either over the Soviet Republic or over world capitalism," Lenin once predicted.[32] Believing that their security would be enhanced if class struggle spread across the globe, Soviet leaders were dismayed by their former wartime allies' efforts to smother communist movements in Japan, Germany, and other states within their occupation zones.

Mistrustful states are prone to see in their own actions only virtue and in those of their adversaries only malice. When such **mirror images** exist, hostility becomes likely.[33] Each side imposes its definition of reality on events, and they then become captives to those nightmarish visions. George F. Kennan, the American ambassador to the Soviet Union in 1952, noted how misread signals, common to both sides, eroded the wartime allies' unity:

The Marshall Plan, the preparations for the setting up of a West German government, and the first moves toward the establishment of NATO were taken in

Moscow as the beginnings of a campaign to deprive the Soviet Union of the fruits of its victory over Germany. The Soviet crackdown on Czechoslovakia (1948) and the mounting of the Berlin blockade, both essentially defensive . . . reactions to these Western moves, were then similarly misread on the Western side. Shortly thereafter there came the crisis of the Korean War, where the Soviet attempt to employ a satellite military force in civil combat to its own advantage, by way of reaction to the American decision to establish a permanent military presence in Japan, was read in Washington as the beginning of the final Soviet push for world conquest; whereas the active American military response, provoked by this move, appeared in Moscow . . . as a threat to the Soviet position in both Manchuria and in eastern Siberia.[34]

Thus, in the Cold War's formative stage, U.S. leaders and their allies in the West saw the many crises that erupted as part of a Soviet plan for world domination. The Soviets viewed these same crises altogether differently—as tests of their resolve and as Western efforts to destroy their socialist experiment. Both states operated from the same "inherent bad faith" image of their rival's intentions, and this precluded their cooperation in postwar planning for peace.

Additional factors beyond those rooted in divergent interests, ideologies, and images undoubtedly combined to transform a wartime Soviet-American alliance into an explosive hegemonic rivalry. Whatever the relative influence of the individual factors that combined to produce it, the Cold War's rise was profoundly affected, in the last analysis, by the realignment of the vanquished World War II powers (Germany and Japan) with two of the victors (the United States and Great Britain). The great schism between the United States and the Soviet Union that converted former allies into Cold War antagonists was accelerated by the Western powers' conciliatory patterns toward Germany and Japan and the Soviet Union's belief that this move was designed to encircle the Soviet Union and smother the communist movement. "Nothing," Harry Truman had argued at the organizing conference of the United Nations in San Francisco, was "more essential to the future peace of the world than the continued cooperation of the nations which had to muster the force necessary to defeat the conspiracy of the Axis powers to dominate the world."[35] That cooperation, however, had collapsed. With its collapse came the collapse of the postwar peace settlement process.

THE LONG ROAD TO A POSTWAR PEACE SETTLEMENT

Once the wartime alliance had splintered into two competing factions, the challenge for the United States and the Soviet Union became that of developing rules to prevent their Cold War from turning hot. The postwar settlement with the Axis powers could not be finalized until this obstacle was overcome. During the treacherous course of the next forty years, the two superpowers struggled in their search to avoid war. Mutual recrimination often poisoned their efforts. However, the challenge was eventually met. A set of rules gradually emerged, through trial and error, and disputes between the Kremlin and the White House never escalated to war. Among the implicit rules in this **security regime** were an acceptance of separate spheres of influence, avoidance of direct military confrontations, maintenance of a sharp distinction between conventional and nuclear weapons, and forgoing the first use of the latter. Still, both sides paid a staggering price for their rivalry. The United States alone spent an estimated ten trillion dollars to contain the Soviet Union, an expenditure equivalent to "enough to buy everything in the United States except the land."[36] The costs of waging the Cold War were not just financial; both sides paid a heavy psychological price. They had to survive in the shadow of possible nuclear annihilation. Throughout the Cold War's long evolution, there were many periods when fears of nuclear war increased as tension mounted and the arms race escalated, interrupted by occasional periods of **détente** when confrontation was replaced by a relaxation of tension between the adversaries. Yet, over the troubled course of this global contest of will, the former allies during World War II managed to coexist peacefully without taking up arms against each other directly. Given a circumstance involving a choice between nonviolence and nonexistence, the enemies choose to peacefully coexist.

Exhausted economically, the Soviet Union under a reform-minded Mikhail Gorbachev sought to reconcile his country's differences with the liberal democracies in the capitalist West in order to halt the Soviet Union's deteriorating global position. His pursuit of **rapprochement**—"normalization" of relations—paid a big and unexpected dividend: The Cold War—which began in Europe and had centered on Europe for over forty years—ended there in 1991, when the Soviet Union dissolved. All communist governments in the Soviet **bloc** in Eastern Europe permitted democratic elections in which Communist Party candidates routinely lost. Capitalist free markets replaced socialism and, to nearly everyone's astonishment, the Soviet Union acquiesced in these revolutionary changes.

This momentous sea change allows us to appreciate how a true peace settlement of the scars of World War II was finally reached when the Berlin Wall was torn down in 1989 and the Warsaw Pact began to disintegrate. It was not really until 1990, when the Soviet Union reversed its long-standing opposition to German reunification and agreed to withdraw its troops from Europe (in exchange for the promise that Germany would not rearm and that the United States would keep a military presence on German soil through NATO), that the Cold War ended and a final settlement of the disagreements that surfaced at the end of the Second World War was truly struck. On September 12, 1990, the Four Powers (the United States, the Soviet Union, Great Britain, and France) and the two Germanys (the "Two plus Four") signed the Treaty on the Final Settlement with Respect to Germany, which terminated the Four Powers' rights over Germany and made the reunification of Germany possible. German leaders agreed to make no territorial claims in Europe, including the territories in

---

CONTROVERSIES TO CONTEMPLATE

- What issues were at stake when the victors in World War II began discussions to fulfill the mission described in December 9, 1941, by Franklin D. Roosevelt: "We are going to win the war and we are going to win the peace"?
- Did the victors learn lessons about how to build peace from the failures of the post-World War I settlement at Versailles a generation earlier? What were those perceived lessons? Were they accurate?
- Is it possible to plan for peace when a war is still being fought? What obstacles interfere with successful postwar planning? Was Winston Churchill wise when he advised, "It is a mistake to look too far ahead. Only one link in the chain of destiny can be handled at one time"?
- Can wartime alliances outlast the defeat of common enemies? What problems bred competition and conflict among the former Allies of World War II?
- Did the Grand Alliance of the victors disintegrate because of their divergent philosophies about lenient vis-à-vis punitive treatment of vanquished enemies? To what extent did the differences in the victors' types of political and economic systems cause them to part ways?
- Why did the United States (and Great Britain) treat Germany and Japan so leniently after World War II, considering the injustice of the aggressors' cause and criminality of their brutal wartime deeds?
- Was the post-World War II settlement successful or flawed? What are the best criteria for evaluating success or failure?
- What international, societal, institutional, and individual variables most influenced the victors' war-making and peace-making decisions?
- Were the postwar peace-keeping approaches of the United States, Great Britain, and the Soviet Union inspired most by realist or liberal thought? What does this case say about the relative benefits and limitations of these two theories?

Poland that were annexed during and after World War II.[37] Moreover, German leaders pledged never to obtain nuclear, biological, or chemical weapons and to reduce their 670,000-person armed forces to 370,000 troops (in exchange for the removal of 370,000 Soviet soldiers from Germany). Afterward, Germany and the Soviet Union signed a bilateral treaty under which the two powers promised never to attack each other but instead to cooperate economically for the next twenty years.

The dramatic change these agreements produced was enshrined in the 1992 Camp David Declaration on New Relations, which proclaimed that "from now on the relationship [between Russia and the United States] will be characterized by friendship and partnership, founded on mutual trust." At long last, the Cold War was over, and with its collapse it was finally possible for the issues left unresolved since the end of World War II to be put to rest.

There is a possible lesson suggested by this exceptional case about the prospects for peace making, because the abrupt end of the Cold War suggested something quite different from the lesson of the two World Wars: that **enduring rivalries** between great-powers are doomed to end in armed conflict. The Cold War was different; it came to an end peacefully. This suggests that great-powers with hegemonic aspirations are capable of settling their struggles without bloodshed and that it is sometimes possible for them to build "enduring détentes" to manage their competition and eventually resolve their disputes.

> "Compromise does not mean cowardice."
>
> —JOHN F. KENNEDY

As we have seen in this chapter, military victory can easily breed conflict among victorious allies unless they manage their relationship carefully. It is important for them to reach a consensus on the terms of a postwar settlement before their guns fall silent. Victors must prepare for peace if they wish it to prevail, and preparations for constructing a satisfactory peace settlement should begin early in the war.

NOTES

1. Hitler is reported to have declared when he heard that the Soviet Union had agreed to the German-Soviet nonaggression treaty on August 23, 1939, "Now Europe is mine. The others can have Asia."
2. Holsti, 1991, pp. 224–225.
3. Ibid., p. 243.
4. Shriver, 1996, p. 77.
5. In Kissinger, 1994, p. 390.
6. Holsti, 1991, p. 243.
7. Morgenthau, 1985, p. 591.
8. In Holsti, 1991, p. 243.
9. See Jenkins, 1995.
10. Shriver, 1995, p. 133.
11. Davies, 1994, p. 23.
12. In Green, 1982, p. 94, citing a speech Bradley delivered on Armistice Day in 1948.
13. Shriver, 1996, p. 79.
14. In Iklé, 1991, p. 54.
15. In Cook, 1989, p. 53.
16. *Public Papers and Addresses of Franklin D. Roosevelt, 1943*, p. 558.
17. In Yergin, 1977, p. 67.
18. *New York Times,* June 23, 1941.
19. In Ardagh, 1987, pp. 10–11.
20. Keylor, 1996, p. 255.
21. In Cook, 1989, p. 44.

22. Puchala, 1996, p. A9.
23. Keylor, 1996, p. 268.
24. Literary critic Shuichi Kato, in Fallows, 1994, p. 149.
25. Keylor, 1996, p. 359.
26. Fallows, 1994, p. 142.
27. In Truman, 1955, p. 71.
28. Truman, 1955, p. 552.
29. In Paterson, 1978, p. 314.
30. Commager, 1983; Morgenthau, 1985; Gardner, 1970.
31. In Schuman, 1958, p. 235.
32. In Kegley and Wittkopf, 1997, p. 83.
33. See Bronfenbrenner, 1971.
34. Kennan, 1976, pp. 683–684.
35. In Kissinger, 1994, p. 424.
36. Sagan, 1992, p. 24.
37. The German-Polish treaty of November 14, 1990, confirmed the continuation of the Oder-Neisse border as the permanent frontier between these two states.

· 9 ·

VACANT VICTORY:
THE PERSIAN GULF WAR

The end game: it was bad.
MAJOR GENERAL BARRY McCAFFREY,
COMMANDER, 24TH U.S. MECHANIZED DIVISION

PREVIEW

World Wars I and II were complex, global wars that radically altered the international distribution of military and economic power. Not every war involves such stupendous collisions between great-powers. Many wars are asymmetrical: they involve contestants that are unequal in military capability and economic resources. While asymmetrical wars may have a significant impact on the belligerents and their immediate neighbors, they seldom have enormous long-term consequences for the structure and processes operating within the larger world system.

Our final case describes the Persian Gulf War of 1991, an asymmetrical conflict between Iraq and a large, diverse coalition led by the United States. Various asymmetrical wars could have been selected to compare with the system-transforming wars covered in previous chapters. We have selected the Persian Gulf War for several reasons. As the first war of the post-Cold War era, it provides an opportunity to probe the limits of multilateral peace enforcement under the auspices of the reinvigorated United Nations. Nothing like this had been approved by the Security Council for four decades. Second, as the world's first electronic war—fought with stealth aircraft, infrared targeting systems, precision-guided weapons, and global positioning satellite devices—it gives us a glimpse of what warfare and the problems of peace making may be in the twenty-first century. Finally, although the outcome of the Persian Gulf War did not transform the world system, it did have wider implications for regional security in the Middle East and for the energy policies of industrialized nations in Europe, Asia, and North America.

As you read this case, think about the cross pressures buffeting the United States as it searched for an appropriate response to the Iraqi invasion of Kuwait. Policymakers in Washington realized they could not afford to conduct the war unilaterally; they had to persuade other states to share the financial costs. But to garner international support they would have to reconcile multiple conflicting interests. Not only did the Bush administration need to be attentive to the mood of a public fixated on live reports from the war zone broadcast by the Cable News Network (CNN), it also had to balance myriad demands from Israel, numerous Arab states, Japan, NATO allies and the Soviet Union. How could the United States hold its unwieldy coalition together during and after the war? How could it defeat Saddam Hussein without making him a martyr? How could a peace be constructed that did not provide opportunities for Iran or other dissatisfied states to increase their influence over the region?

■ ■

Speaking from the Oval Office on February 27, 1991, President George Bush proclaimed a victory "for all mankind, for the rule of law, and for what is right." Kuwait had been liberated from Iraqi occupation. Reminding the nation of his promise that Iraq's aggression against the tiny, oil-rich emirate would not stand, the president announced all military objectives had been achieved. After expressing pride in "the people whose strength and resolve made victory quick, decisive, and just," he concluded by highlighting the next challenge facing the United States: "We must now begin to look beyond victory in war. We must meet the challenge of securing the peace."

At the time of the invasion, Iraqi leader Saddam Hussein possessed the fourth largest army in the world. It was regarded as "a professionally competent, well-equipped, well-led, and well-trained force with considerable experience in combined arms warfare."[1] Seasoned by eight years of war with Iran, Saddam's military machine included an extensive chemical weapons arsenal, an array of medium-range ballistic missiles, and a proven ability to mount a tenacious defense. In view of these strengths, commentators as varied as Patrick Buchanan and Senator Edward Kennedy (D-MA) warned that any attempt by the United States to evict Iraq from Kuwait would cost thousands of Americans their lives.[2] According to conventional wisdom, liberating Kuwait by military means would "most likely be bloody and protracted."[3] Rumors had circulated in Washington that the Pentagon ordered sixteen thousand body bags in preparation for war. But instead of a long, grinding campaign with heavy U.S. casualties, Iraq was routed in one of the most one-sided military engagements in history. "By God," George Bush would later exclaim, "we've kicked the Vietnam syndrome once and for all."[4]

Yet Bush was worried about the future. Saddam Hussein's forces had been crushed but the Iraqi dictator was still in power. The president's trepidation about "screwing up" the war "with a sloppy muddled ending"[5] emerged during his first press conference after the fighting had ended. Responding to a reporter's question about his somber mood, Bush admitted: "I want to see an end. You mention World War II. There was a definite end to that conflict. And now we have Saddam Hussein still there, the man that wreaked the havoc upon his neighbors."[6]

If the military victory over Iraq appeared tainted by unfinished political business, at least the president's position at home looked secure. Buoyed by battlefield success, his approval rating among the American electorate climbed to 89 percent, the highest rating for any president during the five decades that the Gallup organization had been polling public opinion. In the words of the *Arkansas Democrat-Gazette*, George Bush stood over the "political horizon like a colossus."[7] Ironically, just twenty months later, Bush suffered a stunning defeat in the 1992 presidential election at the hands of Arkansas governor Bill Clinton. Meanwhile, Saddam Hussein's tyrannical rule in Baghdad remained as strong as ever.

THE ONE WHO CONFRONTS

Saddam Hussein was born on April 28, 1937, to a peasant family in the impoverished village of al-Auja. Raised by an abusive stepfather, he later moved to Baghdad to live with his maternal uncle, a fervent nationalist who cultivated the belief that Hussein was destined to follow in the footsteps of Nebuchadnezzar, the ancient Babylonian conqueror, and Saladin, the Arab warrior who defeated the Crusaders. In Baghdad, Hussein became immersed in political activism, joining the Baath Party and articulating its rallying cry that "the primary method of achieving [Arab unity] . . . is through armed struggle."[8] In 1956, he supported a failed coup attempt against King Faisal II, and a few years later he participated in an attack on the general who had assumed power after deposing the king. In Hussein's mind, he was the heir to Gamal Abdul Nasser, the Egyptian president seen by many during the 1950s and 1960s as the symbolic leader of the Arab world.

When the Baath Party seized control of Iraq in 1968, Saddam Hussein began his ascent to absolute power. Angered by rifts within the party, he created a secret-police apparatus loyal to himself alone. His reputation for ruthlessness and his alliance with the secret police combined to provide Hussein a foundation for achieving the presidency of Baathist Iraq in 1979. Ever suspicious of potential rivals, he purged the party of many of its senior members and established a cult of personality around Saddam the "father/leader." Massive billboards, murals, and statues across the country depicted him as a triumphant field marshal, a devout Muslim in prayer, or as a simple peasant surrounded by children. Through religious symbolism, he cultivated his image as a fearless defender of the Muslim community who would not submit to anyone but God. In the cutthroat environment of Iraqi politics, Saddam Hussein was a shrewd tactician and savage competitor who demanded unconditional subservience. Underneath his lavish presidential palace sat a vast bunker constructed of steel and prestressed concrete. As one observer of the Iraqi leader has written, "The architecture of this complex is Saddam's psychological architecture: a defiant, grandiose facade resting on the well-fortified foundation of a siege mentality."[9]

It would be difficult to imagine two men from more different backgrounds than Saddam Hussein and George Herbert Walker Bush. The former, whose name in Arabic means "the one who confronts," had a modest education and little experience outside the Middle East. The latter came from elitist stock, attended Andover and Yale, and served as American envoy to China, U.S. ambassador to the United Nations, and director of the Central Intelligence Agency. Whereas Hussein was an opportunist who would eliminate anyone he perceived as an impediment no matter how loyal they might have been in the past, Bush, a self-avowed pragmatist, was a practitioner of consensual politics who valued the camaraderie of old friends. The Iraqi president's pursuit of personal power was boundless. The American president saw public service as a citizen's highest calling. Products of different worlds, neither man understood the personal motives and political calculations of the other. Yet their fates would soon become intertwined.

"I WILL CHOP OFF HIS ARM AT THE SHOULDER "

Early on the morning of August 2, 1990, columns of T-72 tanks from Saddam Hussein's elite Republican Guard crossed their country's southern border and raced down a six-lane superhighway toward Kuwait City (see Map 9.1). Allegedly his troops had been invited by revolutionaries to assist in liberating Kuwait from the rule of a corrupt minority, the al-Sabah family and their minions. Within hours, resistance to the invasion collapsed. Announcing that the new provisional government of Kuwait wanted to rejoin the "motherland" through an "eternal merger," Saddam Hussein issued a decree making the emirate the nineteenth province of Iraq and threatened to "turn Kuwait into a graveyard" if any foreign power intervened.[10]

Iraq's claim to Kuwait stretched back to the days of the Ottoman Empire, when Kuwait was an administrative subdivision of the Iraqi province of Basra. After the dismemberment of the Ottoman Empire following its defeat in World War I, the borders between Iraq and Kuwait were redrawn by the victorious British at the 1922 Uqair conference. Iraqi dissatisfaction with these frontiers was voiced by King Ghazi ibn Faisal during the 1930s, and again in 1961 by President Abdul Karim Qassim. Seizing upon this history of territorial frustration, Saddam Hussein asserted that his recovery of "lost" Iraqi land was just,

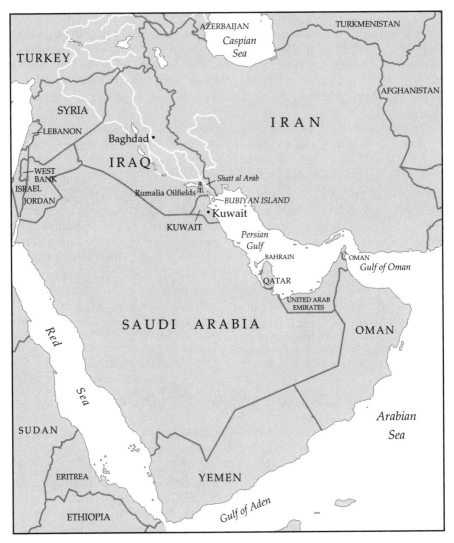

MAP 9.1 The Persian Gulf Region. Iraq is situated in the strategic center of the oil-rich and politically unstable Middle East—a region composed of states with a history of recurrent rivalries and episodic warfare. The Persian Gulf War erupted when Iraqi leader Saddam Hussein sent a powerful army into Kuwait to secure territory that he maintained was within the traditional boundaries of his country.

because it redressed an old wrong. To ensure their petroleum interests, he argued, "Western colonialism divided and established weak states ruled by families . . . [that] kept the wealth away from the masses." Now "the branch had been returned to the tree trunk."[11]

In addition to this historical claim, Hussein spelled out more recent griev-ances to justify his blitzkrieg. Kuwait, he charged, was engaged in economic aggression against Iraq. Rather than behaving like Arab brothers, the al-Sabah family had thrust a poisoned dagger into the back of the Iraqi nation. On the one hand, it had exceeded the oil-production quota set by the Organization of Petroleum Exporting States (OPEC), therein driving prices down at the very moment that Baghdad needed revenue to rebuild after its eight-year war with Iran. On the other hand, Kuwait purportedly had been drilling under Iraq's border in order to extract oil from the Rumalia field. Prior to the invasion, Tariq Aziz, the Iraqi foreign minister, listed a series of demands to be met by Kuwait to avert war. Included among these were demands for (1) $2.4 billion in compensation for the oil "stolen" from the Rumalia field; (2) cancellation of the debt Iraq incurred to Kuwait during the war with Iran, estimated at $40 billion; (3) $10 billion in aid to help Iraq recover from the war; and (4) a long-term lease on Bubiyan and Warba, two strategically important islands guard-ing Iraq's access to the Persian Gulf. If these demands were not met, Saddam Hussein would take what he wanted: "If anyone tries to stop me," he threat-ened, "I will chop off his arm at the shoulder."[12]

"IF KUWAIT'S EXPORT WAS ORANGES . . ."

Iraq's invasion caught the White House off guard. Throughout the previous decade, the United States and Iraq had coinciding interests: Each nation saw Iran as a threat to its position in the region (see Table 9.1). The Ayatollah Ruholla Khomeini had denounced the United States as the "Great Satan" and called for a holy war against Saddam Hussein. When hostilities erupted be-tween Iraq and Iran, the Reagan administration adopted one of the core tenets of realpolitik—the enemy of an enemy is a friend. In search of an ally, the United States removed Baghdad from its list of state sponsors of terrorism, thus making the country eligible for U.S. government–financed export cred-its as well as arms and technology sales. American officials proclaimed Iraq was changing and a prominent foreign policy consultant dismissed Hussein's "Butcher of Baghdad" image as a stereotype.[13] Because Iraq was seen as a modernizing state seeking a respected position within the world community, almost everyone in the Bush White House believed that the threats against Kuwait were a bluff. Even Egyptian president Hosni Mubarak insisted that the dispute between Iraq and Kuwait was "a cloud that would pass with the wind."[14]

Prior to the invasion, the Bush presidency was foundering. Little headway had been made on resolving the problems of crime, poverty, and skyrocketing health care costs. Moreover, the President had reneged on his "no new taxes" pledge and was hounded by suspicions of his earlier involvement in the so-called

TABLE 9.1
A Chronology of the Persian Gulf War

Year	Event
1979	The Shah of Iran relinquishes power in January; the Ayatollah Khomeini leads the new government. Iranians seize U.S. embassy personnel as hostages in November. On July 16, Saddam Hussein becomes president of Iraq and commander-in-chief of the country's armed forces.
1980	The Iran-Iraq War begins.
1982	U.S. forces sent to Lebanon as part of a multinational peace-keeping force. The Reagan administration initiates its opening to Saddam Hussein by removing Iraq from the list of states that sponsor terrorism.
1983	A bombing at Beirut airport kills 241 U.S. Marines in October; the remaining marines withdrawn from Lebanon the following February.
1988	Iran and Iraq agree to a cease-fire.
1990	Iraq invades Kuwait on August 2; UN Security Council Resolution 660 demands Iraq's withdrawal and Resolution 661 calls for economic sanctions against Iraq. Operation Desert Shield begins. In November, Resolution 678 authorizes member states to use all necessary means to evict Iraq from Kuwait.
1991	Operation Desert Storm commences on January 17 with an air assault and is followed by a ground offensive on February 24. A cease-fire is declared one hundred hours later. Kurds in northern Iraq and Shiite Muslims in southern Iraq rebel during March; both rebellions are crushed by the Iraqi military. On April 3, UN resolution 687 specifies terms for a permanent cease-fire between Iraq and the American-led coalition. UN inspection teams begin work in May.
1996	Iraqi armored forces violate the 1991 cease-fire agreement by entering the Kurdish city of Irbil; the United States responds by attacking Iraqi targets with cruise missiles.
1997	Iraq bars UN inspectors from examining suspected weapons sites; the United States responds with a massive military buildup in the region.
1998	UN Secretary-General Kofi Annan reaches an agreement with Saddam Hussein in February over weapons inspections. In March, the UN Security Council warns Iraq of severe consequences if it violates the agreement.

Iran-Contra affair, in which the Reagan administration had secretly sold arms to Iran in order to fund a covert war against the Sandinista government of Nicaragua. A cautious, practical decisionmaker, George Bush valued patience and prudence over impulsiveness and improvisation. Reputed to be a "man of the moment" who tackled problems in an ad hoc fashion, Bush's foreign policy was widely criticized for lacking a "grand design."[15] His detractors scoffed, "He believes in doing nothing—but doing it well."[16]

In a stark departure from his record of temporizing, President Bush's response to the August invasion was strong and unequivocal. With personal ties to the emirate from his days with Zapata Petroleum, he defined the crisis in terms of good versus evil: Kuwait was the victim; Saddam Hussein, the villain. When Treasury Secretary Nicholas Brady spoke of adapting to the situation, Bush snapped: "Let's be clear about one thing: We are not here to talk about adapting. We are not going to plan how to live with this."[17]

George Bush responded to the invasion as if it were a personal affront. Though a patrician heritage encouraged his "kinder, gentler" side, he often lashed out at challengers, a trait satirized by Garry Trudeau when he gave Bush a mean-spirited twin called "Skippy" in his Doonesbury cartoon strip. It was this tougher, more aggressive George Bush who responded in 1988 to jokes about his wimpiness with one of the most negative presidential campaigns in years. Challenges have "always been a critical, self-defining mechanism, which he has used to reinforce positive feelings about himself and to compensate for whatever self-doubts he may have."[18] As Bush acknowledged in his acceptance speech at the 1988 Republican National Convention, "I am a man who sees life in terms of missions . . . missions defined and missions completed."[19]

Iraq's annexation of Kuwait presented George Bush with a new mission. In a speech delivered on August 8, he seized the opportunity to dispel his image as a leader who lacked "vision" and starkly outlined the mission's objectives:

> First, we seek the immediate, unconditional, and complete withdrawal of all Iraqi forces from Kuwait. Second, Kuwait's legitimate government must be restored to replace the puppet regime. And third, my administration, as has been the case with every president from President Roosevelt to President Reagan, is committed to the security and stability of the Persian Gulf. And fourth, I am determined to protect the lives of American citizens abroad.[20]

A pilot whose aircraft had been shot down during battle in World War II, Bush saw the crisis in the Gulf through the lens of the 1930s. As he told the United Nations General Assembly, "Iraq's unprovoked aggression is a throwback to another era, a dark relic from a dark time."[21] In his eyes, Saddam Hussein was another Adolf Hitler, demagogic and maneuvering to conquer defenseless countries. Less than a month later, in a speech delivered before a joint session of Congress, the president added another objective to his mission:

> The crisis in the Persian Gulf, as grave as it is, also offers a rare opportunity to move toward a historic period of cooperation. Out of these troubled times, our fifth objective—a new world order—can emerge: a new era, freer from the threat of terror, stronger in the pursuit of justice, and more secure in the quest for peace.[22]

"We will succeed in the gulf," Bush promised in his 1991 State of the Union Address. "And when we do, the world community will have sent an enduring warning to any dictator or despot, present or future, who contemplates outlaw aggression."[23]

From Bush's perspective, Britain and France failed to deter German aggression at the 1938 Munich Conference due to a series of miscalculations regarding Hitler's character. The Führer was not a prudent leader with limited territorial aims, such as the Prussian chancellor, Otto von Bismarck, who had masterminded German unification over a half century earlier through shrewd diplomacy and the calculated exercise of military might. In contrast, Adolf Hitler was an avaricious and untrustworthy dictator. Anglo-French vacillation in the face of Hitler's remilitarization of the Rhineland, their acquiescence to his annexation of Austria, and their efforts to appease the Nazi leader were among the foreign policy mistakes Bush believed had led to World War II. If London and Paris stood firm and communicated a credible threat to punish aggression, German expansion would have been contained. Each time the Western democracies failed to show resolve, Hitler was emboldened to make further encroachments on contiguous countries.

Vowing not to ignore the lessons of the 1930s, the Bush administration formulated a response based on three rules of **realist** statecraft: (1) Do not make unnecessary concessions to aggressive, deceitful opponents; they cannot be accommodated. If aggressors pocket an easily achieved concession, they will be encouraged to press for more. Expecting a cruel, rapacious opponent to foreswear expansion and adhere religiously to his promises invites more aggression. "A half century ago," the president told those attending the 91st National Convention of the Veterans of Foreign Wars, "the world had the chance to stop a ruthless aggressor and missed it. I pledge to you: We will not make that mistake again."[24] (2) Negotiate with aggressive, deceitful opponents from a position of strength; the language of military might is the only language they understand. A preponderance of power was seen by the president and those around him as a prerequisite for making intransigent opponents bargain in earnest. Conciliatory gestures made after unjustified demands would only be taken as a sign of weakness. As General Colin L. Powell, chairman of the Joint Chiefs of Staff, once put it, "A side that sees an easy victory will go after it."[25] (3) Counter every attempt by aggressive, deceitful opponents to amass more power; it is better to fight a small war now than a big war later. Adversaries such as Saddam Hussein, it was assumed, continually probe for soft spots. Any unchallenged extension of their influence into some new geographic area will produce a **domino effect** on neighboring countries. If these incremental increases in their power are not blocked, they will become progressively more difficult to defeat. As Secretary of State James Baker posed the matter to the House Foreign Affairs Committee: "Do we want to live in a world where aggression is made less likely

> "History teaches that wars begin when governments believe the price of aggression is cheap."
>
> —RONALD REAGAN

because it is met with a powerful response, a world where civilized rules of conduct apply? Or are we willing to live in a world where aggression can go unchecked, where aggression succeeds because we cannot muster the collective will to challenge it?"[26]

Lurking beneath the president's lofty rhetoric about not appeasing aggressors was oil, a commodity on which daily life in industrialized countries had become so dependent that they have been referred to as "hydrocarbon societies."[27] While President Bush preferred to speak in terms of liberal principles such as fighting aggression and upholding the rule of law, he admitted in a speech to Pentagon employees on August 15 that access to energy resources was also important. Secretary of State Baker was more blunt: "The cause, in one word, is jobs."[28] As an advisor to the president put it, "If Kuwait's export was oranges . . . there would be no issue."[29] To add to the gravity of the situation, Saddam Hussein would control almost half of the world's proven petroleum reserves if he followed up his conquest of Kuwait by overrunning Saudi Arabia. In the words of Representative Stephen Solarz (D-NY), "It would be unthinkable for the United States to permit a rampaging dictator like Saddam to have his hands on the economic jugular of the world."[30]

TIGHTENING THE SCREWS

From George Bush's inauguration to the eve of Saddam Hussein's invasion, U.S. policy rested on the premise that Iraq was a war-weary nation that could be converted into a force for stability in the region. Sabers might be rattled in Baghdad from time to time, but pure exhaustion after eight years of war with Iran made any new military adventures unlikely. National Security Directive (NSD) 26 argued that the United States could promote peace in the Middle East by using "economic and political incentives for Iraq to moderate its behavior." Despite Iraq's abysmal human rights record, its pursuit of nuclear and binary chemical weapons, and its work on a "super gun" capable of launching huge projectiles over enormous distances, efforts to reassure Saddam Hussein of the American desire for better relations continued, and expectations were high that he would cooperate if given the proper incentives.

In Baghdad, Washington's reassurances sounded like equivocating. For example, on July 24, when evidence of suspicious troop movements opposite the Kuwaiti border raised questions about Saddam Hussein's intentions, State Department spokesperson Margaret Tutwiler answered: "We do not have any defense treaties with Kuwait, and there are no special defense or security commitments to Kuwait." The next day, in a conversation with the Iraqi leader, U.S. ambassador April Glaspie stated, "We have no opinion on Arab-Arab conflicts, like your border disagreement with Kuwait."[31] Similarly, in his testimony before a House Foreign Affairs subcommittee on July 31, Assistant Secretary of State for Near Eastern and South Asian Affairs John Kelley affirmed,

"We have no defense treaty relationship with any Gulf country."[32] These statements signaled Baghdad that the United States was less fearful of Iraqi expansionism than it was hopeful that Iraq could serve as a bastion against the spread of Islamic fundamentalism in the Middle East.

The day after the invasion, President Bush flew to Colorado to fulfill a previously scheduled speaking engagement at the Aspen Institute and to have an informal meeting with British prime minister Margaret Thatcher. The two leaders compared Iraq's attack to Germany's aggression in the 1930s and agreed that Saddam Hussein had to be stopped. During a press conference held outside the elegant mountain home of Henry Catto, the American ambassador to the Court of St. James in London, Bush told reporters that he was not ruling any options out. Bush had already moved to freeze all Iraqi and Kuwaiti assets in the United States and had ordered his advisors to explore what other sanctions might be imposed. At a National Security Council meeting convened upon the president's return from Colorado, National Security Adviser Brent Scowcroft insisted: "There are lots of reasons why we can't do things [about the invasion], but it's our job."[33] Deputy Secretary of State Lawrence Eagleburger agreed: "It is absolutely essential that the U.S.—collectively, if possible, but individually, if necessary—not only put a stop to this aggression but roll it back."[34]

The initial strategy of the Bush administration, recalled a senior adviser, "was to deny Saddam a chance to expand his aggression . . . [and] to put in place the sanctions to tighten the screws."[35] To deter further aggression, Secretary of Defense Dick Cheney secured an invitation from King Fahd allowing elements of the U.S. Rapid Deployment Force (RDF) to be deployed in Saudi Arabia; meanwhile, President Bush began contacting world leaders by telephone in order to forge a multinational coalition against Iraq. Eventually thirty nations joined, including such traditional U.S. allies as Great Britain and France, as well as Arab states such as Egypt and Syria. To dislodge Iraq from Kuwait, the United States lobbied the United Nations to organize a global arms and economic embargo against Iraq. The UN Security Council had already unanimously adopted Resolution 660, which demanded Iraq's immediate and unconditional withdrawal. On August 6 it spelled out a list of economic sanctions to be levied against Iraq (Resolution 661), and a few weeks later called upon member states with maritime forces in the region to enforce those sanctions by inspecting the cargoes of any ships thought to be assisting Iraq (Resolution 665). Operation Desert Shield was underway.

Iraq provided an ideal target for tightening the screw of **economic sanctions:** its economy was vulnerable, Saddam Hussein was isolated, and the sanctions were applied decisively. Relying heavily upon a single natural resource and highly dependent on foreign sources of finished goods and technical services, Iraq faced the prospect of growing disruptions and deprivation. William Webster, director of the Central Intelligence Agency, testified before the Senate Armed Services Committee that the economic embargo had cut off more than

90 percent of Iraq's imports and more than 97 percent of its exports, depriving the country of approximately $1.5 billion of foreign exchange earnings monthly. At the current rate of depletion, Iraqi foreign exchange reserves would be drained within a few months.[36]

Yet there were drawbacks to a strategy of military **containment** and economic strangulation. The longer sanctions were applied, the greater the likelihood that the diverse military coalition so carefully assembled by George Bush would disintegrate. Friction from the ongoing Israeli-Palestinian dispute, Islamic fundamentalist resentment over the growing number of infidel soldiers in the region, and the staggering cost of maintaining troops in a distant and inhospitable environment were just some of the problems that threatened to weaken coalition resolve as the months wore on. Furthermore, because Saddam Hussein remained indifferent to hardships borne by his own people, there was no guarantee that Iraq's economic suffering would compel him to withdraw from Kuwait. Defiant as ever, the Iraqi leader tried one ploy after another in his attempt to erode the American-dominated coalition that encircled him. To dislodge Syria and other Arab states, he proposed to negotiate an end to the crisis if Israel vacated the Golan Heights, Gaza Strip, and the West Bank of the Jordan River. To shake loose popularly elected Western governments, he threatened to make "human shields" of the hundreds of European nationals captured in Kuwait. He even tried to curry the favor of Iran by returning territory previously captured from his old enemy.

By late fall, few in the White House retained hope that the economic vise around Iraq would pressure Saddam Hussein into giving up Kuwait. Reflecting on his gradual disenchantment with sanctions and his subsequent shift from guarding a line in the sand to an offensive strategy aimed at evicting Hussein from Kuwait, President Bush revealed: "I cannot pinpoint all of this to a certain date, but . . . as the military planners went forward, I was more and more convinced that we could use force and be successful."[37] By the end of October, the president told Secretary of Defense Dick Cheney that he was inclined to use his authority as Commander in Chief to allocate the wherewithal needed to undertake offensive operations, but nothing could be disclosed until after November 6 since any such announcement would be taken as an attempt to influence the upcoming Congressional elections.[38]

On November 8 George Bush declared that he would double U.S. troop strength in the Persian Gulf. Two political steps would be necessary before these troops could be sent into battle. The first step was taken by the end of the month, when the UN Security Council passed Resolution 678 authorizing member states "to use all necessary means" to evict Iraq from Kuwait if it did not leave voluntarily by January 15, 1991. The second step occurred shortly thereafter, when a joint resolution was passed in the U.S. Senate by a vote of 52 to 47 and in the House of Representatives by 250 to 183 authorizing the president to wrest control of Kuwait from Iraq. With nearly one million heavily armed soldiers standing toe-to-toe astride the welter of failed peace proposals littering the diplomatic landscape, the forces of war were gaining momentum. "What is at issue," the American president wrote in a letter to his Iraqi counterpart, "is not the future of Kuwait . . . but rather the future of Iraq."[39]

THE NINTENDO WAR

Early in the morning of January 17, 1991, the USS *Bunker Hill* and the USS *San Jacinto* fired Tomahawk cruise missiles at Baghdad from their respective locations in the Persian Gulf and the Red Sea. As the Tomahawks sped toward the Iraqi capital, a group of F-117A Stealth fighters and a task force of Apache AH-64 and MH-53J Pace Low helicopters were preparing to engage other targets. Their attack would be followed by waves of fighters, bombers, and electronic warfare aircraft, including B-52s, F-15E Strike Eagles, F-4G Wild Weasels, EF-111 Ravens, A-6 Prowlers, British and Saudi Tornados, and French Jaguars. What Saddam Hussein called the "Mother of All Battles" had begun.

The Doctrine of Invincible Force

Although Operation Desert Storm, the U.S. plan for liberating Kuwait, went through many iterations and was an amalgam of contending ideas, its roots reach back to what General Colin Powell called the doctrine of invincible force. Haunted by the ghost of Vietnam, a generation of American military officers was leery of the argument that political leaders in Washington could fine-tune a program of rising military pressure in a **limited war** to persuade an opponent to relinquish territory already won. Threats of further violence after a pause in escalation were supposed to induce enemy forces to withdraw and spare the United States the cost of slugging it out on the ground. This strategy failed. Hence, the Bush administration concluded that military gradualism was counterproductive; it amounted to fighting with one hand tied behind your back.

Rather than orchestrating an alternating pattern of incremental escalations and pauses, Powell advocated marshaling all of the resources necessary to overwhelm an adversary. By harnessing the latest technology, he maintained that U.S. forces could use mobility and firepower to win swift, decisive victories. "I don't believe in doing war on the basis of macroeconomic, marginal-analysis models," the general said. "I'm more of the mind-set of a New York street bully: 'Here's my bat, here's my gun, here's my knife, I'm wearing armor. I'm going to kick your ass . . .' "[40]

Whereas the U.S. military was geared to fight a fast and furious campaign, Saddam Hussein pinned his hopes on a war of attrition, believing he could exploit a fatal weakness in America's democratic policy-making process—a lack of patience with protracted warfare. The United States "is a society that cannot accept 10,000 dead in one battle," he insisted.[41] If Iraq could lure U.S. troops into frontal assaults on heavily fortified "killing zones," Hussein assumed mounting casualties would prompt the Americans to yield. Just as they had done in their earlier war with Iran, the Iraqis constructed an elaborate system of minefields, bunkers, antitank guns, and fire trenches all surrounded by concertina wire. Slowed by these barriers, the American attack would come under a heavy artillery barrage, followed by a counterattack by armored and mechanized divisions of Saddam Hussein's elite Republican Guard. The key to the plan resided in Iraq's ability to ride out the preliminary strikes by coalition air power. "The U.S. may be able to destroy cities, factories, and to kill," Saddam Hussein once proclaimed, "but it will not be able to decide the war with its Air Force."[42]

Operation Desert Storm unfolded in two phases: a relentless air assault (January 17–February 24) followed by a devastating ground offensive (February 24–28). The objectives of the first phase were to (1) achieve air superiority; (2) cripple Iraq's ground forces; and (3) destroy electric power grids, military facilities, bridges, and other strategic targets. By the end of the war, coalition aircraft had flown "52,000 air-to-ground sorties [that] delivered approximately 210,000 unguided bombs, 9,300 guided bombs, 5,400 guided air-to-surface missiles, and 2,000 anti-radar missiles; American forces also hurled more than 300 cruise missiles at the enemy."[43] In addition to pummeling Iraq's infrastructure, logistical network, and armored formations, the air campaign demoralized Hussein's troops. Americans watching tapes of the bombing runs with the lethal accuracy of heat-seeking sensors and laser-guided munitions likened the action to a computer video game.[44] In the words of reporters covering the air assault, it was a Nintendo War.

The second phase of Operation Desert Storm involved deceiving Saddam Hussein into thinking that the ground offensive would be aimed directly at Kuwait City. Instead, taking advantage of air cover and navigational data from global positioning satellites, U.S. general H. Norman Schwarzkopf redeployed the bulk of his forces westward, where they could strike deep into Iraq, pivot, and then quickly circle back to outflank Hussein's forces in Kuwait. The objectives of sweeping around enemy defenses were to envelop and then crush the Iraqi war machine.

Exhausted by weeks of aerial pounding and bewildered by Schwarzkopf's end run, the Iraqis began surrendering in droves. Those who fought were chewed up by the ground offensive. American troops were well-trained professionals; Iraqi front-line conscripts were riddled by poor morale. American equipment allowed soldiers to fire accurately while on the move and attack at night; Iraqi weaponry, though formidable, lacked the same level of technological sophistication and suffered from shortages of spare parts. Simply put, the Mother of All Battles was one of the most lopsided fights in the annals of military history. It quickly degenerated into the Mother of All Retreats.

The End Game

By the third day of the ground offensive, thousands of Iraqi troops began streaming northward out of Kuwait City. Forming a column almost thirty miles long and three or four abreast in places, the broken, defenseless units were ravaged by wave after wave of swarming coalition aircraft. Back in Washington, reports suggesting mass carnage created enormous pressure for a **cease-fire**. Watching television coverage of what the media called the "Highway of Death," Bush worried that his triumph might be marred by charges of brutalization. Informed that the gate was closed on the encircled Iraqis and eradication of their heavy tanks and artillery imminent, the president now looked toward a cessation of hostilities. In the waning hours of the war, one last attempt was made to destroy a hardened command bunker where Saddam Hussein might be hiding. Late on the night of February 27, two five-thousand-pound penetration bombs were dropped on the al-Taji Air Base about fifteen miles outside Baghdad. The bunker was demolished, but it did not house the Iraqi leader. Shortly after the bombing raid, Bush suspended offensive action. "We were 150 miles from Baghdad and there was nobody between us and Baghdad," noted General Schwarzkopf. "If it had been our intention to take Iraq, if it had been our intention to destroy the country, if it had been our intention to overrun the country, we could have done it unopposed."[45]

> "The time of reconstruction and recovery should not be the occasion for vengeful actions against a nation forced to war by a dictator's ambition."
>
> —JAMES A. BAKER

The decision to halt the fighting was made on the basis of erroneous information, however. Contrary to Schwarzkopf's assertion that the gate had been closed, the retreating Iraqis were not completely surrounded. Another six to eight hours would have been needed to entrap them. With key choke points open, roughly half of Saddam Hussein's Republican Guard escaped with their weapons intact. Together with the twenty or so divisions not involved in the Kuwait Theater of Operations, these troops became the cornerstone for a reconstituted Iraqi army that would trouble the region for years to come.

The announcement of the war's end triggered celebrations throughout the United States. The war had been won with less than 150 American deaths. It was an impressive military victory. Unfortunately, the victory was tainted by lingering political problems. Little thought had gone into how the war's termination would affect the peace settlement. Could Saddam Hussein be removed from power without a U.S. march to Baghdad? If not, what would be the long-term consequences of his continued rule? How would the United States deal with those consequences? Anxious to secure a swift victory with minimal U.S. casualties, the Bush administration made a hasty decision to bring the war to a conclusion. Insufficient attention was devoted to how the United States would influence events in a postwar Iraq still ruled by Saddam Hussein, who was now highly motivated to seek revenge for the destruction inflicted upon his country.

On March 3 General Schwarzkopf met with Iraqi representatives at the Safwan airfield in southern Iraq to finalize the terms of the truce. A lack of American planning for the peace settlement and the absence of a clear, coherent design for the future of Iraq soon became evident. The terms presented by the general called for Iraq to release all coalition prisoners of war and Kuwaiti detainees, provide information on the location of all sea and land mines, and comply with all relevant UN Security Council resolutions. When the Iraqis asked whether they would be allowed to fly helicopters over areas not populated by coalition forces, Schwarzkopf agreed. When they asked whether territory seized during the ground offensive would be returned to Iraq's control, he assured them his forces would soon depart. By granting Iraq the right to operate helicopters and promising to withdraw rapidly, Schwarzkopf inadvertently permitted Saddam Hussein to use a frightening weapon against his domestic opposition and relinquished the opportunity to use Iraqi land as leverage to ensure compliance with the terms of the truce. As one senior member of the Bush administration later admitted, "Norm went in uninstructed. He should have had instructions. But everything was moving so fast the process broke down."[46] "We never did have a plan to terminate the war," remarked another official.[47]

Given Iraq's military humiliation, President Bush assumed that a disgruntled army would rise against Saddam Hussein. On several occasions he called for a rebellion against the Baathist leader. A new government, Bush reasoned, would live in peace with its neighbors and act as a counterweight to Iranian ambitions. But rather than the army staging a coup, the Kurds in northern Iraq and the Shiite Muslims in the southern part of the country rebelled. Using the very Republican Guard forces that escaped American grasp and the helicopters he was now allowed to fly, Hussein viciously suppressed both uprisings, razing villages and sending hundreds of thousands of refugees fleeing in terror. Despite pleas for U.S. assistance from the minorities facing **genocide** as the penalty for their rebellion, the Bush administration initially stood on the sidelines. Defense Secretary Cheney explained that another American intervention would raise "the very real specter of getting us involved in a quagmire trying to figure out who the hell is going to govern Iraq."[48] According to another high-ranking official, Bush had "no, I mean absolutely no, intention of putting the United States in the middle of a civil war."[49] Ultimately, Bush responded to the threat against the *pesh marga* (literally, "those who face death") by creating a Kurdish safe haven above the 36th parallel and a Shiite haven below the 32nd parallel, each patrolled by coalition forces. Although this provision of the truce settlement was designed to protect both groups while preventing the disintegration of Iraq, it enmeshed Washington in an ongoing commitment to uphold Gulf security. Aircraft, naval power, and prepositioned ground equipment would have to be maintained in the area for an extended period at considerable expense. On April 3, 1991, the UN Security Council approved Resolution 687, which specified the terms for a permanent cease-fire between Iraq and the American-led coalition. The formal truce went into effect eight days later. Saddam Hussein had been defeated on the battlefield, but he remained as truculent as ever. In the aftermath of the peace settlement, he tested allied determination to prevent him from rebuilding his military infrastructure and projecting his power beyond Baghdad. The following are a few examples of the carefully calculated probes Hussein initiated in the wake of the Gulf War to undermine the victors' resolve in enforcing the punitive terms of the armistice:

- *Weapons of Mass Destruction* UN Resolution 687 called for the disclosure and dismantling of Iraqi production facilities for chemical, biological, and nuclear weapons. The first UN inspection team visited the Al-Tuwaitha nuclear research facility on May 14, 1991, and discovered that much of the equipment had been moved to other locations. On the second inspection a few weeks later, UN personnel were denied entry to the Abu Ghurayb facility but noticed trucks removing uranium enrichment equipment. The next few visits revealed that Iraq had made considerable progress toward developing nuclear weapons, though controversy continued over whether Baghdad provided the United Nations with a complete inventory of its nuclear facilities. On September 13 Iraqi officials took documents away from inspectors and detained the UN team for a number of hours. Subsequent visits over the ensuing years were also marred by Iraqi efforts at evading and obstructing UN inspection, amid complaints that these monitoring activities were an unjust infringement of Iraq's sovereign right to arm for defense.

- *Humanitarian Aid* To prevent Saddam Hussein from rapidly rebuilding his arsenal, economic sanctions preventing the sale of Iraqi oil were maintained after the war. A United Nations formula allowing limited sales to generate revenue for purchasing food and medical supplies was rejected by Baghdad as an unacceptable violation of its sovereignty. Hussein wanted to determine how revenue from the sale of Iraqi oil would be used. While the sanctions did not affect the living standard of Hussein and his entourage, they took a huge toll on ordinary Iraqis. In particular, cases of malnutrition-related diseases among children rose exponentially after the war. Only in the late spring of 1996 did Iraq begin serious negotiations on a deal to sell oil for emergency civilian needs. Until that point, Hussein used the plight of his people to gain sympathy from other Arab states.

- *Troop Movements* On several occasions after the Gulf War, Saddam Hussein massed troops along his borders in defiance of allied warnings. Sometimes they made limited incursions into forbidden areas. In early 1993, for instance, a small contingent of troops crossed into Kuwait to retrieve weapons.

- *Targeting Aircraft* From time to time, Iraqi fighters entered the air exclusion zones, and in one instance on December 27, 1992, an Iraqi jet fired at an American plane. Surface-to-air missiles were moved in and around the exclusion zones over the years, and allied aircraft were tracked with radar from Iraqi antiaircraft batteries.

In a speech delivered on August 20, 1992, during his reelection campaign, George Bush told his supporters that he had "locked a tyrant in the prison of his own country."[50] Each of the probes by Saddam Hussein was a calculated exploration of the walls of that so-called prison. His tenacious poking and prodding served the twin ends of maneuvering for more latitude and demonstrating that he remained unbowed. The United States and its allies responded sporadically to Hussein, as illustrated by the limited retaliatory air strikes launched during January 1993 and the cruise missile attack of September 1996. But more often than not, warnings were issued and the matter was dropped—a strategy of "threat and forget." Whereas Saddam Hussein concentrated all of his energy at making a jailbreak, the guards experienced growing resource scarcities and fatigue. They found themselves frustrated and uncertain over what to do about the Iraqi leader. By not anticipating the political contours of postwar Iraq, the United States and its coalition partners won a vacant victory and lost the chance to show that **collective security** could work.

RETRIBUTION REDUX

The relationship between Saddam Hussein and the U.S.–led coalition that defeated him remained locked in an embittered confrontation for years after the Persian Gulf War ended. Triumph on the battlefield had been a cause for celebration in Washington. But the euphoria soon disappeared in a new round of military thrust and parry. Saddam Hussein desperately sought to overturn the sanctions that had strangled Iraq's economy and made his country an international pariah. With George Bush in retirement following his 1992 electoral defeat, the question of how to deal with a combative Iraq would now challenge U.S. President Bill Clinton.

In September 1996, as Clinton neared the end of his first term in office, Saddam Hussein once again tested American resolve. With the presidential election nearing its critical stage and public attention riveted on domestic issues, Hussein saw an opportunity in a civil war that had erupted among the Kurdish population in northern Iraq. Violating the provisions of the 1991 truce, he sent his tanks into the Kurdish city of Irbil with the intention of

> "No promise of peace and no policy of patience can be without its limits."
>
> —BILL CLINTON

becoming the ultimate power broker between the two factions struggling for control of Kurdistan. By playing these factions against one another, Hussein hoped to reverse the terms of the truce and resume his domination over that war-weary land.

This test of American resolve was met by an immediate response. To cripple Saddam Hussein's capacity to intervene into Kurdish politics, the United States fired twenty-two cruise missiles at Iraqi targets. President Clinton defended the retaliation as fully justified by Iraq's flagrant breach of the peace. Further underscoring his determination to contain Iraqi aggression, Clinton deployed additional forces in the Persian Gulf, where they would be poised to strike Iraq if Saddam Hussein persisted in his efforts to remove the shackles of the 1991 armistice agreement. As it turned out, the deployment proved insufficient. During the fall of 1997, Iraq once again barred UN weapons inspectors from examining key sites in Iraq, insisting on the right to influence the composition and activities undertaken by the inspection team. In addition, Iraq threatened to shoot down U-2 reconnaissance planes on surveillance missions over its territory. The Clinton administration replied by sending more U.S. forces into the region and threatening a military response. Just when a U.S. air strike on Iraq seemed imminent, Saddam Hussein backed down and the crisis appeared to be over.

In early 1998, Hussein resumed his obstreperous behavior, claiming that the American members of the UN team were spies who would not be allowed to inspect Iraqi facilities. The Clinton administration was now in a quandary. Having deployed additional troops, warships, and combat aircraft to the region, it found little international support for a punitive strike. Russia and France, backed by a chorus of African and Arab states, vigorously opposed military action against Iraq. Covert action against Saddam Hussein also appeared unpromising. The two major Iraqi opposition groups in exile—the Iraqi National Congress, based in London, and the Iraqi National Accord, based in Amman, Jordan—had been weakened by internal squabbles. Seven years after winning a crushing victory on the battlefield, the United States was still groping for a final political settlement to the Persian Gulf War.

The search for a viable solution to the problems in the Persian Gulf was complicated by distracting events in Washington. President Clinton, who had been embroiled in several previous controversies stemming from allegations about his sexual improprieties, was now under scrutiny for an alleged affair with a White House intern. Coincidentally, a film titled *Wag the Dog* opened in theaters across the country. Portraying an embattled president who considers using a fabricated war to shift attention away from domestic issues, the film led the president's detractors to speculate about his foreign policy in terms of the **diversionary theory of war.** Thus, at the very time that the United States was poised to attack Iraq for violations of the 1991 cease-fire agreement, the Clinton administration had to deal with an unraveling international coalition and a host of domestic critics searching for evidence of a scandal.

A military showdown was finally averted when UN Secretary-General Kofi Annan traveled to Baghdad in February and negotiated an arrangement that would allow weapons inspectors unrestricted access to sites suspected of housing weapons of mass destruction. The United States hoped to augment the

CONTROVERSIES TO CONTEMPLATE

- Prior to the onset of the Persian Gulf War, the Iraqi economy appeared to be highly vulnerable to economic sanctions. Speaking before a joint session of Congress during the fall of 1990, President Bush indicated that sanctions needed time in order to succeed. However, approximately two months later, he abandoned sanctions in favor of an armed attack. Were sanctions given a chance to work? What would have been the likely consequences of continuing with a policy of economic sanctions in order to expel Iraq from Kuwait?

- What impact did perceived "lessons" from the Vietnam War have on the way the United States conducted the Persian Gulf War? Was the Vietnam experience applicable to Iraq? For the United States, what were the major similarities and differences between fighting in Southeast Asia versus fighting in the Middle East? Did the differences outweigh the similarities? If so, what were the consequences for the conduct of the war and the crafting of a postwar peace plan?

- Many military analysts assert that the armed forces of the U.S.-led coalition could have swept all the way to Baghdad without significant opposition. Why did President Bush decide to stop the war instead of continuing on to the Iraqi capital?

- Following the cease-fire, the Bush administration hoped that Saddam Hussein would be overthrown by an internal uprising. What was known about Saddam Hussein's opposition? What was unclear to policymakers about his opposition? What did they assume about the opposition? Were any of their assumptions unfounded? Were any of them treated as facts?

- Some political realists advised the Bush administration to design its postwar policies around the concept of a regional equilibrium. They cautioned the president against weakening Iraq to the point that it could not offset the power of such rivals as Iran and Syria. Others proposed that any *balance of power* policy would require that the United States play the role of the *balancer*, supporting whichever country was the weakest at a particular point in time. How useful is the balance of power concept as a mechanism for building a durable peace in the Gulf region?

- What has been the strategy behind Saddam Hussein's behavior in the years after the cease-fire? Why has he provoked one crisis after another only to back down when confronted with the threat of retaliation?

agreement by obtaining Security Council authorization for an automatic military response in the event that Iraq violated its provisions. Russia, France, and China balked at the U.S. proposal, however, and only agreed to a more ambiguous resolution that threatened severe consequences would follow if there were any transgressions. With the threat of a U.S. strike now dissipated, Saddam Hussein returned to his long-standing effort to redefine the terms that ended the Persian Gulf War.

To sum up, national leaders make crucial decisions when wars draw to a close. Victors from General Lysander of ancient Sparta to President George Bush of the United States typically think of **grand strategy** in the narrow terms of a military mission designed to coerce the enemy into submission and surrender. Rarely do they articulate the clear, long-term political goals that military missions ultimately serve. This inattention to political planning is troublesome because how an adversary is treated can exert a powerful influence on the prospects for lasting peace. As the Persian Gulf War illustrates, a seat-of-the-pants approach to making vital decisions in the waning days of battle can easily result in political defeat being snatched from the jaws of military victory. Peace is not something that happens spontaneously when the infernal engine of war is shut off; it must be cultivated and nourished by people of vision.

Our aim in this book is to extract lessons from the historical record of war termination to illuminate the obstacles that stand in the way of durable peace settlements. From antiquity to the present, victors have struggled with how they should treat defeated adversaries. Although some political leaders succeeded in their efforts at peace building, too many implemented short-sighted policies that merely set the stage for another round of armed conflict. Having reviewed a variety of noteworthy successes and failures, in Chapter 10 we turn our attention to deriving a set of policy prescriptions that can help guide future decisionmakers in the elusive quest for a lasting peace.

NOTES

1. Aspin, 1991, p. 10.
2. Buchanan, 1991, Kennedy as cited in *Time,* August 20, 1990, p. 82
3. Schlesinger, 1991, p. 268.
4. *Washington Post,* March 2, 1991, p. A13.
5. In Gordon and Trainor, 1995, p. 416.
6. *New York Times,* March 2, 1991, p. 5.
7. In Waterman, 1996, p. 338.
8. Dawisha, 1986, p. 30
9. Post, 1993, p. 55; see also Henderson, 1991; Karsh, 1991; and Miller and Mylroie, 1990.
10. *New York Times,* August 3, 1990, pp. 8, 10.
11. In Frankel, 1991, p. 17.
12. In Stoessinger, 1993, p. 190.
13. Jentleson, 1994, p. 48.
14. In Stoessinger, p. 190.
15. *U.S. News & World Report,* January 27, 1991, p. 31.
16. Bonafede, 1995, p. 99.
17. *New York Times,* March 3, 1991, p. 18.
18. Wayne, 1993, p. 32.
19. In Ibid.

20. Bush, 1990c, p. 674.
21. Bush, 1990a, p. 3.
22. Bush, 1990d, p. 739.
23. Bush, 1991, p. 261.
24. Bush, 1990b, p. 2.
25. Speech to the National Press Club on October 27, 1988, in Kegley and Raymond, 1994, p. 37.
26. Prepared statement delivered on September 4, 1990.
27. See Yergin, 1991.
28. In Vaux, 1992, p. 18.
29. *Time*, August 20, 1990, p. 11.
30. Solarz, 1991, p. 270.
31. In Jentleson, 1994, p. 170.
32. Ibid., p. 174.
33. In Woodward, 1991, p. 237.
34. In Gordon and Trainor, 1995, p. 37.
35. In *Triumph Without Victory*, 1992, p. 63.
36. See Aspin, 1990, pp. 2–3.
37. In *Triumph Without Victory*, 1992, p. 172.
38. Woodward, 1991, p. 311.
39. The letter was delivered to Iraqi Foreign Minister Tariq Aziz by Secretary of State Baker during their meeting in Geneva on January 9, 1991. Aziz refused to deliver it to Saddam Hussein because he felt the tone was inappropriate.
40. In *Triumph Without Victory*, 1992, p. 172.
41. Iraqi transcript of meeting on July 25, 1990, with U.S. ambassador April Glaspie. Hussein voiced the same theme in a February 1990 speech before the Arab Cooperation Council when he reminded the audience that the United States withdrew from Lebanon after marines were killed in the bombing of Beirut airport.
42. In Gordon and Trainor, 1995, p. 180.
43. Cohen, 1994, p. 110.
44. The technology used in the Gulf War was an outgrowth of a strategy devised in the 1970s to offset the numerical superiority of Warsaw Pact forces. According to a 1996 report issued by the General Accounting Office, the Pentagon exaggerated the effectiveness of this technology. See the *International Herald Tribune,* July 10, 1996, pp. 1, 7.
45. In Polmar, 1991, p. 212. Iraqi battle deaths have never been counted carefully. Estimates range from 6,500 to 200,000.
46. In Gordon and Trainor, 1995, p. 444.
47. Ibid., p. 461.
48. *U.S. News & World Report,* April 15, 1991, p. 31.
49. In Schneider, 1992, p. 66.
50. In Bonafede, 1995, p. 119.

PART IV

Paths to Peace in the Twenty-First Century: Moral Dilemmas and Policy Prescriptions

Is it possible to win a war and then win the peace? How should victors treat defeated foes? Are there sound "lessons" that can be derived from historical cases about the paths peacemakers should pursue as they forge peace settlements? What factors are likely to influence their capacity to make prudent and moral choices that can cement a lasting and just peace with an enemy that has been vanquished?

These are questions that were asked in earliest recorded history, they are still being asked today, and will, in all likelihood, be asked in the twenty-first century.

The cases introduced in *How Nations Make Peace* provide a laboratory for seeking out eternal principles to perpetual problems about war and peace. A variety of past wars and peace settlements, from antiquity to the present, have been covered in hope of capturing the complexities and controversies of this conundrum in the study of war and peace. In our concluding chapter, "Waging Peace: Choices and Consequences," we draw on this rich and varied past to pull together the discrepant range of opinions, activities, and outcomes. Our focus centers on four major categories of evaluation.

First, what is the most meaningful way to look at peace-making practices theoretically? What are the major advantages and limitations of the realist and liberal schools of thought in interpreting how nations should make peace? The difficult type of choice selected for inspection in this book—how nations should deal with enemies—is representative of many other kinds of hard decisions confronting policymakers in world affairs and was chosen to emphasize the nature of such dilemmas. *Realism* and *liberalism* provide the primary lens to view most controversies in international decision making. Are either adequate? What are the payoffs and pitfalls of relying on either perspective? Are both, to a degree, based on illusions? Why, and under what conditions? If both fail to provide sound answers, should they be abandoned and a new or different theory be embraced? Or should future policymakers continue to see classical realism and liberalism—or some new fused version—as the only reasonable ways of organizing thought about this topic?

Second, we revisit the perils and politics of peace making and consider the many factors—international, societal, institutional, and individual—that influence the capacity of victors to make rational and moral choices when they seek to promote peace.

Third, we put forth a number of policy prescriptions that the cases in this book and others throughout history suggest are worthy of consideration and ask that an assessment be made about the boundaries of pragmatic and ethical peace-making strategies.

Finally, we frame all the above controversies with a discussion of contrasting ethical arguments about how enemies can reconcile their differences and build a just peace after the war ends.

·10·

WAGING PEACE: CHOICES AND CONSEQUENCES

A phenomenon noticeable throughout history regardless of place or period is the pursuit by governments of policies contrary to their interests.

BARBARA W. TUCHMAN

The victory won by the U.S.-led coalition in the Persian Gulf War has been called a defining moment in military history—a victory as dramatic as those attained by Hannibal at Cannae or Wellington at Waterloo. Hyperbole aside, the coalition's battlefield success was predictable. Throughout modern history, when a significant imbalance of forces favored the side using a strategy of maneuver on flat, open terrain, it tended to win a decisive victory in a relatively short war.[1] What few people anticipated was the inability of the United States to translate its striking victory into a durable peace settlement. Despite numerous American attempts to make Saddam Hussein adhere to the UN resolutions that defined the terms of the Gulf War armistice, the truculent Iraqi leader continued for more than seven years after the war to flout the will of the international community. His successful defiance ultimately prompted columnist George Will to grouse that most Americans now "do not believe in the 'community of nations' any more than they believe in the Big Rock Candy Mountain."[2]

The German philosopher Johan Wolfgang Goethe once defined genius as knowing when to stop. According to Nissan Oren, political genius has been rare among victors: Some have gone too far, plundering the defeated in fits of avarice and rage; others have not gone far enough, humiliating them without weakening their capability to retaliate in the future. Prudent victories, he concludes, "are but small islands engulfed by an ocean of imprudence, like small specks of rationality afloat in a sea of insanity."[3]

225

THINKING THEORETICALLY ABOUT WAR TERMINATION

Mortal combat between states is rare, but its consequences are staggering. In the almost two centuries since the Congress of Vienna, 150 members of the interstate system never experienced warfare. Those which did suffered more than 30 million battle-connected fatalities and tens of millions of additional civilian deaths.[4] The human tragedy behind this horrific toll has led many scholars to undertake rigorous, systematic analyses of how wars begin. The question of how they end has received far less attention, despite the fact that the end of fighting "does not necessarily mean the resolution of a conflict."[5] Because a cessation of hostilities can be engineered in ways that either dampen or inflame the underlying disagreement between combatants, some theorists maintain that the "transition from war to peace constitutes a more serious problem than does the reverse."[6]

To build a theory that provides meaningful guidelines about how nations can successfully wage peace, one must begin with an inspection of past cases. The last seven chapters provide examples of efforts to build peace that illustrate the magnitude of the challenge.[7]

In thinking theoretically about the origins and outcomes of different types of peace treaties, we will find that most interpretations have been informed by ideas derived from the so-called "realist" and "liberal" intellectual traditions. As discussed in Chapter 1, realists "earn their label by emphasizing consequences over moral principles and necessity over choice. Liberals begin with opposite premises, emphasizing duty over consequences and moral imperatives over expediency."[8] These bodies of thought, Joel Rosenthal observes, provide the storehouse of concepts from which nearly all controversies in international politics can be examined, because "most of the literature of the past fifty years is an unwitting and curious combination of the two approaches."[9] The challenge now, Rosenthal cogently argues, "is to relate the insights of these traditions to the problems of our age."[10]

Waging peace remains our most important problem today, because failure can lead to mass destruction. For that reason, we advise readers to inspect and interpret the wars and peace settlements we have covered in previous chapters by applying the rich insights of both realism and liberalism to those cases.[11]

Comparing the Cases Considered

Although it is common for data-based analyses of interstate conflict to overlook temporal dynamics and treat violent incidents between the same pair of states as if they were independent of one another, these clashes generally do not happen out of the blue. Only 21 percent of the militarized disputes that erupted between 1816 and 1985 and 16 percent of the wars occurred in isolation.[12] Most violent clashes occurred within the context of a rivalry. Not only do states in protracted rivalries adopt more coercive bargaining strategies with each other in successive confrontations,[13] but the longer these altercations continue, the greater the likelihood of war.[14]

How belligerents conduct themselves on the battlefield, as well as how victors treat the vanquished, have far-reaching implications for the durability of peace settlements between bitter rivals. Decisive military outcomes and imposed political settlements may temporarily reduce the prospects that the defeated will retaliate,[15] but people harboring an acute sense of injustice do not easily forget suffering at the hands of others. As the last seven chapters illustrate, history is replete with examples of settlements that provoked a new round of hostilities by creating a sense of injustice among those on the losing side. Peace, in these situations, never endures; it is an interlude when one side or the other longs for revenge, and neither can overcome the rancor of their collective past to restore amicable relations.

The cases covered in this book comprise a special category of wars, namely, those where one side was a decisive winner on the battlefield and the other side a loser.[16] To introduce the timeless issue of how victors—be they the initiators or the targets of aggression—should treat the vanquished after the fighting stops, we began by describing the outcomes from some of the most famous ancient conflicts: the Peloponnesian War and the Punic Wars. After juxtaposing the relative advantages and disadvantages of the Spartan policy of leniency with the Roman policy of subjugation, we turned to consider how victors in the modern state system have acted. Was it prudent for them to be magnanimous in victory and seek a conciliatory peace? Or, was it more advantageous to impose a punitive peace? Table 10.1 lists the modern wars that we have examined in response to these these questions. Whereas some were short, resulting in limited casualties (e.g., the Second Schleswig-Holstein, Austro-Prussian, and Persian Gulf Wars), others stretched on for years, causing enormous destruction (e.g., the Napoleonic and the two World Wars). By selecting several cases from each type of war, we provided a basis for investigating whether the behavior of the winners in decisive military victories followed a general pattern. Concentrating on a few cases allows us to examine the war-termination process in greater detail than if we had employed additional cases.[17] Of course, the drawback is that our ability to generalize is less than it would have been with a larger sample. Trade-offs exist between studies based on the focused comparison of a small number of cases and those based on numerous cases. Whereas the former approach allows for more complete and complex accounts of the phenomena under investigation, the latter offers greater confidence when generalizing to the wider population from which a sample is selected. There are costs and benefits to whichever choice a researcher makes, and these should be kept in mind when evaluating the results from our analysis.

Not only did the wars in our sample vary in terms of their duration, magnitude, and severity, but the termination agreements that ended them were also

TABLE 10.1
Selected Characteristics of the Modern Wars under Investigation

Wars	Dates	Number of Participants	Battle Deaths
Napoleonic	1803–1815	6	1,380,000
Second Schleswig-Holstein	1864	3	4,500
Austro-Prussian	1866	11	36,100
Franco-Prussian	1870–1871	5	187,500
World War I	1914–1918	15	9,000,000
World War II	1939–1945	29	15,000,000
Persian Gulf	1990–1991	30	100,000

Source: Small and Singer, 1982; Persian Gulf war estimates based on United Nations Information Office.

different. As shown in Table 10.2, victors' peace-making strategies ranged from the highly punitive (e.g., the Franco-Prussian War and World War I) to the conciliatory (e.g., the Napoleonic and Austro-Prussian Wars). Occupation, territorial losses, forced disarmament, financial reparations, and at times even assistance for economic recovery were used by the victors. Because winners employed so many approaches to deal with the defeated, we have ample opportunity to compare the results of callousness toward a former foe with the results of magnanimity.

What Can History Teach Us?

Although the formal academic study of international relations is relatively new, attempts to theorize about state behavior date back to antiquity. Thucydides' pioneering realist history of the Peloponnesian War is perhaps the best example of such an effort. He believed "knowledge of the past" would be "an aid to the interpretation of the future" and therefore wrote his book "not to win the applause of the moment, but as a possession for all time."[18] Heavily influenced by the Hippocratic school of medicine, Thucydides examined the war between Athens and Sparta like an ancient Greek physician diagnosing a patient. His detailed clinical observations were recorded as a case study which described the symptoms of war-prone periods and offered the reader a prognosis of the probable consequences of malevolent versus benevolent approaches to making peace.

Thucydides was not the only writer in antiquity to present us with historical cases as tools to improve decision making. Livy, one of our primary sources of information on the Punic Wars between Rome and Carthage, believed that history provided "the lessons of every kind of experience plainly set forth as on a conspicuous monument; from these you may choose for yourself and for your

TABLE 10.2
A Comparison of Selected War Termination Agreements

| Treatment of Loser | Napoleonic War | Wars of German Unification | | | World War I | World War II | | Persian Gulf War |
		Second Schleswig-Holstein War	Austro-Prussian War	Franco-Prussian War		Germany	Japan	
Accused of Responsibility for War	×				×	×	×	×
Condemnation of Leaders	×			×	×	×	Yes, but Emperor was not indicted	×
Occupied	×			×	×	×	×	×
Disarmed	×			×	×	×	×	×
Reparations	×			×	×	Light in U.S., British, and French occupation zones; heavy in Soviet occupation zone	Light	
Territorial Loss	×	×	Austria lost its rights in Schleswig-Holstein; Venetia ceded to Italy	×	×	×	×	
Economic Assistance					×	×		

Source: Adapted from Clemens, 1998, pp. 43, 53.

own state what to imitate [and] from these mark for avoidance what is shameful."[19]

Whereas some foreign policy fiascoes are the result of circumstances beyond the control of decisionmakers, what Thucydides and Livy warn of are preventable failures caused by lapses in human judgment. The relations among nations are shaped by chance and the sequence of choices made by the interacting parties. From antiquity down to the present, history has been used as a laboratory for discovering which choices in what contexts reduce the probability of committing those errors that precipitate avoidable policy disasters. "The future can never look exactly like the past," note Richard Neustadt and Ernest May, "but past conditions can offer clues to future possibilities."[20] Focused, structured comparisons of historical cases have the potential to stimulate our imagination and help us frame sharper questions about how to build a durable peace.[21]

If the past can help us frame sharper questions about peace making, can victors learn from history? Learning from experience involves a change in beliefs or the degree of confidence in one's beliefs based on the interpretation of past events.[22] Unfortunately, there is mounting evidence that decisionmakers have difficulty learning from the experience of others. Rather than learning from the past, they often use it "to buttress pre-existing policy preferences."[23] To borrow a phrase from Edmund Burke, history for decisionmakers is "a magical mirror where everyone sees what he wants."[24]

> "What history teaches us is that men have never learned anything from it."
>
> —GEORG WILHELM HEGEL

One reason why decisionmakers have such problems with learning from the past can be found in their belief that history's "lessons and insights lie on the surface for anyone to pick up, so that one can go at history like a looter at an archeological site."[25] Victors may remember a rousing success or a traumatic failure in postwar peace building and assume that the situation they now confront is an exact parallel. Familiar episodes from the past are not always instructive, however. Drawing analogies between events that share only a superficial correspondence distorts reality, encourages premature cognitive closure, and may needlessly trigger negative feelings about the vanquished.[26] But when used carefully, history can provide a source of ideas, suggest alternatives that might otherwise have been overlooked, and encourage the search for additional information.[27]

What follows are ten policy prescriptions suggested by the historical cases we have examined. Taken together, they sketch out an approach to peace making that abstains from heavy-handed oppression without embracing hope-for-the-best beneficence. As discussed in Chapter 2, harsh treatment and leniency are polar extremes on a continuum of possible peace settlements. Rather than conceiving of the victor's choice in dichotomous terms, these prescriptions embody a more nuanced approach to dealing with the defeated.

MORAL PRINCIPLES AND POLICY PRESCRIPTIONS FOR THE RESOLUTION OF ARMED CONFLICT

On November 7, 1941, with German tanks only eighty kilometers from Moscow, Soviet leader Joseph Stalin spoke to local Communist Party workers at the Mayakovsky underground railway station. The invaders, he promised, "would get their war of annihilation and be exterminated without mercy. Our task is revenge," he thundered.[28]

The role of emotions in decision making has generally been neglected by contemporary students of international security. Yet, as suggested by recent neurological research, deep-seated emotions like Stalin's anger are central to decision making.[29] Emotions are like filters that narrow alternatives: they eliminate some options and draw those driven by passion to others.

Different emotions are brought into play by the manner in which a war begins and how it is conducted. For example, victors who have been targets of brutal, unprovoked aggression will have to grapple with feelings of treachery and betrayal, something unlikely to color the postwar policies of victors who initiated wars for opportunistic reasons. Regardless of how a war may have started and whether one was fighting to defend or overthrow the status quo, the longer the duration and the greater the costs, the more angry emotions will constrict the range of choices available to victor and vanquished alike. **Mirror imaging,** the propensity of each side in a conflict to see in its own actions only rectitude and in those of the adversary only malice, reduces the prospects for leniency by the winner and acquiescence by the loser. In such an atmosphere of mutual distrust, victors face difficult choices in sorting out short-term desires from long-term interests. What they want may not be what they need. Even from an advantaged position in which the enemy surrendered unconditionally, the victor still must decide what kind of peace agreement would enhance security. Should the peace be lenient or punitive? Can it combine elements of conciliation with retribution? How will the prostrate adversary respond? What countermoves are likely once the loser recovers from defeat? Military triumph solves certain problems but creates new ones. As we have seen in the preceding chapters, many wars have ended with a victor's peace rather than a victory for peace.

Given the far-reaching repercussions that result from how victors deal with the defeated, what steps can be taken to solidify a durable peace settlement? Based on the cases examined, we suggest the following policy prescriptions.

Prescription 1: *Military strategy in war fighting should be coordinated with the political strategy for peace making.*

Throughout this book we have argued that victory is not an end in itself. Military forces should be deployed for national purposes, not for promoting the interests of the military doing the fighting. However, this principle is sometimes overlooked, and that exacerbates the problem of making peace.

At the root of the danger is the difficulty of separating military objectives from basic national goals. Although people tend to see a country's foreign policy as the product of a single calculating intelligence, in fact most governments are amalgams of large, semiautonomous bureaucratic organizations that have their own interests and hold different conceptions of national security. Since policy is often formulated by a small group of senior officials, each of whom may occupy a leadership position within one of these organizations, it can be difficult to orchestrate words and deeds in a coherent program that will be implemented faithfully by subordinates.[30] Fearing that **bureaucratic politics** contaminate military decisions, the armed forces sometimes are given substantial leeway in shaping the conduct of the war. Yet when crucial military and political decisions are compartmentalized, battlefield triumphs may not advance vital political aims. As one observer of this problem has noted, "Making peace is not a military operation, and even when a military response is unavoidable, tactical considerations ought to be tempered by greater political goals."[31]

How wars are fought and won influence how peace agreements are designed and maintained. Without a mechanism to integrate the conduct of war with planning for peace, questions of grand strategy can devolve to questions of operational art.[32] In such circumstances, insufficient attention is devoted to the geopolitics of military victory. Where and when an adversary is forced to lay down its arms can have long-term political consequences. Consider the case of the German *Dolchstoss* legend, the stab-in-the-back interpretation of Germany's defeat in World War I. At the end of the war, the German army was still in France. Given that a civilian government surrendered to the Western allies, and no allied offensive ever reached Germany, disgruntled German officers later said that their army had not been defeated. Rather, it was betrayed by traitors who had negotiated a treaty of shame. This association between the allegedly perfidious Weimar Republic and the humiliating Treaty of Versailles haunted German political life for the next fourteen years.[33] Adolf Hitler made it a staple in his bombastic appeals to the German masses. To prevent a similar reinterpretation of history from souring the peace after World War II, the United States and Great Britain called for the "unconditional surrender" of the Axis powers at the 1943 Casablanca conference.

Harmonizing military and political strategy does not mean politicians should consider themselves field commanders. Just as military leaders may be inattentive to how their actions affect the contours of the postwar settlement, political leaders ignorant of military matters may interfere with the conduct of crucial operations. According to Geoffrey Regan, Winston Churchill's "meddling in the military affairs of the Middle East Command in 1940–1941 contributed to four separate yet connected disasters: the Greek expedition, the fall of Crete, Rommel's recapture of Cyrenaica, and the fall of Singapore."[34] Backseat driving by impatient political leaders may lead to assaults being launched too soon or in the wrong place. During the 1982 war between Argentina and Great Britain over the Falklands Islands, for example, British general Julian Thompson was ordered by his political superiors in London to seize an Argentinian position at Goose Green, despite its lack of military significance and serious logistical problems inherent in mounting the attack.[35] The purpose of coordinating political and military strategy is to ensure that the process of war termination facilitates postwar peace building. Although political leaders decide war aims, they must avoid the temptation to micromanage the war effort and never lose sight of their responsibility for seeing that military action should service the political goal of making peace.

Prescription 2: Planning for the postwar era must begin early.

The eve of victory is not the time to begin formulating plans for dealing with the many complicated problems that arise when wars end. Decisions must be made on the evacuation of wounded soldiers, the exchange of prisoners of war, the release of interned civilians, the repatriation of displaced persons, and the restitution of property. National leaders must also wrestle with questions pertaining to how many troops should be demobilized, how to absorb them into the labor force, and how to compensate those who have borne the costs of fighting. In some instances, they may have to confront additional challenges, including stationing occupation forces in conquered territory, retiring war-related debts, rebuilding damaged infrastructure, and converting armament industries to the production of consumer goods. The nature of a war determines the complexity of these issues. Generally speaking, the longer the fighting continues and the greater the number of belligerents involved, the more difficult management of these issues becomes.[36]

Regardless of whether a war is terminated by a series of piecemeal agreements while the fighting drags on or through a comprehensive settlement after a truce, the bargaining position of victors erodes over time. As the United States discovered after the Persian Gulf War, whatever is not exacted from an adversary during the shock of defeat becomes far more difficult to attain later.[37]

Unfortunately, as our cases reveal, postwar policies rarely emerge from deliberative plans; they unfold incrementally through a tyranny of small decisions, owing more to impulse than design. Lacking a grand strategy for the world of their making, victors usually improvise and **muddle through** the immediate aftermath of the war. "Few indeed are the occasions on which any statesman sees his objective clearly before him and marches toward it with undeviating stride," observed Harold Nicolson.[38] Most decisions "are like Topsy—they just grow."[39] Indeed, there "may be no policy at all but simply a drift with events."[40]

To prevent policy drift, victors need to project what is likely to occur at the end of the war, anticipate the potential obstacles to a lasting peace settlement, and design a plan for surmounting them. Planning means forecasting the range of plausible futures, setting clear goals for attaining a specific desired future, and recommending actions for realizing that future. The sooner a formal attempt is undertaken to accomplish these tasks, the greater the chances that decisionmakers will be alerted to peace-making opportunities they might otherwise miss.

Prescription 3: Prepare the public for the transition from war to peace.

Nationalistic fervor, so important for mobilizing the population for war, can become an obstacle to concluding a reasonable peace. Political leaders frequently stoke the fires of **xenophobia** on the home front to encourage sacrifice in the war effort. Denigrating the enemy's character is among the most common techniques to fuel these flames. Rhetorical appeals containing derogatory assertions about an enemy's character are a form of "ethotic" argument.[41] Typically, the thrust of these arguments during a war is to emphasize something diabolical about the character of the opponent in order to arouse a strong negative response. After highlighting these traits, an attempt is made to transfer the negative response to a conclusion about the intentions, actions, and motivations of the opponent.[42] Ethotic arguments appeal to the well-documented tendency of people to attribute their own behavior to situational factors while attributing the same behavior to an adversary's dispositional characteristics.[43] For example, if the leader of a particular country authorizes the strategic bombing of an enemy city, he might plead that he was driven to it by the exigencies of military necessity. However, when a rival engages in the same behavior, the leader probably would explain it by referring to his counterpart's inherent character flaws. Given that most people habitually overestimate the importance of dispositional causes when explaining the behavior of others, it is not surprising that ethotic arguments are common, politically acceptable, and persuasive during wartime.

Another reason for the effectiveness of ethotic arguments is the tendency of people to make facile connections between current problems and certain past events that they have personally or vicariously experienced. Research in cognitive psychology has found evidence that people are "classifiers" who attempt to understand the world by matching what is presently occurring with experiences that are stored in the form of memory schemata.[44] Simply put, **schematic reasoning** involves comparing the current situation with prototypes in one's memory. Among the types of schemata that influence decision making are stereotypical images that represent the character traits of vividly recalled or easily imagined individuals—the ruthless gangster, the sadistic bully, and so on. Despite the fact that an adversary may bear only a superficial resemblance to one of these "stock" characters, when little is known about someone our expectations will be shaped by presumed similarities to these stereotypes.

Finally, ethotic arguments are compelling because they allow people to evade responsibility. Combatants fall back on negative stereotypes and other discrediting devices to reduce guilt over their own repugnant acts by projecting blame on the enemy. Since the enemy allegedly is unscrupulous, one's own unethical behaviors are interpreted as pre-emptive measures.[45] According to the old saw, sometimes you have to fight fire with fire, and this way of thinking easily leads to the conviction that the end justifies the means, regardless of how evil are those means.

Heavy doses of ethotic argumentation have a dangerous side effect. When the war ends, the public may have little empathy for the losing side and expect to receive what it believes are the justifiable spoils from victory over a sinister enemy. For example, when it was learned that Russia refused to pay an indemnity or cede territory at the end of the Russo-Japanese War of 1904–1905, the

Asahi Shimbun, a Japanese newspaper, printed the peace terms in a black frame, above a picture of a weeping soldier's skeleton. In response to this and similar editorials in other newspapers, tens of thousands of Japanese demonstrators clashed with police and set fire to government buildings on September 5 and 6, 1905, prompting the government to declare martial law and prohibit further criticism of the treaty.[46] Accentuating a diabolical image of the enemy may rally the populace when morale is low, but it will distort the peace settlement unless public expectations regarding the fruits of victory are attenuated before the fighting halts. Praise for an opponent's valor, differentiating between those who fought with honor and those who committed war crimes, and reminding one's own citizens of the plight of victims on both sides are critical in reversing the effects of wartime propaganda that denigrates the enemy's character.

Prescription 4: *Victors should not ignore the passion for vengeance.*

A passion for vengeance resides at the very core of our sense of justice. The moral vocabulary we use when discussing how to deal with perpetrators of grievous offenses is permeated with metaphors about debt ("repaying a wrong") and balance ("getting even") that underscore the central place of vengeance in our conception of punishment.[47] From the ghost of Clytemnestra who implores the Furies to avenge her murder by Orestes to the ghost of Hamlet's father who demands Hamlet avenge his murder by Claudius, playwrights through the ages have fascinated us with tales of wrathful anger. Although revenge themes are still common in film and literature today, we usually regard vengeance as the "sick vestige of a more primitive stage of human development," something that "falls within the province of detectives and other specialists in abnormal psychology."[48] Yet it is difficult to deny the satisfaction most humans feel when those guilty of some moral outrage receive their comeuppance, regardless of whether the penalty deters others from engaging in offensive conduct. Indeed, we often speak of "poetic justice" when miscreants who have evaded formal punishment experience a misfortune that nullifies ill-gotten gains.

The need for vengeance derives from powerful emotions that peacemakers ignore at great risk. It generally arises in the aftermath of premeditated campaigns of aggression that violate international humanitarian norms,[49] such as the those undertaken by the Axis powers in World War II. If the victims of these campaigns believe that wrongdoers failed to receive their just desserts, a sense of closure is never reached and private acts of retaliation are likely to follow.[50] Evil must be condemned and its perpetrators held responsible for their appalling deeds. The issue for victors is not whether angry emotions that demand punishment for wrongs are irrational and therefore inappropriate for consideration when crafting a peace settlement, but rather when and how it is reasonable to satisfy these demands.

Prescription 5: Avoid taking revenge, but seek retributive punishment for the culpably guilty.

To assert that a passion for vengeance is sometimes warranted is not to advocate wanton vindictiveness. Unrestrained vengeance has the potential to degenerate into an endless blood feud. In the culture of the vendetta, retaliation for an injury involves more than "an eye for an eye, a tooth for a tooth."[51] It is "an overpowering and consuming fire that burns away every other thought" and creates "the wildest, sweetest kind of drunkenness."[52] Under such a code of conduct, revenge is a duty. "He who cannot revenge himself is weak," proclaims an old Italian proverb. "He who will not is contemptible."

The dangers of spiteful, measureless retaliation lead many theorists to differentiate between revenge and retribution. Revenge is an attempt "to impose suffering upon those who have made one suffer, because they have made one suffer."[53] It is a personal act—a self-righteous returning of wrong for wrong in which the avenger seeks pleasure from the suffering inflicted on the culprit. In Homer's *Iliad*, Achilles embodies the concept of revenge when he turns his wrath toward Hector, the Trojan warrior who slew his friend Patroclos. "Lions and men make no truce, wolves and lambs have no friendship—they hate each other for ever," Achilles tells his opponent. "So there can be no love between you and me, and there shall be no truce for us." After killing Hector and mutilating his body, Achilles declares: "Fare thee well, Patroclos . . . . See now I am fulfilling all that I promised! I said said I would drag Hector to this place and give him to the dogs to devour raw; and in front of your pyre I would cut the throats of twelve noble sons of the Trojans, in payment for your death."[54]

Retribution lacks the resentful, vindictive spirit of revenge; it avenges a moral transgression dispassionately, without personal rancor. In contrast to the paroxysm of violence shown by Achilles, retribution has limits.[55] Since revenge has no objective limits, it is normally restricted by social norms that specify what constitutes an affront, who is obliged to respond, what means may be used, when it can occur, and what will be done to those who fail to live up to their obligations. In some societies, these norms transform revenge into ritualized acts of violence that extinguish smouldering disagreements before they ignite into full-scale fighting.[56] More typically, acts of revenge "overpay" rather than "even the score," thereby adding new injuries that reinforce old hatreds.[57] Retributive justice attempts to halt this escalatory momentum by taking jural-like activity out of private hands, distinguishing between crimes and their punishment, and placing limits on the penalties wrongdoers pay.

Two basic schools of thought exist on the nature of retributive justice. The *maximalist* school, represented by Immanuel Kant, holds that there is a duty to punish anyone who is guilty and culpable for wrongdoing and that the punishment should be equal to the seriousness of the offense.[58] *Minimalism*, the second school of thought, also expresses moral indignation over the behavior of the culpable. However, it asserts that punishment should be relative to the seriousness of the offense and, unlike in a strict liability system, allows for mitigating circumstances that can partially or completely absolve the offender.

For victors seeking a durable peace, a minimalist conception of retributive justice offers several important benefits. First, by holding specific individuals accountable for any war crimes or crimes against humanity that they may have committed, it defuses the possibility that charges of **collective guilt** will be leveled against an entire defeated nation, as happened to Germany following World War I. Second, avoiding collective condemnation facilitates the normalization of relations between victor and vanquished after the war. Third, by showing that international humanitarian law cannot be violated with impunity, it helps those who were victimized bring closure to the experience. Finally, by eschewing revenge in favor of retributive justice through a fair and impartial judicial process (ideally through an international tribunal), reconciliation and the pursuit of restorative justice can begin.

Prescription 6: *Victors should forgive the forgivable, but not forget.*

Reconciliation is a process of developing a mutually conciliatory accommodation between former enemies.[59] It is a dynamic, sequential process that requires actions by those who have suffered wrongs as well as by those who have committed them. The former consists of forgiving; the latter, apologizing. Although it is common to hear references to forgiveness and apology in our everyday conversations, rarely does anyone seriously reflect on their precise meaning. Because both are complex, multidimensional concepts, let us briefly discuss each in turn.

Perhaps the most systematic contemporary work on the elusive concept of forgiveness has been done by Donald Shriver.[60] Genuine forgiveness, he explains, has four dimensions. First, forgiveness begins with a memory of past evils suffused with a moral judgment of injustice. Second, forgiveness entails forbearance; past wrongs are neither overlooked nor excused, but punishment is not reduced to revenge. Third, forgiveness includes empathy for the enemy; that is, a recognition of the other side's humanity. Finally, genuine forgiveness is restorative; it seeks to repair fractured human relationships and promote social healing.

For social healing to occur, wrongdoers must shoulder the responsibility for apologizing. Like forgiveness, a sincere apology entails several things. First, it involves feelings of sorrow and regret for the injurious act.[61] Second, it expresses shame over what was done and repudiates that kind of behavior.[62] Third, it contains an avowal henceforth to conduct oneself in the proper way.[63] Finally, it includes a gesture of penance to atone for the transgression. In certain societies, apologies inaugurate a process of lustration. Rather than just stigmatizing the offender, the members of these societies follow their denunciations with a highly visible ritual of reacceptance.[64] In this way, the wrongdoer is reintegrated into the fold instead of remaining an outcast, forever condemned to the margins of public life. Public ceremonies of reconciliation, such as the ancient practice observed by some native Americans of burying war axes, can help reverse relations among former adversaries.

Apology and forgiveness can jointly soothe raw postwar feelings, but not necessarily in every situation. No victor can force the vanquished to have feelings of sorrow and remorse for injurious acts. Even when someone has suffered directly from the misdeeds of a truly repentant person, deep introspection normally is required before the relationship can be repaired. Forgiving under ordinary circumstances is difficult. What happens when the injustice is far greater in scope and magnitude? Are certain offenses of such moral gravity and some perpetrators at such moral fault that apology is an empty gesture and forgiveness beyond human reach? Does anyone have the moral agency to forgive massive atrocities committed against others? How should we respond to existential evil? Consider the plight of Simon, a Jewish internee at a Nazi concentration camp.[65] One day he encountered a mortally wounded SS officer who asked forgiveness for the many heinous crimes he committed against other Jews. Did Simon have the power or the right to forgive him for his unspeakable acts? Perhaps there are some deeds so horrific that recompense for the victims and forgiveness for the perpetrators are outside of the victors' human capability.[66]

Prescription 7: A dictated peace is a precarious peace; victors should involve the vanquished in settlement negotiations.

History judges a nation as a winner in war if it can force the enemy to surrender. But winners can ultimately lose the peace if they fail to include the defeated at the conference table. There are many perils to the art of peace making. Perhaps none is as perilous as summoning the courage and skill to negotiate the terms of surrender with an enemy.

A classic example of the dangers of imposing a settlement is provided by the harsh treatment forced upon on France in 1871 at the conclusion of the Franco-Prussian War. The prostrate French were instructed about the terms of the peace treaty and were not given much of a chance to modify the settlement. Their thirst for revenge over this humiliation "was a prime combustible leading to the global conflagration of 1914–1918. The Germans forgot one of their own proverbs: 'Revenge does not long remain unrevenged.' "[67]

Victors should avoid treating grievances voiced by the defeated as if they were simply outrageous bargaining tactics. The losing side in a war may believe it has legitimate complaints and a right to express them. When victors deny that perceived right and proclaim that they alone can define the meaning of justice, they deprive the defeated a chance to express its ideas about what constitutes a fair peace settlement. Not only does this cause a loss of face, but it removes any stake the defeated might have had in upholding the settlement. Even concessions by the victor on issues of low priority can assuage an adversary. As Roger Fisher and William Ury point out, giving the other side a small role in drafting the settlement creates a sense of ownership: "An outcome in which the other side gets absolutely nothing is worse for you than one which leaves them mollified."[68]

Showing disrespect to an adversary by precluding their participation in discussion about peace terms is risky for another reason besides the likelihood that insulting treatment will evoke future efforts to vindicate a wounded sense of honor. It is also bad policy because it overlooks the possibility that yesterday's enemy may be needed as tomorrow's friend. Peace settlements must look forward rather than backward. Victors should be aware of the interests underlying their opponents' stated position and look for opportunities to work toward achieving superordinate goals that neither side could achieve alone.[69] Shared interests may not be immediately obvious, but there will almost always be features in a peace settlement where victors can satisfy some interest of the other side without damaging a significant interest of their own."[70]

In sum, victors in search of a durable peace settlement should apply the Golden Rule to diplomacy, treating the vanquished the way they would wish themselves to be treated were they in the same position. So long as one is not dealing with an utterly ruthless, depraved opponent, restraint and a readiness for conciliation can evoke gratitude and set in motion a positive spiral of tension-reducing reciprocation. Victors who couple firmness regarding their own interests with fairness toward the interests of others encourage defeated powers to work within the postwar system. Nowhere is this more important than in resolving outstanding territorial issues. A fair disposition of territorial claims, coupled with simple, unambiguous, and prominent lines of demarcation, are critical to building a lasting peace.

Prescription 8: Beware of allies whose interest in the peace negotiations centers on gaining the spoils of victory.

Alliances are formal agreements between sovereign states "for the putative purpose of coordinating their behavior in the event of certain specified contingencies of a military nature."[71] Coordination may range from a detailed list of armed forces that will be furnished by each party to the broader requirement of consultation should a serious dispute occur. In addition to differing according to the level of coordination, **alliances** also vary in terms of the target and duration of their accords. The target of an alliance may be left implicit or may be identified as a single country, a group of states, or a geographic region. Alliance duration may be limited to a relatively short period of time or constructed to last indefinitely.

Rarely are alliances formed just to express friendship or some vague ideological affiliation. They are constructed for clear, calculated advantage. In the first place, alliances help states acquire benefits that might not have been attained by acting unilaterally. In the second place, they reduce the costs associated with foreign policy undertakings by spreading them among several partners. If the perceived benefits exceed the costs, and if the costs are politically sustainable, states worried about their security will join alliances despite the uneven burdens they necessitate and the unequal returns they provide.

It is always uncertain whether an alliance will serve the purposes for which it was originally created. Will it deter external attacks? If not, will the members uphold their treaty commitments when faced with the possibility of war? And if they do, will the alliance be able to defeat the aggressors? Fighting in concert with allies is a challenge. Enormous amounts of time and energy must be invested in resolving interallied disagreements on strategy. Even when a consensus exists, friction may still arise over the priorities assigned to specific theatres of the war. Further complicating matters, units from various countries—trained under different philosophies, armed with different weapons, and configured for different missions—must somehow work in tandem, occasionally in the midst of petty rivalries among allied commanders. As one observer of military partnerships has put it, alliances are "like a house built by jealous carpenters with no boss and with many different plans for the design of the building."[72]

Alliances, in other words, are rickety constructions whose structural integrity diminishes when the common external threat that brought them into being recedes. With victory in sight, aggressively self-interested members of large wartime coalitions will likely be tempted by the chance for booty and begin jockeying for a peace settlement that furthers their own selfish aims. At this point it is crucial for those states with aspirations of building a durable peace settlement to use the waning days of the war to unite behind a collective peace plan. If major issues are left unresolved until a formal peace conference, the most determined ally will end up in possession of important assets which then can be removed only through a perilous confrontation.[73]

The success of a multilateral peace conference depends on the victors' capacity to transcend the desire for short-term relative gains and embrace the goal of avoiding mutual loss. Perhaps no statesman in the cases we have covered was better at framing the settlement process in these terms than Austria's Metternich. At the Congress of Vienna he was able to control events by defining their moral framework. Keenly aware of the importance of reducing the grandiose claims put forth by others—rather than simply promoting his own—Klemens von Metternich made concessions appear as sacrifices to a common cause. The legitimacy of a peace settlement, he always said, rests on acceptance, not imposition.[74]

Prescription 9: Victors should be prepared to use military force after the war ends.

Thomas Schelling has written, "It takes at least as much skill to end a war properly as to begin one to advantage."[75] Losers may still possess bargaining assets, even when they have no hope of winning a war. Not only can they struggle on and extract a price from the winner by making victory more costly, they may, like Saddam Hussein following the Persian Gulf War, be able to undermine postwar stability. The durability of a peace settlement hinges on the victor's ability to (1) anticipate how dissatisfied parties may challenge new security arrangements and (2) develop effective contingency plans for arresting these challenges. Ironically, "military victory is often a prelude to violence, not the end of it," notes Schelling.[76] The successful victor generally holds the threat of more pain to come in reserve as a way of inducing the vanquished to accommodate itself to defeat. Conciliation is unlikely to succeed without the backing of a credible deterrent.

By itself, restraint in victory may not be enough to defuse the losers' desire for revenge. Occasionally, restraint toward the vanquished must be combined with a convincing use of military force against someone else. Take, for instance, relations between Prussia and Austria after the Seven Weeks War. As early as December 1866, Bismarck had sought a **rapprochement** with Austria, but was rebuffed. With Prussia's shocking victory over France at the Battle of Sedan, attitudes in Vienna began to change. Austrian foreign minister Friedrich Ferdinand Baron Beust, an ardent opponent of Bismarck, concluded that it was now in Austria's interest to distance itself from the French. In a memorandum written on May 18, 1871, Beust stated that Austria was detrimentally affected by the French loss at Sedan in two ways. First, Prussia could exert its immense military power against Austria directly. Second, it could interfere indirectly with Austria by manipulating German nationalist sentiments within Austria's multinational empire. Given the leverage Berlin would have over Austria, he recommended seeking an accommodation with Prussia.[77]

Prescription 10: The vanquished have responsibilities in making peace.

Winners in war have the power to exercise their will. As a result, they have received most of the praise when peace settlements succeeded and most of the blame when they failed. Indeed, it is tempting to believe that the responsibilities for making peace rest exclusively with the choices of victors. That temptation should be overcome, however, because the actions of the defeated can influence the peace plans of the victors.

Losers, like winners, must also make hard choices. Should they resent their loss and strive to undermine the new postwar order? Or should they adjust to the painful turn of events and work within the new order? The choice is difficult even when the loser is guilty of wrongdoing; it becomes agonizing when the loser is innocent. How should the vanquished respond when it was responsible for the war? Conversely, what should it do when the winner provoked the showdown and then violated prevailing codes of military conduct? What should it do when blame is relatively equal? The answers depend in large measure on whether the war effort was regarded by the loser as being worth the costs. Wars perceived as not having been worth their costs engender a domestic political environment where accommodationists rather than defiant hard-liners prevail. According to John Vasquez, a repeat of war between the same two parties is less likely when accommodationists govern political life within the country that has lost the war.[78]

Defeated nations are always in poor bargaining positions. Yet they are not without power. In certain circumstances, a principled posture by accommodationists within the defeated country can influence how victors behave once the fighting ends. Assuming the loser is not annihilated (like Carthage after the Third Punic War), the victor must confront a series of questions about the role of its former enemy in the postwar world. Can the vanquished be trusted? Do they intend to stand by the peace agreement? Will they recoil into battle at the first opportunity to avenge their losses? Uncertainty over the answers to these questions can plague a victor, leading it to expend scarce resources for contingencies it would prefer to avoid.

Consider the following scenario: What would a victor do if a defeated country accepted its part of the blame for the war's onset and its accommodationist government sought to work dutifully within the new international order? A pacific response by the subjugated can sometimes disarm the conqueror. Losing parties can win by practicing "moral jiujitsu," in the terminology of Richard B. Gregg. Jiujitsu is an Oriental martial art that throws the powerful off balance by countering its attack. In Gregg's conception, a repentant former enemy can encourage the victor to be merciful by throwing him off moral balance:

> He suddenly and unexpectedly loses the moral support which the usual violent resistance of most victims would render him. He plunges forward, as it were, into a new world of values. He feels insecure because of the novelty of the situation and his ignorance of how to handle it. He loses his poise and self-confidence . . . . [In this way, the vanquished party] uses the leverage of a superior wisdom to subdue the rough direct force of his opponent.[79]

Suffering may be a viable strategy for a state defeated in war. Principles can produce power. "Most advocates of principled nonviolence believe that unmerited suffering is the most forceful way to affect an opponent's conscience." Self-imposed suffering and "the willing acceptance of sanctions imposed for noncooperation are considered most effective for bringing about a change of heart in one's opponents."[80] As the twentieth century's leading prophet of this philosophy, Mahatma Gandhi, explained,

> Things of fundamental importance to the people are not secured by reason alone, but have to be purchased with their suffering. Suffering is the law of human beings; war is the law of the jungle. But suffering is infinitely more powerful than the law of the jungle for converting the opponent and opening his ears, which are otherwise shut, to the voice of reason.[81]

To heed his advice about encouraging compassion through *satyagraha* (or "truth force") is to ask the loser in war to respond in an unusual way. Disarming the victor by appealing to its morality is not easy. Tempers flare in the heat of battle, and enemies often dehumanize each other as accusations fly back and forth. Memories of war continue to smolder long after a truce is struck, threatening to ignite once again into an inferno of hatred. But if the defeated duti-fully serves the victor after the war, and if it can identify itself with principles the victor accepts as just, it may be able to embarrass the victor into living up to its own beliefs about fair play. Of course, such a strategy assumes that the victor believes in fair play and is not committed to a policy of genocide.[82]

FROM JUST WAR TO JUST PEACE

"The real puzzle for social scientists is not war and violence," observe an-thropologists Thomas Gregor and Clayton Robarchek, "but a more unusual phenomenon: peace."[83] While scholars rightly devote enormous effort to scien-tifically studying the causes of war, complementary research efforts on how nations make peace lag far behind. "Much more is known about how conflicts escalate," conclude psychologists Dean Pruitt and Jeffrey Rubin, "than about how they de-escalate."[84]

Attaining peace is more difficult than desiring it. Sustaining peace once it has been attained is even more demanding. The victor in search of a lasting accord with the vanquished must somehow blend demands for security from domestic constituencies with policies the former enemy accepts as fitting. It must be able to quash challenges to the new international order while develop-ing procedures that allow complaints to be aired and peaceful change to occur. Postwar settlements that harmonize these competing concerns are fragile and require constant care because mistrust is endemic in world politics.

Building Trust, Building Peace

While scholars have argued for centuries about the conditions under which it is just to wage war, far less thought has gone into how to craft a just peace. Achieving a just and lasting peace is difficult because suspicion is pervasive among sovereign states in an anarchic world. Without a higher authority pos-sessing the legitimacy and coercive capability to preserve peace, states must fend for themselves while struggling with multiple fears: the fear of attack by enemies, the fear of exploitation by allies, and the fear of being victimized by an unfair treaty. These fears peak as war clouds gather, but scarcely dissipate when the fighting ends. As the belligerents face the task of rebuilding their rela-tionship, insecurity persists. The parties to every war face uncertainty as they look to the future.

The chronic suspicion infecting world politics does not auger well for build-ing a lasting peace. Entrenched doubts about promises voiced by a former foe inhibits mutually beneficial collaboration and encourages defensive noncoop-eration. Yet, building peace requires building trust, even among states that have few reasons to have confidence in one another. At war's end, the victor must consider actions that seem counterintuitive, such as reconciling with an adversary previously perceived as without scruples. Obviously, many authorities recommend against this risky approach. They recognize that "to trust is to act as if the uncertain future actions of others were indeed certain in circumstances wherein the violation of these expectations results in negative consequences for those involved."[85] Trust can invite betrayal. Building trust by trusting unreliable former enemies is therefore highly controversial. As Bernhardt Lieberman has written, embedded within most foreign policy debates on these matters are two contending positions:

> Without doing lethal damage to the essence of the arguments, it is possible to dichotomize the various views about these questions. One group argues it is irrelevant, and possibly dangerous, to consider the notion of trust in the conduct of international relations. Nations, it is said, will act in their own self-interest and abrogate treaties, agreements, or their word informally given, whenever it is believed to be necessary to do so. It is said that a nation that does not act in its own self-interest is difficult to deal with; trustworthy behavior contrary to national interests is irresponsible and dangerous. Therefore there is no point in concerning oneself with such a value-laden notion as trust. Trust is irrelevant in the conduct of international affairs, it is said, and if we seek to resolve conflicts among nations rationally, before they become harmful and mutually destructive, we must not trust our opponents at all; we must not even consider such a notion seriously.
>
> A second group believes that at the root of the difficulty in international affairs is the fact that nations cannot and do not trust each other. Aggressive behavior and conflicts arise not so much from genuinely irreconcilable conflicts, but more from mistrust, suspicion, and untrustworthy acts. They believe that one should impress upon one's opponent one's good intentions. One should take actions that do not endanger one's own security, but that promote trust and demonstrate good will. One should sign arms agreements that will build mutual trust and positive feelings.[86]

These rival ideas about making peace are nested within the two major traditions of theoretical inquiry introduced in Chapter 1: liberalism and realism. As summarized in Table 10.3, liberals like Woodrow Wilson maintain that trust is possible and from it peace can be built. Realists from Cleon to Bismarck aver that it is better to put faith in your own power than to trust others. Let us briefly return to the ongoing conversation between these two traditions on how to craft a durable peace settlement.

Liberal Ideals and Illusions?

Observing the dismal regularity with which harsh peace settlements throughout history have disintegrated, liberal reformers have questioned the wisdom of punitive postwar policies. In fact, some liberal thinkers, like John Locke,

TABLE 10.3
Liberal and Realist Theories: Premises and Policy Prescriptions

	Liberalism	Realism
Premises		
Human Nature:	Cooperative, altruistic	Competitive, selfish
Chief Global Condition:	Interdependence	Anarchy and self-help
Conception of Politics:	A struggle about principles	A struggle for power
Core Concern:	Global interests	National interests
Philosophical Outlook:	Optimistic	Pessimistic
Prescriptions		
	Do what is right.	Do what is necessary.
	Moral duties supercede state sovereignty.	State sovereignty is inviolable.
	Seek mutual gains.	Seek relative gains over rivals.
	If you want peace, prepare for it by constructing international institutions.	If you want peace, prepare for war.
	Negotiate rather than fight, but adjudicate when negotiations stall.	Negotiate rather than fight, but fight rather than risk losing on an issue of importance.
	Limit national power through international law.	Increase national power.
	Promote international integration.	Resist any reduction of national autonomy.

believed that victors have ethical obligations to the vanquished.[87] Although there are several distinct theoretical traditions within liberalism, they share many elements of commonality. For liberals, foreign policy unfolds in a nascent global society populated by actors who recognize the costs of conflict and share significant interests. Believing in altruism, reason, and the capacity of people to change those practices that foster conflict, liberals emphasize how well-designed international institutions can bind victor and vanquished together in a web of overlapping and converging interests.

The European Coal and Steel Community (ECSC), formed by France, Germany, Italy, Belgium, Luxemburg, and the Netherlands in 1952, exemplified this integrative liberal approach to peace building through institutions. The ECSC contained a **supranational** body called the High Authority, which made binding decisions by majority vote on the production and marketing of coal and steel. As part of the ECSC, Germany could revive its heavy industry after

World War II without alarming its neighbors, who now possessed some degree of control over key German resources by virtue of their representation in the High Authority. Unfortunately, note some liberals, an earlier opportunity to build institutions in the metallurgical sector that could have brought the governments in Paris and Berlin closer together after World War I was missed, even though French iron ore complemented German coking coal.

> "Wars occur because people prepare for conflict, rather than for peace."
>
> —TRYGVE LIE

Several steps are considered necessary in order to get former foes to participate in institutions like the ECSC: repentance, restitution, and reciprocity. To the liberal faith, admitting injury and injustice are essential to the healing process. Peace making is not merely a matter of letting bygones be bygones. Reconciliation depends on a sincere effort to set the record straight through repentance and to build a new record through restitution.[88] Liberal theory also suggests that reconciliation depends on victors showing mercy to the defeated. Although mercy is a virtue that can conflict with the demands of justice, it nonetheless serves as a potential source of influence for the victor as well as a source of constraint for the vanquished. Recipients of magnanimity are placed in a position of social indebtedness. The greater their feeling of indebtedness, the greater their subsequent attempts to reduce it. Over time, this kind of exchange relationship is thought to create obligations that generate **reciprocity**.[89]

Many liberals stress the importance of commerce in reinforcing the web of interdependence spun by international institutions. Free trade creates material incentives to resolve disputes peacefully. The cosmopolitan business elites who benefit most from trade are seen as comprising a powerful transnational interest group with a stake in promoting amicable solutions to festering disagreements. Furthermore, many liberal theorists argue that the flow of trade between former enemies increases communication, erodes parochialism, and encourages both sides to construct new institutions to coordinate their behavior in other issue areas.

Liberalism also advances a large number of other proposals for making peace between nations. It advocates, for example, human rights, international law, and democratic forms of governance. For our purposes, the important element in liberal theory is moral. Liberals see power in adherence to ethical principles and see in conformity to rules the possibility of converting feuds into friendships. This applies directly to the question of the proper code of conduct for disputants after wars end. At the risk of oversimplifying the liberal argument, we can assert that most liberals would concur with the proposition that "Men will pay you back with the same measure you have used with them."[90] Good will be returned for good, bad for bad. Compassionate settlements, therefore, maximize the prospects for a lasting peace because they encourage the vanquished to return that good will.

The liberal approach to peace making is not without its problems, however. Ruthless opponents throughout history have taken advantage of mercy and forbearance, returning ill will for magnanimity. For this reason, various people have concluded that liberalism's peace proposals are illusory. The most severe of these critics are found in the realist camp.

The Realism of Realpolitik?

Any assessment of the virtues of repentance, restitution, and reciprocity must be balanced by a realist account of the dangers in this approach. Like liberalism, realism contains many strains of thought. As a political theory, realism traces its intellectual roots to the ancient Greek historian Thucydides, the Italian Renaissance theorist Niccolò Machiavelli, and the sixteenth-century English philosopher Thomas Hobbes. International politics, according to realists, is a ceaseless and repetitive struggle for power that occurs among territorially organized states of varying military and economic strength. Since the anarchic structure of the state system makes lasting peace impossible, realists envision the highest purpose of statecraft to be national survival. Wise leaders, they argue, will carefully weigh the perceived costs and benefits of alternative foreign policies with an eye toward marshaling the wherewithal needed to ensure security and advance national interests. From the realist perspective, security is a function of power, and power is primarily a function of military preparedness.

> "Diplomacy without arms is like music without instruments."
> —FREDERICK THE GREAT

According to some versions of realist thought, concern over moral principles interferes with the pursuit of national power. Ethical preferences are neither good nor bad—what matters is whether the state's self-interest is served. When it comes to designing a peace settlement, victors should be unrestrained in their sovereign right to choose whatever action they think is most likely to enhance their prospects for self-preservation. Any attempt to import moral principles into the settlement process would prove self-defeating. Looking at failed peace-making policies of the past, realist thought rivets attention on scenes of malevolence, deceit, and broken promises, concluding that postwar diplomatic conferences provide an opportunity to practice deception. Harsh punishment is the best way to keep a defeated enemy permanently down so it cannot rise again in retaliation. As a counter to the liberal claim that enemies should be forgiven, realists predict that crime unpunished will be repeated.

Like liberal theory, hard-boiled realism is not without its shortcomings. Contrary to what the nihilistic versions of this theory would predict, moderate treatment of France after the Napoleonic Wars ushered in a period of prolonged peace. Thus, while many realists scoff at the liberal suggestion that a defeated adversary will reciprocate goodwill, some realists assert that pure power politics may not be as effective in dealing with the defeated as the exercise of power within a framework of accepted legitimacy.

Kautilya, the ancient Hindu practitioner of realism, embodied this tension between the roles of power and justice in a peace settlement. Kautilya urged caution when interacting with subjugated powers.[91] "An enemy who was defeated earlier and who has since become a friend should not be trusted," he warned, "as a burnt cave filled with smoke is not trusted by the crow, even after the fire is extinguished." Because the remnants of such an enemy can spark an uprising, even "children of enemies who have surrendered" will "prove dangerous in due course." The "power born out of sorrow and resentment," he cautioned, "bestows bravery." Yet Kautilya recognized the importance of justice when dealing with the defeated. Wrong punishment angers while "good behavior wins even an enemy." He "who punishes severely is hated by the people, he who punishes mildly is despised, one who metes out deserving punishment is respected."

Proponents of liberalism and realism have long debated one another about the paths to peace and the perils of peace making, as this brief synopsis of their philosophies suggests. Whereas liberals believe in progress and place their faith in the improvement of individuals and institutions, realists discern no such capability in the human condition.[92] Notwithstanding these important distinctions, it would be wrong to conclude that there are no areas of agreement between the two traditions. Both concur on the importance of peace treaties in constructing a durable settlement, and both recognize the problems in designing such treaties. More importantly, all but the most vulgar exponents of realpolitik agree that "political expedience itself has to consult the moral sense of those it will affect" and be "softened into prudence."[93] Peace agreements encapsulated by a web of collaborative, partner-specific norms of prudence are more resilient than those lacking normative support, because international norms add predictability to future relations by communicating the scope of each state's entitlements, the extent of its obligations, and the range of its jurisdiction. Liberals and realists agree that postwar diplomacy cannot be divorced from the normative climate in which it occurs. If victors do not reinforce international norms that buttress the war termination agreements they sign, the vanquished will attempt to establish alternative norms that can be used to undermine the peace settlement.

From Reconciliation to Resolution

How can bitter adversaries overcome the rancor of their collective past and restore amicable relations? Peace making is a process without rigid rules. The only guidelines are those the winners choose. We have seen that victors tend to make up the rules as they go along. Sometimes their choices are made under time constraints. At other times, the peace-making process is protracted, with no perceived incentives for a prompt settlement. Whether constructed quickly or patiently, either procedure is likely to bring a series of problems in their wake if little thought has been given to questions of grand postwar strategy.

Like war itself, peace making can be likened to the game of chess. The players are able to make a vast number of interconnected moves and countermoves, each of which will alter the costs and benefits of the next round of decisions. Neither side can be sure of the opponent's sequence of moves over the course of the game, and each move alters the possibilities and payoffs of subsequent countermoves—thereby preventing anyone from knowing the long-term consequences of their choices. Just as there is no single formula to win at chess, there is no simple formula for how nations should make peace. As Charles Doran has written, victors "must consider the unique aspects that characterize the [international] system" at the time of their victory and the impact the war's outcome will have on other "major actors."[94] In addition, they must recognize the moral dilemmas involved.

Recognition involves acknowledging the past. Wartime adversaries may have to face unpleasant truths about themselves and their enemies. They must both give up the self-righteous belief that virtue resided in their own behavior and that all blame can be ascribed to the enemy. Wars are seldom a struggle between total virtue and vice, between an honorable nation and a wicked nation. But when so conceived, they become crusades that remove the possibility of finding common ground after the battles are over.

Empathy is crucial for finding common ground.[95] The architect of a peace settlement "must be able to comprehend the innermost interests of the vanquished and to empathetically assess the particular world of the defeated if he is to serve his own interests."[96] Victors must overcome what has been called "compassion fatigue" and the vanquished must move beyond recrimination.[97] Both parties need to see how their fates are intertwined. This requires that there be some general agreement as to the wrongs committed during the war, a consideration of the impact that those wrongs have had, and an attempt to atone for them.[98] As one scholar has put it,

> To achieve a comprehensive mutual accommodative relationship requires that significant members of the antagonistic parties combine a minimal level of [understanding of each other's] view and actions. First, the injured and the perpetrators openly acknowledge that reality of the terrible acts that were committed. Second, the injured are provided with prospects for security and well-being. Third, those who experienced injustices receive redress in some measure. Finally, the injured accept with compassion those who committed injurious conduct as well as acknowledge each other's suffering. The injured and the perpetrators of injury may refer to individuals, groups, organizations, peoples, or countries. The injured and the perpetrators are not to be regarded as mutually exclusive categories.[99]

In conclusion, when we think about making peace, we must think about **justice**. The end of a war requires calculations to be made about the allocation of benefits and burdens, rewards and punishment. These are ethical choices, not legal ones; they are decisions about values, not rights; they are occasions where winners can determine what goods will be received and what goods will be lost.

The decision-making problem confronting winners is complicated by the pull of several competing dimensions of justice: (1) distributive justice—the ethics of dividing the spoils of war at the loser's expense; (2) retributive justice—the ethics of administering punishment for wrongful deeds; (3) corrective justice—the ethics of compensating victims; and (4) **restorative justice**—the ethics of rebuilding broken relationships. All war-ending events raise difficult questions in each of these areas of moral inquiry. If this book inspires greater awareness of, and attention to, the broader ethical and policy issues of building a just world order, it will have accomplished its primary educational goal.

NOTES

1. For statistical findings that describe this pattern, see Bennett and Stam, 1996, pp. 251–253.
2. *Newsweek,* March 2, 1998, p. 92.
3. Oren, 1982, p. 153.
4. Geller and Singer, 1998, p. 1. Of those nations that have experienced war, forty-nine fought in one or two wars, sixteen participated in three or four, and only eight were involved in more than ten.
5. Massoud, 1996, p. 491.
6. Georg Simmel' in Beer and Mayer, 1986, p. 195.
7. A practical, didactic (advice-giving) theory of peace making identifies the decision rules and conditions associated with lasting settlements. Such a theory draws upon past patterns to identify those factors (independent variables) most strongly linked to peace-making success and failure (the dependent variable). If predictions about how to act are based on a correct reading of historical regularities, the theory can offer guidance to victors on how to craft durable peace settlements. For discussions of explanations that account for particular cases by reference to general patterns, see Hempel, 1965 and 1966, and Raymond, 1975. A discussion of how applied empirical research can be used to evaluate foreign policy can be found in Raymond, 1987.
8. Rosenthal, 1995, p. 317.
9. Ibid.
10. Ibid., p. 328.
11. The literature on realism and liberalism is vast, and it is beyond the scope of this book to give a full account of the many variations within each tradition. The reader will note that we also draw on a wide variety of theories beyond realism and liberalism (from such fields as moral philosophy, sociology, and international law) and that here, too, an attempt to describe the divergent orientations is hopelessly outside what we can cover in this book. For summaries and syntheses that cover realist and liberal thinking about international peace, see Baldwin, 1993; Doyle, 1997; Kegley, 1995; Nardin and Mapel, 1992; Rosenthal, 1991; and Smith, 1986.
12. Bennett, 1996, p. 158.
13. Leng, 1983.
14. See Brecher, 1984; Goertz and Diehl, 1992a and 1992b; and Diehl, Reifschneider, and Hensel, 1996.
15. Maoz, 1984, p. 239; Hensel, 1994. Although winners tend to initiate new wars sooner than states that suffer a loss, the inhibiting effect of losing on future aggression is seldom long-lasting

because losers have a high probability of initiating another war roughly a generation after they recover from a loss, largely due to treasured memories of previous victories. Nevin, 1996, p. 105.

16. As discussed earlier, for analytic reasons we have excluded the many armed conflicts that ended without a clear victor; hence, we have not focused on how to build peace following a military stalemate. Obviously, how nations make peace after an inconclusive war is an important topic. Believing that it merits a separate study, we plan to address it in subsequent research.

17. We recognize that our sample was not randomly drawn from the population of all decisive victories in the modern era. Instead, we have focused on those wars that have been most frequently cited by policymakers as evidence of why victors should act in a particular way when combat ends. Based on a comparison of those wars, we have advanced a prescriptive argument composed of didactic propositions about how nations should act after wars to sustain durable peace settlements. In the spirit of building policy-relevant theory that advances recommendations for making peace, we envision this tentative first step as preliminary to subsequent empirical testing. From our perspective, the process of moving back and forth between making arguments and testing them against new data lies at the heart of the social-scientific enterprise.

18. Thucydides, 1951, pp. 14–15.

19. Livy, 1919, p. 7.

20. Neustadt and May, 1986, pp. 91–92.

21. For suggestions on how policy-relevant theories can be built from the comparative study of cases, see George, 1979. Also see Fry and Raymond, 1983, pp. 1–9; Eckstein, 1975; and McGowan, 1975.

22. Levy, 1994; Stern, 1997.

23. Levy, 1994, pp. 306–310.

24. Burke, 1989, p. 155.

25. Schroeder, 1994a, p. 148.

26. Khong, 1992, p. 225; Hybel, 1990.

27. Vertzberger, 1986, p. 243.

28. In *The European*, November 8–10, 1991, p. 6.

29. Human behavior appears to be heavily influenced by "somatic markers," biases generated by emotions that give people a feeling about the outcome of doing one thing versus another. When a negative marker is associated with an anticipated future outcome, it functions like an alarm that warns against behaving in a certain way; but when a positive marker exists, it functions like a beacon of incentive. See Damasio, 1994, pp. 173–174; also Devlin, 1997.

30. See Thies, 1980, pp. 376–383.

31. Oz, 1996, p. A17. As Bailey, 1968, p. 247, observes, "Professional soldiers are seldom professional diplomats."

32. Operational art refers to managing tactical encounters during a sustained campaign to achieve strategic objectives. No single organizational mechanism can ensure the effective coordination of political and military strategy. But the absence of such a mechanism virtually guarantees that harmonization will not occur. What mechanism is ultimately chosen depends upon the preferences of the leader, and to a lesser extent upon the type of government and national civil-military traditions. Some leaders prefer formal, hierarchical structures where standing committees with carefully delineated roles present policy proposals for consideration. Other leaders gravitate toward collegial structures built around ad hoc, interdepartmental committees. And still other leaders rely on structures that foster conflict and debate by giving departmental working groups overlapping assignments and few explicit operating rules. For a discussion of the linkages among strategy, operational art, and tactics, see Luttwak, 1987.

33. On September 29, 1918, General Erich Ludendorff, who had assumed dictatorial powers over the war effort, informed the kaiser that Germany's military position on the western front was untenable and that he must seek immediate peace negotiations. Ludendorff called for the creation

of a new democratic government, apparently so the military would not have to admit defeat and sue for peace. Our purpose in pointing out that the way World War I ended gave reactionaries an opportunity to propagate a stab-in-the-back myth is not to suggest that the allied powers should have refused the peace overtures and fought on until they could seize German territory. With some 10 million men killed and twice as many wounded, it was important to bring the fighting to a close as soon as possible. We use this case merely to illustrate the proposition that the geographic position of victorious troops has political consequences for the postwar period. Of course, we recognize that stab-in-the-back myths can surface even when the territory of the losing side is occupied. Following the Franco-Prussian War, for example, Captain Alfred Dreyfus, a Jewish officer in the French army, was falsely convicted of treason in a shameful effort to suggest that the war had been lost due to espionage rather than military failure.

34. Regan, 1987, p. 131.
35. Hastings and Jenkins, 1983, pp. 362.
36. Randle, 1973, pp. 36–52, 478–480.
37. Kissinger, 1994, p. 257.
38. Nicolson, 1946, p. 19.
39. Millar, 1969, p. 61.
40. Seabury, 1963, p. 5.
41. The term "ethotic" is derived from Aristotle's discussion of *ethos* (character) in deliberative rhetoric. An example can be found in his discussion of Dionysius's request for a bodyguard: because in the past Peisistratus, Theagenes, and other schemers sought bodyguards as part of their masterplans to become despots (and presumably because Dionysius and the others are alike in certain important character traits), Dionysius should not be trusted since he probably has the same purpose in mind. For an analysis that applies Aristotle's example to foreign policy, see Raymond, 1991.
42. Brinton, 1986.
43. Nisbet and Ross, 1980.
44. Larson, 1985, pp. 50–57.
45. Blalock, 1989, p. 138. An illustration of this point can be found in Hume, 1948, p. 188. If "a civilized nation" was in a conflict with barbarians "who observed no rules even of war, the former must also suspend their observance of them . . . and must render every action or recounter as bloody as possible."
46. Shillony, 1982, p. 96.
47. Solomon, 1990, pp. 299–300. An example of this kind of language can be found in the novel *Lonesome Dove*, when Augustus McCrae warned Arkansas sheriff July Johnson not to seek revenge for the murder of his deputy and two children: "Don't be trying to give back pain for pain," he said. "You can't get even measures in a business like this." McMurtry, 1985, p. 507.
48. Jacoby, 1983, p. 17. An example of the view that vengeance and justice are antithetical can be found in the criticisms Senator Robert A. Taft (R-Ohio) made of the Nuremberg and Tokyo war crimes trials at the end of World War II. In a speech delivered at Kenyon College, he asserted that a trial of the vanquished by the victors is animated by a "spirit of vengeance" and cannot be impartial. See Taft, 1946.
49. Some theorists differentiate between premeditated wars and two types of unwanted, unexpected wars: accidental and *inadvertent wars*. Whereas "a war that starts as a result of actions *not* properly authorized either by central decisionmakers or their legitimately predelegated command to those lower in the chain of command" is an accidental war, "a war that *is* authorized during the course of a crisis, even though at the outset of the crisis central decisionmakers did not want or expect a war," is an inadvertent war. Of course, both of these types of unwanted, unexpected wars may be conducted without restraint and involve actions that violate international humanitarian law. See George, 1991, p. 8.
50. Reflecting on the "accumulated passion" and "demand for retribution that rose like a plaintive chant from all the desolated lands" in the aftermath of World War II, Herbert Wechsler defended the International Military Tribunal at Nuremberg on the grounds that a failure by

the Allied Powers to proceed would have forsaken those who had suffered at the hands of the Nazi regime. "Who can doubt," he asked rhetorically, "that indiscriminate violence, a bloodbath beyond the power of control, would have followed an announcement by the responsible governments that they were unwilling to proceed?" Wechsler, 1972, p. 126.

51. *Exodus* 21: 24–25; *Leviticus* 24: 17–20. Cf. *Matthew* 5: 38–42 and the comments on returning a wrong made by Socrates in Plato's *Crito*.

52. Djilas, 1958, pp. 105–107. Private acts of retaliation have a long history. In ancient Greece, the practice of *androlepsia* was a special form of reprisal. If an Athenian was unjustly put to death in another state and the perpetrators went unpunished, relatives were empowered to seize three citizens of that state and hold them as hostages until restitution was made. During the Middle Ages in western Europe, a person who suffered an injustice abroad could obtain letters of marque from his sovereign to authorize reprisals against the nationals of the foreign state. Sometimes these private retaliations became a matter of public policy. For example, in 1292 an English sailor murdered a Norman in the port of Bayonne. Associates of the victim retaliated by seizing an English ship and hanging several members of the crew. After the English responded in kind, a flotilla of Norman vessels scoured the seas with the objective of hanging as many English sailors as could be found. When the English sent out a stronger fleet and offered no quarter to captured Normans, the conflict escalated beyond a private feud and led to hostilities between the two countries. Private reprisals of this type were gradually abolished in the eighteenth century. Ward, 1795, pp. 295–296.

53. Elster, 1990, p. 862.

54. Homer, 1938, pp. 260, 265–266.

55. Nozick, 1990, pp. 281–283. Some of these limits derive from an acceptance of the distinction between intentional and unintentional wrong.

56. Kiernan, 1989, p. 21.

57. Wolgast, 1987. For an analysis of social dynamics created by a code of revenge, see Marongiu and Newman, 1987.

58. The distinction between maximalist and minimalist schools of retribution is made by Golding, 1975, p. 85.

59. See Kriesberg, 1998a.

60. See Shriver, 1995, pp. 6–9.

61. Tavuchis, 1991, p. 31.

62. Scheff, 1994, p. 135.

63. Goffman, 1971, p. 113.

64. Braithwaite, 1989.

65. See Wiesenthal, 1976.

66. See *Deuteronomy* 32: 35.

67. Bailey, 1968, p. 267.

68. Fisher and Ury, 1981, p. 75.

69. Sherif and Sherif, 1953.

70. Fisher, Kopelman, and Schneider, 1994, p. 39.

71. Bueno de Mesquita and Singer, 1973, p. 241.

72. Gulick, 1955, p. 86.

73. Kissinger, 1994, p. 405.

74. Kissinger, 1973, pp. 21, 312.

75. Schelling, 1966, p. 128.

76. Ibid., p. 12. For a discussion of the role of spoilers in peace processes aimed at ending civil wars, see Stedman, 1977.

77. Orme, 1996, p. 110.

78. Vasquez, 1993, pp. 202, 208–210. Accommodationists are defined as "individuals who have a personal predisposition (due to beliefs they hold) that finds the use of force, especially war, repugnant, and advocates a foreign policy that will avoid war through compromise, negotiation, and the creation of rules and norms for nonviolent conflict resolution."

79. Gregg, 1966, p. 52.

80. Burgess and Burgess, 1994, p. 14.
81. In Gregg, 1966, p. 150.
82. Obviously, pacific responses are not viable against everyone. The sack of Hamanu in the seventh century B.C.E. by the Assyrian leader Assurbanipal is one of many examples that testify to the inability of a vanquished people to prevent their utter destruction by a brutal conqueror. Even rulers who labored to integrate diverse populations into unified states occasionally responded to military adversaries with unmitigated fury. The sixteenth-century Mughal emperor Akbar, for example, was so enraged by the resistence of the Rajput fortress of Chitor, that after overrunning the stronghold his forces massacred thousands of people.
83. Gregor and Robarchek, 1996, p. 160.
84. Pruitt and Rubin, 1986, p. 184.
85. Lieberman, 1968, p. 361.
86. Ibid., p. 360.
87. Locke, 1952, pp. 104–105.
88. Graybill, 1998; Shriver, 1995, p. 224.
89. Dimuccio, 1998, p. 250.
90. *Matthew* 7: 1–2.
91. Kautilya, also known as Chanakya, lived during the period of approximately 350–275 B.C.E. He is credited with helping overthrow the last ruler of the Nanda Dynasty and making Chandragupta Maurya the emperor of India. The citations that follow come from two of his most important works, the *Arthasastra* and the *Chanakyanitidarpana*, as reprinted and translated in Subramanian, 1990, pp. 42, 110–112, 161–162, 178.
92. Rosenthal, 1995, p. 322.
93. Wight, 1968, p. 128.
94. Doran, 1971, p. 194.
95. Sherman, 1998, p. 119. The concept of empathy, as originally developed by psychologists Walter Lipps and Edward Titchener, involves the cognitive capacity to imagine oneself in others' circumstances. Recent research indicates that empathy predisposes people to altruistic behavior. See Sherman, 1998, pp. 110–115.
96. Oren, 1982, pp. 150–151.
97. Ignatieff, 1998.
98. Graybill, 1998, p. 49.
99. Kriesberg, 1998b, p. 5.

GLOSSARY

absolute gains A condition in which all participants in exchanges and bargains become better off in contrast with situations of *relative gains,* in which some participants benefit more than others.

adjudication A conflict-resolution procedure in which a third party makes a binding decision through an institutionalized tribunal.

alignments When a state threatened by foreign enemies forms a special relationship short of formal alliance with a stronger state able to protect it from attack.

alliance A formal agreement among states to coordinate their behavior in the event of certain specified military contingencies.

anarchy The absence of governmental authority to keep peace and enforce rules.

appeasement, appease A policy that attempts to satisfy a potential aggressor with significant concessions.

arbitration A conflict-resolution procedure in which a third party makes a binding decision through an ad hoc forum.

arms control Agreements designed to regulate arms levels.

arms race Intense competition between states in the acquisition of more or better weaponry.

balance of power The tendency of states to form counterpoised defensive alliances to prevent any single power or bloc from dominating the others.

balancer The role played by a great-power that supports one side of a dispute to ensure that no one achieves preponderance, thus maintaining the international balance of power and deterring war.

bandwagoning The tendency for weak states to seek alliance with the strongest state, irrespective of that state's ideology or form of government, in order to increase national security.

bilateral Relationships affecting reciprocally two nations or parties to an exchange, such as both members of an alliance or trade agreement between two states.

bipolarity, bipolar An international system containing two dominant power centers.

bloc A rigid, highly cohesive alliance among a group of states that share a sense of solidarity about goals.

bounded rationality A concept which acknowledges that the decision-making capacity to choose the best option is often constrained by human and organizational factors.

bureaucratic politics model An interpretation of policy making that stresses the bargaining among contending governmental organizations that exert influence on the foreign policy choices of political leaders.

cease-fire A military decision to stop the firing of weapons in warfare to suspend active military hostilities.

chain-reaction cycle An action-reaction sequence that results when one state increases its military capabilities to offset the expected growth of an adversary's capabilities, which in turn prompts the adversary to increase its defense capabilities.

coercive diplomacy The use of threats or limited armed force to persuade another nation to take an action it would otherwise not take.

255

cognitive dissonance The tendency of people to ignore new information when it produces a distressing psychological reaction because it differs from their existing beliefs.

collective guilt The belief that all members of a nation conducting a war are collectively responsible for the wrongs committed in pursuit of victory.

collective security A system of world order in which aggression by any state will be met by a collective response from other nations in the international community.

concert A cooperative agreement among great powers to jointly manage international relations.

conciliation The procedure where a third party assists both sides in resolving their disputes.

containment A policy to prevent the expansion of an adversary's territory or influence beyond its present geostrategic reach.

corrective justice The ethical arguments in favor of inflicting either injury or providing rewards as a way to change another's behavior.

crisis decisions Made in high-threat situations, such as a probable war, these choices must be made under conditions of surprise and time pressure by the highest level of decision makers.

customs union A form of economic integration where member states eliminate duties on commodities they trade among themselves while levying a common external tariff on commodities imported from non-member states.

decision-making theory, decision making An analytic approach to the determinants of states' foreign policy behavior that focuses on the settings and situations in which leaders find themselves when they make decisions.

democratic peace The propensity of democratically governed nations to settle conflicts among themselves through peaceful means rather than resorting to war.

détente The relaxation of tension between adversaries.

deterrence A preventive strategy designed to dissuade an adversary from doing what it would otherwise do.

disarmament Agreements designed to reduce or eliminate weapons.

distributive justice The ethical criteria used to evaluate how collective goods should be allocated to different parties.

diversionary theory of war The contention that leaders initiate conflict abroad as a way to increase their personal popularity and national cohesion at home.

domino effect A situation where an expansionist state conquers another country and its aggression leads to the subsequent conquest of other neighboring countries.

domino theory A metaphor popular in the United States during the Cold War which predicted that the fall to communism in one country would in turn cause the fall of its neighbors.

economic sanctions Governmental actions designed to change an adversary's policies by inflicting deprivation on that state through the limitation or termination of economic exchanges.

embargo An order of a government prohibiting the export of commerce to a target state as a method of coercive diplomacy.

empire A political unit comprising extensive territory and many nations that is ruled by a single supreme authority.

enduring rivalries A condition pertaining to pairs of nations that, over a long period of time, relentlessly compete with one another and frequently take up arms to gain supremacy.

entente An agreement between states to consult if one side is attacked by another party.

extended deterrence A strategy to deter an adversary from attacking one's allies.

genocide The deliberate extermination of an ethnic, a religious, or a minority group.

grand strategy A nation's conception of its core security goals, military and nonmilitary methods for pursing them, and allocation of resources to support the means selected.

great-powers The most powerful countries, militarily and economically, in the international system.

groupthink The propensity of members of cohesive, insulated groups to engage in excessive efforts to seek agreement at the expense of objectively analyzing policy problems and rigorously searching for solutions.

gunboat diplomacy A show of naval force by one nation to intimidate another.

hegemon, hegemony A dominant military and economic state that uses its unrivaled power to create and enforce rules aimed at preserving the existing world global or regional system and its own position in that order.

hegemonic stability theory A theory that focuses on the stabilizing impact of a preeminent state (a hegemon) in maintaining international cooperation.

high politics Geostrategic issues of national and international security that pertain to matters of war and peace.

imperialism, imperial The intentional imposition of one state's power over another, usually through territorial conquest and denial of the victim population's freedom to have a voice in the conquering regime's decisions.

imperial overstretch The condition where a great-power makes foreign commitments that exceed its ability to fulfill them.

inadvertent war A war that results from uncertainty, confusion, and circumstances beyond the control of those involved, rather than as the result of anyone's master plan.

international regime The set of rules, norms, and decision-making procedures that coordinates national behavior within a given area of activity, such as a security regime's rules to manage conflicts without recourse to war.

intervention An overt or covert use of force by one or more countries that crosses the borders of another country in order to affect the government and policies of the garget country.

irredentism, irredentist The desire by one state to annex or reclaim territory held by another that was historically connected to the first state.

isolationism A national policy of withdrawing from active participation with other actors in world affairs by abstention from alliances and other politcal and economic relations.

justice The principles of morality governing ethical belief and behavior.

levels of analysis Alternative perspectives on world politics that may focus on the personal characteristics of decisionmakers, the attributes of nations' societies and governing institutions, or the structure of the international system as factors influencing choices about war and peace.

liberalism, liberal The school of thought in international relations predicated on the assumption that applying reason to international relations can lead to institutional reforms conducive to the development of a more just and peaceful world.

limited war The restrained use of armed force for limited objectives.

long cycle theory A theory that focuses on the rise and fall of the leading global power as the central political process of the modern world system.

long peace A prolonged period of peaceful great power relations, such as that extending from the end of World War II until the present.

machtpolitik The German term for the practice of power politics.

mediation A conflict-resolution procedure where a third party offers a nonbinding solution to the disputants.

militarized dispute Confrontations short of war, characterized by the reciprocated threat, deployment, mobilization, or use of limited armed force.

military intervention The overt or covert use of armed force by one or more countries, with troops crossing the border of another country to exercise influence over the decisions of the target county's government.

military necessity The legal doctrine that permits violations of the rules of warfare to be excused during periods of extreme emergency.

mirror images The tendency for each party in a conflict to see the other as the other sees it.

morality A system of ideas about right and wrong behavior.

muddling through A model that stresses the tendency for foreign policy decisions to be made incrementally through trial and error rather than according to a comprehensive long-term strategy.

multiple advocacy The concept that high-quality decision making is most likely when leaders hear various policy recommendations from many different agencies within their government.

multipolarity, multipolar An international system containing three or more dominant power centers.

nation A collection of people who, on the basis of ethnic, linguistic, cultural affinity, or historic tradition, perceive themselves to be members of the same group.

nationalism The belief that one's nation is the ultimate object of political loyalty.

nation-state A polity (system of government) holding territory controlled by members of some nationality recognizing no higher authority.

negotiation The process of conferring with others when a conflict arises so disputing parties can reach a mutually satisfactory agreement that resolves the issue.

neorealism A variant of realism that emphasizes the anarchic structure of world politics rather than human nature to explain why nations go to war.

neutral, neutrality A state that formally abstains from participating in a war between other states.

neutralization, neutralized The condition of permanent neutrality conferred on a state through treaties with guarantor states.

nonalignment, nonaligned A policy rejecting the decision to join either side when competitive alliances oppose each other.

noninterference principle The legal duty of states to refrain from uninvited involvement or intervention in another's internal affairs.

opportunity costs The lost chance to undertake one rewarding activity because of involvement in another activity.

pacifism A philosophy that rejects violence as a method of exercising political influence, even for a just cause.

pacta sunt servanda The legal norm that treaties are binding and should not be violated even when defection would be expedient.

paradigm A set of beliefs that give direction to research by indicating what problems in a field of inquiry are more important than others and what criteria should govern their investigation.

peace building Post-conflict actions, predominately diplomatic and economic, that strengthen and rebuild governmental infrastructure and institutions in order to avoid a relapse into conflict.

peace enforcement Military actions undertaken to impose a peace settlement, truce, or agreement to surrender by a warring party or to prevent the resumption of fighting by the participants in a past war.

peacekeeping The use of a military force as a buffer between disputants in order to prevent fighting.

peace making The process of diplomacy, mediation, negotiation, or other forms of peaceful settlements that seeks to end a war and resolve the issues that led to the original conflict.

polarization The clustering of smaller nations in alliances around the dominant power centers in the international system.

political integration The process or the product of efforts to build new political communities and supranational institutions that transcend nation-states.

politics The exercise of influence by one actor to affect the behavior and beliefs of another actor.

popular sovereignty The belief embedded in liberal democratic theory that citizens should have a voice in governmental decisions and that government leaders should be accountable to the public.

power The capacity to influence others to continue a course of action, change what is being done, or refrain from acting in a particular way.

power transition A circumstance that occurs when the military capabilities of one great power overtake those of its nearest rival.

power transition theory The contention that war is most likely when the differentials between the capabilities of rival states begin to narrow and that change provokes a pre-emptive attack to prevent the ascending rival from gaining supremacy.

prospect theory A body of thought contending that policymakers are more risk acceptant with respect to gains than they are risk averse with respect to potential losses.

rapprochement In diplomacy, a policy to reestablish normal relations between enemies.

rational actor model, rational actor Decision-making procedures guided by a clear definition of the policy problem, the prioritization of goals, a careful weighing of all options, and the selection of the option most likely to achieve the highest priority goals.

rational decision making An idealized portrayal of decision making wherein the individual uses the best information available to choose the response most likely to maximize goals.

rationality, rational A conceptualization of decision making that assumes people have preferences and, when faced with two or more alternatives, will choose the one that yields the preferred outcome.

realism, realists A school of thought in international relations based on the premise that world politics is a struggle among self-interested nations for power and position within an anarchical global environment.

realpolitik The theoretical outlook prescribing that countries do whatever is expedient to advance their self-interests defined in terms of maximizing national power.

rebus sic stantibus The legal norm that reserves the right of states to terminate treaties unilaterally if conditions at the time of signing have since changed.

reciprocity A principle about international conduct holding that states should treat other states as they are treated.

regime A set of rules agreed to by states to regulate their interactions, for the purpose of managing common problems.

reparations Compensation paid by a defeated state for damages or expenditures sustained by the victor during hostilities.

reprisal Hostile and illegal retaliatory acts.

restorative justice The ethical criteria addressing the means by which broken relationships can be restored and rebuilt.

retorsion Hostile but legal retaliatory acts.

retributive justice The ethics of administering punishment for evil or illegal deeds.

sanctions Punitive actions by one state against another to retaliate for previous objectionable behavior.

satisficing The tendency for decision makers to choose policy alternatives that are readily available and to select the first choice that meets minimally acceptable standards, even though it is barely satisfactory.

schematic reasoning Processing new information according to a memory structure that contains a network of genetic scripts, metaphors, and stereotypical characters.

security dilemma The propensity for one state's arming for ostensibly defensive purposes to be perceived by others as threatening, provoking them to arm in response, with the result that the security of all is reduced.

security regime Rules, norms, and decision-making procedures designed for the peaceful management of security problems or among countries.

self-determination The doctrine that asserts nationalities have the right to determine what political authority will represent and rule them.

self-help The dependence of the state on its own resources to promote its interests and protect itself against external attack.

sovereignty The legal principle that no authority is above the state to establish or enforce rules about national foreign or domestic conduct.

sphere of influence A region or nations within a particular territorial area dominated by a foreign great power.

spiral model A metaphor used to describe the tendency of efforts aimed at enhancing defense to result in escalating arms races.

standard operating procedures (SOPs) Established methods to be followed in performing designated tasks when bureaucratic units within governments make decisions about foreign policy choices and their implementation.

state A legal entity that possesses a permanent population, a well-defined territory, and a government capable of exercising sovereignty.

strategic surrender A tactic, when facing certain defeat in continued fighting, of accepting surrender in the hopes of evoking a lenient peace settlement from the victor.

structural realism A theory favored by some contemporary realists that sees the changing distribution of power within the global system as the primary determinant of nations' choices about international behavior and of whether peace will prevail.

summit conference Personal diplomatic negotiations between national leaders.

supranational International institutions authorized to make decisions binding on its national members without being subject to their individual approval, transcending national boundaries and authority in order to regulate shared problems.

theory A set of interrelated propositions that purports to explain or predict phenomena.

total war Unrestrained battle against an enemy state's civilian population and economic resources to drive it into surrender.

two-level games A concept referring to the propensity for national policymakers to forge foreign policy decisions that attempt to simultaneously address domestic and foreign priorities.

ultimatum A final, uncompromising demand that normally contains a threat and a time limit for compliance.

unilateralism A go-it-alone, self-reliant strategy for dealing with threats from another actor or global problem, as opposed to multilateral approaches or collective problem-solving.

unipolarity, unipolar An international system with a single dominant power center.

war-weariness hypothesis The proposition that a state experiencing war will become exhausted after prolonged fighting and, whether victor or vanquished, will lose its enthusiasm for participating soon thereafter in another war.

world-system theory The conception that the global capitalist system determines the rise and fall of nations in the international hierarchy of power.

xenophobia A fear of foreigners.

zero-sum The perception that gains for one side in a rivalry are losses for the other side.

REFERENCES

Adcock, F. E. "Fear of Carthage and Irrationality." In *Imperialism in the Roman Republic*, edited by Erich S. Gruen, 77–84. New York: Holt, Rinehart and Winston, 1970.

Agard, Walter R. *The Greek Mind*. Princeton, NJ: D. Van Nostrand, 1957.

Albrecht-Carrié, René. *A Diplomatic History of Europe since the Congress of Vienna*. New York: Harper and Row, 1958.

Allison, Graham T. "Conceptual Models and the Cuban Missile Crisis." *American Political Science Review* 63 (September 1969): 689–718.

———. *Essence of Decision: Explaining the Cuban Missile Crisis*. Boston: Little, Brown, 1971.

Allison, Graham T., and Morton H. Halperin. "Bureaucratic Politics: A Paradigm and Some Policy Implications." In *American Foreign Policy: Theoretical Essays*, edited by G. John Ikenberry, 378–409. Glenview, IL: Scott, Foresman, 1989.

Anderson, Paul A., and Timothy J. McKeown. "Changing Aspirations, Limited Attention, and War." *World Politics* 40 (October 1987): 1–29.

Andocides. *Minor Attic Orators*. Vol. 1. Translated by K. J. Maidment. London: William Heinemann, 1941.

Angell, Norman. *The Great Illusion: A Study of the Relationship of Military Power in Nations to Their Economic and Social Advantage*. London: William Heineman, 1910.

Ardagh, John. *Germany and the Germans*. New York: Harper and Row, 1987.

Aristotle. *Nicomachean Ethics*. Translated by David Ross. London: Oxford University Press, 1925.

———. *The Athenian Constitution*. Translated by H. Rackham. London: William Heinemann, 1935.

Armstrong, Donald. "Unilateral Disarmament: A Case History." In *Peace and War in the Modern Age: Premises, Myths, and Realities*, edited by Frank R. Barnett, William C. Mott, and John C. Neff, 5–13. Garden City, NY: Doubleday, 1965.

Aron, Raymond. *Peace and War: A Theory of International Relations*. Translated by Richard Howard and Annette Baker Fox. New York: Praeger, 1968.

Arquilla, John. *Dubious Battles: Aggression, Defeat, and the International System*. Washington, DC: Crane, Russak, 1992.

Aspin, Les. "The Role of Sanctions in Securing U.S. Interests in the Persian Gulf." White Paper based on Hearings of the House Armed Services Committee, December 21, 1990. Washington, DC: U.S. Department of Defense.

———. "The Military Option: The Conduct and Consequences of War in the Persian Gulf." White Paper based on Hearings of the House Armed Services Committee, January 8, 1991. Washington, DC: U.S. Department of Defense.

Astin, Alan E. *Cato the Censor*. Oxford: Oxford University Press, 1978.

Bailey, Sydney D. *How Wars End: The United Nations and the Termination of Armed Conflict, 1946–1964*, 2 vols. Oxford: Clarendon Press, 1982.

Bailey, Thomas A. *The Art of Diplomacy*. New York: Appleton-Century-Crofts, 1968.

Baldwin, David A., ed. *Neorealism and Neoliberalism: The Contemporary Debate*. New York: Columbia University Press, 1993.

Barnet, Richard J. "Reflections," *The New Yorker* (March 9, 1987): 78 et passim.

Bartlett, C. J. *The Global Conflict, 1880–1970.* London: Longman, 1984.

Beck, Robert J., Anthony Clark Arend, and Robert Vander Lugt, eds. *International Rules: Approaches from International Law and International Relations.* New York: Oxford University Press, 1996.

Beer, Francis A., and Thomas F. Mayer. "Why Wars End: Some Hypotheses." *Review of International Studies* 12 (April 1986): 95–106.

Bennett, D. Scott. "Security, Bargaining, and the End of Interstate Rivalry." *International Studies Quarterly* 40, (June 1996): 157–184.

————. "Democracy, Regime Change, and Rivalry Termination." *International Interactions* 22, no. 4 (1997): 369–397.

Bennett, D. Scott, and Allan C. Stam, III. "The Duration of Interstate Wars, 1816–1985." *American Political Science Review* 90 (June 1996): 239–257.

Bismarck, Otto von. "A Letter to Minister von Manteuffel." In *The Quest for a Principle of Authority in Europe 1715–Present,* edited by Thomas C. Mendenhall, Basil D. Henning, and Archibald S. Foord, 219–220. New York: Holt, Rhinehart and Winston, 1948.

————. *The Memoirs.* Translated by A. J. Butler. New York: Howard Fertig, 1966.

Blachman, Morris J., and Donald J. Puchala. "When Empires Meet: The Long Peace in Long-Term Perspective." In *The Long Postwar Peace: Contending Explanations and Projections,* edited by Charles W. Kegley, Jr., 177–201. New York: HarperCollins, 1991.

Blainey, Geoffrey. *The Causes of War.* New York: Free Press, 1968.

————. *The Causes of War,* 2nd ed. New York: Free Press, 1973.

Blalock, Hubert M., Jr. *Power and Conflict: Toward a General Theory.* Newbury Park, CA: Sage, 1989.

Bonafede, Dom. "George Bush and the Gulf War: A Tainted Triumph." *Miller Center Journal* 2 (Spring 1995): 95–123.

Bonfils, Henry. *Manuel de droit international public.* 4th ed. Paris: Paul Fauchille, 1905.

Botero, Giovanni. *The Reason of State.* Translated by P. J. Waley and D. P. Waley. New Haven, CT: Yale University Press, 1956.

Boulding, Kenneth E. *Stable Peace.* Austin: University of Texas Press, 1978.

Bozeman, Adda B. *Politics and Culture in International History.* Princeton, NJ: Princeton University Press, 1960.

Bradford, Ernle. *Hannibal.* New York: McGraw-Hill, 1951.

Braithwaite, John. *Crime, Shame, and Reintegration.* Cambridge: Cambridge University Press, 1989.

Brams, Steven J., and Ben D. Mor. "When Is it Rational to Be Magnanimous in Victory?" Paper presented at the annual meeting of the International Studies Association, Vancouver, Canada, March 20–23, 1991.

Brecher, Michael. "International Crises, Protracted Conflicts." *International Interactions* 11, nos. 3–4 (1984): 237–298.

Bremer, Stuart A. "Dangerous Dyads: Conditions Affecting the Likelihood of Interstate War, 1816–1865." *Journal of Conflict Resolution* 36 (June 1992): 309–341.

Brinton, Alan. "Ethotic Argument." *History of Philosophy Quarterly* 3, (July 1986): 245–258.

————. "Appeal to the Angry Emotions." *Informal Logic* 10 (Spring 1988): 77–87.

Brodie, Bernard. *War and Politics.* New York: Macmillan, 1973.

Bronfenbrenner, Urie. "The Mirror Image in Soviet-American Relations." *Journal of Social Issues* 27, no. 1 (1971): 46–51.

Brown, Seyom. *The Causes and Prevention of War.* New York: St. Martin's Press, 1994.

Buchanan, Patrick. "Have the Neocons Thought This Through?" In *The Gulf Reader: History, Documents, Opinions,* edited by Micah L. Sifry and Christopher Cerf, 213–215. New York: Times Books/Random House, 1991.

Bueno de Mesquita, Bruce. *The War Trap.* New Haven, CT: Yale University Press, 1981.

Bueno de Mesquita, Bruce, and David Lalman. *War and Reason.* New Haven, CT: Yale University Press, 1992.

Bueno de Mesquita, Bruce, and J. David Singer. "Alliances, Capabilities, and War: A Review and Synthesis." In *Political Science Annual Review,* Vol. IV, edited by Cornelius Cotter, 237–280. Indianapolis, IN: Bobbs-Merrill, 1973.

Bull, Hedley. *The Anarchical Society: A Study of Order in World Politics.* New York: Columbia University Press, 1977.

Burgess, Guy, and Heidi Burgess. "Justice without Violence: Theoretical Foundations." In *Justice without Violence,* edited by Paul Wehr, Heidi Burgess, and Guy Burgess, 7–36. Boulder, CO: Lynne Rienner, 1994a.

Burgess, Heidi, and Burgess, Guy. "Justice without Violence: Theorectical Synthesis." In *Justice without Violence,* edited by Paul Wehr, Heidi Burgess, and Guy Burgess, 257–290. Boulder, CO: Lynne Rienner, 1994b.

Burke, Edmund. *Reflections on the Revolution in France.* New York: Anchor, 1989.

Bush, George. "Aggression in the Gulf." *Vital Speeches of the Day,* no. 1 (1990a): 2–4.

———. "America's Stand against Aggression." No. 1294. Washington, DC: U.S. Department of State, Bureau of Public Affairs, 1990b.

———. "Iraq's Invasion of Kuwait." *Vital Speeches of the Day* 56, no. 22 (1990c): 674–675.

———. "The Persian Gulf." *Vital Speeches of the Day* 56, no. 24 (1990d): 738–741.

———. "State of the Union." *Vital Speeches of the Day* 57, no. 9 (1991): 258–261.

Buruma, Ian. *The Wages of Guilt: Memories of War in Germany and Japan.* New York: Farrar, Straus, Giroux, 1994.

Carr, Edward Hallett. *International Relations Between the Two World Wars, 1919–1939.* New York: Harper and Row, 1947.

———. *The Twenty Years' Crisis, 1919–1939.* New York: Harper and Row, 1964.

Carr, William. *The Origins of the Wars of German Unification.* London: Longman, 1991.

Caven, Brian. *The Punic Wars.* New York: St. Martin's Press, 1980.

Chazan, Naomi. *Irredentism and International Politics.* Boulder, CO: Lynne Rienner, 1991.

Churchill, Winston. *Closing the Ring.* Boston: Houghton Mifflin, 1951.

Cicero, Marcus Tullius. *On Duties.* Edited by M. T. Griffin and E. M. Atkins. Cambridge: Cambridge University Press, 1991.

Cimbala, Stephen J., and Keith A. Dunn, eds. *Conflict Termination and Military Strategy: Coercion, Persuasion, and War.* Boulder, CO: Westview, 1987.

Clark, Ian. *Waging War: A Philosophical Introduction.* Oxford: Oxford University Press, 1990.

Claude, Inis L., Jr. *States and the Global System: Politics, Law, and Organization.* New York: St. Martin's Press, 1988.

Clausewitz, Karl von. *On War.* Edited and translated by Michael Howard and Peter Paret. Princeton, NJ: Princeton University Press, 1984.

Clemens, Walter C., Jr. *Dynamics of International Relations: Conflict and Mutual Gain in an Era of Global Interdependence.* Lanham, MD: Rowman and Littlefield, 1998.

Cohen, Eliot A. "The Mystique of U.S. Air Power." *Foreign Affairs* 73 (January–February 1994): 109–124.

Cohen, Eliot A., and John Gooch. *Military Misfortunes: The Anatomy of Failure in War.* New York: Free Press, 1990.

Commager, Henry Steele. "Misconceptions Governing American Foreign Policy." In *Perspectives on American Foreign Policy,* edited by Charles W. Kegley, Jr., and Eugene R. Wittkopf, 510–517. New York: St. Martin's Press, 1983.

Cook, Don. *Forging the Alliance: NATO, 1945–1950.* New York: Arbor House/William Morrow, 1989.

Coplin, William D. *Introduction to International Politics: A Theoretical Overview*. Chicago: Markham, 1971.

Coser, Lewis. "The Termination of Conflict." *Journal of Conflict Resolution* 5 (December 1961): 351–357.

Cox, Robert W., with Timothy J. Sinclair. *Approaches to World Order*. New York: Cambridge University Press, 1996.

Craig, Gordon A. *The Battle of Koniggratz*. Philadelphia: J. B. Lippencott, 1964.

———. *The Germans*. New York: New American Library, 1982.

Craig, Gordon A., and Alexander L. George. *Force and Statecraft: Diplomatic Problems of Our Time*, 2nd ed. New York: Oxford University Press, 1990.

———. *Force and Statecraft: Diplomatic Problems of Our Time*. 3rd ed. New York: Oxford University Press, 1995.

Crankshaw, Edward. *Bismarck*. New York: Viking, 1981.

Crocker, Chester A., and Fen Osler Hampson. "Making Peace Settlements Work." *Foreign Policy* 104 (Fall 1996): 54–71.

Damasio, Antonio. *Descartes' Error: Emotion, Reason, and the Human Brain*. New York: G. P. Putnam's Sons, 1994.

Davies, Norman. "The Misunderstood War." *New York Review of Books* 41 (June 9, 1994): 20–24.

Dawisha, Adeed. *The Arab Radicals*. New York: Council on Foreign Relations, 1986.

Dean, Jonathan. "No NATO Expansion Now." *Bulletin of the Atomic Scientists* 52 (May/June 1996): 18–19.

Dehio, Ludwig. *The Precarious Balance*. Translated by Charles Fullman. New York: Vintage Books, 1962.

De Sousa, Ronald. *The Rationality of Emotion*. Cambridge, MA: MIT Press, 1987.

Destler, I. M., Leslie H. Gelb, and Anthony Lake. *Our Own Worst Enemy: The Unmaking of American Foreign Policy*. New York: Simon and Schuster, 1984.

Detwiler, Donald S. *Germany: A Short History*. Carbondale: Southern Illinois University Press, 1976.

Devlin, Keith. *Goodbye Descartes: The End of Logic and the Search for a New Cosmology of Mind*. New York: John Wiley and Sons, 1997.

De Waal, Frans B. M. "The Biological Basis of Peaceful Coexistence." In *A Natural History of Peace*, edited by Thomas Gregor, 37–70. Nashville, TN: Vanderbilt University Press, 1966.

Diehl, Paul F. "What Are They Fighting For? The Importance of Issues in International Conflict Research." *Journal of Peace Research* 29 (August 1992): 333–344.

Diehl, Paul F., Jennifer Reifschneider, and Paul F. Hensel. "United Nations Intervention and Recurring Conflict." *International Organization* 50 (Autumn 1996): 683–700.

Dimuccio, Ralph B. "The Study of Appeasement in International Relations." *Journal of Peace Research* (March 1998): 245–259.

Diodorus of Sicily. *Fragments*. Translated by Francis R. Walton. London: William Heinemann, 1967.

Djilas, Miloven. *Land Without Justice*. London: Methnen, 1958.

Doran, Charles F. *The Politics of Assimilation: Hegemony and Its Aftermath*. Baltimore, MD: Johns Hopkins University Press, 1971.

Dorsey, T. H., and D. R. Dudley. *Rome against Carthage*. Garden City, NY: Doubleday, 1972.

Dower, John W. *War without Mercy: Race and Power in the Pacific War*. New York: Pantheon Books, 1986.

Doyle, Michael W. *Ways of War and Peace*. New York: W. W. Norton, 1997.

Duchhardt, Heinz. "Münster/Osnabrück as a Short-Lived Peace System." In *Great Peace Congresses in History, 1649–1990*, edited by Albert P. van Goudoever, 13–19. Utrecht: Utrechtse Historische Cahiers, vol. 14, no. 2, 1993.

Dunnigan, James F., and William Martel. *How to Stop a War: The Lessons of Two Hundred Years of War and Peace.* New York: Doubleday, 1987.

Dyer, Gwynne. *War.* Homewood, IL: Dorsey Press, 1985.

Eckstein, Harry. "Case Study and Theory in Political Science." In *Strategies of Inquiry: Handbook of Political Science,* VII, edited by Fred I. Greenstein and Nelson W. Polsby, 104–113. Reading, MA: Addison-Wesley, 1975.

Eden, Anthony. *Full Circle: The Memoirs of Anthony Eden.* Boston: Houghton Mifflin, 1960.

Elrod, Richard. "The Concert of Europe: A Fresh Look at an International System." *World Politics* 28 (January 1976): 159–174.

Elster, Jon. "Norms of Revenge." *Ethics* 100 (July 1990): 862–885.

Esposito, David M. *The Legacy of Woodrow Wilson: American War Aims in World War I.* Westport, CT: Praeger, 1996.

Etheredge, Lloyd S. *Can Governments Learn?* New York: Pergamon, 1985.

Eyffinger, Arthur. *The Peace Palace.* The Hague: Carnegie Foundation, 1988.

Fair, Charles. *From the Jaws of Victory.* New York: Simon and Schuster, 1971.

Fallows, James. *Looking at the Sun: The Rise of the New East Asian Economic and Political System.* New York: Pantheon, 1994.

Farnham, Barbara, ed. *Avoiding Losses/Taking Risks: Prospect Theory and International Conflict.* Ann Arbor: University of Michigan Press, 1994.

Fay, Sidney B. *The Origins of the World War.* 2nd ed., vol. I. New York: Free Press, 1966.

Ferrill, Arther. "The Grand Strategy of the Roman Empire." In *Grand Strategies in War and Peace,* edited by Paul Kennedy, 71–85. New Haven, CT: Yale University Press, 1991.

Festinger, Leon. *A Theory of Cognitive Dissonance.* Evanston, IL: Row, Peterson, 1957.

Finer, Samuel E. "State and Nation-Building in Europe: The Role of the Military." In *The Formation of Nation States in Western Europe,* edited by Charles Tilly, 84–163. Princeton, NJ: Princeton University Press, 1975.

Fisher, Roger, Elizabeth Kopelman, and Andrea Kupfer Schneider. *Beyond Machiavelli: Tools for Coping with Conflict.* Cambridge, MA: Harvard University Press, 1994.

Fisher, Roger, and William Ury. *Getting to Yes.* Boston: Houghton Mifflin Company, 1981.

Fowler, Wilton. *British-American Relations, 1917–1918.* Princeton, NJ: Princeton University Press, 1969.

Fox, William T. R. "The Causes of Peace and Conditions of War." *The Annals* 392 (November 1970a): 1–13.

———, ed. *How Wars End.* Vol. 392, *The Annals.* New York: American Academy of Political and Social Science, 1970b.

Frankel, Glenn. "Lines in the Sand." In *The Gulf Reader: History, Documents, Opinions,* edited by Micah L. Sifry and Christopher Cerf, 16–20. New York: Times Books/Random House, 1991.

Freedman, Lawrence, ed. *War.* Oxford: Oxford University Press, 1994.

Frensley, Nathalie J. "Ratification Processes and Conflict Termination." *Journal of Peace Research* 35, (March 1998): 167–191.

Friedjung, Heinrich. *The Struggle for Supremacy in Germany, 1859–1866.* Translated by A. J. P. Taylor and W. McElwee. New York: Russell and Russell, 1966.

Friedrich, Carl J., and Charles Blitzer. *The Age of Power.* Ithaca, NY: Cornell University Press, 1957.

Fry, Earl H., and Gregory A. Raymond. *The Other Western Europe: A Political Analysis of the Smaller Democracies.* 2nd ed. Santa Barbara, CA: Clio Press, 1983.

Gallie, W. B. *Philosophers of Peace and War: Kant, Clausewitz, Engels, and Tolstoy.* Cambridge: Cambridge University Press, 1978.

Gardner, Lloyd C. *Architects of Illusion.* Chicago: Quadrangle, 1970.

Geller, Daniel S., and J. David Singer. *Nations at War: A Scientific Study of International Conflict.* New York: Cambridge University Press, 1998.

George, Alexander L. "The Operational Code." *International Studies Quarterly* 13 (June 1969): 190–222.

———. "The Case for Multiple Advocacy in Making Foreign Policy." *American Political Science Review* 66 (September 1972): 751–785.

———. "Case Studies and Theory Development: The Method of Structured, Focused Comparison." In *Diplomacy: New Approaches in History, Theory, and Policy,* edited by Paul Gordon Lauren, 43–68. New York: Free Press, 1979.

———. "Plan of the Study." In *Avoiding War: Problems of Crisis Management,* edited by Alexander L. George, 7–12. Boulder, CO: Westview, 1991.

———. *Bridging the Gap: Theory and Practice in Foreign Policy.* Washington, DC: U.S. Institute of Peace Press, 1993.

Gibbard, Alan. *Wise Choices, Apt Feelings.* Cambridge, MA: Harvard University Press, 1990.

Gibbon, Edward. *The Decline and Fall of the Roman Empire.* New York: Viking, 1952.

Gibler, Douglas M. "Control the Issues, Control the Conflict: The Effects of Alliances That Settle Territorial Issues on Interstate Rivalries." *International Interactions* 22, no. 4 (1997): 341–368.

Giesberg, Robert I. *The Treaty of Frankfort: A Study in Diplomatic History, September 1870–September 1873.* Philadelphia: University of Pennsylvania Press, 1966.

Gilbert, Martin. *The Roots of Appeasement.* New York: Plume Books, New American Library, 1966.

Gillis, John R. "Germany." In *Crises of Political Development in Europe and the United States,* edited by Raymond Grew, 313–345. Princeton, NJ: Princeton University Press, 1978.

Gilpin, Robert. *War and Change in World Politics.* Cambridge: Cambridge University Press, 1981.

Glahn, Gerhard von. *Law among Nations,* 7th ed. Boston: Allyn and Bacon, 1996.

Goertz, Gary, and Paul F. Diehl. "The Empirical Importance of Enduring Rivalries." *International Interactions* 18, no. 2 (1992a): 151–163.

———. *Territorial Changes and International Conflict.* London: Routledge, 1992b.

———. "Enduring Rivalries: Theoretical Constructs and Empirical Patterns." *International Studies Quarterly* 37 (June 1993): 147–171.

———. "The Initiation and Termination of Enduring Rivalries: The Impact of Political Shocks." *American Journal of Political Science* 39 (February 1995): 30–52.

Goffman, E. *Relations in Public.* New York: Harper, 1971.

Golding, Martin P. *Philosophy of Law.* Englewood Cliffs, NJ: Prentice-Hall, 1975.

Goldstein, Erik. *Wars and Peace Treaties 1816–1991.* London: Routledge, 1991.

Goldstein, Joshua S., and Jon C. Pevehouse. "Reciprocity, Bullying, and International Cooperation." *American Political Science Review* 91 (September 1997): 515–529.

Goodman, Allan E., and Sandra Clemens Bogart. *Making Peace: The United States and Conflict Resolution.* Boulder, CO: Westview, 1992.

Gordon, Michael R., and Bernard E. Trainor. *The Generals' War: The Inside Story of the Conflict in the Gulf.* Boston: Little, Brown, 1995.

Graybill, Lyn S. "South Africa's Truth and Reconciliation Commission: Ethical and Theological Perspectives." *Ethics and International Affairs* 12 (1998): 43–79.

Green, Jonathan. *The Book of Political Quotes.* New York: McGraw-Hill, 1982.

Gregg, Richard B. *The Power of Nonviolence.* Rev. ed. New York: Schocken Books, 1966.

Gregor, Thomas, ed. *A Natural History of Peace.* Nashville, TN: Vanderbilt University Press, 1996.

Gregor, Thomas, and Clayton A. Robarchek. "Two Paths to Peace: Semai and Mehinaku Nonviolence." In *A Natural History of Peace,* edited by Thomas Gregor, 159–188. Nashville, TN: Vanderbilt University Press, 1996.

Grey, Edward. *Twenty-Five Years, 1892–1916.* New York: Frederick Stokes, 1925.

Gulick, Edward Vose. *Europe's Classical Balance of Power*. Ithaca, NY: Cornell University Press, 1955.

Hall, William Edward. *International Law*. 7th ed. Oxford: Clarendon Press, 1917.

Hamilton, Edith. *The Greek Way to Western Civilization*. New York: Norton, 1942.

Hammond, Grant T. *Plowshares into Swords: Arms Races in International Politics, 1840–1991*. Columbia: University of South Carolina Press, 1993.

Hampson, Fen Osler. *Nurturing Peace: Why Peace Settlements Succeed or Fail*. Washington, DC: U.S. Institute of Peace, 1996.

Handel, Michael I. "War Termination—A Critical Survey." *Jerusalem Papers on Peace Problems*, no. 24. Jerusalem: Leonard Davis Institute for International Relations, Hebrew University of Jerusalem, 1978.

Harkavy, Robert E. "Defeat, National Humiliation, and the Revenge Motif in International Politics." Paper presented at the annual meeting of the International Studies Association, San Diego, CA, April 1996.

Harris, Marvin. *Cultural Materialism*. New York: Random House, 1979.

Harris, W. V. *War and Imperialism in Republican Rome, 327–270 b.c.* Oxford: Oxford University Press, 1979.

't Hart, Paul. *Groupthink in Government*. Amsterdam: Swets & Zeitlinger, 1990.

't Hart, Paul, Eric K. Stern, and Bengt Sundelius, eds. *Beyond Groupthink: Political Group Dynamics and Foreign Policy-making*. Ann Arbor: University of Michigan Press, 1997.

Hartmann, Frederick H. *The Relations of Nations*. 6th ed. New York: Macmillan, 1983.

Hastings, Max, and Simon Jenkins. *The Battle for the Falklands*. New York: Norton, 1983.

Hempel, Carl G. *Aspects of Scientific Explanation*. New York: Free Press, 1965.

———. *Philosophy of Natural Science*. Englewood Cliffs, NJ: Prentice Hall, 1966.

Henderson, Simon. *Instant Empire: Saddam Hussein's Ambition for Iraq*. San Francisco: Mercury House, 1991.

Hensel, Paul R. "One Thing Leads to Another: Recurrent Militarized Disputes in Latin America, 1816–1986." *Journal of Peace Research* 31, no. 3 (1994): 281–297.

Hermann, Margaret G., and Joe D. Hagan. "International Decision Makers: Leadership Matters." *Foreign Policy* 110 (Spring 1998): 124–137.

Hermann, Margaret G., and Charles F. Hermann. "Who Makes Foreign Policy Decisions and How: An Empirical Inquiry." *International Studies Quarterly* 33 (December 1989): 361–387.

Herodotus. *The Histories*, 4 vols. Translated by A. D. Godley. London: William Heinemann, 1920.

Hershey, Amos S. *The Essentials of International Public Law and Organization*. Rev. ed. New York: Macmillan, 1930.

Herz, John H. *Political Realism and Political Idealism*. Chicago: University of Chicago Press, 1951.

Hinsley, F. H. *Power and the Pursuit of Peace: Theory and Practice in the History of Relations between States*. Cambridge: Cambridge University Press, 1963.

Hoffmann, Stanley. "International Law and the Control of Force." In *The Relevance of International Law*, edited by Karl Deutsch and Stanley Hoffmann, 34–66. Garden City, NY: Doubleday-Anchor, 1971.

———. *The Political Ethics of International Relations*. New York: Carnegie Council on Ethics and International Affairs, 1988.

Holborn, Hajo. *A History of Modern Germany, 1840–1945*. New York: Alfred A. Knopf, 1969.

———. "Moltke and Schieffen: The Prussian-German School." In *Makers of Modern Strategy: Military Thought from Machiavelli to Hitler*, edited by Edward Meade Earle, 172–205. Princeton, NJ: Princeton University Press, 1943.

Holbraad, Carsten. *The Concert of Europe*. New York: Barnes and Noble, 1970.

Holsti, Kalevi J. *Peace and War: Armed Conflicts and International Order 1648–1989*. Cambridge: Cambridge University Press, 1991.

———. *The State, War, and the State of War*. Cambridge: Cambridge University Press, 1996.

Holsti, Ole R. "Theories of International Relations, and Foreign Policy: Realism and Its Challengers." In *Controversies in International Relations Theory*, edited by Charles W. Kegley, Jr., 35–66. New York: St. Martin's Press, 1995.

Holt, Robert J., and John E. Turner, eds. *The Methodology of Comparative Research*. New York: Free Press, 1970.

Homer. *The Iliad*. Translated by W. H. D. Rouse. Edinburgh: Thomas Nelson and Sons, 1938.

Hopmann, P. Terrence. *The Negotiation Process and the Resoultion of Internatioal Conflicts*. Columbia: University of South Carolina Press, 1996.

Horne, Alistair. *The Fall of Paris: The Siege and the Commune, 1870–71*. New York: St. Martin's Press, 1965.

Howard, Michael. *The Franco-Prussian War: The German Invasion of France, 1870–1871*. New York: Macmillan, 1962.

———. *The Lessons of History*. New Haven, CT: Yale University, 1991.

Hume, David. *A Treatise on Human Nature*. In Henry D. A. Ken, ed. New York: Hafner Publishing, 1948.

Hunt, Michael H. *Crises in U.S. Foreign Policy*. New Haven, CT: Yale University Press, 1996.

Hybel, Alex Roberto. *How Leaders Reason*. Oxford: Basil Blackwell, 1990.

Ignatieff, Michael. *The Warrior's Honor: Ethnic War and the Modern Conscience*. New York: Metropolitan, 1998.

Ikenberry, G. John. "After Victory: Constitutionalism, Commitment and the Building of Order After Major War." Paper presented at annual meetings of the American Political Science Association, Washington, DC, August 29, 1997.

Iklé, Fred Charles. *How Nations Negotiate*. New York: Frederick A. Praeger, 1964.

———. *Every War Must End*, 2nd ed. New York: Columbia University Press, 1991.

Isard, Walter. *Understanding Conflict and the Science of Peace*. Cambridge, MA: Blackwell, 1992.

Jacobini, H. B. *International Law: A Text*. Homewood IL: Dorsey Press, 1962.

Jacoby, Susan. *Wild Justice: The Evolution of Revenge*. New York: Harper and Row, 1983.

Janis, Irving L. *Victims of Groupthink*. Boston: Houghton Mifflin, 1972.

———. *Groupthink: Psychological Studies of Policy Decisions and Fiascoes*. 2nd ed., Boston: Houghton Mifflin, 1982.

———. *Crucial Decisions: Leadership in Policymaking and Crisis Management*. New York: Free Press, 1989.

Jayatillike, K. N. "The Principles of International Law in Buddhist Doctrine." *Recueil des Cours, 1967*. Vol. I, no. 120. 445–567. Leyden: A. W. Sijthoff, 1968.

Jenkins, Simon. "Dresden: Time to Say We're Sorry." *Wall Street Journal* (February 14, 1995): A22.

Jentleson, Bruce W. *With Friends Like These: Reagan, Bush, and Saddam, 1982–1990*. New York: W. W. Norton, 1994.

Jervis, Robert. "Cooperation under the Security Dilemma." *World Politics* 30 (January 1978): 167–214.

———. "Introduction: Approach and Assumptions." In *Psychology and Deterrence*, edited by Robert Jervis, Richard Ned Lebow, and Janice Gross Stein, 1–12. Baltimore, MD: Johns Hopkins University Press, 1985.

———. "The Future of World Politics: Will It Resemble the Past?" *International Security* 16 (Winter 1991–1992): 39–73.

Joffe, Josef. " 'Bismarck' or 'Britain'? Toward an American Grand Strategy After Bipolarity." *International Security* 19 (Spring 1995): 94–117.

Joll, James. *The Origins of the First World War*. London: Longman, 1984.

Kagan, Donald. *The Fall of the Athenian Empire*. Ithaca, NY: Cornell University Press, 1987.

———. *On the Origins of War and the Preservation of Peace*. New York: Doubleday, 1995.

Kaplan, Morton A. *System and Process in International Politics*. New York: John Wiley and Sons, 1957.

Kaiser, David. *Politics and War: European Conflict from Philip II to Hitler*. Cambridge, MA: Harvard University Press, 1990.

Karsh, Efraim. *Saddam Hussein: A Political Biography*. New York: Free Press, 1991.

Kecskemeti, Paul. *Strategic Surrender: The Politics of Victory and Defeat*. Stanford, CA: Stanford University Press, 1958.

Keegan, John. *A History of Warfare*. New York: Vintage, 1993.

Kegley, Charles W., Jr. "Decision Regimes and the Comparative Study of Foreign Policy." In *New Directions in the Study of Foreign Policy*, edited by Charles F. Hermann, Charles W. Kegley, and James N. Rosenau, 247–268. Boston: Allen & Unwin, 1987.

———, ed. *Controversies in International Relations Theory: Realism and the Neoliberal Challenge*. New York: St. Martin's Press, 1995.

———. "International Peacemaking and Peacekeeping." *Ethics & International Affairs* 10 (1996): 25–46.

Kegley, Charles W., Jr., and Gregory A. Raymond. *When Trust Breaks Down: Alliance Norms and World Politics*. Columbia: University of South Carolina Press, 1990.

———. *A Multipolar Peace? Great-Power Politics in the Twenty-First Century*. New York: St. Martin's Press, 1994.

Kegley, Charles W., Jr., Gregory A. Raymond, and Margaret G. Hermann. "The Rise and Fall of the Nonintervention Norm: Some Correlates and Potential Consequences." *Fletcher Forum* 22 (Winter–Spring 1998): 81–101.

Kegley, Charles W., Jr., and Richard A. Skinner. "The Case for Analysis Problem." *In Search of Global Patterns*, edited by James N. Rosenau, 308–318. New York: Free Press, 1976.

Kegley, Charles W., Jr., and Eugene R. Wittkopf. *World Politics: Trend and Transformation*, 5th ed. New York: St. Martin's Press, 1995.

———. *World Politics: Trend and Transformation*, 6th ed. New York: St. Martin's Press, 1997.

———. *World Politics: Trend and Transformation*, 7th ed. New York: St. Martins/Worth, 1999.

Kennan, George F. *American Diplomacy, 1900–1950*. New York: New American Library, 1951.

———. "The United States and the Soviet Union, 1917–1976." *Foreign Affairs* 54 (July 1976): 670–690.

———. *The Fateful Alliance: France, Russia, and the Coming of the First World War*. New York: Pantheon, 1984.

Kennedy, Paul. *The Rise and Fall of the Great Powers*. New York: Random House, 1987.

Kent, James. *International Law*. Edited by J. T. Abdy. Cambridge: Deighton, Bell and Company, 1866.

Keohane, Robert O. *After Hegemony*. Princeton, NJ: Princeton University Press, 1984.

———. "International Liberalism Reconsidered." In *The Economic Limits to Modern Politics*, edited by John Dunn, 165–94. Cambridge: Cambridge University Press, 1992.

Keylor, William R. *The Twentieth-Century World: An International History*. 3rd ed. New York: Oxford University Press, 1996.

Khong, Yuen Foong. *Analogies at War*. Princeton, NJ: Princeton University Press, 1992.

Kiernan, V. G. *The Duel in European History*. Oxford: Oxford University Press, 1989.

Kissinger, Henry A. *A World Restored*. Boston: Houghton Mifflin, 1973.

————. *Diplomacy*. New York: Simon and Schuster, 1994.

Klingberg, Frank L. "Predicting the Termination of War: Battle Casualties and Population Losses." *Journal of Conflict Resolution* 10 (June 1966): 129–171.

Knock, Thomas J. *To End All Wars: Woodrow Wilson and the Quest for a New World Order*. New York, NY: Oxford University Press, 1992.

Koning, Hans. "Germanian Irredenta." *Atlantic Monthly* 278 (July 1996): 30–33.

Korman, Sharon. *The Right of Conquest*. New York: Oxford University Press, 1996.

Kranzberg, Melvin. *The Siege of Paris, 1870–1871*. Ithaca, NY: Cornell University, 1950.

Kriesberg, Louis. *Constructive Conflicts: From Escalation to Resolution*. Lanham, MD: Rowman & Littlefield, 1998a.

————. "Reconciliation: Conceptual and Empirical Issues." Paper presented at the annual meeting of the International Studies Association, Minneapolis, MN, March 17–21, 1998b.

Lamb, Christopher J. *How to Think about Arms Control, Disarmament, and Defense*. Englewood Cliffs, NJ: Prentice-Hall, 1988.

Lane, Frederic C., Eric F. Goldman, and Erling M. Hunt. *The World's History*. 3rd ed. New York: Harcourt, Brace and Company, 1959.

Langhorne, Richard. "Reflections on the Significance of the Congress of Vienna." *Review of International Studies* 12 (October 1986): 313–324.

————. "Establishing International Organisations: The Concert and the League." *Diplomacy & Statecraft* 1, no. 1 (March 1990): 1–18.

Langsam, Walter Cunsuello. *The World since 1919*. New York: Macmillan, 1954.

Larson, Deborah Welch. *Origins of Containment*. Princeton, NJ: Princeton University Press, 1985.

Lazenby, J. F. *Hannibal's War: A Military History of the Second Punic War*. Warminster, UK: Aris and Phillips, 1978.

Lederach, John Paul. *Building Peace: Sustainable Reconciliation in Divided Societies*. Washington, DC: U.S. Institute of Peace Press, 1997.

Lefever, Ernest W. *The Irony of Virtue*. Boulder, CO: Westview Press, 1998.

Leng, Russell. "When Will They Ever Learn? Coercive Bargaining in Recurrent Crises." *Journal of Conflict Resolution* 27 (September 1983): 379–419.

————. *Interstate Crisis Behavior, 1816–1980: Realism Versus Reciprocity*. Cambridge: Cambridge University Press, 1993.

Levy, Jack S. "Learning and Foreign Policy: Sweeping a Conceptual Minefield." *International Organization* 48 (Spring 1994): 279–312.

————. "An Introduction to Prospect Theory." *Political Psychology* 13 (June 1992): 171–186.

————. *War and the Modern Great Power System, 1495–1975*. Lexington: University of Kentucky Press, 1983.

Levy, Jack S., and T. Clifton Morgan. "The War-Weariness Hypothesis: An Empirical Test." *American Journal of Political Science* 30 (February 1986): 26–49.

Liberman, Peter. *Does Conquest Pay? The Exploitation of Occupied Industrial Societies*. Princeton, NJ: Princeton University Press, 1996.

Liddell Hart, Basil Henry. *Strategy*. 2nd ed. New York: Praeger, 1967.

Lieberman, Bernhardt. "I-Trust: A Notion of Trust in Three-Person Games and International Affairs." In *Social Processes in International Relations*, edited by Louis Kriesberg, 359–371. New York: John Wiley and Sons, 1968.

Lindblom, Charles E. "The Science of 'Muddling Through.'" *Public Administration Review* 19 (Spring 1959): 79–88.

Link, Arthur S. *Wilson the Diplomatist*. Baltimore, MD: Johns Hopkins University Press, 1957.

Liska, George. "Wars in Rounds: Termination and Erosion." In *Termination of Wars: Processes, Procedures and Aftermaths*, edited by Nissan Oren, 114–146. Jerusalem: Magnes Press, Hebrew University, 1982.

Livy. *History of Rome*. Volume 1. Translated by B. O. Foster. London: William Heinemann, 1919.

———. *The War With Hannibal*. Translated by Aubrey De Sélincourt. Baltimore, MD: Penguin, 1965.

Lloyd, Alan. *Destroy Carthage! The Death Throes of an Ancient Culture*. London: Souvenir Press, 1977.

Locke, John. *The Second Treatise of Government*. Indianapolis, IN: Bobbs-Merrill, 1952.

Luttwack, Edward N. *Strategy: The Logic of War and Peace*. Cambridge, MA: Harvard University Press, 1987.

Lyons, William E. *Emotion*. Cambridge: Cambridge University Press, 1980.

Machiavelli, Niccolò. *The Prince*. Translated by Luigi Ricci. New York: Random House, 1950.

Mann, Golo. *The History of Germany Since 1789*. Translated by Marian Jackson. New York: Praeger, 1968.

Manuel, Frank E. *The Age of Reason*. Ithaca, NY: Cornell University, 1951.

Maoz, Zeev. "Peace by Empire? Conflict Outcomes and International Stability, 1816–1976." *Journal of Peace Research* 21, no. 3 (1984): 227–241.

Margolis, Howard. "Equilibrium Norms." *Ethics* 100 (July 1990): 821–837.

Marongiu, Pietro, and Graeme Newman. *Vengeance*. Toronga, NJ: Rowman and Littlefield, 1987.

Massoud, Tansa George. "War Termination." *Journal of Peace Research* 33, (November 1996): 491–496.

May, Ernest R. *"Lessons" of the Past: The Use and Misuse of History in American Foreign Policy*. New York: Oxford University Press, 1973.

McGowan, Patrick J. "Meaningful Comparisons in the Study of Foreign Policy." In *International Events and the Comparative Analysis of Foreign Policy*, edited by Charles W. Kegley, Gregory A. Raymond, Robert M. Rood, and Richard Skinner, 52–87. Columbia: University of South Carolina Press, 1975.

McMahon, Matthew M. *Conquest and Modern International Law: The Legal Limitations on the Acquisition of Territory by Conquest*. Washington, DC: Catholic University of America Press, 1940.

McMurtry, Larry. *Lonesome Dove*. New York: Simon and Schuster, 1985.

Merritt, Richard, and Dina Zinnes. "Democracies and War." In *On Measuring Democracy: Its Consequences and Commitments*, edited by Alex Inkeles, 207–234. New Brunswick, NJ: Transaction Books, 1991.

Midlarsky, Manus I. "Hierarchical Equilibria and the Long-Run Instability of Multipolar Systems." In *Handbook of War Studies*, edited by Manus I. Midlarsky, 55–81. Boston: Unwin Hyman, 1989.

———. "Polarity and International Stability." *American Political Science Review*. 87 (March 1993): 173–177.

Millar, T. B. "On Writing about Foreign Policy." In *International Politics and Foreign Policy*, 2nd ed., edited by James N. Rosenau, 57–64. New York: Free Press, 1969.

Miller, Judith, and Laurie Mylroie. *Saddam Hussein and the Crisis in the Gulf*. New York: Times Books/Random House, 1990.

Miller, Lynn H. *Global Order: Values and Power in International Politics*. Boulder, CO: Westview, 1985.

Modelski, George, and William R. Thompson. *Leading Sectors and World Powers*. Columbia: University of South Carolina Press, 1996.

Monoson, S. Sara, and Michael Loriaux. "The Illusion of Power and the Disruption of Moral Norms: Thucydides' Critique of Periclean Policy," *American Political Science Review* 92 (June 1998): 288–297.

Montross, Lynn. *War through the Ages*. New York: Harper and Row, 1960.

Morgan, Patrick. "Examples of Strategic Surprise in the Far East." In *Strategic Military Surprise: Incentives and Opportunities*, edited by Klaus Knorr and Patrick Morgan, 43–76. New Brunswick, NJ: Transaction Books, 1983.

Morgenthau, Hans J. "Defining the National Interest—Again." In *Perspectives on American Foreign Policy*, edited by Charles W. Kegley Jr. and Eugene R. Wittkopf, 32–39. New York: St. Martin's Press, 1983.

———. *Politics among Nations: The Struggle for Power and Peace*. 6th ed. Revised by Kenneth W. Thompson. New York: Alfred A. Knopf, 1985.

Nardin, Terry. *Law, Morality, and the Relations of States*. Princeton, NJ: Princeton University Press, 1983.

Nardin, Terry, and David R. Mapel, eds. *Traditions of International Ethics*. New York: Cambridge University Press, 1992.

Neustadt, Richard E., and Ernest R. May. *Thinking in Time: The Use of History for Decision Makers*. New York: Free Press, 1986.

Nevin, John A. "War Initiation and Selection by Consequences." *Journal of Peace Research* 33 (February 1996): 99–108.

Nicolson, Harold. *The Congress of Vienna*. New York: Viking, 1946.

Niebuhr, Reinhold. *Moral Man and Immoral Society: A Study of International Politics*. New York: Scribner's, 1932.

———. *Christianity and Power Politics*. New York: Scribner's, 1940.

Nino, Carlos Santiago. *Radical Evil on Trial*. New Haven, CT: Yale University Press, 1996.

Nisbet, Richard, and Lee Ross. *Human Inference*. Englewood Cliffs, NJ: Prentice-Hall, 1980.

Nozick, Robert. "Retribution and Revenge." In *What Is Justice?*, edited by Robert C. Soloman and Mark C. Murphy, 281–284. Oxford: Oxford University Press, 1990.

Ober, Josiah. "Classical Greek Times." In *The Laws of War: Constraints on Warfare in the Western World*, edited by Michael Howard, George J. Andreopoulos, and Mark R. Shulman, 12–26. New Haven, CT: Yale University Press, 1994.

O'Loughlin, John, Tom Mayer, and Edward S. Greenberg, eds. *War and Its Consequences: Lessons from the Persian Gulf Conflict*. New York: HarperCollins, 1994.

Oppenheim, Felix E. *The Place of Morality in Foreign Policy*. Lexington, MA: Lexington Books, 1991.

Oren, Nissan. "Prudence in Victory." In *Termination of Wars: Processes, Procedures, and Aftermaths*, edited by Nissan Oren, 147–163. Jerusalem: Magnes Press, Hebrew University, 1982.

Organski, A. F. K., and Jacek Kugler. *The War Ledger*. Chicago: University of Chicago Press, 1980.

Orme, John. "The Unexpected Origins of Peace: Three Case Studies." *Political Science Quarterly* 111, (Spring 1996): 105–125.

Oz, Amos. "Israel's Wrath, Iran's Sweet Grapes." *New York Times* (April 25, 1996): A17.

Paskins, Barrie. "Obligations and the Understanding of International Relations." In *The Reason of States: The Study of International Political Theory*, edited by Michael Donelan, 153–170. London: Allen & Unwin, 1978.

Paterson, Thomas G. *On Every Front: The Making of the Cold War*. New York: Norton, 1978.

Pavithran, A. K. *Substance of Public International Law: Western and Eastern*. Bombay: N. M. Tripath, 1965.

Pflanze, Otto. *Bismarck and the Development of Germany: The Period of Unification, 1815–1871*. Princeton, NJ: Princeton University Press, 1963.

Phillimore, Robert Joseph. *Commentaries upon International Law*. 3rd ed. 4 vols. London: Butterworth, 1879–1889.

Phillimore, Walter Frank George. *Three Centuries of Treaties of Peace*. London: John Murray, 1917.

Phillipson, Coleman. *The International Law and Custom of Ancient Greece and Rome.* Vol. 2. London: Macmillan, 1911.

———. *Termination of War and Treaties of Peace.* London: Sweet & Maxwell, 1916.

Picard, Gilbert Charles, and Colette Picard. *The Life and Death of Carthage.* London: Sidgwick & Jackson, 1968.

Pillar, Paul R. *Negotiating Peace: War Termination as a Bargaining Process.* Princeton, NJ: Princeton University Press, 1983.

Pinson, Kappel. *Modern Germany.* New York: Macmillan, 1966.

Plato. *Laws.* Translated by R. G. Bury. London: William Heinemann, 1926.

Plutarch. *Fall of the Roman Republic.* Translated by Rex Warner. Baltimore, MD: Penguin, 1958.

Plutarch. *The Lives of the Noble Grecians and Romans.* Translated by John Dryden and revised by Arthur Hugh Clough. New York: Modern Library, 1864.

Polmar, Norman, ed. *CNN War in the Gulf.* Atlanta, GA: Turner Publications, 1991.

Polybius. *Polybius on Roman Imperialism.* Translated from the text of F. Hultsch by Evelyn S. Shuckburgh. Abridged, with an introduction by Alvin H. Bernstein. South Bend, IN: Regnery/Gateway, Inc., 1980.

Popper, Karl R. *The Logic of Scientific Discovery.* New York: Basic Books, 1959.

Porter, Bruce. *War and the Rise of the State.* New York: Free Press, 1994.

Posen, Barry. *The Sources of Military Doctrine: France, Britain, and Germany Between the Wars.* Ithaca, NY: Cornell University Press, 1984.

Post, Jerrold M. "The Defining Moment of Saddam's Life: A Political Psychology Perspective on the Leadership and Decision Making of Saddam Hussein during the Gulf Crisis." In *The Political Psychology of the Gulf War: Leaders, Publics, and Processes of Conflict,* edited by Stanley A. Renshon, 49–66. Pittsburgh, PA: University of Pittsburgh Press, 1993.

Pruitt, Dean G., and Jeffrey Z. Rubin. *Social Conflict: Escalation, Stalemate, and Settlement.* New York: Random House, 1986.

Puchala, Donald J. "Fifty-Year Friendship with Germany: A Legacy of South Carolina's James F. Byrnes." *The State* (Columbia, SC), September 6, 1996: A9.

Putnam, Robert D. "Diplomacy and Domestic Politics: The Logic of Two-Level Games." *International Organization* 42 (Autumn 1988): 427–460.

Quester, George H. *Offense and Defense in the International System.* New York: John Wiley and Sons, 1977.

Raemdonck, Dirk C., and Paul F. Diehl. "After the Shooting Stops: Insights on Postwar Economic Growth." *Journal of Peace Research* 26 (August 1989): 249–264.

Raff, Diether. *A History of Germany from the Medieval Empire to the Present.* Translated by Bruce Little. New York: St. Martin's Press, 1988.

Randle, Robert F. *The Origins of Peace.* New York: Free Press, 1973.

Rasler, Karen A., and William R. Thompson. *Great Powers and Global Struggle, 1490–1900.* Lexington: University of Kentucky Press, 1994.

Ray, James Lee. *Democracy and International Conflict: An Evaluation of the Democratic Peace Proposition.* Columbia: University of South Carolina Press, 1995.

Raymond, Gregory A. "Comparative Analysis and Nomological Explanation." In *International Events and the Comparative Analysis of Foreign Policy,* edited by Charles W. Kegley, Jr., et al., 41–51. Columbia: University of South Carolina Press, 1975.

———. "Evaluation: A Neglected Task for the Comparative Study of Foreign Policy." In *New Directions in the Study of Foreign Policy,* edited by Charles F. Hermann, Charles W. Kegley, and James N. Rosenau, 96–110. Boston: Allen & Unwin, 1987.

———. "Demosthenes and Democracies: Regime-Types and Arbitration Outcomes." *International Interactions* 22, no. 1 (1991): 1–20.

———. "The Use of Ethotic Argument in Foreign Policy." In *Proceedings of the Second International Conference of Argumentation,* edited by Frans H. Van Eemeren, et al.,

1036–1040. Amsterdam: Stichting International Centrum voor de Studie van Argumentatie en Taalbeheersing, 1991.

———. "Democracies, Disputes, and Third-Party Intermediaries." *Journal of Conflict Resolution* 38 (March 1994): 24–42.

Regan, Geoffrey. *Great Military Disasters*. New York: M. Evans and Company, 1987.

Ritter, Gerhard. *The Sword and the Scepter: The Problem of Militarism in Germany*. Vol. 1, *The Prussian Tradition, 1740–1890*. Translated by Heinz Norden. Coral Gables, FL: University of Miami Press, 1969.

Rock, Stephen R. *Why Peace Breaks Out: Great Power Rapprochement in Historical Perspective*. Chapel Hill: University of North Carolina Press, 1989.

Rodzinski, Witold. *A History of China*. Oxford: Pergamon Press, 1979.

Rorty, Amelie, ed. *Explaining Emotions*. Berkeley: University of California Press, 1980.

Rosecrance, Richard. *Action and Reaction in World Politics: International Systems in Perspective*. Boston: Little, Brown, 1963.

Rosecrance, Richard. *The Rise of the Trading State: Commerce and Conquest in the Modern World*. New York: Basic Books, 1986.

Rosenau, James N. "Pre-Theories and Theories of Foreign Policy." In *Approaches to Comparative and International Politics*, edited by R. Barry Farrell, 27–92. Evanston, IL: Northwestern University Press, 1966.

———. "A Pre-theory Revisited: World Politics in an Era of Cascading Interdependence." *International Studies Quarterly* 28 (September 1984): 245–305.

Rosenthal, Joel H. *Righteous Realists*. Baton Rouge: Louisiana State University Press, 1991.

———. "Rethinking the Moral Dimensions of Foreign Policy." In *Controversies in International Relations Theory*, edited by Charles W. Kegley, Jr., 317–329. New York: St. Martin's Press, 1995.

Ruggie, John Gerard. *Winning the Peace*. New York: Columbia University Press, 1996.

———. *Constructing the World Polity: Essays on International Institutionalization*. New York: Routledge, 1998.

Russett, Bruce. *Grasping the Democratic Peace: Principles for a Post–Cold War World*. Princeton, NJ: Princeton University Press, 1993.

Sagan, Carl. "Between Enemies." *Bulletin of the Atomic Scientists* 48 (May 1992): 24–26.

Sagey, I. "International Law Relating to Occupied Territory: Can Territory Be Acquired by Military Conquest under Modern International Law?" *Revue Egyptienne de droit international* 28 (1972): 56–64.

Santayana, George. *The Life of Reason: Or the Phases of Human Progress*. New York: McGraw-Hill, 1953.

Santoro, Carlo M. "Bipolarity and War: What Makes the Difference?" In *Hegemonic Rivalry: From Thucydides to the Nuclear Age*, edited by Richard Ned Lebow and Barry S. Strauss, 71–88. Boulder, CO: Westview, 1991.

Scheff, Thomas J. *Bloody Revenge: Emotions, Nationalism, and War*. Boulder, CO: Westview, 1994.

Schelling, Thomas C. *The Strategy of Conflict*. Oxford: Oxford University Press, 1960.

———. *Arms and Influence*. New Haven, CT: Yale University Press, 1966.

———. *Choice and Consequence*. Cambridge, MA: Harvard University Press, 1984.

Schenk, H. G. *The Aftermath of the Napoleonic Wars: The Concert of Europe—An Experiment*. New York: Howard Fertig, 1967.

Schlesinger, Arthur M., Jr. "White Slaves in the Persian Gulf." In *The Gulf Reader: History, Documents, Opinions*, edited by Micah L. Sifry and Christopher Cerf, 265–268. New York: Times Books/Random House, 1991.

Schneider, William. "The Old Politics and the New World Order." In *Eagle in a New World Order: American Grand Strategy in the Post–Cold War Era*, edited by Kenneth

A. Oye, Robert J. Lieber, and Donald Rothchild, 35–68. New York: HarperCollins, 1992.

Schroeder, Paul W. "The 19th-Century International System: Changes in the Structure." *World Politics* 39 (October 1986): 1–26.

———. "The Nineteenth Century System: Balance of Power or Political Equilibrium?" *Review of International Studies* 15 (April 1989): 135–153.

———. "Historical Realty vs. Neo-realist Theory." *International Security* 19 (Summer 1994a): 108–148.

———. *The Transformation of European Politics, 1763–1848.* Oxford: Oxford University Press, 1994b.

Schuman, Frederick L. *International Politics.* 7th ed. New York: McGraw-Hill, 1958.

Schwebel, Stephen M. *Justice in International Law.* Cambridge: Cambridge University Press, 1994.

Seabury, Paul. *Power, Freedom, and Diplomacy.* New York: Random House, 1963.

Seldes, George. *Great Thoughts.* New York: Ballantine, 1985.

Sengupta, Bama Prasanna. *Conquest of Territory and Subject Races in History and International Law.* Calcutta: Gouranga Press, 1925.

Sherif, M., and C. W. Sherif. *Groups in Harmony and Tension.* New York: Harper and Row, 1953.

Sherman, Nancy. "Empathy, Respect, and Humanitarian Intervention." *Ethics & International Affairs* 12 (1998): 101–119.

Shillony, Ben-Ami. "The Japanese Experience." In *Termination of Wars: Processes, Procedures, and Aftermaths,* edited by Nissan Oren, 91–101. Jerusalem: Magnes Press, Hebrew University, 1982.

Shriver, Donald W., Jr. *An Ethic for Enemies: Forgiveness in Politics.* New York: Oxford University Press, 1995.

Sibert, M. "L'armistice dans le droit des gens." *Revue générale de droit international public* 40 (1933): 657–714.

Sigal, Leon V. *Fighting to a Finish: The Politics of War Termination in the United States and Japan, 1945.* London: Cornell University Press, 1988.

Simon, Herbert A. *Administrative Behavior: A Study of Decision-Making Processes in Adminstration Organizations.* 2nd ed. New York: Macmillan, 1957.

———. *Models of Bounded Rationality.* Cambridge, MA: MIT Press, 1982.

Sinclair, T. A. *A History of Greek Political Thought.* Cleveland, OH: World Publishing Company, 1967.

Singer, J. David. "Threat-Perception and the Armament-Tension Dilemma." *Journal of Conflict Resolution* 2 (1958): 90–105.

———. "The Level-of-Analysis Problem in International Relations." In *The International System: Theoretical Essays,* edited by Klaus Knorr and Sidney Verba, 79–92. Princeton, NJ: Princeton University Press, 1961.

———. "Peace in the Global System: Displacement, Interregnum, or Transformation?" In *The Long Post-War Peace: Contending Explanations and Projections,* edited by Charles W. Kegley, Jr., 56–84. New York: HarperCollins, 1991.

Singer, J. David, and Thomas Cusack. "Periodicity, Inexorability, and Steersmanship in International War." In *From National Development to Global Community,* edited by Richard L. Merritt and Bruce M. Russett, 404–422. London: Allen & Unwin, 1981.

Singer, J. David, and Melvin Small. *The Wages of War, 1816–1965: A Statistical Handbook.* New York: Wiley, 1972.

Small, Melvin, and J. David Singer. *Resort to Arms: International and Civil Wars, 1816–1980.* Beverly Hills, CA: Sage, 1982.

Smith, James D. *Stopping Wars: Defining the Obstacles to Cease-fire.* Boulder, CO: Westview Press, 1995.

Smith, Michael Joseph. *Realist Thought from Weber to Kissinger*. Baton Rouge: Louisiana State University Press, 1986.

Solarz, Stephen. "The Case for Intervention." In *The Gulf Reader: History, Documents, Opinions*, edited by Michael L. Sifry and Christopher Cerf, 269–283. New York: Times Books/Random House, 1991.

Solomon, Robert C. *The Passions*. Garden City, NY: Doubleday, 1976.

———. "Justice and a Passion for Vengeance." In *What is Justice?*, edited by Robert C. Solomon and Mark C. Murphy, 292–302. New York: Oxford University Press, 1990.

Soren, David, Aicha Ben Abed Ben Khader, and Hedi Slim. *Carthage: Uncovering the Mysteries and Splendors of Ancient Tunisia*. New York: Simon and Schuster, 1990.

Stam, Allan. *Win, Lose, or Draw: Domestic Politics and the Crucible of War*. Ann Arbor: University of Michigan Press, 1996.

Starke, J. G. "Distinction Between a Suspension of Hostilities and a Cease-Fire." *Australian Law Journal* 65 (May 1991): 293–294.

Starr, Harvey. *Anarchy, Order, and Integration: How to Manage Interdependence*. Ann Arbor: University of Michigan Press, 1997.

Stedman, Stephen John. "Spoiler Problems in Peace Processes." *International Security* 22 (Fall 1997): 5–53.

Steefel, Lawrence D. *Bismarck, the Hohenzollern Candidacy, and the Origins of the Franco-German War of 1870*. Cambridge, MA: Harvard University Press, 1962.

Stein, Janice Gross. "War Termination and Conflict Reduction or, How Wars Should End." *Jerusalem Journal of International Relations* 1 (Fall 1975): 1–27.

Stern, Eric. "Crisis and Learning: A Balance Sheet." *Journal of Contingencies and Crisis Management* 5 (June 1997): 69–86.

Stoessinger, John. *Crusaders and Pragmatists: Movers of Modern American Foreign Policy*. New York: Norton, 1985.

———. *Why Nations Go to War*, 6th ed. New York: St. Martin's Press, 1993.

Strauss, Barry S., and Josiah Ober. *The Anatomy of Error: Ancient Military Disasters and Their Lessons for Modern Strategists*. New York: St. Martin's Press, 1990.

Subramanian, V. K. *Maxims of Chanakya*. New Delhi: Abhinav Publications, 1990.

Suganami, Hidemi. *On the Causes of War*. New York: Oxford University Press, 1996.

Sylvan, David. "A World Without Security and Foreign Policy: Thinking about the Future by Reflecting on Ancient Greece." *Mediterranean Quarterly* 6 (Spring 1995): 92–116.

Taft, Robert A. "Equal Justice Under Law: The Heritage of the English-Speaking Peoples and Their Responsibility." *Vital Speeches* 13 (November 1, 1946): 44–48.

Tavuchis, N. *Mea Culpa: A Sociology of Apology and Reconciliation*. Stanford, CA: Stanford University Press, 1991.

Taylor, A. J. P. *The Origins of the Second World War*. New York: Atheneum, 1962a.

———. *The Course of German History*. New York: Capricorn, 1962b.

———. *The Struggle for Mastery in Europe, 1847–1918*. Oxford: Oxford University Press, 1971.

Taylor, William J., Jr., and James Blockwell. "The Ground War in the Gulf." *Survival* 33 (May/June 1991): 230–245.

Taylor, William J., Jr. *The Tears of Germany*. In *Renaissance and Reformation*, edited by G. R. Elton, 237–239. New York: Macmillan, 1963.

Thies, Wallace. *When Governments Collide: Coercion and Diplomacy in the Vietnam Conflict, 1964–1968*. Berkeley: University of California Press, 1980.

Thompson, William R. *On Global War: Historical-Structural Approaches to World Politics*. Columbia: University of South Carolina Press, 1988.

Thucydides. *The Peloponnesian War*. Translated by Richard Crawley. New York: Modern Library, 1951.

Timmerman, Kenneth R. "West Is Poised to Rearm Saddam." *Wall Street Journal* (September 27, 1994): A16.

Towle, Philip. *Enforced Disarmament*. New York: Oxford University Press, 1997.

TRB. *New Republic* 214 (June 3, 1966): 6.

Treitschke, Heinrich von. "What We Demand from France." In *The Quest for a Principle of Authority in Europe 1715–Present*, edited by Thomas C. Mendenhall, Basil D. Henning, and Archibald S. Foord, 226. New York: Holt, Rinehart, and Winston, 1948.

Triumph without Victory: The Unreported History of the Persian Gulf War. New York: U.S. News & World Report, 1992.

Truman, Harry S. *Memoirs*. Vol. I. Garden City, NY: Doubleday, 1955.

Tuchman, Barbara W. *The Guns of August*. New York: Macmillan, 1962.

———. *The March of Folly: From Troy to Vietnam*. New York: Ballantine Books, 1984.

Tucker, Robert W. "An Inner Circle of One: Woodrow Wilson and His Advisers." *The National Interest* 51 (Spring 1998): 3–26.

Vasquez, John. *The War Puzzle*. Cambridge: Cambridge University Press, 1993.

———. "Why Do Neighbors Fight—Territoriality, Proximity, or Interactions." *Journal of Peace Research* 32 (August 1995): 277–293.

———. "Distinguishing Rivals that Go to War from Those that Do Not." *International Studies Quarterly* 40 (December 1996): 531–558.

Vaux, Kenneth L. *Ethics and the Gulf War: Religion, Rhetoric, and Righteousness*. Boulder, CO: Westview, 1992.

Verba, Sidney. "Assumptions of Rationality and Non-Rationality in Models of the International System." In *International Politics and Foreign Policy*, 2nd ed., edited by James N. Rosenau, 217–231. New York: Free Press, 1969.

Vertzberger, Yaacov Y. I. "Foreign Policy Decisionmakers and Practical-Intuitive Historians: Applied History and Its Shortcomings." *International Studies Quarterly* 30 (June 1986): 223–247.

Virgil. *Aeneid*. Translated by Rolfe Humphries. New York: Scribner's, 1951.

Vitoria, Francisco de. *De Indis et de Jure Belli Relectiones*. Translated by John Pawley Bate. Washington, DC: Carnegie Institution, 1917.

Von der Glotz, K. "The Growing Scale of Warfare." In *Basic Texts in International Relations: The Evaluation of Ideas about International Society*, edited by Evan Luard, 252–255. New York: St. Martin's Press, 1992.

Wallace, Michael D. "Arms Races and Escalation: Some New Evidence." *Journal of Conflict Resolution* 23 (March 1979): 3–16.

Wallach, Jehuda L. *The Dogma of the Battle of Annihilation: The Theories of Clausewitz and Schlieffen and Their Impact on the German Conduct of Two World Wars*. Westport, CT: Greenwood Press, 1986.

Wallensteen, Peter. "Recurrent Detentes." *Journal of Peace Research* 26 (August 1989): 225–231.

Wallerstein, Immanuel. "The Rise and Future Demise of the World Capitalist System: Concepts for Comparative Analysis." *Comparative Studies in Society and History* 16 (September 1974): 387–415.

Walt, Stephen M. "The Case for Finite Containment: Analyzing U.S. Grand Strategy." *International Security* 14 (Summer 1989): 5–49.

Waltz, Kenneth N. *Man, the State, and War*. New York: Columbia University Press, 1954.

———. *Theory of International Politics*. Reading, MA: Addison-Wesley, 1979.

Walzer, Michael. *Just and Unjust Wars*. New York: Basic Books, 1977.

Ward, Robert Plummer. *An Enquiry into the Formation and History of the Law of Nations in Europe*. Vol. 1. London: Butterworth, 1795.

Warmington, B. H. *Carthage*. London: Robert Hale, 1960.

Warner, Rex. *The Greek Philosophers*. New York: New American Library, 1958.

Waterman, Richard W. "Storm Clouds on the Political Horizon: George Bush at the Dawn of the 1992 Presidential Election." *Presidential Studies Quarterly* 26 (Spring 1996): 337–349.

Watson, Adam. *The Evolution of International Society: A Comparative Historical Analysis.* London: Routledge, 1992.

Wayne, Stephen J. "President Bush Goes to War: A Psychological Interpretation from a Distance." In *The Political Psychology of the Gulf War: Leaders, Publics, and Processes of Conflict,* edited by Stanley A. Renshon, 29–48. Pittsburgh, PA: University of Pittsburgh Press, 1993.

Wechsler, Herbert. "The Issue of the Nuremberg Trial." In *From Nuremberg to My Lai,* edited by Jay W. Baird, 125–136. Lexington, MA: D.C. Heath, 1972.

Wedgwood, C. V. *The Thirty Years' War.* New York: Doubleday Anchor, 1961.

Weinberg, Gerhard L. *A World at Arms: A Global History of World War II.* Cambridge: Cambridge University Press, 1994.

Weiner, Tim. "U.S. Holds Iraqis Who Aided CIA Plot to Oust Saddam." *International Herald Tribune* (May 12, 1997): 2.

Weir, William. *Fatal Victories.* New York: Avon, 1993.

Welch, David A. *Justice and the Genesis of War.* Cambridge: Cambridge University Press, 1993.

Westlake, John. *International Law.* 2nd ed. 2 vols. Cambridge: Cambridge University Press, 1910–1913.

White, Ralph K. "Why Aggressors Lose." *Political Psychology* 11 (June 1990): 227–242.

Wiesenthal, Simon. *The Sunflower.* New York: Shocken, 1976.

Wight, Martin. *Power Politics.* London: Royal Institute of International Affairs, 1946.

———. "Western Values in International Relations." In *Diplomatic Investigations,* edited by Herbert Butterfield and Martin Wight, 89–131. Cambridge, MA: Harvard University Press, 1968.

Williamson, Samuel R., Jr. "World War I." In *The Oxford Companion to Politics of the World,* edited by Joel Krieger, 987–991. New York: Oxford University Press, 1993.

Wittman, Donald. "How a War Ends: A Rational Model Approach." *Journal of Conflict Resolution* 23 (1979): 743–763.

Wolfers, Arnold. *Discord and Collaboration.* Baltimore, MD: Johns Hopkins Press, 1962.

Wolgast, Elizabeth. *The Grammar of Justice.* Ithaca, NY: Cornell University Press, 1987.

Woodruff, Paul, ed. *On Justice, Power, and Human Nature.* Indianapolis, IN: Hackett, 1993.

Woodward, Bob. *The Commanders.* New York: Simon and Schuster, 1991.

Wright, Morehead. "Reflections on Injustice and International Politics." *Review of International Studies* 12 (January 1986): 67–73.

Wright, Quincy. *A Study of War.* Chicago: University of Chicago Press, 1964.

———. "How Hostilities Have Ended: Peace Treaties and Alternatives." *The Annals* 392 (November 1970): 51–61.

Xenophon. *Hellenica.* Translated by Rex Warner. London: Penguin, 1979.

Yergin, Daniel. *Shattered Peace.* Boston: Houghton Mifflin, 1977.

———. *The Prize: The Epic Quest for Oil, Money, and Power.* New York: Simon and Schuster, 1991.

Yetiv, Steve A. *America and the Persian Gulf.* Westport, CT: Praeger, 1995.

Zartman, I. William. "Resolving the Toughness Dilemma." Paper presented at the 39th annual meeting of the International Studies Association, Minneapolis, MN, March 17–22, 1998.

Zartman, I. William, and Jeffrey Z. Rubin. *Power and Negotiation.* Ann Arbor: University of Michigan Press, 1998.

Ziegler, David W. *War, Peace, and International Politics.* 6th ed. New York: HarperCollins, 1993.

INDEX

2